BRITAIN, NATO AND NUCLEAR WEAPONS

Also by Ken Booth

AMERICAN THINKING ABOUT PEACE AND WAR (*co-editor*)
CONTEMPORARY STRATEGY: Theories and Policies (*joint author*)
LAW, FORCE AND DIPLOMACY AT SEA
THE MILITARY INSTRUMENT IN SOVIET FOREIGN POLICY, 1917–72
NAVIES AND FOREIGN POLICY
SOVIET NAVAL POLICY (*co-editor*)
STRATEGY AND ETHNOCENTRISM

Also by John Baylis

*ALTERNATIVE APPROACHES TO BRITISH DEFENCE POLICY (*editor*)
*ANGLO–AMERICAN DEFENCE RELATIONS, 1939–84
 BRITISH DEFENCE POLICY IN A CHANGING WORLD (*editor*)
 CONTEMPORARY STRATEGY: Theories and Policies (*joint author*)
*NUCLEAR WAR AND NUCLEAR PEACE (*joint author*)
 SOVIET STRATEGY (*co-editor*)

**Also published by Macmillan*

Britain, NATO and Nuclear Weapons

Alternative Defence versus Alliance Reform

Ken Booth and John Baylis

© Ken Booth and John Baylis 1989

All rights reserved. No reproduction, copy or transmission of this publication may be made without written permission.

No paragraph of this publication may be reproduced, copied or transmitted save with written permission or in accordance with the provisions of the Copyright Act 1956 (as amended), or under the terms of any licence permitting limited copying issued by the Copyright Licensing Agency, 33–4 Alfred Place, London WC1E 7DP.

Any person who does any unauthorised act in relation to this publication may be liable to criminal prosecution and civil claims for damages.

First published 1989

Published by
THE MACMILLAN PRESS LTD
Houndmills, Basingstoke, Hampshire RG21 2XS
and London
Companies and representatives
throughout the world

Typeset by Footnote Graphics,
Warminster, Wiltshire

Printed and bound in Great Britain at
The Camelot Press plc, Southampton

British Library Cataloguing in Publication Data
Booth, Ken
Britain, NATO and nuclear weapons :
alternative defence versus alliance reform.
1. North Atlantic Treaty Organization.
Role of Great Britain
I. Title II. Baylis, John, *1946–*
355'.031'091821
ISBN 0–333–43403–X (hardcover)
ISBN 0–333–43404–8 (paperback)

To Emma and Katie
and to Rob and Tom

Contents

Preface	x
Acknowledgements	xii

PART I   ALTERNATIVE DEFENCE   1
           Ken Booth

1	**A Debate to be Won**	**3**
	The Advent of Alternative Defence	3
	The Broken Consensus	6
	The 1987 General Election: Defence and Democracy	14
	The Myths, Threats and Promises of the Double-Zero Agreement	25
	Towards a Critical Non-Nuclear Mass?	42
2	**What is Wrong with Britain's Existing Defence Policy?**	**66**
	Strategic Dangers	66
	Political Problems	68
	Economic Costs	70
	Has the Deterrent Deterred?	72
	Operational, Moral and International Security Issues	76
3	**Towards a Stable Peace**	**87**
	A 'Legitimate International Order'	87
	'The Soviet Threat'	90
	'Process Utopians'	95
4	**Towards a Non-Provocative Defence Policy**	**103**
	The Principle of Non-Provocative Defence	104
	From Pro-Nuclear to Non-Nuclear	109
	From Flexible Response to Defensive Deterrence	112
	From an Atlanticist to a more European NATO	124
	The Military Balance	142
	An Alternative Agenda	144
5	**Criticisms of a Non-Nuclear Defence Policy**	**156**
	Would it be Hypocritical for a Non-Nuclear Britain to remain within NATO?	162

	Would the Renunciation of Nuclear Weapons by Britain make War more Likely?	162
	Would Conventional Defence be more Costly?	168
	Would British Nuclear Disarmament Weaken if not Shatter NATO?	173
	Can a Non-nuclear Strategy be Successful in War?	189
	Would a Non-nuclear Britain be Exposed to Nuclear Blackmail?	194
	Would Soviet Russia Reciprocate?	204
6	**Conclusion**	**211**
	Reciprocal Security	214
	Living with Soviet Russia	221
	World Order Building	228
	Losing a Burden, Finding a Role	232

PART II   ALLIANCE REFORM   237
             John Baylis

7	**Nuclear Deterrence and the Preservation of Peace**	**239**
	Has Nuclear Deterrence Kept the Peace?	240
	Is Nuclear War More likely in the Future than in the Past?	243
	Defending the Status Quo	245
8	**How Valid are the Criticisms of Nuclear Deterrence?**	**248**
	Morality and Nuclear Deterrence	248
	The Dangers of Nuclear Deterrence	255
	The Credibility of Nuclear Deterrence	261
	Nuclear Deterrence and Proliferation	264
	Nuclear Deterrence, the United States and British Independence	266
	Nuclear Deterrence and East–West Tensions	268
	The Cost of Nuclear Weapons	272
	Nuclear Weapons, Political Prestige and Influence	275
	The Utility of Nuclear Weapons in Lesser Contingencies	277
	A Summary of the arguments	278

9	**The Political Problems of Non-nuclear Strategies**	**284**
	The Nature of Non-Nuclear, Non-Provocative Strategies	284
	Alliance Difficulties	287
	The Question of Nuclear Blackmail	293
10	**The Military Problems of Non-nuclear Strategies**	**300**
	The Difficulty of dealing with Armoured Forces	300
	The Difficulty of dealing with Nuclear-armed Forces	301
	The Case of Yugoslavia	307
	The Balance of Risk	309
11	**Towards a New Strategic Concept for NATO**	**312**
	The Future of British Defence Policy	312
	The Reform of NATO Strategy	320
	The Advantages of an Extended Firebreak Strategy	327
	Is the Strategic Defence Initiative (SDI) the Long-term Solution?	340
	The Implications of the Global Double-Zero Agreement	346
12	**Towards a Broader Conception of Security**	**353**
	The Political Aspects of Security	354
	The Notions of 'Common', 'Cooperative' and 'Reciprocal' Security	355
	An Agenda for the Future	359

Index   365

Preface

This book, written at a time when so many issues in European security are at a crossroads, is by two friends and colleagues who are on opposite sides of the nuclear debate. It has been written in the hope that our own mind-clearing and dialogue will help others who continue to agonise over this most complex and important issue in British public policy. The reader will find the book an unusual contribution to the subject, since it is neither a debate between ideological rivals who talk past each other, nor is it one of those ostensibly 'balanced' surveys which actually stack the cards one way or the other. We do not have radically different views of the nature of international politics or of the preferred direction for British society. In foreign policy we both rejected Cold War stereotypes and endorse notions of common or reciprocal security, while in domestic matters we belong in the centre. At the root of our differences over nuclear weapons are divergent assessments of the balance of the strategic, political and moral risks we all face.

The book is divided into two parts, in which we each make our case. We have avoided addressing each other's arguments point by point, in a pedantic fashion, but instead have concentrated on presenting our own coherent and comprehensive explanations. However, we have criticised (or endorsed) each other's arguments where appropriate, and have also criticised the views of others who advocate different versions of the non-nuclear or pro/nuclear cases. The different approaches adopted mean that there is one major asymmetry in the book. Since Part I seeks to advance an alternative way of thinking about the problem, and how to cope with it, it has been necessary to deal with a much wider range of issues there (foreign and domestic, political and strategic) than is the case in Part II, which is concerned to improve the existing structure of policies and attitudes.

We have deliberately avoided attempting to achieve a final compromise position, although this might be cause for criticism. We thought that such an ending would have been spurious, for what we could have accepted as friends and colleagues would not necessarily have been possible or relevant for those involved in the hurly-burly of daily politics; in any case, we both believe that our individual cases are to be preferred to compromise positions. Before compromising, people should be clear where they stand, and why.

Preface

Despite the result of the 1987 general election, which could be read as a striking endorsement of the Conservative government's policy on defence, the latter will remain a major issue in British politics. The hitherto impressive consensus on defence has cracked, and there is no immediate prospect of its revival while Labour remains committed to a non-nuclear policy. And as the arguments presented later will reveal, even the centre of British politics is torn. It should not be forgotten in this regard that the 1983 and 1987 Tory victories did not represent resounding national support for the government's defence policy. After 1983 for example, the vagaries of the British electoral system meant that while 61 per cent of the seats in the House of Commons were occupied by Conservatives, almost 60 per cent of the popular vote had gone to other parties – parties which in one way or another had reservations about Conservative defence policy. As long as the fractured character of British politics remains, the defence issue will be the focus for strong opinions and lively debate. Should we remain a nuclear power? Should NATO's strategy of flexible response be reformed or abolished? Is the Europeanisation of NATO a good thing? Are Anglo-American relations 'special' any more? Should we change the character of US base rights in Britain? What should our role be in relation to super power relations? How much can we afford to spend on defence? What should our defence priorities be? And so on. The 1990s could be a time of considerable change in British defence policy. Economic difficulties might force a Defence Review which calls for radical choices to be made between commitments and missions. There may be major changes in the international arena if the super power commitment to deep cuts in strategic forces actually begin to materialise, or if anti-nuclear parties come to power in the capitals of various European allies. In such circumstances, the Conservative government's belief in nuclear deterrence could increasingly come under pressure in the 1990s. It is not inconceivable that the next general election could bring to power a government committed to denuclearising British defence policy. Even if future British governments of whatever complexion remain committed to nuclear weapons, the views expressed in both Parts of this book indicate the real public concern which is felt about a wide range of issues relating to established nuclear policies. The issues discussed below will be with us for many years.

KEN BOOTH
JOHN BAYLIS

Acknowledgements

For typing this manuscript Ken Booth wishes to thank Jane Guest, Doreen Hamer and Marian Weston. He thanks John Roper of the Royal Institute of International Affairs for giving permission to use as the basis of Part I his chapter on non-nuclear defence which appeared in John Roper's edited volume *The Future of British Defence Policy* (London: Gower, 1985). He also wishes to thank General Sir Hugh Beach and Brigadier Kenneth Hunt for their vigorous criticisms of that chapter, some of which had a big effect. In addition he wishes to thank members of the Alternative Defence Working Group organised by the Institute for Defence and Disarmament Studies (Brookline, MA) for their less adversarial encouragement during 1986–87.

John Baylis wishes to thank Becky Noah, Kathleen Braine and Sherlaine White who typed the final version of Part II, and to Professor Denis Thompson and the Department of Political Science at Brigham Young University, Utah, USA, for financial support.

We both give special thanks to Jane Davis, who compiled the index.

KEN BOOTH
JOHN BAYLIS

Part I
Alternative Defence
Ken Booth

1 A Debate to be Won

The Cold War is over, and we have won it.[1] The West is secure, and its societies enjoy considerable material comfort. There are general and particular problems, of course, but there is also a high degree of social satisfaction. The military and ideological threats posed by 'Stalinism' and 'communism' have faded. Indeed, the systems ostensibly committed to communism present a sorry picture when compared with their Western rivals. Just as it is becoming clearer to many of us that the Cold War is well over, and that we won it, so it is dawning in the East that history was not on their side, in the way they had hoped. At different rates, and everywhere with difficulty, we are seeing the 'mellowing' in the Soviet bloc that the 'father of containment', George Kennan, looked forward to forty years ago.[2] It is not unilinear and it is not guaranteed; but the trend, however unsteady, looks set. Instead of the command economies of the past, we now have glimmers of what might be called socialism with a consumer's face. It may become consumerism with a socialist face; it is too soon to see where the balance will lie in the different countries. It is also too soon to say whether we both – East and West – can jointly win the next struggle: that of living together, indefinitely, free of the fear of war.

Characteristics that identified the first post-Second World War era have changed and are changing before our eyes. Nevertheless, some of our thinking has not caught up with the new realities and too many of the policies pursued by our governments are static. As new problems replace or add to the familiar ones, the old mindsets are unhelpful in managing the transition to the second postwar era. The aim of Part I of this book is to suggest how we should think about the new and interesting times which face us, and how we might survive them so that we will then have some energy and resources to deal with the fresh difficulties the future is bound to dump upon us.

THE ADVENT OF ALTERNATIVE DEFENCE

The case to be argued below is that, if done sensibly and given enough time to evolve, a non-nuclear policy allied to a strategy of non-provocative defence and a commitment to common security would represent the optimum contribution by Britain to the changing character of the international landscape. The package of proposals to be discussed represents an alternative yet realistic approach to thinking about our predicament; its ideas do not dominate the policies of any government, but their time may yet be coming. In contrast to the static thinking that has dominated British attitudes to defence, offering no future other than more-of-the-same and the 'stability' offered by the arms race, the 'alternative defence' approach is forward-looking. In the present argument it takes a thirty-year perspective; it sets a long-term goal, identifies the intermediate steps necessary to achieve it, and lays down an agenda from which we have to choose priorities.

The alternative defence policy to be explained below is not neutralist, pacifist, naive, anti-American, or military irrelevant – the familiar jibes of the critics. It is based on a realistic assessment of Britain's political, economic and military potential, the increasing irrationality of war in Europe, the evolving pattern of relations between the United States and Western Europe, the changing character of the Soviet challenge to Western interests, and the prospects for more sensible super power relations in the late 1980s than were witnessed in the first part of the decade. A shift by Britain to a non-nuclear defence policy is one of the processes that need to be encouraged if we are to bring about a more secure and peaceful world. By denuclearising British strategy, and then NATO's, British governments can help to change the character of European security and so move relations with the Soviet Union towards that of a 'stable peace'.[3] The latter represents a condition in which war is thought unlikely not because of the threat of mutual annihilation but because of mutual satisfaction with the prevailing situation. In short, it is a peace based on a political relationship rather than on cosmic fear.

In Britain in the early 1980s, 'Ban the Bomb' was transformed from a slogan on the banners of peace-marchers to a strategy – or rather a set of strategies – going under the label 'alternative defence'. In the 1970s thinking about non-nuclear strategies had been marginal to defence issues, but in the 1980s it forced itself on to the national agenda. Alternative defence thinking began as an irritant to the defence establishment and those party politicians who preferred to repeat old slogans rather than adjust to new realities and possibilities. It quickly became more. In a remarkably short time for Britain a radical idea about defence achieved a toe-hold on respectability, and came to be taken seriously. One token of the growing significance was the way the government felt it necessary to attack it in the *Statement on the Defence Estimates 1987*: 'defensive defence', it was argued, could never provide a satisfactory deterrent while any suspicion of Soviet expansionism remained.

Although faced by a Maginot Line of traditional defence attitudes, alternative defence ideas have advanced. There is a lively literature, and some of it has been creative and sophisticated, as well as radical – a combination of qualities that do not always go hand-in-hand.[4] This body of ideas crystallised in the late 1970s and early 1980s, though some of its doctrinal and philosophical roots can be traced back earlier.[5] There is no simple definition of 'alternative defence', as is often the case with relatively new and dynamic concepts. It is best understood as an umbrella term for a body of ideas that range across military tactics, strategic doctrine and philosophies about security. It is not, as is sometimes supposed, simply concerned with changing NATO's strategy and weapons; ultimately, it is concerned with the way we approach the problem of security in international politics.

Alternative defence seeks an escape from the 'security dilemma' that grips many states, that is, the condition whereby what one state does to enhance its own security provokes fears on the part of others, and so countervailing military efforts.[6] Alternative defence does not accept that this is a necessary condition between states, or that in the case of the East–West confrontation we are bound to live with high and permanent levels of insecurity. We can choose to change the situation. Instead of relying indefinitely on order based on fear, as at present, alternative defence schemes seek to maintain a level of deterrence against aggression, but to do so in such a way that the arms race will be reversed, crisis-stability will be increased, and arms reduction will be encouraged. Political stability will evolve and eventually there will be more security for all at less cost. In short, a stable peace (as defined earlier) will have arrived.

Under the umbrella notion of alternative defence there is a rich interplay of ideas about strategies, tactics, weapons and priorities. These range from the goal of complete nuclear disarmament in the foreseeable future to the indefinite acceptance of minimum nuclear deterrents, and from non-violent resistance to more modest reforms of NATO's existing doctrines. There are, however, two interdependent elements in all the schemes, however radical or however reformist. The first is an emphasis on denuclearisation rather than nuclear deterrence. At all levels, from tactical to strategic, the aim is to move towards increasingly non-nuclear postures. The second is the objective of achieving non-provocative military postures. While retaining a defensive military posture (to continue to raise the entry-price of aggression) offensive strategies and weaponry are ruled out as far as possible. Security will be based on 'defensive deterrence' and reassurance rather than on threats of retaliation. By this means the bonds of the insecurity trap will be progressively loosened. Alternative defence, therefore, is a set of ideas seeking to reshape the security landscape – our images of it, and then the reality – in such a way that, in the course of time, we will have a predictable peace based upon politics rather than a dangerous order based upon fear.

THE BROKEN CONSENSUS

The expansion of alternative defence, in ideas and support, was one of the manifestations of the break in consensus which began in British politics over the defence issue in the late 1970s, and which has lasted until the present day. For the previous thirty years, the British public had been generally quiescent on defence matters. It had been in favour of 'defence' in general, but uninterested in the details; these were left to the experts. Public opinion polls showed that the majority of the British public supported the retention of nuclear weapons, and the defence roles more-or-less agreed by successive governments of both major parties. This bipartisan approach to defence consisted of a triad of principles: maintaining the 'special relationship' with the United States, retaining an independent strategic nuclear deterrent, and playing a major role in NATO's conventional and nuclear strategies.

Against the background of general public quiescence and bipartisanship about defence policy there were occasional rumblings. The flourishing of the Campaign for Nuclear Disarmament (CND) at the turn of the 1950s and 1960s was the biggest and noisiest challenge to the consensus. This stimulated public debates outside its ranks, in a country where the disastrous Suez intervention in 1956 had shaken the national self-image. In party-political terms, many members of the Labour and Liberal parties became anti-nuclear at this time, though their numbers were not sufficiently strong to direct party policy. As in the 1980s the Labour Party became the main hope for the anti-nuclear cause. Given the pressures on it, it proved an unsteady hand. The idea of 'unilateralism' was endorsed by many supporters for the first time, but this was overthrown in the Party Conference of 1961. When Labour went on to win the general election of 1964, the Wilson government was persuaded by officials to maintain the Polaris system negotiated between the Macmillan government and the Kennedy administration. Hitherto, Harold Wilson and Denis Healey, who became his Defence Secretary, had opposed the idea of an independent nuclear deterrent, though they had supported the idea of Britain making a nuclear contribution to NATO.[7] In the years that followed, Labour continued the established outlines of British defence policy, though they did carry out a withdrawal from the country's major extra-European military commitments. Public interest in the nuclear issue, and defence in general lay quite dormant through the rest of the 1960s and most of the 1970s.

In the late 1970s this situation changed dramatically. Defence policy became a live issue in the British political arena, in the streets, outside US bases, and also in Parliament. The reasons are not difficult to find, especially when the events of the late 1970s and early 1980s are set against the images people had of the early 1970s; these were seen as years of super power *détente*, dialogue about European security and arms control. A drastically more threatening image arose in the late 1970s. The restraints on super power relations slackened, witnessed by the Soviet intervention in Afghanistan and the US refusal to ratify the SALT II Treaty. A 'new Cold War' developed. Sections of British opinion became extremely worried by the belligerent posture in world affairs of the recently-elected Reagan administration. The latter engaged in vigorous arms-racing, an unprecedented peacetime military build-up, and the accumulation of weaponry for 'nuclear war-fighting'. Members of the administration talked in what was widely seen in Europe as an irresponsible and irrational fashion, about limited nuclear options, demonstration shots, fighting nuclear wars and 'surviving' and even 'prevailing'. Military sabre-rattling was accompanied by a simultaneous verbal attack on the nature and legitimacy of the Soviet state. As a result of this shocking and seemingly irrational rise in tension, fear of nuclear war increased sharply. Public opinion in Western Europe, where *détente* with the East was still a widely-preferred option, felt vulnerable under the darkening shadow being cast by the deteriorating super power relationship. In Britain these gathering fears become focused upon the prospective arrival of US cruise missiles on to bases in Britain and by the government's decision to replace the ageing

Polaris by the enormously more destructive Trident system. The consequence of this convergence of developments was the swelling of peace-movements across Western Europe. They not only grew in size, but also became increasingly articulate and knowledgeable. Their midwife had been Ronald Reagan and US strategic fundamentalism, not Brezhnev and Kremlin gold.

At the turn of the 1970s and 1980s, therefore, nuclear weapons, once a pacifier in the politics of British defence policy, became a divisive issue. They were divisive both in general (should we have a nuclear or non-nuclear policy?) and in particular (should be have Trident or a cheaper option?). Whereas the majority of the public still favoured an independent deterrent, opinion polls showed that the gap was narrowing. It also showed that the public at large was not well-informed on defence. But, whatever the level of expertise, defence was now a major issue in British politics; it had entered the party-political arena in a way which had not been seen in the postwar period.

The politicisation of defence became apparent when the anti-nuclear cause came to be advocated not only on the streets but also in Parliament. The Labour Party became 'unilateralist' and adopted alternative defence ideas. Particularly after its defeat in the 1983 general election, it determined to place a more coherent non-nuclear policy before the electorate. The Labour Party's role had both positive and negative results for the idea of alternative defence. On the positive side, the fact that non-nuclear ideas were endorsed by a major political party meant that they had some hope of actual implementation. On the negative side it meant that these ideas became a party-political matter, with the prospect for rational debate inevitably becoming entangled with loyalty tests and the other complications of party politics. Nevertheless, politicisation was unavoidable if alternative defence was to advance beyond the protest stage; and Labour was naturally the political party most likely to pick up the banner.

In the 1983 general election, the Labour Party under Michael Foot could offer only bad thought-out 'unilateralism' and deep divisions of opinion, even among its major spokesmen. In the aftermath of defeat and Neil Kinnock's becoming leader, a greater degree of unity was seen in the party than for many years, and this was evident on defence as well as other issues. The party achieved unity as well as greater electoral respectability on defence, by stressing that it was pro-NATO as well as anti-nuclear, and that it favoured robust conventional defence as well as unconditional nuclear disarmament. Whether Labour in power would act differently from Labour in opposition was another matter, but there was a sense in the country in the mid-1980s that, if elected, a Kinnock government would be more radical on defence than its Labour predecessors since 1945. By placing an increasingly coherent and thought-out package of non-nuclear ideas before the electorate, Labour decisively broke with over thirty years of bipartisanship on British defence policy.

The Labour recovery continued in the mid-1980s. After the heavy defeat of 1983 some people had written it off for the foreseeable future, but with an election on the horizon, public opinion in 1986 occasionally showed that the Labour Party had some chance of achieving office. This revival suggested, at the minimum, that large numbers of voters were not sufficiently hostile to Labour's non-nuclear defence policy to reject the party as a possible government. Some sections of public opinion were much more positive on defence than that. The 1983 election and subsequent public opinion polls showed that a majority was opposed to such nuclear centrepieces of Margaret Thatcher's defence policy as the deployment of long-range US cruise missiles in Britain, US nuclear bases in Britain and the development of Trident as the follow-on to Polaris. At the same time, however, a majority favoured some type of 'independent nuclear deterrent' and was worried about the likely effect of Labour's policies on the future of NATO, which most believed to be the key to British security.[8]

Labour therefore had a reservoir of support, both active and passive. But if it was to be electorally successful it still needed to put considerable effort into the explanation of its defence policies to both the British people and its allies; the criticism of some of the latter, especially the United States, intruded into British politics. Without better presentation Labour threatened to lose the debate by having people at home and abroad see its non-nuclear policy solely through the jibes of critics and old slogans about 'unilateralism'. In the background the anti-nuclear movement continued to provide a large constituency for alternative ideas about defence, though much of the energy predictably went out of street demonstrations once the campaign to stop the deployment of cruise missiles had been lost in 1983. Nevertheless, what the anti-nuclear movement lost in marching power it gained in intellectual strength, as will be seen at the end of this chapter. It was not the nuclear issue that died, it was the postwar consensus on nuclear weapons.

In comparison with the lively thinking taking place among the proponents of alternative defence, and also less radical critics of existing policy,[9] spokesmen of Margaret Thatcher's government in the early 1980s sometimes proved reluctant to debate their views,[10] or they simply wrapped themselves in the military clichés of the past, Cold War Sovietology, unending trust in Atlanticism, and an infinite commitment to the security offered by extended deterrence. Conservative governments after 1979 placed their faith, with some justification, in the British love of the status quo, the forces of inertia, the tendancy of the public to defer to experts, the robust pro-defence gut-feeling of the majority of the British voters, and an understandable confidence that public opinion would remain satisfied with a nuclear defence policy which appeared to have 'worked'. For Conservatives, defence has never been something to theorise about: it is something to be done.

In defence as well as other matters, Mrs Thatcher's government took much satisfaction from the events of 1983 and 1987. In May 1983 her opponents were shaken by the general election result, which gave her party a huge majority in the House of Commons, though hardly the mandate claimed in terms of the popular vote. With the 'Falklands factor' and Labour's confusion and disunity in the foreground the cards were stacked heavily on the government's side. Not surprisingly the victors argued that the election result represented a resounding endorsement of Tory defence policy and a crushing defeat for the confused and confusing ideas of their Labour opponents. Nevertheless, the precise importance of the defence issue was uncertain. What is evident, is the fact that the size of the Conservative victory owed more to the distorting mathematics of our electoral system than to the party's actual nationwide popular appeal. Despite the landslide of parliamentary seats, the majority of the popular vote went to parties embracing non-nuclear policies or at least critical of important elements of the government's position. This disparity between parliamentary seats and the popular vote is but one illustration of a general malaise in British politics, namely the uncertain legitimacy of governments which gain only minority support from the electorate. Despite such minority status, these governments claim a 'mandate' for their whole programme. This is tenable on bipartisan issues, but illogical where there are major differences of position. In the 1980s defence joined that list.

In addition to winning the election, the government's other success in the defence field in 1983 occurred in December, when the deployment began of cruise and Pershing II missiles in Western Europe. This was an outcome which it had been a major objective of the peace movement to stop. The government's list of triumphs continued to come in pairs. In 1987, as will be seen in the following sections, Mrs Thatcher won a third term as Prime Minister, though again without a true mandate in terms of the popular vote, and this was followed in December by the signing of the INF Treaty by the super powers, thereby vindicating, the government claimed, the multilateralist approach it had adopted since 1979.

The trumpeted victories of the government are not the full story, nor are they the end of it. This will be made clear in the chapters that follow. Nuclear weapons will remain an important, emotive and expensive issue, and anti-nuclear opinion is not now likely to sink into the sands as it did in the early 1960s. Disarmament slogans have now been transformed into the new realism of alternative defence ideas, the international context is now changing and favourable, and the nuclear issue is now politicised. By the mid-1980s one political party, Labour, was endorsing a non-nuclear defence policy, and doing so with a unity and conviction that had not previously been apparent.[11] Elements of two other parties, the Liberals and the SDP, were both aiming to divert British defence policy and NATO strategy away from the traditional pro-nuclear orientation towards a more 'conventional' emphasis. And the Welsh and Scottish Nationalist parties were also anti-nuclear in outlook.

As they emerged from the discussions of the mid-1980s and faced up to the election of 1987, the main party positions were clearer than they had been, but there were some important differences of emphasis within each. There was a wide gap within the Labour Party, for example, between those firmly favouring the NATO framework, like Denis Healey, and the neutralism of some on the far left. Within the Alliance there was a sizeable body of CND supporters within the Liberal Party, but also pro-nuclear advocates behind David Owen in the SDP. Much less evident or important were the differences within the Conservative Party, between the Gaullists (non-nuclear in the case of Enoch Powell) and the traditional Atlanticists represented by Margaret Thatcher. Inevitably, Table 1 overleaf is cruder than reality.

The table represents a snapshot of the positions of the major parties on the defence issue on the eve of the 1987 election. How important this issue turned out to be, what the voters thought, and the significance of the results is the subject of the next section.

Table 1 The 1987 election: the position of the major parties on defence

	The Alliance (Liberal and SDP)	The Conservative Party	The Labour Party
Basic defence posture	Acquire, if possible, a cheaper nuclear deterrent and more conventional emphasis; reform 'flexible response' in the direction of 'no early first use'; strengthen ties with Europe.	Maintain a powerful independent deterrent and maintain the main elements of flexible response and post-war Atlanticism.	Unilaterally give up British nuclear weapons; shift to a conventional posture ('defensive deterrence'); and seek to denuclearise NATO strategy.
Trident	Cancel.	Build and deploy.	Cancel.
Polaris	Place Polaris on the table in arms-control negotiations. If not negotiated away, maintain until obsolete and then replace with a cheaper alternative if possible. Options under consideration include Anglo-French cooperation and sea-launched cruise missiles. Maintain 'minimum deterrent' only.	Phase out as necessary and replace with Trident.	Decommission.
Cruise missiles	Freeze pending outcome of arms control negotiations; establish 'dual key' arrangement with the United States if negotiations fail.	Continue the 1979 NATO deployment programme, and the zero-option in the negotiations with the Soviet Union.	Negotiate their withdrawal from UK soil.
Conventional forces	Strengthen, with funds saved from cuts in the nuclear programme, if possible. Accept the NATO strategy of Flexible Response, but move to no early first use.	Support the established NATO strategy of Flexible Response, including deep strike and the threat of first nuclear use. Stress the defensive/reactive character of NATO posture: 'no first use of force'. Level funding after a period of build-up.	Base deterrence on conventional forces: strengthen them, with funds saved from nuclear programme. Change doctrine to a more obviously defensive posture.

US bases in Britain	Maintain, but seek to clarify the arrangements and establish closer control.	Maintain under long-established arrangements.		Maintain US conventional weapons and bases and communication facilities, but negotiate the removal of nuclear bases.
NATO	Stay in. Strengthen the European pillar and conventional defence. Attempt to bring about greater cooperation and rationalisation in European defence procurement. Accept Flexible Response as NATO's basic doctrine.	Stay in. Attempt to maintain the 'special relationship' with the United States while exploring the possibilities of closer collaboration with Europe. Support NATO's established posture of nuclear deterrence and flexible response.		Stay in. Attempt to persuade the allies that European security will be enhanced by a less provocative NATO defence posture *vis-à-vis* the Warsaw Pact. Negotiate a withdrawal of battlefield nuclear weapons. Support no-first-use policy.
Disarmament/arms control	Support existing treaties, a nuclear test moratorium, a European nuclear weapons-free zone, an INF agreement, deep reductions in the super power arsenals, chemical disarmament, mutual and balanced conventional force reductions in Europe, and further confidence- and security-building measures. Strengthen the ABM treaty and oppose SDI deployment. Stop British nuclear testing and place Britain's weapons on the negotiating table.	Support existing treaties, reject the Comprehensive Test Ban, seek zero-option in the INF negotiations and the elimination of disparities in conventional forces, work for further confidence- and security-building measures, and a global, comprehensive, verifiable ban on chemical weapons. Allow SDI within the limits of the ABM Treaty. Favour super power strategic arms reductions, but withhold Britain's strategic deterrent from negotiations. Consider what to do in the light of their progress, or otherwise. Favour only multilateral restraints.		Support existing treaties, favour Comprehensive Test Ban, and a European nuclear weapons-free zone. Oppose SDI and support the ABM Treaty. Favour chemical disarmament, beginning with a chemical weapons-free zone on both sides of the Inner German Border. Support a super power nuclear-freeze as a start to progress towards deep reductions. Favour zero-option in INF talks. Stop British nuclear testing, and work with NATO for reduction and elimination of nuclear forces. Employ both unilateral and multilateral steps.

13

THE 1987 GENERAL ELECTION: DEFENCE AND DEMOCRACY

The result of the 1987 British general election put yet another government impregnably in Westminster claiming a 'mandate' from the people on the basis of only minority of the popular vote. This third success in a row for the Conservative Party, and Labour's disappointing showing, together constituted a major blow for the non-nuclear cause. Labour had become the hope of anti-nuclear opinion, including those who were not necessarily supporters of the party's policies in other areas. But whether Labour supporters or not, the hopes of the anti-nuclear movement for positive action on Britain's part were squashed for another four or five years at least; indeed, given the outlook of Mrs Thatcher's cabinet, it could be expected that Britain would be a negative influence on whatever negotiations took place about the reduction of nuclear weapons. With the apparent historical decline of the Labour Party, and the messy post-election *hara-kiri* of the SDP/Liberal Alliance, the anti-nuclear voice in British politics was understandably dejected in the summer of 1987.

As summer turned to autumn, however, the situation did not look nearly so gloomy. The passage of time threw more perspective on the defence issue in the election. Some comfort could be gained from evidence of growing interest in a range of countries in 'common security', 'non-provocative defence', 'definsive deterrence', 'de-nuclearisation' and other ideas encompassed by the notion of 'alternative defence'. And, to cap it all, the US–Soviet INF talks, culminating in the signing of a treaty in Washington in December 1987, placed denuclearisation and détente firmly on the international agenda. The INF agreement, following on from the mini-summit at Reykjavik in the previous year, promised (some would say threatened) to alter the European security landscape in ways that conformed more to the ideas of the Western European peace meovements in the early 1980s than to the pro-nuclear logic and Cold War instincts by Mrs Thatcher, and the then leaders of the super-powers. The implications of these developments, beginning with the general election, will be discussed in the rest of this chapter.

It is obvious that political parties cannot shackle themselves to decisive electoral liabilities and remain in contention for power. If, therefore, the verdict becomes set in concrete that Labour lost the election in 1987 because of its commitment to non-nuclear defence, then the pressure within the party might one day become irresistible to abandon nuclear disarmament as a practical as opposed to a propaganda goal. Before that comes about, careful examination should be given to both the recent and future roles that the nuclear issue might play.

To begin with, there is some room for debate about the actual importance of defence as an issue in the 1987 election. Opinion polls offer a range of evidence. The Labour Party's own survey after the election indicated that defence had been a significant factor for only three out of one hundred voters, but other polls have suggested that the figure should be much higher.[12] A Gallup-based survey by Ivor Crewe shortly after the election suggested that 35 per cent of voters thought that defence was one of the two most important issues influencing their vote, just before the NHS and hospitals, but far behind unemployment. Had the electors voted only on the main issues, according to this survey, Labour would have won; it was considered more capable on three out of the four leading issues. Only on defence was it vulnerable, and then only among those for whom this issue mattered; but the 35 per cent for whom it did matter obviously represented a significant proportion of the electorate. Furthermore, the defence issue constituted a net loss among actual Labour voters: while 25 per cent of Labour recruits pointed to defence, so did 38 per cent of party defectors. Opinion polls cited by Peter Shore, a former Labour Cabinet Minister and former Shadow Foreign Secretary, were even more negative.[13] In support of his argument that Labour should change its defence policy, he quoted polls showing that 52 per cent of the electorate were less likely as opposed to 18 per cent more likely to vote Labour because of defence; this represented a negative score of 34 per cent. He also quoted a figure of 57 per cent who believed that the Tories would ensure that Britain was safely defended, whereas only 17 per cent were confident in Labour.

The verdict of opinion polls is therefore clearly negative to Labour, though how decisively is open to some discussion. The fallibities of opinion polls are well known. It is not unlikely that those individuals who told pollsters that they did not vote Labour because of defence did so for reasons unrelated to Labour's actual defence programme. How many of those individuals could actually have explained Labour's position? To what extent was defence simply a convenient answer to satisfy a pollster? There can be little doubt that, under Conservative Party guidance, 'defence' became a fashionable code word to criticise the alleged extremism of the left of the Labour Party. In any case, most responses on the defence issue were probably quite visceral; and compared with Labour's message, the government's image of Britain with its own 'bomb' appealed to that jingoism that is never far below the surface. Some comfort for Labour could be taken from the possibility that its defence policy may have been less of a problem among younger voters; this is presumably a factor that will increase in significance as more voters grow up whose outlooks have not been shaped by rigid Cold War Sovietology. A more relaxed international environment, if it comes about, will also help Labour's case. With these possibilities in mind it is worth remembering that an anti-nuclear Labour Party was elected to power a quarter of a century ago (1964) after losing the three previous elections.

Opinion polls measure only quantities of opinion, not qualities; and whatever their numerical verdicts, there can be no denying that the quality of the defence 'debating' that preceded the election was generally low. For the government, Mrs Thatcher and her supporters in the press and elsewhere were far more interested in winning seats than in having a serious discussion about defence. The same was true regarding foreign policy, which, in any case, hardly surfaced; and when it did, the discussion was not always reassuring. Following the Prime Minister's apparently constructive meetings with Mr Gorbachev in Moscow shortly before the election, for example, Mrs Thatcher during the campaign returned to playing up the 'Soviet threat'. It was not only the government that preferred to trade slogans rather than engage in discussion. One of David Owen's 'war-mongering jibe(s)' against non-nuclear defence provoked a Liberal member of the Liberal/SDP Joint Commission on Defence and Disarmament to leave the Alliance and join Labour.[14] The nadir of the defence issue in the campaign, without doubt, occurred when the Conservative Party displayed posters and newspaper 'advertisements' showing a frightened British soldier holding up his arms in surrender, under the heading 'Labour's Policy on Arms'.[15] This was a travesty of the non-nuclear position, but it presumably helped to cultivate further the belief that because Labour was against Trident it was also against defence. Slogans were undoubtedly enough for many people, and to this extent those who 'won' the defence debate should not take much satisfaction from the quality of that victory. Henry Stanhope, a former defence correspondent for *The Times* commented during the campaign that 'Half the people of Britain still think that Trident is a shop which sells tumble-driers and refrigerators.'[16] A proper debate requires a much higher level of public education, and until we have that, we cannot really know what the British people really *think*. We know how they vote, but that is not always the same thing.

Whatever the level of the debate, there is no doubt that the non-nuclear case could have been better presented by many Labour spokespeople. In addition to a general unfamiliarity with the issues in the case of many candidates, several gaffes were made by leading figures. Denis Healey made a notable one. After a session with the Central Committee of the Communist Party of the Soviet Union the Shadow Foreign Secretary commented that the Kremlin was 'praying for a Labour victory';[17] these words, easily quoted out of context, were obviously greeted with amusement and derision by the Tory faithful. More trouble was caused when Neil Kinnock talked on TV about using the country's resources to make the occupation of Britain untenable. This led to 'Dad's Army' jibes and the images of surrender.[18]

Although Labour's defence proposals were put forward with more unity and generally in a more articulate fashion than had been the case in 1983, there was still room for improvement. In particular, the weaknesses of the government's defence policy were not sufficiently exposed; this was in part because Labour itself was so forced on to the defensive that it was distracted from counter-attacking. Alliance critics of the independent deterrent or of the implications of the government's priorities for conventional strength failed equally; they were distracted by the uncertainties of voters regarding the Alliance's position on a range of issues, not least the two-headed leadership problem. Labour's counter-attack could have been stronger and more effective against several areas of government policy: these included the widely-recognised weaknesses and dangers of flexible response, the almost-certain run-down of conventional strength as a result of Trident and other decisions, and the government's negative approach in view of the changing international context. Significantly, when voters were given the opportunity to hear an articulate exponent of the anti-nuclear case, as with Joan Ruddock, the former chairperson of CND, Labour's defence programme did not prove to be an electoral liability.

For its part, the Conservative Party vigorously attacked Labour's vulnerabilities on defence. If, after the election, Labour attracted admiration for the media presentation of its campaign, the Tories won the in-fighting. They exploited Labour's weaknesses and divisions and cultivated the man-in-the-street's gut feelings on defence: the more 'strength' the better, the government knows best, the Russians cannot be trusted, and nuclear weapons work. The government also began its campaign from the high ground with the Prime Minister being able to exploit her visit to Moscow just before the election to project an image of her being a world statesman. But when it came to the election, as was mentioned earlier, there was regression from dialogue to confrontation, and no evidence was given that the government had any ideas about furthering the efforts of those within the Soviet Union who were trying to bring about the changes many of us would like to see.

The non-nuclear argument had not only to withstand the criticism of political opponents, it also had to face the almost-combined forces of the press. Several mass circulation dailies carried out a strong attack, making no attempt either to understand or present the non-nuclear argument in a sophisticated manner. The conservative press took up the theme of 'Kinnock: the man with the white flag' as the *Mail* put it, or incompetence: 'Brother Neil says nowt because he knows nowt' declared the *Sun*,[19] managing at the same time to make both an anti-left and an anti-regional slur. With widespread and hostile press opinion it is surprising that defence did not count even more negatively in the final outcome.

In addition to the press, Labour had also to withstand the adverse opinion of Britain's most powerful ally. Although the Reagan administration ostensibly sought to maintain a position of 'studied neutrality', everybody was clear that Ron stood firmly behind Maggie. At one point officials in Washington were reported as being worried that there might be an upset in the election (that is, a Conservative defeat), and they stressed that the close relationship between the United States and Britain had 'survived Labour governments before'. The officials let it be known that President Reagan would seek to work with a new government to change its non-nuclear policy. The President himself wisely kept a relatively low profile during this time, in order not to provoke British sensibilities. His Defense Secretary, Casper Weinberger, was less reticent. He appeared on a platform with Norman Tebbit, the Conservative Party Chairman, and referred in his speech to threats to NATO 'from within'; this remark was clearly taken to be aimed at Labour's defence policy.[20]

Finally, whatever one's verdict about the importance of the

defence issue in the 1987 election, its future role will be affected considerably by the evolution of the international situation. This is always an unpredictable factor: we do not know whether Mikhail Gorbachev will survive, or whether Ronald Reagan will be succeeded by a more-or-less fundamentalist and/or sophisticated President. If the trends of 1987 continue, on the other hand, and the relaxation in super power relations produces further progress in arms control, then British voters at the next election might decide that Mrs Thatcher's commitment to nuclear deterrence is as out-of-touch and unhelpful as they believed Michael Foot's 'unilateralism' to be in the early 1980s. If deep cuts in strategic arms are agreed there will inevitably be pressure from the Soviet Union and in all likelihood the United States, for Britain to throw its own strategic forces into the ring. If Britian refuses, as Mrs Thatcher shows every evidence of doing, then Britain will be criticised for obstructing further progress in international security; this criticism will come not only from the super powers, but also presumably from the signatories of the Non-Proliferation Treaty. Many floating voters in 1983 and 1987 were not ready to contemplate a shift in a non-nuclear direction; in what might be the significantly different international environment of the early 1990s this might not be the case. There is a growing feeling that we face a rare opportunity to place East–West relations on a more peaceful footing. If the opportunity is still there in the early 1990s, the forward-looking parties should prosper; if the opportunity has been squandered, the government might suffer.

It is clear when we reflect on the 1987 election that defence will remain a sensitive problem for Labour. How it deals with its future is clearly a matter for the party itself; nevertheless, since it will remain the main political platform for the anti-nuclear cause (even if it changes position somewhat) its electoral fortunes are of interest to a much wider body of people than its actual members. For those anti-nuclear supporters who are not also supporters of the Labour Party it is regrettable that their hopes about defence policy have become entangled with the alleged historical decline of the old Labour Party. It is clearly important for anti-nuclear opinion to broaden the political base of their cause. This will include trying to shape the thinking of whatever party emerges from the SDP-Liberal merger. It also means, at the grass-roots level, trying to change the outlooks of those who presently cannot imagine that there is any safer future than indefinitely pursuing the guidelines set down in the late 1940s.

When Labour works on its defence proposals in the months and years of opposition ahead, the public can expect a lively and somewhat acrimonious show. There were signs of this in September 1987, in the first post-election Party Conference. The main passion in the defence debate followed Ken Livingstone's remarks that any attempt to abandon the party's non-nuclear defence policy 'would lead to a civil war inside the party which would render it inelectable in 1991.'[21] In the event various MPs have not restrained themselves; widely differing positions have been advocated. On the right of the party, Peter Shore for one has called for the abandonment of 'unilateralism' (though he agreed that the Party was right to emphasise the 'primacy' of conventional weapons and the need to persuade the allies progressively to abandon their heavy reliance on nuclear weapons in favour of strong conventional forces).[22] On the left of the party, Tony Benn has argued not only for unilateral nuclear disarmament but also for a radical disentanglement from the East–West bloc system. Between these extremes there was a strong support in the Party to retain the programme adopted before the election, but many were tempted to adjust to positions on defence believed to be acceptable to a wider range of public opinion. It would be surprising if there was no shift in the latter direction; in fact, evidence of such movement even predated the election when – with little fanfare – Labour argued that NATO strategy was 'indivisible'. This meant that a Labour government would not have a non-nuclear BAOR fighting alongside nuclear-armed allies; it would cooperate in current strategy until it succeeded in changing it.[23] Further evidence of a willingness to adjust occurred at the Party Conference, when Neil Kinnock declared that he wanted the Trident system, whose deployment was now inevitable, put into the multilateral negotiations that were taking place.[24] The impression that emerged from this first post-election Conference was that Labour would maintain the objective of a 'non-nuclear defence policy' but that it would be flexible in deciding on the means to that goal; in particular, programmes would be adjusted to the prevailing international circumstances. The implication of this sensible approach, according to John Carvel, political correspondent of the *Guardian*, was that with further super power disarmament promised, 'multilateralism' had now become feasible as well as electorally acceptable.[25] Without ruling out unilateral actions when appropriate, Labour could now feel free to support multilateralism.

It was not only Labour's anti-nuclear supporters who had been disappointed by the 1987 election. The anti-nuclear section of the Liberal Party was equally downcast; and their spirits did not rise as the discussions moved forward through the rest of the year regarding the merger with the SDP. The Liberal Party leader, David Steel, had always been opposed to unilateralism, but the SDP merger threatened to confront the nuclear disarmers in his party with an even more hostile hierarchy; Robert McLennan, the SDP's new leader, committed himself at the Liberal Assembly in September to 'retaining a nuclear element in Britain's defence capability for the foreseeable future'.[26] David Steel, for his part, saw the British deterrent as essentially something to 'put on the table', in order to promote a next and more comprehensive stage of disarmament. Steel's position on NATO was that there would be a need for a nuclear strategy as long as there was a need to deter 'a perceived Soviet threat'. Even so, he claimed that 'What we cannot, and will not, accept is the Gaullist doctrine that in all circumstances any self-respecting nation needs its own nuclear weapons – and that such a commitment is absolute, regardless.' These words drew applause from the Assembly. The contrast between this, and McLennan's commitment suggests that the scope for civil war is just as deep among the sons and daughters of the Alliance as it is among the brothers and sisters in the Labour Party.

The uncertain future of the merged SDP and Liberal Party probably means that Labour will continue as the primary vehicle for the anti-nuclear cause in Britain. In this role it is now on the horns of a classic dilemma: if it changes its policy it will be criticised by some of its supporters for selling out, and be attacked by its critics for admitting error; if it does not change, it might harm its electoral chances, and so leave defence policy indefinitely in the hands of a government whose policies would be much less desirable than a modified version of its own. While the Party leadership will have the last word, the following pointers might be borne in mind from the preceding discussion.

(1) The verdict on the true significance of defence in the 1987 election is still open for discussion. It was clearly a net vote-loser for Labour but the extent and implications of this are less clear. The same is true of its relevance. As the international situation changes in striking ways, opinion in 1991–92 might be quite different from what it was thought to be in 1987. Whatever conclusions are drawn about the election, therefore, eyes should be set on the future rather than the past. This approach has the support of Peter Shore, otherwise a critic

of his party's defence policy: he has written that 'The elimination of nuclear weapons is, however tenuously, now on the agenda of world politics. Labour's central aim should be to keep it there.'[27] Instead of rejecting or apologising for its desire to change the character of British defence policy from pro-nuclear to conventional, Labour should stress that this is the way forward: it is what Western defence needs and it would strengthen benevolent trends in the international situation. A reforming political party must never be afraid of public opinion; it can and has been moved. If 'reconstruction' continues in the Soviet Union in ways that Western opinion finds encouraging, then Cold War slogans and nuclear ideology will resonate less and less with younger voters. The outlooks of the latter were not shaped by the 'Zinoviev letter'; but the sympathy of many of them was touched by *Letter to Brezhnev*.

(2) In voting terms, Labour's defence policy has been negative. However, the record of the last twenty-five years shows that the public is not so hostile to an anti-nuclear stance that they will not vote Labour when the party is thought to offer an all-round improvement to the party in power. Politics, of course, is the art of the possible, and political parties need to adjust their ideas in order to get elected; nevertheless, parties that are not merely collections of cynical power-seekers believe that their duty is to lead opinion, and not merely reflect it. There is little virtue in being a party of the lowest common denominator, and it is the role of the Opposition to oppose. Against those who have argued that Labour needed market research, not philosophy, Roy Hattersley has eloquently argued that politicians earn their keep by ideas, and trying to win over opinion. Public opinion polls cannot be allowed to be the arbiter of policies, particularly for those parties wanting change. If Labour had simply followed opinion polls of a century ago it would have contributed little to the development of social attitudes in Britain. The health service and the welfare state as a whole did not come about simply by listening. By definition, those who want change start with adverse opinion polls.

As it contemplates its future, the Labour Party can take some comfort from the recent history of its counterpart in New Zealand. The latter's anti-nuclear stance did not stop it achieving power, nor retaining it in its own 1987 elections; this result was achieved despite (or because of) the bullying by its ostensible allies (the United States, Britain and Australia). The anti-nuclear cause grew in popularity in this strongly independent country, and the Lange government was therefore able to withstand the external pressure. Rather than the government change its anti-nuclear line, the Opposition party felt obliged to adjust its policies in an anti-nuclear direction. Britain's Labour Party would do well to become less insular, and to learn from and build ties with those sharing similar outlooks in other countries; this is particularly true of Western Europe. Denis Healey rightly told the Party Conference in October 1987 that it had to work to find common ground with the 'growing worldwide coalition' in favour of disarmament.[28]

(3) In the time ahead the 'lessons' of 1987 must be learned carefully. In particular, more attention must be given to attacking the weaknesses of a pro-nuclear policy (see Chapter 2) rather than simply defending against the government's criticism. There are likely to be plenty of occasions for counter-attack. Several have presented themselves since the election. In autumn 1987 we had the revelation that the missiles from the Trident system are to be 'rented' from the United States, rather than being independently 'British';[29] this underlines the argument put effectively during the election campaign by Lord Kennet and others that whatever else it achieves Trident does not promise independence: in Kennet's words, 'Deference to the present American president is not so much thanks for help over the Falklands as part of the deposit on Trident.'[30] Another area of vulnerability is the likelihood during 1988 and afterwards that we will see the British government standing out against the spirit of super power denuclearisation. And in the longer term we will understand more clearly that one of the costs of Trident and various other nuclear modernisations will be a decline in our conventional forces. There will undoubtedly be an attempt to hide this by first allowing the erosion of the unglamorous facets of this capability such as ammunition stocks and training; before too long it may be a comprehensive defence review. In order that a more effective campaign be conducted thoughout the parliament, it is necessary that a greater number of MPs become both interested and knowledgeable about the defence issue; it is, after all, one on which fabulous sums of national money are spent.

(4) As well as attacking established policies more effectively, Labour must also be able to defend its own. And nowhere is it more vulnerable than on the question of 'unilateralism', a term that is not well understood.[31]

Since the late 1960s, the debate about how best to approach disarmament has polarised around the 'multilateralists' and the 'unilateralists'. The former argue that national security requires that any disarmament should be negotiated, 'properly balanced', based on agreed-on verification systems, and enshrined in a treaty. The latter argue that security can sometimes be enchanced by independent and informal disarmament on the part of single states, especially where this might encourage reciprocal gestures of disarmament on the part of other states. The sorry record of both unilateral and multilateral disarmament does not strengthen either case and largely feeds the 'realists' and disarmament critics who believe that security most surely rests on a high and balanced level of armaments between the major powers.

The unilateralists argue that the mutlilateralist approach is a sham. It is criticised on the grounds that it has not worked in the past and is merely a fine-sounding method by which governments can obstruct real disarmament. In contrast, unilateralism is advocated on the grounds that it is something individual nations can do to promote disarmament in a dangerous world – since 'progress' does not depend on endless talks – and that it might lead to a spiral of reductions as a result of reciprocal actions by others. Noting the gap between words and deeds on the part of governments, unilateralists sometimes say that they are 'multilateralists who mean it'. Multilateralists, on the other hand, argue that unilateralists exaggerate the danger of nuclear war, misconceive the nature of the arms race, and are naive about the role of military force in world affairs. Unilateralism, they fear, can upset power balances and provoke the ambitious by showing weakness. As a result, what multilateralists like to call 'one-sided disarmament' might bring about the insecurity and war it was designed to forestall. There are merits and demerits to both approaches, and there is also common ground. Some steps might be taken unilaterally, while others are best done through negotiations leading to a treaty. The fact is that those who want disarmament cannot afford to neglect either approach, though 'unilateralism', to date, does not attract majority support, while multilateralism has generally failed to achieve results because of the lack of trust between nations.

For its future general posture, it would be helpful as well as proper if Labour played down its 'unilateralist' image. This should be done not because unilateral actions are to be ruled out as a matter of policy, but because the tag is an unsatisfactory and misunderstood label to describe the posture being advocated. It is better that Labour identify its aim – a non-nuclear defence policy – rather than one of the possible means to achieve it. Unilateral actions are *means* or *tactics*; 'unilateralism' should never be thought of as a *principle*. It is as irrational to be a unilateralist on principle as it would be to be a multilateralist on principle (that is, being willing to reduce forces only if negotiated and verified). Since 1945 there has been a great deal of informal and unverified disarmament, not least on the part of the Soviet Union. British multilateralists would presumably not oppose a unilateral Soviet withdrawal from Afghanistan, or a unilateral cut in Soviet tank strength in Eastern Europe. If we would welcome unilateral restraints on the part of our adversary, because we believed they would contribute to regional, arms-race, or crisis-stability, we should be sometimes willing to undertake such actions ourselves. There are times when unilateral actions are rational, and they are undertaken by all countries; but this is not inconsistent with the pursuit of multilateral negotiations when appropriate. The key is to know when to employ each tactic. To think of the problem as one of 'unilateralism *versus* multilateralism' is therefore false; it should be stressed that the very aim of unilateral actions is to encourage reciprocal behaviour.

Rather than suffer under the misleading tag of 'unilateralism', anti-nuclear opinion should instead stress and become more identified with the basic themes of alternative defence: common security, non-provocative defence, denuclearisation, conventional strength and so on.

(5) Finally, when thinking about its future defence proposals, the Labour Party at this point in opposition should not tie itself too closely to exact policies and timetables; it could say what it would do if it were in power now, but it cannot say what it might do in four or five years' time, when the international and domestic context will have changed. This is a time for comment, learning and building foundations. As the rest of the chapter will reveal, it is not a hopeless prospect despite the 1987 election result.

THE MYTHS, THREATS AND PROMISES OF THE DOUBLE-ZERO AGREEMENT

Some of the reasons for the hope just discussed were strengthened by the signature of the INF Treaty in Washington in December 1987.

This agreement promised a global ban on missiles with ranges between 500 and 5000 kilometres. To be removed will be intermediate-range missiles (108 Pershing IIs and 64 cruise missiles on the US side, and 441 SS-20s and 112 SS-4s on the Soviet side) and shorter-range systems (72 West German/US Pershing IAs and 120 SS12/22s and 20 SS-23s on the Soviet side). It is the first agreement bringing about actual reductions in nuclear weapons.

Despite the hullabaloo that naturally surrounded the signing of the Treaty, it is difficult not to have mixed feelings about it. On the one hand there is reason to be satisfied that it happened, and to have hope that the momentum towards denuclearisation will continue. On the other hand, there is also reason to be cynical about the motives for its signing, and sceptical about future behaviour. However we arrived at this point – and the journey is already surrounded by much mythology – we are at a crossroads in European security; the double-zero agreement offers us both threats and promises.

The story of the double-zero agreement is extremely revealing. It throws a great deal of light on official arguments, assumptions and rationalisations; and shows both how things in nuclear strategy are not always as they are presented and how outcomes can be different from intentions. As a microcosm of our security predicament, and with potentially major implications for the future, the story and lessons of the double-zero agreement are too important to be left to governments.

The official version of the INF story, as told and retold by Western governments, is both familiar and remarkably straightforward. It goes, with minor national and individual variations, as follows: In December 1979 NATO agreed to the 'twin-track' decision; this involved deploying new US ground-launched missiles in Western Europe and at the same time negotiating arms control with the Soviet Union. On the military side this deployment was necessary to counter the growing threat of Soviet SS-20 missiles; politically it represented a US response to the worries of the European allies, articulated most notably by Chancellor Schmidt, about the strength of the US guarantee to Western security. The new US missiles, ground-based in Western Europe and capable of hitting the Soviet Union, would 'couple' the United States and its allies and create a 'seamless web of deterrence'. While plans for the missile deployment went ahead, President Reagan in 1981 proposed the 'zero-option' to the Soviet Union: NATO would forgo its missile deployment if the Soviet Union would scrap its growing arsenal of SS-20s. In the talks that followed, the Soviet Union did not negotiate seriously, and when NATO began deploying its own new systems at the end of 1983, the Soviet representatives walked out and broke down the whole arms-control process. Despite this, and despite the vociferous protests of the Western 'peace movements', the NATO allies stood together, and the deployment of the cruise and Pershing II missiles continued. In time this determination shown by the West forced the Soviet Union back to the negotiating table. Under its new leader, Mr Gorbachev, the Soviet Union proved more flexible and inventive in its approach, even to the extent of expropriating Mr Reagan's zero-option proposal. NATO responded positively to the new Soviet approach, and through 1986–87 worked towards an agreement. This was signed in Washington in December 1987; it represents the first concrete achievement in nuclear disarmament. Not only will reductions take place for the first time, but a whole class of weaponry will be eliminated. Furthermore, NATO's determination led to asymmetrical cuts, with the Soviet Union showing a novel willingness to accept bigger reductions than the West. This vindication of the multilateral approach to arms control now promises good tidings for progress in super power negotiations on strategic forces, where the declared aim is to achieve 50 per cent cuts in the near future.

The above version of the story of the double-zero agreement is now the Western defence establishment's litany. But at best it gives only a partial view of what happened and, if widely accepted, it will lead to false lessons for the future. Because of the distorting mirror which our officials are holding up to the recent past, we should therefore be sceptical about the crystal ball through which they ask us to look at the future. Space forbids an extensive discussion of all these matters, so what follows are brief comments on those areas that are most relevant to the main issues of this book: alternative and more accurate ways of thinking about the Soviet threat, the value of nuclear weapons, the character of NATO strategy, and the role of arms-control. The discussion will show that there is good reason to be sceptical of the official version of 'reality'.

(1) Did NATO need to counter the SS-20?

The SS-20 has an undeservedly large role in this story. For nearly twenty years before they started the deployment of the SS-20s, the Soviet Union had targeted ground-based missiles (SS-4s and SS-5s) against Western Europe. NATO during this period had not thought it necessary to 'counter' these systems like-for-like in order to maintain an effective deterrent. Aircraft and sea-launched systems had performed the theatre nuclear role for NATO: extended deterrence was not seen as requiring precise balances between all systems. In the light of this, NATO's decision to introduce a new category of systems (and in the case of the Pershing II a dramatically more capable system than its predecessor) gives support to the Soviet claim that NATO, not itself 'escalated' the arms race in Europe.[32]

The original Soviet Euro-missiles were primitive. They were inaccurate (their large warheads were a partial compensation for this) and they were vulnerable in a crisis. The latter was particularly important; their vulnerability made them classic use-them-or-lose-them weapons. Soviet modernisation (and hence improvement) was predictable. When the SS-20 arrived, many Western analysts claimed that it represented an escalation rather than a modernisation.[33] This was unnecessary alarm. Its greater accuracy and smaller warhead made it a more discriminating weapon, and therefore one less likely to cause wanton destruction in war, while its mobility gave it crisis-stability. As a result of the latter the SS-20 could have been seen as a unilateral arms control measure, whether intended or not. The SS-20 had the same stabilising potential in the theatre context that the US deployment of Polaris had earlier represented in the strategic: NATO planners have no interest in the Soviet Union possessing vulnerable nuclear systems that predispose them to first use in a crisis. The NATO allies should therefore have regarded the SS-20 as an improvement on what had confronted them before, and then ignored it. It did not increase the threat we faced.

The SS-20 did not 'need' to be 'countered', and indeed was not, in the sense that the new US missiles deployed in Europe were designed to take out the SS-20s in the event of war. That would have been a logical military purpose, but it was not the reason for the NATO deployment. The latter had little directly to do with the SS-20. The new Soviet missile was not so much the cause as the occasion for the deployment of cruise and the Pershing IIs; the role of the SS-20 was therefore to provide a convenient rationalisation for various Western motives. If the United States had not been developing ground-launched cruise missiles and did not have a qualitatively different Pershing system, then it is unlikely that the SS-20 would have been 'countered' in the way chosen. It had been evident by the mid-1970s that the US military–industrial complex was doing and would do its utmost to see that the relatively cheap and accurate cruise systems would be deployed in many modes and in large numbers. Development had gone too far to be ignored. At the same time, the very fast and accurate Pershing II promised to be of considerable value to the military as a nuclear war-fighting system; it represented a technological leap over its predecessor rather than the incremental development implied in the progression in nomenclature from Pershing I to II. Technological inertia was clearly one explanation for NATO's decision; these new US weapons were a textbook example of solutions looking for problems.

A second reason for the deployment was the US desire to establish 'parity plus'. Parity had been codified in SALT I, and was a principle in the SALT II negotiations which were going on during the period when the INF decisions were taking place. NATO's new systems were categorised as 'intermediate', since they were obviously not of intercontinental range: but they were regarded as 'strategic' systems by the Soviet Union, since they could hit Soviet territory. They were therefore effectively an attempt to regain a degree of superiority over the Soviet Union by circumventing the notion of parity.[34] This again underlines the Soviet claim that it was the West rather than itself which escalated this dimension of the arms race. Western governments failed to understand the Soviet viewpoint and dismissed their arguments; any comparable attempt on the Soviet side to extend and increase its deterrent power (siting the equivalent of Pershing IIs in Cuba or Nicaragua, for example) would obviously have been met by fierce, perhaps world-threatening US opposition.

The third set of reasons for the development – again unrelated to the SS-20 – were more political than military, and, as will be seen, concerned the intra-NATO problem of the evolving relationship between the two parts of the alliance.

(2) What role did the Europeans have in the deployment?

By the late 1970s some Europeans were becoming nervous about the strength of the US nuclear guarantee. For those of this opinion, and it was not widespread until governments made a loyalty test out of it, the INF deployment had a political dimension: to 'couple' the United States and Western Europe, to show alliance 'resolve', and to reassure West Germany in particular. Given the fever NATO had to overcome in the early 1980s in order to achieve these aims, we are justified in concluding that the cure was worse than what the nuclear hypochondriacs considered to be the disease.

Support for the INF deployment, even among Western governments, was less enthusiastic than the official story of the twin-track decision might suggest. The arms control track, for example, was not laid down because of any belief on the part of NATO hardliners in the virtue of arms control, but because of the need to buy the support of the more sceptical allies (particularly the Belgians and the Dutch), and to help them all sell the deployment to their publics. Arms-control was not originally integral to NATO's 1979 decision; it was a last-minute addition, to manage opinion. From the start, therefore, the twin-track policy was always rather lopsided.

Even those Europeans strongly in favour of the deployment were not at the time exercised about the SS-20s, as subsequent mythology suggests. In his famous 1977 Alistair Buchan lecture, Chancellor Helmut Schmidt did not mention the SS-20, though it is often assumed he did. His anxieties about the Western European–United States relationship sprang from the conventional military disparity at a time of strategic nuclear parity.[35]

(3) How serious is NATO about the 'seamless web' of deterrence?

In strictly military terms, even many of the supporters of the INF deployment did not think that NATO's new missiles served a necessary purpose, while their critics believed them to be positively dangerous. The Pershing II in particular was very provocative to the Soviet Union since it cut down warning time and so, in a crisis or at the outbreak of war would put them under great pressure to pre-empt. The effect of the deployment of these missiles on the Soviet Union has been justifiably compared with the intolerable pressure that the Americans believed themselves to be under when the Soviet Union deployed intermediate systems in Cuba in 1962.

As was pointed out earlier, before the late 1970s NATO had not felt the need for a seamless web of deterrence. Nevertheless, once the decision to deploy was taken the idea of a 'seamless web' was elevated to a principle. A role was found for the new weapons in the doctrine of flexible response, which, as will be discussed later has always been heavily pro-nuclear and escalatory. In war the seamless web of deterrence threatens to be a seamless web of escalation in that strategy, 'Flexible Response', which is a pact to nuclear suicide in order to avoid the risk of fighting to death.

The idea of the seamless web of deterrence had not been NATO doctrine but was brought out to justify the deployment of unpopular new systems. After the INF agreement, however, this principle looks set to rebound on its supporters. If it is necessary for deterrence to be 'seamless', was it not irresponsible to tear such a large hole in the middle of our doctrinal veil?

(4) Whose zero-option was it, and why should we be cynical about it?

It is becoming widely assumed that the original idea for the zero-option emanated from the Reagan administration. The latter cannot claim the idea; they only coined the phrase and made the first formal diplomatic proposal. Like so many ideas on the agenda these days, this one originated in the peace movement. The 1980 END (European Nuclear Disarmament) Appeal called for the non-deployment of the US systems and the removal of SS-20s; and demanding a 'no' to each of these systems was a prominent feature of peace-movement banners. Reflecting this, an informal proposal on these lines was made to the Soviet Union by Michael Foot and Denis Healey during a visit to Moscow.

The reasons for the Reagan administration's interest in the zero–zero idea are not difficult to find. Believing that the Soviet Union would be most unlikely to respond positively to the proposal, the White House proceeded with the zero-option in order to deflate the growing anti-nuclear and anti-American criticism in Western Europe by endorsing a dramatic disarmament initiative. In the course of time it also served as a tactic by which to undercut the increasingly influential nuclear-freeze movement in the United States. Furthermore, because the zero-option, as presented, would be unacceptable to the Soviet Union, the White House could expect to win important propaganda points in the new Cold War: the USSR would be seen as the obstacle to a simple and dramatic disarmament proposal. It was hoped that this image of Soviet obstructionism would help change the minds of any wavering Western opinion about the need to deploy the new US INF systems.

There are several reasons for believing that the zero-option was not a 'serious' offer by the US administration. First, it was asking Moscow to give up something for nothing. The Soviet Union was being asked to reverse its long-established posture based on land-based INF; in return, NATO was offering not to change its existing posture, which was based on not having land-based INF. The zero-option did not therefore involve equal sacrifice. There can be no doubt that the White House would not have agreed to a zero-option had the United States been in a comparable position to the Soviet Union. Strobe Talbott expressed the predicament in the vernacular of Washington: 'it was like the Redskins trying to persuade the hated Dallas Cowboys to trade Tony Dorsett for a future draft pick.'[36] Second, when, as expected the Soviet Union refused to trade something for nothing, Western officials went out of their way to assert that this showed that the Kremlin was not serious about arms-control; it was claimed that they would negotiate, if at all, only when NATO had begun or was on the point of deploying its own new missiles. The Russians, it was argued, only respond to power. Naturally, the Soviet Union did not react positively to such diplomatic bullying. To have done so in the face of such crude tactics would have created a weak image. Again, the United States would have been equally obdurate if forced into the same corner.

The record suggests that there is more reason for being cynical about the motives of the Reagan administration than for imagining it to have been serious about the zero-option. When he was elected, Ronald Reagan was the most hostile critic of arms-control ever to have become president. His first director of the Arms Control and Disarmament Agency was Eugene Rostow, a fellow member of the hawkish Committee for the Present Danger. He was later replaced by Kenneth Adelman, who thought arms negotiations were a 'sham'; their real value, he once said, was in their usefulness in managing public opinion.[37] This attitude was echoed in a phrase used by Assistant Secretary of State Richard Burt to describe the aim of the zero-option: 'alliance management'.[38] The zero-option was a 'gimmick' not intended to produce an agreement but instead to show the Soviet Union in a bad light and so encourage unsteady allies to stay on the deployment-track of the 1979 decision. Alexander Haig, then Secretary of State, later described the zero-option as a killer proposal, designed in order that the Soviet Union would reject it.[39] NATO's Supreme Allied Commander at the time, General Bernard Rogers, called the White House's 1981 proposal a 'magnificent political ploy', but one that gave him 'gas pains' when it later came to be discussed seriously.[40] Like other officials, Rogers had gone along with the zero-option only because he believed the Russians would reject it.

There is therefore abundant reason to be cynical about the administration's motives in proposing the zero-option during 1981–83. The Soviet Union rejected it, as expected, and when the deployment of US systems began in Western Europe at the end of 1983, the Soviet negotiators left the table; their counterparts in any major power would have done the same. They had been outmanoeuvred. To make matters worse, from the Soviet point of view, the unaccommodating and blustering behaviour of their government during the previous few years had exactly fitted the propaganda image that had been designed in Washington. In the first half of the 1980s the Kremlin could not have performed more perfectly the White House's anti-Soviet script.

(5) Who disrupted the arms control process?

In the official NATO story of arms control in the 1980s the role of good guys and bad guys is clearly delineated. The reality is more complicated and this is evident in the apportionment of blame for the collapse of the super power arms control process. The NATO story places all the blame on the Soviet Union, but more objective analysis suggests that the responsibility was less one-sided.

It was obviously the Soviet Union which formally walked out of the INF talks, but it was argued earlier that they were pushed into it by a White House policy that had Soviet non-cooperation rather than mutual agreement as its main objective. Which super power in these circumstances is the more blameworthy? The responsibility for the breakdown was shared. This is also the case when we consider the arms control process more broadly. While the Kremlin gave up on the INF round of talks, it had been the Reagan administration that had earlier disrupted the process by refusing to ratify the SALT II Treaty which President Carter had signed with General Secretary Brezhnev in 1979. The White House would argue that this decision had been in reaction to unacceptable Soviet behaviour in Afghanistan and elsewhere. It was, but it also reflected the new administration's general hostility to arms control, and its particular opposition to the 'fatally flawed' SALT II Treaty.

Between 1980 and 1985 neither super power had an impressive arms control record. Both engaged in gamesmanship, played the numbers game, and sought to further their own interests at the expense of the other. Flexibility and imagination was only seen in propaganda, not in sticky issues such as verification. When the super powers accept mutual (if not always equal) responsibility for past failures, they might get on track to create the basis for a more cooperative future.

(6) Did the Kremlin come to accept the zero-option only because of Western strength?

As with other aspects of the INF story, the claim about the decisiveness of Western 'strength' in the eventual outcome of the negotiations gives an incomplete and in this case misleading picture of what happened. The December 1987 Treaty, whose signature seemed impossible only a short time earlier, owed at least as much to President Reagan's growing political weakness as to NATO's earlier determination to see the deployment through. Success also depended upon Mr Gorbachev's flexibility and commitment to arms control; previous Soviet leaders, without his flair, may not have been able to have brought an agreement about, even had they wished to do so.

The Soviet Union resumed negotiations on INF for several reasons other than the fact that NATO held together on this issue. In the first place it was predictable that the Kremlin would resume talking, following a cooling-off period after the US missiles had been deployed. Although the exhibition of Western 'strength' (such as the White House's determination to press on with SDI) made it urgent for the Soviet Union to try to impose mutual restraints, Gorbachev wanted to reduce the defence burden regardless. Talks were resumed by the Soviet Union because they served several interests: arms restraint promised economic benefits; the negative reputation of the Soviet Union caused by the collapse of the talks was harming Soviet relations with a range of countries, including Japan and those in Western Europe; and the resumption of talks might improve the international atmosphere and alleviate the wasteful confrontation with the United States.

Given Ronald Reagan's history of opposition to arms control, it is doubtful whether a strong and confident President Reagan would have come to pursue a disarmament agreement with his sworn enemy. The events of 1986 and 1987 show President Reagan to have become a remarkable convert to disarmament, in practice if not in theory. Reagan became a willing negotiator because of weakness, not because of strength. As the problems of the second Reagan administration accumulated (from the record budget deficit to the scandal of the Iran-Contra deal), and as its reputation visibly sank, the appeal of a super power summit and an arms-control treaty has grown for Ronald Reagan, a lifelong anti-Soviet and anti-arms controller. A summit and a treaty would be a distraction from less savoury matters and might improve the image of an increasingly lonely and marginal President, 'nearly all [of whose] closest friends and allies are retired, sacked or facing indictment'[41]

(7) Does the INF agreement vindicate the 'multilateralist' approach?

It is of course true that if NATO had not deployed cruise and Pershing II, the Soviet Union would not now be planning to remove its SS-20s. Leaving aside the argument that that would not matter – since the SS-20s represent an economic cost to the Soviet Union rather than leverage in the daily game of nations – what is significant is not simply the successful multilateral negotiations at the end of the INF story but the flexibility and unilateralism shown by Gorbachev just before; it was this that made a successful agreement possible. Since 1985 Gorbachev has regularly outflanked the West over arms control. The domestic problems he faced also concerned his predecessors: the new factor in the equation – the one that made agreement possible – was Gorbachev's personality, including his willingness to travel the next step. By unilaterally announcing and maintaining a nuclear-test moratorium, by unilaterally accepting that US scientists could monitor Soviet tests, by unilaterally conceding asymmetries in the INF agreement. Gorbachev showed himself, in the words of the old peace movement definition of a unilateralist, to be a 'multilateralist who means it'. This unilateralism on the Soviet side, added to changes in the US position, made agreement possible.

The change in the Reagan administration's position was partly due to the President's weakness, mentioned earlier, but also to the continuing strength of the pro-arms control constituency throughout the West. This body of opinion kept arms control on the agenda through the 1980s when Western defence was in the hands of leaders who equated security with strength, and stability with the adversary's fear; they favoured arms control only as gamesmanship, not as a necessary ingredient in a stable relationship.

In sum, the 1987 agreement was at least as much the result of Presidential weakness and Kremlin unilateralism as of allied unity and Soviet weakness. It showed that multilateralism can work, but that its success may depend upon uniltateral actions. Ultimately, success in arms control rests not on tactics but on the recognition by the leaders of the super powers that the accumulation of overkill is wasteful and unproductive, and that security can only be improved by agreement.

(8) Does the agreement eliminate a whole class of weapons and represent the first real progress in nuclear disarmament?

Whether the Treaty eliminates a 'whole class' depends on the way the class is defined. If it is defined as 'cruise missiles' then a whole class is not eliminated, for extensive programmes exist for sea and air-launched versions. These programmes might be expanded, and so reverse the reductions to take place in the sub-class of ground-launched systems.

While some officials were negotiating the double-zero agreement NATO planners and their defence ministers – and probably their Soviet counterparts – were pursuing a different aim. They were seeking 'compensations' to plug the hole that would allegedly be left by the removal of the missiles. Their plan was to circumvent the agreement. Instead of seeing it as the start of a process, they were seeing it as the end.[42] If both alliances go ahead with 'compensations', or if one proceeds hastily and the other responds, by the end of the century there will be even more air- and sea-launched cruise missiles than those already planned. If restraint is not exercised, the agreement could simply channel the arms race into different areas. In particular, it could boost the already vigorous nuclear arms race at sea.[43]

Various alternatives are possible on the NATO side to plug the alleged 'gaps' left by the departing missiles. More F-111s could be deployed in Britian, or B-52s with air-launched cruise missiles; at sea, more cruise missiles could be deployed either on submarines or surface ships. Britain's Trident might also figure in this role; while not quite as accurate as the missiles it would replace, it has bigger warheads. There has been some talk that our 'independent deterrent' might be employed in this Treaty-circumventing role.[44] Other possible initiatives to repair the seams ripped from flexible response include more Tornados with stand-off missiles, an improved Lance missile to be deployed in West Germany, and neutron shells for artillery on the central front. If the NATO allies rush ahead with these 'compensations' the spirit of the double-zero will be wrecked, and the pressure on the Soviet Union to follow suit will be enormous. The problem will be the same if the Soviet Union blunders first into a compensations race. Those now pressing for compensations and modernisations are certainly exhibiting the paranoia that often accompanies addiction to nuclear deterrence, and are probably hoping to spoil the new pro-arms control spirit.

The case for compensations and modernisation is weak. In the West we regularly scare ourselves with the thought that deterrence might break down as a result of deliberate Soviet aggression. To suggest that a reduction of approximately 1.4 per cent of NATO's nuclear stockpile will significantly increase the risk that a Soviet war-planner would contemplate conventional attack is mind-boggling in its underestimation of Soviet rationality. To hear some people talk, one would think that the elimination of about 4 per cent of the super powers' nuclear arsenals was turning Europe into a Nuclear Free Zone, and so 'open for conventional war'. Compensations and modernisations at this point would wreck the spirit of the 1987 agreement, and for no urgent deterrent purpose. We have such an excess of nuclear deterrent potential that even if one element of it is on the road to obsolescence, the military case for updating should be outweighed by the political case for restraint.

In addition to the problems just discussed, the Treaty's future will also depend upon whether it is ratified. Although this seems likely in the immediate aftermath of the signing, there is plenty of evidence of right-wing opposition in the United States; and there is always the danger of an unexpected and unhelpful international situation developing. If the US Senate were to fail to ratify the Treaty at this stage, the adverse consequences for relations between the United States and its allies in Western Europe, not to mention those with the Soviet Union, would be difficult to exaggerate.

It remains to be seen therefore whether the double-zero agreement is the first step in nuclear disarmament, or the last. Certainly from the viewpoint of all those now wanting more reductions – the declared aim of the super powers – the true measure of the Treaty will be whether it leads to further denuclearisation. If it is not followed by progress in conventional arms reductions or by movement towards a 50 per cent cut in strategic warheads, we will almost certainly have more nuclear weapons by the end of the century than we have today. Unfortunately, both technically and politically, the START negotiations are far more complex than even those that led to the INF agreement, since they involve sensitive issues such as SDI and the problem of mutually acceptable sub-ceilings. In the best of circumstances progress will not be easy. If the post-Treaty atmosphere is poisoned by compensations, modernisation, or non-ratification, further progress will be impossible.

(9) Were the cuts as 'asymmetrical' (in favour of the West) as has been claimed?

Not only did Western determination bring the Soviet Union back to the negotiating table – so it is claimed – it also led to the Soviet Union agreeing to scrap approximately four times more warheads than the United States. As a rider, it is sometimes added that this asymmetrical cut will not have been welcomed by the Soviet military, and so represents yet another threat to Gorbachev's future.

Needless to say, the actual picture is more complex, and must begin with an appreciation that a consistent Soviet objective since the talks began had been to remove from European territory US missiles that could hit the Soviet Union. Just as the United States did not want forward-based Soviet intermediate range missiles on Cuba, or elsewhere on the American continent, neither did the Kremlin want US ground-based nuclear missiles on any offshore islands of Europe, or on the continent itself. From the Soviet perspective US INF were 'strategic' systems, since they could hit the Soviet homeland; their own Euromissiles (SS-20s and SS-4s in the intermediate range and SS-12/22s and SS-23s in the shorter range) could not hit the United States. When this important asymmetry in geography and technology is appreciated, it should be apparent that there is less asymmetry in the actual agreement than at first appears. If the weapons to be removed are defined only in a Western sense, as INF systems, then the Soviet Union is removing more – about four times the number of warheads (1575 as against 436). On the other hand, if some of these weapons are seen as 'strategic', as they are by the Soviet Union, then the asymmetry is on the US side (it is conceding 364 'strategic' warheads against zero).[45] The US concession also includes the removal of the very threatening Pershing IIs, which, as pointed out earlier, had been a particular concern for the Soviet Union.

In the light ot this more symmetrical assessment of the agreement, the Soviet military has little reason to grumble about Gorbachev's achievement. The growth of Soviet military opposition to Gorbachev is wishful thinking on the part of his critics in the West, while in Moscow, only those who are the General Secretary's enemies for other reasons will publicise the Western claim that the Treaty terms are asymmetrical. In actuality, it is a rather good deal for the Soviet Union as well as the West. This is not surprising, since Gorbachev, who has Soviet interests at heart, wants socialism to work, and is a hard-headed political leader.

Conclusions

As can be seen from this discussion, the story and implications of the zero–zero agreement are rather more subtle and multifaceted than the official NATO account suggests. It is a microcosm of many of the problems discussed in this book. If we are to succeed in living in peace and security with Soviet Russia, we need to see the world in a balanced rather than in an ethnocentric fashion. Our security prospects are threatened more by one-sided analysis than by what the government likes to call 'one-sided disarmament'.

While much of the history of the INF talks can be interpreted cynically, the outcome could be beneficial. But there are many obstacles and negative possibilities. If the parties involved do not act within the spirit as well as the letter of the Treaty, the arms race will merely be rechannelled, we might end up with even more nuclear weapons, cynicism about arms control will deepen, strain will develop in super power relations, there will be a political crisis within NATO, and the risks and waste of present European security relations will be prolonged for another indefinite period. These outcomes are not inevitable; if followed up with skill and imagination the Treaty might come to have a number of intended and unintended beneficial results.

In the first place, the agreement could reduce the number of nuclear weapons in the world. This would be a breakthrough. The agreement is a signal of our overdependence on these systems and might help to undermine the belief that more is better. Among the benefits of this, money could be saved and it could be the start of further steps in denuclearisation. Although the leaders of the super powers talk about the complete elimination of nuclear weapons, this is not at present realistic; but movement towards minimum deterrent postures are now becoming conceivable, as well as being politically and strategically desirable.

If it is not undermined, the Treaty will help to restore serious arms control (as opposed to gamesmanship) to the centre of the super-power relationship. Success here would help to strengthen Gorbachev's position within the Soviet Union, which appears to be in our interests as well as his own; it might also encourage candidates in the US presidential race to support arms-restraint policies rather than the racing for primacy that was the basis of Ronald Reagan's first bid for the presidency.

If arms control is restored, there is some reason to be more confident of the prospects for success. The learning process involved in the negotiation of the double-zero, the precedents established by some of the terms, and the limited trust built up may have created a momentum that will help achievements in other and more difficult areas, notably strategic arms reduction and the halting of the weaponisation of space. The precedents established in the traditionally sensitive problem of verification are particularly important, since the very intrusive system that was agreed is much better than could have been hoped for several years earlier. The reassurance it should create could have important spillover for other talks. In addition, the Treaty reflected a willingness by both parties to accept 'unbalanced cuts'; the Soviet Union gave up 'theatre' systems; the United States, 'strategic' ones. If 'balance' is to be achieved in security, unbalanced cuts will be essential, for example in conventional forces.

If the Treaty could prove a boost for arms control, it could have just the opposite effect for nuclear strategy. While its significance in the latter respect can be exaggerated, the Treaty does add to the gathering uncertainties about nuclear deterrence. Elements of flexible response and extended deterrence are being eroded, willy-nilly, just as many of them grew. The INF deployment was justified according to the virtues of flexibility, the need for a seamless web of deterrence and coupling. But the INF link between the battlefield and strategic nuclear systems upon which NATO's strategy of escalation is based is now about to be removed. It is bound to lead to further questioning: if it can be removed, was it needed in the first place? Futhermore, the confusion about what is best for NATO – why remove the missiles if compensations are needed? – must lead more people to wonder whether the NATO hierarchy really knows what it is doing when it comes to the management of nuclear weapons. Confusion and the potential for discord within the alliance could be seen in the immediate aftermath of the Treaty in the debate in West Germany about battlefield nuclear weapons. Supporters of both government and opposition parties started asking why they should bear a disproportionate nuclear risk. Why, they asked, if NATO is removing new nuclear systems capable of hitting the Soviet Union, should West Germany support the modernisation of shorter-range systems whose warheads would explode on German soil? Out of these concerns might grow powerful pressure for the 'third zero', the removal of battlefield nuclear weapons. This has been proposed by the Soviet Union, and it could become another area where there is scope for trouble within NATO, which does not seem to have a coherent doctrine. In this and other areas, NATO's seams have been prised open by the removal of just those weapons whose difficult deployment was supposed to have achieved the opposite.

As a result of reducing the nuclear component of deterrence, albeit by a small amount, the Treaty has thrown more light on the role of conventional forces in Europe. This should stimulate the ingenious Mr Gorbachev to think even more carefully about his force posture. If he wants further progress in denuclearisation, and wants to undermine NATO justifications for INF compensations, he will have to address, unilaterally or multilaterally, Western worries about imbalances in conventional and chemical forces. If Western fears about Soviet strength decrease, then further progress in denuclearisation will become easier. The adoption of a no-first-use doctrine will become more thinkable, even for a NATO hierarchy conditioned to think nuclear.

Whether intended or not, the INF Treaty shows a victory for political sense over military logic. While the weapons to be removed could all be justified in relation to particular doctrines and targets, their removal indicates that some notion of 'sufficiency' has broken through both the traditional Soviet preference for over-insurance and the early Reaganite dream of superiority. When sufficiency takes hold, further arms control, including a comprehensive test ban, becomes feasible.

In addition to its effects on deterrence, doctrine and arms control, the agreement may also have positive political repercussions. Most immediately, it has boosted the desire for *détente*. As a result of the way the Treaty was negotiated, and the terms agreed, the exaggerated image of the 'Soviet threat' has been rolled back a little more. The agreement obviously does not wipe out East–West differences, and there is a rocky road ahead, but it is undoubtedly a step to better relations as yet more people realise the anachronistic character of Cold War attitudes and behaviour.

If the agreement might lead to a relaxation in East–West relations, it might have just the opposite effect on West–West relations. In addition to causing trouble over doctrinal issues, it could lead to a major reassessment of US–Western European relations, by creating for the Europeans a more accurate picture of the direction being taken by their super power ally. The Treaty, which at a stroke removed vaunted symbols of the US nuclear guarantee, can be seen as a step in the nuclear decoupling of the two parts of the alliance; the Reykjavik preliminaries (and other cases) showed that the US President was willing to contemplate far-reaching changes in NATO strategy without consultation. All this, and the image of the superpowers acting together over the heads of the Europeans, might push the latter together to take more responsibility for their own defence. De Gaulle's instincts are approaching being vindicated.

The double-zero agreement could therefore help to unravel some of the military infrastructure and political mindsets that have sustained Cold War behaviour. Appetites have been whetted for more denuclearisation, for changes in NATO strategy, and for revisions in the image of the Soviet Union. Such trends threaten to undermine some of the basic assumptions on which British government policy has been based. Cruise missiles and Pershing II were brought in to show that the way to deal with the Soviet Union was by acting tough, and that effective nuclear deterrence needed coupling, flexibility and seamlessness. Ironically, the decision to remove these missiles is teaching the opposite: we can do business with the Soviet Union, denuclearisation is not dangerous, and extended deterrence and flexible response are flawed. The INF Treaty is a crossroads on the security landscape of Europe. But if we are to take the safer road, a significant body of support is needed to sustain the new thinking. Whether there is any hope for this is the subject of the final section.

TOWARDS A CRITICAL NON-NUCLEAR MASS?

The previous two sections have shown that the year 1987, with the general election and the double-zero agreement, was one of mixed fortunes for British supporters of alternative defence. Some immediate hopes were dashed, notably that of halting Trident, but other possibilities became more thinkable as a result of developments in superpower relations. The weight of official opinion, together with the mindsets and vested interests that sustain Cold War postures, remain powerful obstacles to change. Nevertheless, the prospects for advancing the cause of denuclearisation have never been brighter. Change is in the air, as debate and situation interact. Commenting on the influence of pro-nuclear vested interests, Enoch Powell has written that 'Reason is not sufficient to overcome so formidable an inertia. Only events can topple a thesis buttressed so securely. It may be however that both in the West and in the East those very events are now taking shape.'[46] This final section of Chapter 1 will identify some of the proponents of alternative ways of proceeding; these are the individuals and groupings that must combine to form a critical mass if Cold War mentalities and behaviour are to be superseded by ideas and policies that promise a more stable peace.

There is abundant evidence of interest in alternative defence. It is not going too far to suggest that alternative defence ideas are shaping the agenda in the debate about defence and East–West relations today as effectively as the hawkish tendency, notably the Committee for the Present Danger, shaped the agenda in the late 1970s.

Given the strength of opinion on both sides of the nuclear debate in Britain today, it could mean that we will never again see a consensus on defence. More likely, given Britain's political traditions and the pressures of the electoral system, a consensus of sorts will re-emerge. If and when it does, it will be surprising if it is as pro-nuclear as hitherto. In Britain and other countries evidence of the new 'alternative' thinking can be detected at various levels of opinion. The discussion about the proponents of these ideas begins, appropriately, at the grassroots.

(1) *Public opinion*   The early 1980s were a formative time in British public opinion. They revealed that we had become complacent about nuclear weapons in the 1970s; the situation was not as comfortable as we had come to imagine. There was a dramatic rise in the fear of nuclear war, and growing numbers of people decided that they did not want to learn to love and live with the bomb. Anti-nuclear opinion swelled, grew more sophisticated, and become politicised.

Although the anti-nuclear movement today is less vociferous than in 1980–84, a provoked peace movement in future cannot be ruled out. Contingent factors – another Chernobyl or a nuclear crisis – could energise people. A more predictable source of provocation would be the determination of allied governments, pushed by their military commanders, for 'compensations' to replace the systems removed by the INF agreement. 'Plugging the holes' would make a nonsense of the agreement; it would reveal it (on our side) to have been a cynical exercise in the management of public opinion. That officials have some anxieties about public opinion in this regard is suggested by the fact that although NATO commanders looked early for compensations, the issue was played down before the election, for fear of creating an anti-nuclear storm. If the NATO allies do press for compensations and nuclear modernisation, it will be necessary to manipulate public opinion. To do this they will have to revert to emphasising Soviet conventional strength, and the disparity in chemical weapons. To meet this possibility, Mr Gorbachev must exert himself to meet legitimate Western fears in this regard.

The nuclear issue in the years ahead could become entangled with other issues in British politics. These include questions of civil rights, secrecy, accountability and the role of unelected military, scientific and political bureaucracies. If there is to be a reassertion of British democracy, it must include more openness about nuclear policy. The history of Britain and nuclear weapons reveals that it is not only the public that is kept in the dark about nuclear decisions: even the Cabinet sometimes is.[47]

The direction public opinion takes on defence matters will depend upon a range of factors. Some of these will be domestic, such as the state of the British economy. Others will be international, pre-eminently the state of super power relations, and US–Western European relations. If, as seems likely, the image of the 'Soviet threat' continues to ameliorate, then expending scarce resources on the military confrontation will be increasingly difficult to justify. There is already a widespread perception that we have more than enough for deterrence, and that fuelling the arms race is less necessary than progressively reducing the risks of nuclear war. More than ever the public wants control on armaments. This is well illustrated by the support – across the parties and from the general public to 'celebrities' – given to the UK Nuclear Weapons Freeze. A Marplan Poll in mid-1987, for example, revealed that 79 per cent wanted Britain to freeze its nuclear testing if the super powers did.[48] On British relations with the United States, the unique Reagan–Thatcher personal relationship will soon come to an end; then it will just be a matter of time before the 'special relationship' is fully revealed to be special only in its one-sidedness. At that point Trident could develop an increasingly negative image, when it is realised that it gives us less independence than we imagined. The 'rent-a-missile' revelation in the autumn of 1987, which led to a wider questioning of the extent to which our 'independent deterrent' is really a 'sub-branch of US defence policy'[49] was a harbinger of this.

There is often scepticism about what public opinion can achieve, especially in a well-guarded domain like defence. Apathy is induced if people believe that nothing can be done. The evidence, however, suggests that when mobilised and channelled, public opinion can have a significant effect. The 1980s, so far, are a testimony to that. Despite the weight of opposition – the dominance of right-wing governments and the 'new Cold War' – opinion in the West critical of official policies has actually achieved a great deal. Among the victories of public opinion in several Western countries, to set against such failures as the deployment of cruise missiles, the following stand out: arms control was kept on the agenda despite the hostile instincts of Reagan, Thatcher and Kohl; anti-nuclear slogans evolved into the concrete policy options of alternative defence; the language of common security and alternative defence has spread horizontally and vertically (including into Eastern Europe, as will be seen below); the desirability of *détente* was kept alive during a wasteful period of East–West sabre-rattling; limits were maintained on the extreme military and political ideas of the strategic fundamentalists in the United States; President Reagan was kept from temptation or prevented from indulging his beliefs in such areas as intervention in Central America, the deployment of the MX-missile, breaking out of the SALT II limits, or embarking full-steam-ahead (and damn the ABM Treaty) on Star Wars; throughout the West public consciousness was raised on nuclear issues to an unprecedented level; in West Germany popular opinion discouraged Kohl from stopping the progress towards an INF agreement, by deciding to keep the Pershing IA missiles; it is most unlikely that an INF agreement would have been pursued, and then welcomed by the major Western governments had there not been such large pro-arms control constituencies in their countries; when, in the early 1980s, confrontation and boycott were the preferred official postures towards the East, the dissatisfaction of interested opinion led to a great expansion of 'personal diplomacy' in East–West relations; and finally, the peace movement has led the way in so many matters, not least seeing the problem of European security from an all-European rather than a simply nationalistic perspective, and thinking about security with a view to the long term (measured in decades) rather than year-to-year. All these successes were achieved by public opinion in the 1980s when the international atmosphere was particularly inclement. They should be better publicised. If such successes could be achieved in bad times, what cannot be achieved now, when the conditions are becoming brighter, there are positive results to build upon, and many of the notions of alternative defence are being taken seriously at all levels, as will be seen below?

(2) *Authorities* One of the most interesting features of the defence debate since the late 1970s has been the questioning of the Cold War/pro-nuclear norms that dominated Western thinking about defence for thirty years by a growing number of individuals who are specialists in defence or defence-related fields. This is a recent development,

and its impact has not run its course. As it does, its implications could be enormous.

The catalogue of authorities and specialists who have become more outspoken in their criticism of established thinking about nuclear deterrence has increased markedly in the last ten years.[50] Instead of the comfortable consensus, we see questioning and the proposing of different options. Since the late 1970s the very concept of nuclear deterrence has been under challenge from a range of experts, both on the left and right of the spectrum, and in the United States as well as Western Europe. We have seen Generals and Air Chief Marshals criticising NATO strategy in public. Former defence scientists, who have held the highest positions, point to the waste and increasing insecurity that the arms race brings. Soviet specialists in the West give a more relaxed interpretation of the 'Soviet threat'. Computer programmers and scientists stand out against the waste, ineffectiveness and danger threatened by Star Wars, and back measures like a Comprehensive Test Ban Treaty to restrain the arms race. Old nuclear-deterrers oppose the British decision to deploy Trident. Supporters of NATO question the military utility of the GLCM deployment. Leading US defence specialists, including former 'insiders' (ex-Secretary of Defense Robert McNamara, ex-National Security Adviser McGeorge Bundy and Admiral Noel Gaylor, for example) make serious criticisms of the direction of US nuclear strategy and advocate radical changes such as no-first-nuclear-use. Defence analysts cast a sceptical eye over old assumptions about nuclear diplomacy ('blackmail', 'coercion' etc.). Prominent philosophers erode the moral standing of nuclear deterrence. Retired military officers, academic specialists and researchers devise 'alternative defence' schemes. Some academics, researchers and military figures interested in changing doctrine in a defensive direction promote exchanges of view across the Iron Curtain. And doctors, lawyers and people from other professions campaign against the trends in and thinking behind the pro-nuclear postures and anachronistic Cold War attitudes that has dominated Western policy for decades.

An important phenomenon within this trend has been the rise to prominence of a number of women specialists in international security. Prominent in Britain have been Mary Kaldor and Scilla McLean, the former for her writing and work for the Labour Party and END (European Nuclear Disarmament), the latter as Director of the Oxford Research Group. In the United States Randall Forsberg,

Director of the Institute for Defense and Disarment Studies (IDDS) wrote the initial tract for the influential US Nuclear Freeze movement and has made IDDS a major centre for the study of alternative defence and the dissemination of its ideas at all levels.[51] Women have also come to play important roles in activist positions; in Britain Joan Ruddock was chair of CND during its years of expansion in the early 1980s.

Such voices are rightly being taken more seriously than hitherto. A multinational group of women defence analysts and leaders, for example, including some of the above, and also political figures like Mai-Britt Theorin, Sweden's Minister for Disarmament, and Margaret Papandreou of Greece, had an audience with the US Congress before the Reagan–Gorbachev summit in December 1987.[52] Among other matters, they presented evidence that the NATO governments had already taken steps to introduce new nuclear weapons to replace those being removed by the Treaty. This venture was the result of an earlier initiative by an International Assembly of Women, which discussed disarmament topics and led to a high-level visit by a group of women leaders to NATO in June 1987. There the group was 'stunned to learn' that no formal channel of communication existed between NATO and the Warsaw Pact. As a result, the Warsaw Pact's 29 May invitation to discuss military doctrine, to be mentioned later, had to be conveyed through the media. The women leaders – correctly as events have shown – received the impression that NATO officials were not enthusiastic about discussing military doctrine with the WTO. As a result of meeting officials, the group concluded that unless there were significant changes in attitude and behaviour, the arms race would continue to escalate regardless of any agreements that might be signed. Women leaders such as these represent a swelling tide of public and specialist opinion which did not want such an escalation to continue.

The impact of alternative defence ideas on proponents of establishment thinking has been variable. Some individuals remain unmoved, but others, who a few years ago would have been unresponsive to such ideas, now take them seriously. In the summer of 1987, for example, Zbigniew Brzezinski, former National Security Adviser to President Carter, expressed support for disengagement rather than confrontation as the key to European security.[53] Noting the loosening ties between the two halves of Europe and their super power allies, he wrote that 'This might even lead to the revival of a genuine reassociation of the two halves of Europe. We should welcome such a movement.' He then suggested that NATO propose a 'tank-free' zone in central Europe, to build confidence and reduce the risks of surprise attack. This approach (emphasising building-down rather than negotiating from strength, bringing the blocs together rather than drawing lines between them, and favouring reassurance rather than confrontation) would not have been heard from such a voice at the start of the decade.

The spreading influence of alternative defence notions on growing numbers of authorities in the field is a phenomenon that should not be minimised. Pro-nuclear opinion is mistaken if it believes that the anti-nuclear movement is beaten because the membership of CND declined after the peak of 1983–84. Those who want to reform the way we approach the problem of security are more extensive than those who march, and their influence is spreading. In future, anti-nuclear opinion will gain confidence from the changing attitudes of some authorities in the field. At the same time these authorities will offer an alternative set of ideas and policy options to doubters, don't-knows, and young people yet to think about it. The experts in the debate are by no means as one-sided as formerly.

The days when the critics of extended nuclear deterrence and Britain's own bombs and missiles could be dismissed as 'lefties', 'pinkos', or the 'woolly-hatted brigade' have passed. Indeed, the centre-of-gravity of opinion has moved so much that negative images are now recognised in profusion on the other side: Michael Heseltine and his camouflage jacket, Lady Olga Maitland and her platoon of strident followers, anti-Soviet party hacks who do not want to be disturbed by knowledge, and (in future) a Prime Minister who may well be the most hectoring leader in the West in asserting the virtues of nuclear deterrence.

So, just as the experts and pundits are by no means on the side of the pro-nuclear status quo, neither are negative images and 'ill-informed' and 'emotional' attitudes only to be found on the side of those wanting change. They never were; but that fact is now clearer.

(3) *Organisations* While alternative defence ideas were originally developed by a few individuals, a number of organisations have been responsible for helping to develop and spread them. The health of these organisations is important to develop theoretical and practical ideas, to serve as repositories of knowledge, and to transmit ideas upwards to policymakers and downwards to the interested public.

Furthermore, if a critical mass of opinion is to be achieved these organisations will need to provide mutual support; in this way they can foster alternative defence, as other organisations fostered nuclear deterrence 30–40 years ago. The big difference is that the earlier organisations in the United States received large amounts of money, as they still do, from government contracts.

Organisations involved in alternative defence now exist in most Western countries; and, as will be seen later, interest has also been stimulated within the Soviet bloc. The various organisations have different emphases in their work. Some make an explicit effort to promote public education. Others notably university departments, involve individuals pursuing and publishing their own research. Some undertake the important and novel task of making contact with and seeking to influence the work of political and military leaders. Although lacking both the routine and informal contacts of the 'establishment', progress has been made.

In Britain there have been a number of organisational initiatives. Much publicity was given in the early 1980s to the Alternative Defence Commission (ADC). Set up in 1980, the ADC was sponsored by the Lansbury House Trust Fund in conjunction with the School of Peace Studies at Bradford University. Its stated purpose was a simple one: 'to say No to nuclear weapons is not a defence policy. The question then arises: if Britain does renounce nuclear weapons, what defence policy should it adopt? The remit of the Commission was to address itself to this question, and to review a wide range of alternative non-nuclear policies for Britain.' The ADC published two weighty reports, one on the military and the other on the political dimensions of alternative defence.[54]

Out of the turmoil of the early 1980s there arose two other similar organisations, the Common Security Programme and Just Defence. The first Common Security Programme was initiated by an independent group of defence experts on both sides of the Atlantic to consider how the common security interests of East and West could be developed in Europe. *Common Security in Europe* studies were complete in 1987 and the Foundation for International Security was then established to carry forward the work in three areas: specialised studies; a 'task force' to identify solutions to common security problems; and education. The charter for Just Defence has, as one of its basic articles, the provision that 'Defence policy must be for defence only, and clearly seen as non-provocative to others'. The nine articles of its Charter are an excellent expression of the aims and spirit of alternative defence thinking. A rather different type of organisation is the Oxford Research Group, which has specialised in nuclear weapons decision-making: how the decisions are made, and who makes them. Several invaluable studies have revealed the extent to which nuclear weapons decisions across the world are concentrated in the hands of about 800 people (5 women) and that power of decision has moved steadily away from politicians into the hands of insulated defence bureaucracies. Governments are not accountable in this area.[55]

Good work is being done in Britain, but much of the seminal thinking and writing about alternative defence began in Western Europe. Academics, researchers, and retired (and sometimes active) officers have contributed to a lively school of thought. The Centre of Peace and Conflict Research at the University of Copenhagen is an academic centre where relevant research takes place, and in Germany there is the European Study Group on Alternative Security Policy (SAS) whose staff have connections with the SDP. Current research work, conference activity, and the publications of these and similar institutions worldwide is monitered in the *NOD International Research Newsletter*.[56]

Not surprisingly, the United States has not been the most fertile ground for this kind of thinking. Nevertheless, progress is being made. IDDS, referred to earlier, has been in the forefront of efforts 'to define, study, and popularize' alternative defence policies. Since 1986 it has developed an Alternative Defense Project which consists of four initiatives: an Alternative Defense Working Group, an international network of alternative defence analysts and activists, an Alternative Defense Annual, and a US-focused Alternative Defense Network.[57]

On the international front the concept of non-provocative conventional defence in Europe has been promoted by the Pugwash Conferences on Science and World Affairs since its first workshop on the subject in 1984. Under the aegis of the Pugwash organisation, scientists and other specialists from East and West have met together to address urgent security problems away from immediate political pressures; they have sought solutions 'with both technical validity and political workability', and have made their findings available to policymakers and interested public alike.[58] The aim of Pugwash, like other organisations of similar outlook, is to work out alternatives to the current situation, in which both alliances see the other's forces as a threat because of their offensive potential. Pugwash seeks to improve stability by achieving 'Mutual Defensive Superiority', by drastic cuts in the weapons most suitable for offensive operations, by a buildup of 'robust defensive postures', and by a reduction of the danger of surprise-attack by defining zones of separation.

In addition to such research organisations as those just described, attention must also be paid to the role of campaigning bodies. Of these the most important in Britain have been CND and END. The revival of the former and the birth of the latter were again related to the increased fears of nuclear war starting in the late 1970s. Although the membership and demonstrating impact of CND has subsided since the deployment of cruise missiles, there is still a substantial membership of around 75 000 people. CND's main contribution to the public debate in the 1980s has been in raising awareness that all is not well in the security arrangements of the world; END's special role has been to stimulate thinking in a Europe-wide perspective. During these years both organisations have become more 'professional', and maintain contact with members and attempt to raise wider consciousness through journals and other publications.[59] Both movements were confronted by a dilemma when the super powers decided to remove the missiles that had been such an important focus for their activity. But even though this campaigning focus was removed, decades of other struggles remain.

If alternative defence is to progress there seems to be a general understanding among the interested bodies that there needs to be better contact between them, that campaigning has to be less single-issue, and that more attention has to be given to foreign policy and the non-military dimensions of security. Many outstanding issues remain on the nuclear scene; the zero–zero should be an encouragement to press on, not relax. There is a need for both a vertical and a horizontal proliferation of ideas and consciousness; people need to be persuaded that alternatives do exist, that there are choices.

(4) *Political parties* If new ideas are to become effective they need to be articulated and packaged by political parties. There has been some progress in this respect for alternative defence in the 1980s.

As will be seen in later chapters, several political parties in Western Europe have adopted elements of alternative defence thinking, in addition to the British Labour Party's non-nuclear commitment described earlier. As in Britain, notions of alternative defence, denuclearisation and common security have been embraced most readily by parties on the left of the Western European political spectrum. For US opinion the label 'left' is scary, but in the European context it does not have the same extreme connotations. The most significant Western European political party to have shown interest in alternative defence notions is the West German Social Democratic Party, since one day this party could form the government of a powerful and pivotal state.

Interest in alternative defence has been shown by political parties in other parts of the world. The most intersting examples have been the anti-nuclear stance adopted by the New Zealand Labour Party and the anti-NATO, anti-cruise missile programme proposed by the revived NPD in Canada. In the United States some political figures have shown interest in adopting a more conventional emphasis in military postures, but none of the political parties have shown any serious interest in alternative defence.

The future attitude of British parties towards alternative defence ideas will depend upon a range of factors. The way the international situation evolves will be important, but perhaps even more so will be local issues, largely unrelated to the outside world: much will depend upon the evolution of the ideologies and organisation of the centre and left parties following their electoral defeats of 1987. Defence will be something of a plaything of political developments which may have little to do with ideas about the military chessboard of Europe. This prospect is encouraged by the fact that few British MPs are either interested in or knowledgeable about defence matters, a problem in turn compounded by the country's notoriously secretive and largely unaccountable decision-making structure on defence.

Because of the British parliamentary system, the progress of the anti-nuclear cause in inhibited by the fact that support for non-nuclear defence is too narrowly party-based at present. This is true elsewhere in Western Europe, though occasionally somewhat less so. In West Germany, for example, both the opposition and the government are now against the modernisation of battlefield nuclear weapons. Another obstacle to progress is the traditional insularity of Britain's political parties; the problem in this case is the Labour Party's lack of enthusiasm about Europe. Again the situation is better on the continent, where parties are less inward-looking in attitude and behaviour. Talks on non-nuclear defence have been held, for example, among a number of continental social democratic parties under the initiative of the Danes; they also included several governing parties from the Warsaw Pact countries.[60]

Sympathetic political parties, like research and campaigning organisations, will need to give each other more mutual support. If progress is made anywhere, this could encourage a spill-over effect. Confidence will be engendered by a belief that alternative defence is an idea whose time is coming. And the more impact the idea has in Western Europe, the more it will have on the super powers.

(5) *The super powers* Alternative defence has crept on to the super power agenda. The campaigning and ideas that grew out of the anti-nuclear activity in Western Europe and the United States during the 1980s has had an impact on the behaviour of both the US and Soviet governments. Its impact can be exaggerated, but not ignored.

In the case of the US government, the Reagan years have not been fruitful for those wanting new as opposed to nostalgic and nationalistic attitudes to the problems of international security. In the area of arms control, for example, the efforts of the Reagan administration have largely been negative, designed to undercut support for anti-nuclear supporters. This objective explained at least a part of the White House's commitment to SDI. Despite the hostile environment created by the fundamentalist attitudes of the Reagan administration, critical opinion in the United States and Western Europe succeeded in restraining the worst excesses of which the White House seemed capable. Arms control was kept on the agenda, a more sensible relationship with the Soviet Union was sought, military spending became controlled, some weapons development and deployment was restrained, military interventions were successfully opposed (so far) and the 'fatally flawed' SALT II agreement was lived up to. Public opinion in the West helped limit Reagan being Reagan. And in due course, inadvertently rather than by choice, and because of weakness rather than strength, the President became a summiteer with the 'evil empire' and helped bring about some nuclear disarmament.

Signs of official US interest in the details of alternative defence can only be described as 'modest'.[61] But there have been some straws in the wind. In 1987 the US Ambassador to the UN Conference on Disarmament publicly stated his support for the long-term policy options being discussed by the alternative defence school, while the US Ambassador to NATO reported that NATO had initiated studies to identify the most destabilising elements of NATO and Warsaw Pact forces in Europe and to consider 'restructuring' as well as reducing these forces. One test of 'alternative' thinking, of course, is when it ceases to be 'alternative' and becomes part of official thinking, as in the case just mentioned. Such straws in the wind must, of course, be set against the countervailing attitudes and interests of the military–industrial complex, which dominates the official mind. Nevertheless, looking towards the future, the potential contribution of some of the authorities referred to earlier, including prominent former insiders, may result in the build-up of a significant counterweight in the US debate.

Little responsiveness to alternative defence ideas could be expected from the Reagan administration, and little resulted. But at least pro-arms control and anti-intervention opinion had a significant restraining effect. Little responsiveness to alternative defence ideas could have been expected from the Kremlin in the early 1980s, so what has emerged since 1985 under Gorbachev must represent one of the most remarkable changes in postwar strategic affairs. Its permanence is uncertain since in important respects it flies in the face of traditional attitudes and doctrines. Soviet committment might not last, in the event of Gorbachev's fall from power or a lack of responsiveness on the part of Western governments. But for the moment what it indicates in terms of the opportunities for European security and the potential for change in the Soviet Union can hardly be exaggerated. If the trend is consolidated, and substantial actions follow hopeful words, then it could have a decisive influence on the future of European security.

Gorbachev's 'new thinking' has affected Soviet foreign and defence policy, as well as other areas of life. In all areas achievements lag behind aims and exhortations, but there has been as much change as was feasible in the time available. The hardest test is in the next few years ahead. As yet we are only beginning to receive hints of the origins of new defence thinking and the degree of support behind it, but the signs so far are promising. Where the ideas come from is less important than what is done with them, of course, but it is interesting that there has been recognition by Soviet analysts that many elements of their new thinking about strategy 'originated in the ranks of the peace movement'.[62] Certainly some of the writing emerging from Moscow's research institutes, like some of Gorbachev's language, directly echoes alternative defence thinking. Jonathan Steele is only one Western observer who has reported conversations with Soviet specialists (retired generals and an admiral in his case) who have argued that the Warsaw Pact should change its posture in Central Europe to reduce Western fears.[63] Non-provocative defence has received approving references in Moscow, and the value of the

Warsaw Pact's preponderance in tanks has been questioned aloud. In Moscow alternative non-provocative defence has not been dismissed as utopian or too hard to define, as it has been by major Western governments. The forces of inertia are always strong in the Soviet Union, but it would be irresponsible for us to ignore the change that is taking place. The defence field is one of lively debate.[64] Soviet researchers are talking about the need for civilians and military officials in both blocs to take non-offensive defence seriously, and of there now being an opportunity for 'a historic breakthrough'.[65] An alternative defence research group has been set up in the USSR's Institute for USA and Canada Studies.[66]

It should be a cause for less surprise that there is special interest in alternative defence in Eastern Europe. Interest in Western research in this area has been shown by scholars and diplomats in several Warsaw Pact countries.[67] In the political realm Eastern European attitudes were given some expression in May 1987 by the revival of the 1957 Rapacki plan by the Polish government. Unlike the original plan, the 1987 initiative includes proposals for the removal of offensive conventional weapons in addition to nuclear arms. It was also proposed that weapons making surprise attacks possible should be removed, and that there should be movement towards military doctrines that can be mutually recognised as strictly defensive.[68]

All these developments within the Soviet bloc are significant; what we can be less sure of is the exact nature of that significance. Is it propaganda? Are the leaders of WTO countries simply telling us what we want to hear? Are they fooling themselves about their ability to change the behaviour of their own military? So far words have not been matched by deeds, and one can look with pessimism at some of the WTO positions (for example, its claim that its posture is already non-provocative). Only time will tell, but even time will not tell the whole truth if the West does not help to provide the negotiating and other contexts in which these innovations in the East can flourish. The West must watch and test the new thinking in the Soviet bloc. It cannot dismiss it, since the new ideas have been canalised into a distinctive set of Warsaw Pact proposals to NATO.

(6) *The alliances* Alternative defence ideas have so far found more responsiveness from, and have been given more publicity by the countries of the Warsaw Pact than has been the case with NATO. Whether this interest is for propaganda purposes or represents

promise remains to be seen, but unless it is tested by the West we will never know.

The most dramatic initiative so far occurred on 29 May 1987, when the Political Consultative Committee (PCC) of the Warsaw Pact, meeting in Berlin, indicated its adherence to the general principles of alternative defence.[69] At the end of a long communiqué the PCC committed itself to the following agenda: working to maintain the military equilibrium in Europe at progressively lower levels; maintaining forces within the limits sufficient for defence; prohibiting nuclear testing; eliminating chemical and other weapons of mass destruction; reducing conventional armaments in Europe to levels that rule out surprise attack or offensive operations in general; encouraging strict verification; establishing nuclear-weapons-free and chemical-weapons-free zones and 'zones of thinned-out arms concentration'; withdrawing the most dangerous categories of offensive weapons from the zone of direct contact'; and entering into consultations to compare the military doctrines of the two alliances in order to reduce suspicion and guarantee that military concepts and doctrine are based on defensive principles. It was also proposed that the consultations could discuss the 'imbalances and asymmetrical levels' that have emerged, and search for ways to eliminate them 'through a reduction by the side holding an advantage over the other'.

On the face of it, the 29 May communiqué represented a massive endorsement by the Warsaw Treaty Organisation of the non-provocative defence ideas developed earlier in Western Europe. The proposals contain a number of problems, not least the suspicion that they may simply be a propaganda exercise, telling the West what it wants to hear in order that the international atmosphere can be relaxed to the Soviet Union's advantage. This suspicion will remain in the West until there is a follow-up in deeds. But there is also reason to suppose that it is not merely propaganda, and the West will play a part in determining whether the Soviet Union feels able to move forward; as President Reagan is fond of saying, 'It takes two to tango'. If, in the event, the Warsaw Pact proposals do simply turn out to be propaganda, or get nowhere because of NATO's unresponsiveness and the spoiling tactics of some governments, the discredit should not attach to the notion of alternative defence. It should be addressed to one or both of the military blocs. A second problem in the communiqué is its identification of present Warsaw Past doctrine as 'strictly defensive in nature', alongside talk of 'maintaining the military equilibrium', albeit at lower levels. From NATO's perspective, the Pact's doctrine and disposition have never appeared to be 'strictly defensive', while it has always been claimed that the conventional military equilibrium is clearly tipped in the Pact's favour. While some of these problems with the communiqué might be tempered by the Pact's proposals for mutual withdrawals of offensive weaponry, and the removal of imbalances (in a downward direction) Western concerns about the Pact's posture and numerical superiority in some areas is likely to remain strong. The general problem with the communiqué is its lack of specificity, and the suspicion, bred by the MBFR exeperience, that talks about conventional weaponry will just end up in deadlock, with no change on the ground. There is certainly plenty of scope for deadlock in this area. Which 'offensive' weapons should be cut? Which 'zones' should be identified? Where are the 'imbalances'? How 'thinned-out' should the forces become? What sort of verification is acceptable? How much 'lower' should 'equilibrium' be? The issues are undeniably complex, but there is only one way to find out how serious are the Warsaw Pact's answers to such questions.

So far, the West has not responded positively to various Warsaw Pact attempts to begin a dialogue about military doctrine. Because of a mixture of deep distrust and a lack of confidence in their own future the NATO allies have done the minimum possible. Studies have been initiated, as was mentioned earlier, but formal responses are still awaited. NATO's position has been cautious, following the avenues it knows well, such as seeking to devise CBMs (Confidence-Building Measures) designed to minimise the risk of a successful Pact surprise attack. A communiqué issued by NATO's Defence Planning Committee at the end of May 1987 spoke of the need to strengthen stability by increased openness and 'undiminished security' at lower levels. It then went on to note that the focus of attention should be upon the elimination of the 'serious imbalance' of forces in favour of the Warsaw Pact and of the latter's 'capability for surprise-attack and for the initiation of large-scale offensive action'. This NATO statement was somewhat more one-sided than the almost simultaneous one issued by the Warsaw Pact, but at least the communiqués issued by both alliances now share an understanding that the essence of the problem is that which had been identified and addressed by supporters of alternative defence for several years.

If serious talks about military disposition and doctrine do take place between the alliances, the Warsaw Pact is presently in an advantageous position. Its members have thought about the issues; they appear to have a coherent doctrine; and they seem to believe that it represents their objective interests. The Soviet Union has a real interest in proposing and bringing about cuts in conventional forces, primarily for economic reasons, while the Eastern European countries have every interest in loosening the militarised framework of East–West and East–East relations. NATO, in comparison, appears to be in some disarray, both with respect to future doctrine and whether and how to begin the dialogue proposed by the Warsaw Pact. NATO is reluctant to change; old Atlanticists equate change with threat rather than growth. Nevertheless, the momentum of the INF agreement, together with changing perceptions of super power and West–West relations, suggest that there might be more problems for the NATO establishment if it tries to shore up the status quo rather than confront change. The atmosphere in arms control today provides a better opportunity for progress on the conventional front than has existed hitherto; and were agreements to be reached in this area, lessening fears of surprise attack, the European security landscape would be transformed. On the NATO side it would result in the erosion of the residual fears about Soviet intentions, which are largely kept alive by the image of their looming military might. If these fears were to be reduced, the argument that we need thousands of nuclear weapons to maintain a deterrent against Soviet conventional power would lose even more credibility.

The discussion so far has shown that while support for the whole package of alternative defence ideas has not yet achieved a critical mass, these ideas are now on the agenda in the discussion of European security. The supporters of these ideas are getting stronger and more sophisticated and developments in the international situation are favourable. There is a growing sense, in both the East and West of Europe, that we are at a pivotal point in the affairs of the continent.

Shifts are taking place not only in anti-nuclear opinion but also in establishment circles. Compared with the self-assurance of the 1960s and 1970s, the pro-nuclear defence community has become more divided and apologetic. Less confidence is shown towards the old ideas. Insiders speak about the problems of Flexible Response, a doctrine which hitherto was thought so logical. Nuclear deterrence has been under pressure as more people appreciate that its vaunted stability is less than infinite, because of constant political and technological change. Supporters of existing policies have seemed less comfortable about defending the proposition that stockpiling nuclear overkill is a desirable and rational way to enhance security; even the Ministry of Defence feels the need to apologise for deterrence. The opposition of the former Chief of the Defence Staff, Lord Carver, to Britain's independent deterrent is well-known, but even such a staunch supporter of present policy as Brigadier Hunt has admitted that if the nuclear deterrent did not exist, it would not need reinventing.[70] If Britain ever became an ex-nuclear state, subsequent Conservative governments would presumably adjust in a similar way.

Moving from the national self-image as a nuclear and therefore major power will be difficult for the establishment in Britain. We need only look at their pain at adjusting to Britain's position after the Second World War. Some will not be able to change their outlooks. The defence bureaucracy will surely remain hostile and obstructionist to the idea of a non-nuclear Britain. But times are changing in at least some areas. This was evident for example, in the aftermath of the raids on Libya by US aircraft based in Britain in April 1986. This event made many Conservatives, as well as opponents of the government, both conscious of and unhappy with what had formerly been a fixed element of British defence policy, namely the stationing of US forces on British soil. The deployment of additional F-IIIs to circumvent the INF Treaty, would surely attract considerable hostility, as will future non-monetary repayments to the United States for the purchase of Trident.

In different ways, therefore, the proponents of established policies have become somewhat more defensive about important elements of our posture. There is no reason why this should decrease. While the leaders of the super powers talk about moving security towards less dependence on escalating levels of nuclear overkill, Britain under Margaret Thatcher's government looks like remaining the most enthusiastic supporter of nuclear deterrence except for that of France. Piling up nuclear overkill, with all it implies for policies and attitudes, could become an unappealing message for British voters at a time when new opportunities are seen to be opening up in the international situation. Developments that seemed unthinkable only a few years ago are now happening in front of our eyes: the Soviet Union has allowed intrusive verification, the Warsaw Pact has proposed mutual defensive doctrines, nuclear reductions are taking place, Ronald Reagan has become committed to disarmament.... Only our old mindsets prevent us from recognising these benevolent changes; many of us are too cautious even to believe them, never mind explore them.

Britain is in a position to obstruct or build upon the hopeful trends in the international situation. We can stick with the balance of nuclear terror we know, and hope that it will work until infinity. To do this our government will simply have to employ spoiling tactics with regard both to arms control and East–West relations. On the other hand, we can try to explore the possibilities in the present situation and try to bring about a safer future.

From the account in this chapter of the spread of alternative defence ideas – a school of thought virtually without form or substance ten years ago – it was clearly not too fanciful earlier to suggest that these ideas, though still far from being 'official' rather than 'alternative', are on the verge of respectability. There are some positive developments at all levels and there are hopeful trends in a number of countries. Britain is not destined to remain a nuclear power.

Old strategies, like old ideologies and leaders, have their day. Behaviour which in one generation seems profitable, morally acceptable and almost eternal, can be changed in the next. Slavery was ended because of changing attitudes towards what was socially acceptable, and the British Empire collapsed when colonialism was delegitimised. In both cases the immorality and costs of the traditional policies became recognised and alternative futures were defined. The emergence of an anti-nuclear consensus in Britain would represent a comparable transformation. It would require a shift in attitude on the part of only a relatively small but very influential sector of the community about the role of nuclear deterrence in British security, the morality of basing security on the threat of nuclear weapons, the character of the Soviet threat, and Britain's proper role in international affairs. When thinking about this possible transformation, let us not forget Shaw's comment that all great truths begin as blasphemy.

This first chapter has revealed that we are living in interesting times as far as British defence policy is concerned. The 1990s could see major changes in the landscape of European security. After nearly a decade of strained super power relations there is cause for some optimism. The turn of events is anti-nuclear. Further benevolent progress cannot be guaranteed, but neither can the irrelevance of anti-nuclear attitudes.

Having looked briefly at the domestic and international context to the debate about alternative defence, the chapters that follow will offer an outline of a more secure future, and how it might be achieved. In contrast to the static and unappealing programme offered by proponents of nuclear deterrence, what is offered below is more helpful and hopeful. The objective sought is that of a 'legitimate international order', and the means consist of denuclearisation, movement towards non-provocative defence postures, and constructive East–West engagement. Such ideas face a good deal of inertia, but change is in the air. Before the future can be recast, however, the defence debate has first to be won.

Notes

1. See Milovan Djilas, 'The East's "West"', *Encounter*, Vol. LXIX(5), December 1987, pp. 6–8.
2. See his famous 'X' article, 'The Sources of Soviet Conduct', *Foreign Affairs* XXV(No.4), July 1947, pp. 566–82.
3. See Kenneth Boulding, *Stable Peace* (Austin: University of Texas Press, 1979).
4. For a good example, and survey, see Michael Clarke, *The Alternative Defence Debate: Non-Nuclear Defence Policies for Europe*, ADIU Occasional Paper No.3 (University of Sussex, ADIU, August 1985). See also, Bjorn Moller, *Non-Offensive Defence Bibliography* (University of Copenhagen: Centre of Peace and Conflict Research, n.d.), and Marc Stein and Kathleen Fahey, *Bibliography of Alternative Defense Research* (Brookline, MA.: Institute for Defense and Disarmament Studies, July 1987).
5. Notable precedents include the 'Bonin Plan' of the early 1950s and the GRIT scheme ('Graduated Reciprocation of Tension-reduction') of the early 1960s. See David Gates, 'Area defence concepts: the West German debate', *Survival*, Vol. XXIX(No.4), July–August 1987, pp. 301–17, and Charles E. Osgood, *An Alternative to War or Surrender* (Urbana: University of Illionois Press, 1962).
6. On the 'security dilemma' see Robert Jervis, *Perception and Misperception in International Politics* (Princeton: Princeton University Press, 1976), pp. 62–71.
7. On this interesting period see A.J.R. Groom, *British Thinking about Nuclear Weapons* (London: Frances Pinter, 1974), pp. 421–58; A. Pierre, *Nuclear Politics* (London: Oxford University Press, 1972), pp. 262–5.
8. Peter Kellner, 'Britain's Bomb, the Reagan factor and the next election', *New Statesman*, 17 October 1986. Useful information about British opinion can be found in Philip A.G. Sabin, *The Third World War Scare In Britain* (London: Macmillan, 1986).

9. See John Baylis (ed.), *Alternative Approaches to British Defence Policy* (London: Macmillan, 1983).
10. Ibid., p.3; note also the infamous refusal of Michael Heseltine, on becoming Minister of Defence, to debate with CND spokesmen.
11. The basic statement of its position is in The Labour Party, *Defence and Security for Britain* (Statement to Annual Conference, 1984, by the National Executive Committee). See also *The Power to Defend our Country* (London: The Labour Party, December 1986).
12. See Ivor Crewe, 'Tories prosper from a paradox', *Guardian* 16 June 1987. For an interesting analysis of the election, see Tim Lister and Bruce George, 'Defence: The 1987 Election and Beyond', *RUSI Journal*, September 1987, pp. 69-71.
13. Peter Shore, 'The despair of unilateralism', *New Statesman*, 13 November 1987; and *Guardian* 21 December 1987.
14. Brian May, 'How I was sandbagged out of the Alliance and into Labour', *Guardian*, 5 June 1987.
15. For example, *Guardian*, 5 June 1987.
16. *Times*, 29 May 1987
17. *Guardian*, 12 May 1987.
18. Ibid., 30 May 1987.
19. See the press survey by Hugh Stephenson, 'Nuke not that ye be not nuked', *Guardian*, 30 May 1987.
20. Ibid., 5 June 1987.
21. Ibid., 2 October 1987.
22. Ibid., 21 December 1987 and the *New Statesman*, 13 November 1987.
23. Shore, 'The despair of unilateralism', op.cit.
24. *Guardian*, 2 October 1987.
25. Ibid.
26. *The Times*, 19 September 1987.
27. Shore, 'The despair of unilateralism', op.cit.
28. *Guardian*, 2 October 1987.
29. Hugo Young, 'The now you see it, now you don't Trident', *Guardian*, 27 October 1987.
30. Letter, *Guardian*, 25 May 1987.
31. The following paragraphs are based on Ken Booth, 'Disarmament and Arms Control', pp. 153–4 in John Baylis et al. (ed.), *Contemporary Strategy*, Vol.1 (London: Croom Helm, 1987).
32. A senior Soviet official recently admitted that the SS-20 modernisation was 'a mistake'; it was, he said, the result of technical inertia rather than political analysis. It also appears that, as early as the late 1970s, some Soviet officials had come to recognise that the accumulation of more weaponry such as the SS-20 did not necessarily bring more security. *Guardian*, 21 November 1987.
33. Those who believe Britain's Trident is a 'modernisation' rather than an 'escalation' are well placed to understand the Soviet justification for the SS-20.
34. See Richard K. Betts, *Nuclear Blackmail and Nuclear Balance* (Washington, DC: The Brookings Institution, 1987), p.205.

35. Helmut Schmidt, The 1977 Alistair Buchan Memorial Lecture, *Survival*, Vo. XX(1), January/February 1978, pp. 2–10.
36. Strobe Talbott, 'The Road to Zero', *Time*, 14 December 1987, p.10.
37. Quoted by Jeff McMahon, *Reagan and the World* (London: Pluto Press, 1984), p.53.
38. Talbott, 'The Road to Zero', op.cit., p.10
39. Alexander Haig, *Caveat* (London: Weidenfeld & Nicolson, 1984), p.229.
40. *The Times*, 19 June 1987.
41. Simon Hoggart and Nigel Hawkes, 'Second Time Around', *Observer*, 6 December 1987.
42. *Washington Post*, 12 and 16 May 1987; *Wall Street Journal*, 8 May 1987; *Los Angeles Times*, 12 May 1987; *Aviation Week & Space Technology*, 18 May 1987.
43. *Guardian* 28 October 1987.
44. Paul Rogers, 'Trident becomes Mrs Thatcher's surprise ace', *New Statesman* 4 December 1987.
45. The discrepancy between the figure of 364 and the earlier one of 436 is explained by the removal of the 72 Pershing IAs, with a 120 km range.
46. Enoch Powell, 'Would they have said No Minister?', *Guardian*, 3 August 1987.
47. See Hugh Miall, *Nuclear Weapons: 'Who's in Charge?'* (London: Macmillan/Oxford Research Group, 1987).
48. William Howard, Letter, *Guardian*, 18 July 1987.
49. Hugo Young, 'The now you see it, now you don't Trident', *Guardian*, 27 October 1987.
50. Illustrations of opinions referred to in this paragraph include the following: Field-Marshal Lord Carver, *A Policy For Peace* (London: Faber & Faber, 1982); *The Defense Monitor* (10 issues a year), the journal of the Center for Defense Information, a 'liberal' research organisation whose staff includes several retired US military commanders; Morton H. Halperin (former deputy assistant secretary of defence), *Nuclear Fallacy* (Cambridge: Ballinger, 1987); General Michael N. Harbottle, et al., *The Arms Race to Armageddon: Generals Challenge US/NATO Strategy* (Leamington Spa: Berg, 1984); Herman Kahn, *Thinking About the Unthinkable in the 1980s* (New York: Simon and Schuster, 1984); George F. Kennan, *The Nuclear Delusion* (London: Hamish Hamilton, 1984); Anthony Kenny, *The Logic of Deterrence* (London: Firethorn Press, 1985); Robert Jervis, 'Why Nuclear Superiority Doesn't Matter', *Political Science Quarterly*, Vo.94(4), Winter 1979–80 pp. 617–33; Michael MccGwire, 'Deterrence: the problem – not the solution', *International Affairs*, Vol.62(1), Winter 1985-86, pp. 55–70; McGeorge Bundy, George F. Kennan, Roberts S. McNamara, Gerald Smith, 'Nuclear Weapons and the Atlantic Alliance', *Foreign Affairs*, Vol.60, Spring 1982, pp. 753–68; Hans J. Morgenthau, 'The Fallacy of Thinking Conventionally about Nuclear Weapons', pp. 255–64 in David Carlton and Carlo Schaerf (eds), *Arms Control and Technological Innovation* (London: Croom Helm, 1977); Robert S. McNamara, *Blundering into*

Disaster: Surviving the First Century of the Nuclear Age (New York: Pantheon, 1986); Union of Concerned Scientists, *No-First-Use* (Cambridge: UCS, 1983); Bernard Williams, 'Morality, Scepticism and the Nuclear Arms Race', pp. 99–114 in Nigel Blake and Kay Pole (eds), *Objections To Nuclear Defence. Philosophers On Deterrence* (London: Routledge and Kegan Paul, 1984); Herbert York, *Race to Oblivion* (New York: Simon and Schuster, 1970); Lord Zuckerman, *Star Wars in a Nuclear World* (London: William Kimber, 1986). The list could be expanded. It deserves to be stressed, for the evolution of some of the thinking of the arch-'realists' of contemporary international relations is not sufficiently well known: Morgenthau came to support nuclear disarmament, Kennan is 'dovish' about the Soviet Union and denuclearisation, Kahn supported no-first-use, and so on. The 'experts' are no longer just on the side of establishment thinking about nuclear weapons.

51. For sample, see Mary Kaldor, *The Baroque Arsenal* (London: Andre Deutsch, 1982); Scilla McLean (ed.), *How Nuclear Decisions Are Made* (London: Macmillan, 1986); Randall Forsberg, 'The Freeze and Beyond: Confining the Military to Defense as a Route to Disarmament', *World Policy Journal*, Vol.1 (Winter 1984), pp. 285–318.
52. Scilla McLean, 'A regiment of women takes up arms', *Guardian*, 30 November 1987; and Michael Davie, 'Women's quest in world of weapons', *Observer*, 29 November 1987.
53. *Washington Post*, 7 June 1987
54. Alternative Defence Commission, *Defence without the Bomb* (London: Taylor and Francis, 1983) and *The Politics of Alternative Defence* (London: Graftan Books, 1987); Defence Information Groups, funded by various charitable trusts, were founded in 1983 to provide alternative information and a variety of expert interpretation on important issues of arms control and disarmament (St. James's Church, Piccadilly, London).
55. Davie, 'Women's Quest', op. cit.
56. The NOD ('Non-Offensive Defence') *International Research Newsletter* (hereafter NOD) is published by the Centre of Peace and Conflict Research at the University of Copenhagen.
57. Information about the project is reported in the Institute's *Defense of Disarmament News* (bimonthly). Hereafter cited as *DDN*.
58. 'Inside Pugwash Newsletter', p.l, *Bulletin of the Atomic Scientists*, Vol.5(1), January/February 1988.
59. CND's journal *Sanity* is published monthly; the *END Journal* five times a year.
60. *NOD*, No.7, September 1987, p.14.
61. 'IDDS Alternative Defense Project', *DDN*, Vol.3(1), August–September 1987, p.8.
62. Walter Schwarz, 'Life after cruise', *Guardian*, 8 December 1987.
63. *Guardian*, 5 August 1987.
64. See, for example, Stephen Shenfield, *The Nuclear Predicament. Explorations In Soviet Ideology* (London: Routledge & Kegan Paul, 1987).

65. *NOD*, No.7, September 1987, p.27
66. *DDN*, Vol.3(1), August–September 1987, p.8.
67. Ibid.
68. *NOD*, No.7, September 1987, pp. 9–10.
69. Ibid., pp. 4–8 reprints the text.
70. Carver, *A Policy for Peace*, op.cit., and Kenneth Hunt, 'Comment', pp. 75–6 in John Roper (ed.), *The Future of British Defence Policy* (London: Gower, 1985).

2 What is Wrong with Britain's Existing Defence Policy?

In the opinion of its supporters, Britain's nuclear deterrent has been a success. They argue that it has helped to keep the peace in Europe for a record period of time, that it has given Britain status in the world and that it has been relatively cheap. In short, they assert that it has worked at an acceptable cost: so why change a winner? On first sight these sound plausible arguments: but they are too simple. As will be seen below, the criticisms which can be levelled against the 'independent nuclear deterrent' are numerous. Some of them will be quite familiar, and need not be rehearsed at length. Others, made against the particular policy of the present government by pro-nuclear strategists, will be addressed by John Baylis in Part II.

The major criticisms of existing policy are categorised below as strategic, political and economic. Some are more important than others, and different critics would package them in different ways. For the moment the main aim is to establish that there is something seriously wrong.[1] Chapter 1 pointed out that in the general election campaign of 1987 the Labour Party and other critics of the Thatcher government's pro-nuclear attitudes were so busy defending their own ideas that the weaknesses of existing policy never received a satisfactory airing. The years ahead will expose some, but one hopes not all of those weaknesses.

STRATEGIC DANGERS

British nuclear strategy lacks credibility. The British so-called independent deterrent is not credible. The only 'last resort' scenario in which it might be employed is almost unimaginable; it would be tantamount to a British leader deciding to commit national suicide. *Britain is particularly vulnerable.* If nuclear deterrence were to fail, the consequences for Britain would be catastrophic beyond imagination. At worst it would mean the onset of nuclear winter; at best the massacre of millions. In either case, a small overcrowded country such as Britain is peculiarly vulnerable to the effects of nuclear war. The disaster at Chernobyl in 1986 made almost everybody more sensitive to the horror and pervasiveness of nuclear mistakes. The breakdown of deterrence would be the ultimate nuclear mistake.

Nuclear deterrence is dangerous. The balance of terror has become somewhat more unstable since the mid-1970s because of doctrinal and weapons innovation. Western nuclear policy (ideas about limited nuclear war and the development of counterforce weapons, and especially those with short flight-times) threaten to increase the risks of nuclear war. Crisis-stability erodes as pressures to pre-empt increase. The Achilles' heels of modern military systems – satellites for reconnaisance and communication – will become tempting targets for anti-satellite weaponry, unless the deployment of the latter is restrained. No increase in the risk of nuclear war, however small, is acceptable.

Britain is a priority target. Under existing arrangements Britain is likely to be a priority nuclear target for the Soviet Union. With its own nuclear potential, together with its role as the 'unsinkable aircraft carrier' of the United States, Britain poses a massive threat to the Soviet homeland in the event of war. If, in a crisis, Soviet planners believe that nuclear war is inevitable, they will feel compelled to eliminate Britain in the first salvo.

NATO strategy is dangerously inflexible. NATO's strategy of Flexible Response, in which Britain's defence efforts are intimately enmeshed, is incredible, inflexible and escalatory. Even the supporters of Flexible Response have come to recognise the need for reform. Britain at present participates in a complacent and dangerous system of extended deterrence.

Britain is not strategically independent. As will be made evident in Part II, Britain has tied itself to US systems, priorities, and policies as a result of its desire to take advantage of the special nuclear relationship symbolised by Polaris and Trident. In doing so, British governments have lost an important degree of independence. The problem of the loss of political independence will be dealt with later. In strategic affairs, supporters of Polaris and Trident argue that a British government remains independent since it has the ability, in the last resort, to fire its nuclear missiles without consultation with or veto from the White House. Carrying out this 'acid test' of independence, as it is called,[2] would be the most irrational act of any British government in history.

The nuclear deterrent contributes to military weaknesses. There is a direct relationship between Britain's pro-nuclear exertions and the weaknesses in its conventional forces. The allocation of funds for the research, development and deployment of nuclear weapons has resulted in a decline in Britain's ability to contribute to NATO's conventional forces. The acquisition of Trident represents an unwise distortion of Britain's defence efforts. The shortages in the conventional field include limitations in training and equipment for the Army, delays in acquiring a new helicopter for the RAF, and fewer frigates for the RN. These problems will grow worse.

Britain adds overkill. Since any nuclear war might quickly become uncontrollable, and since nuclear winter might be the outcome of firing even a fraction of existing arsenals – who knows? – reducing the world's stock of nuclear weapons is imperative. Despite this, and the fact that our fears of an attack by the Soviet Union have receded over time, the Conservative government is increasing Britain's stock of nuclear warheads by an enormous amount. It is an odd strategy that adds overkill in direct proportion to the decrease in the threat.

British policy encourages nuclear proliferation. The Conservative government's actual nuclear behaviour undermines its declared commitment to non-proliferation. Indeed, the arguments used by the government to justify its deployment of Trident strengthen the hands of those in near-nuclear countries who want their own governments to take the nuclear option. Since it is widely believed that a world of many nuclear powers would be proportionately insecure, the British government's behaviour is dangerous as well as hypocritical. A nuclear war in a region of the Third World could be the spark which might finally explode the European powder keg.

POLITICAL PROBLEMS

British political independence is curtailed rather than strengthened. Britain's existing nuclear posture requires a very close relationship with the United States. This dependence on the United States for our ultimate symbol of independence undermines the political case for a Polaris or Trident force. Outside the nuclear sphere the benefits which Britain gets from the 'special relationship' with the United States are marginal. Furthermore, our ties entail an unacceptable risk that Britain might be dragged into a war between the super powers. The quality – or lack of quality – perceived by Europeans in recent White House occupants adds to these fears. Britain should have separated itself from the irrational global struggle which the Reagan administration has been carrying on with the Soviet Union. The special relationship, especially in the Thatcher–Reagan period, has resulted in an overly-deferential attitude on the part of Britain to US foreign and defence policy.

Nuclear weapons do not bring international status for Britain. Nuclear weapons have not brought Britain a ticket to a 'seat at the top table' in international diplomacy. Status in the modern world depends on more than sheer destructive power. In any case, British governments have in practice shied away from sitting at the top table in strategic arms reduction talks, since they did not want their 'irreducible deterrent' included in the bargaining, nor did they want their opposition to nuclear arms reduction clearly exposed. This opposition has become increasingly evident, however, as a result of Mrs Thatcher's forthright hostility to nuclear disarmament in the aftermath of the super power summit at Reykjavik in November 1986, and during the INF negotiations in 1987. If the momentum of super power denuclearisation continues, Mrs Thatcher's obstinate belief in the virtues of nuclear weapons will attract growing unpopularity in the eyes of those who believe in the desirability of the winding-down of the arms race.

Nuclear strategy is immoral. It is immoral to threaten or use weapons of mass destruction. The use of nuclear weapons would violate the 'just war' principles of proportionality and discrimination; and it is wrong to threaten that which it would be grossly immoral to do. It is immoral to base our security on a strategy which threatens to destroy civilised life in order to 'save' the free world.

Nuclear weapons are irrelevant to British diplomacy. Not only is the so-called independent deterrent incredible as a weapon of last resort, it is useless in lesser contingencies. It does not give leverage and is therefore of no diplomatic consequence. In the numerous conflicts in which British troops have been involved in the last thirty years, from the Suez Crisis through 'Confrontation' to the Falklands War, British power has gained nothing from the possession of nuclear weapons.

The balance of terror obstructs the progress of European security. The Soviet military threat to Western Europe has been exaggerated, in terms of both intention and capability. Nuclear deterrence, as it has been practised, exacerbates East–West conflict and undermines the prospects for stable long-term relations. The nuclear addiction distracts attention from the political dimension of security.

Nuclear weapons are illegal. International law, and specifically the laws of war, seek to impose restraints on the horrors of war. They seek to minimise or eliminate unnecessary suffering, the killing of civilians, genocide, mass destruction, the use of uncontrollable weapons, the violation of neutral rights and environmental damage. The use of nuclear weapons would violate formal agreements and practices pertaining to such matters. The possession of nuclear weapons and the devising of strategies to use them is therefore tantamount to planning to break these laws.

Nuclear status fosters delusions. For successive British governments nuclear weapons have been seen as the way of compensating for the country's political and economic decline as a world power. They have signally failed to achieve this result. Instead they have only perpetuated inflated beliefs about Britain's role as a major power and special ally of the United States. Such delusions have retarded Britain's efforts to adjust to its diminished postwar circumstances.

Nuclear power threatens democracy. Decisions about nuclear weapons by successive British governments have been taken in great secrecy. There are already too many secrets in Britain, and nuclear weapons help to justify excessive governmental control of information. Important nuclear decisions have been kept from Cabinet Ministers, let alone Parliament. There is no proper accountability.

ECONOMIC COSTS

Britain cannot compete in the super power league. In the last thirty years Britain's nuclear exertions have been regularly outflanked by technological leaps by one or other super power. The innovation of new technology by the United States has made British systems prematurely obsolescent, while Soviet progress in ballistic missile defence (BMD) has provoked the need for costly efforts in order that Britain stay in the nuclear business. Weapon-innovation by the super powers has undermined the independence and credibility of British efforts. The prospect of future super power achievements in BMD, together with the possibility of deep cuts in their strategic forces, will place additional pressures on 'independent' deterrents.

Britain spends too much on defence. The British economy has done badly since the war, and in the last thirty years the country's rate of economic growth has been lower than that of other Western European states. Despite (and because of) this, Britain has consistently spent more on defence. In the mid-1980s Britain was spending 5.2 per cent of its national income, while its Western European allies, on average, were spending only 3.6 per cent.[3] Even though facing economic hardship at home, Britain proved a most loyal ally to NATO in terms of meeting the 1978 commitment to increase defence spending by 3 per cent per annum.

The nuclear commitment is not cost-effective. Nuclear weapons consume scarce economic and human resources, and in both the military and civilian fields Britain could make more effective use of them. Some of the resources could be redeployed to strengthen Britain's conventional forces, or used to advance the non-military side of Britain's external relations. Britain's influence in the world is not unrelated to its industrial strength, and scarce scientific and engineering resources could be profitably transferred from the military to the civil sector of the economy.

Britain's nuclear role weakens its conventional strength. Britain cannot afford to have the most effective conventional forces possible while trying to maintain nuclear independence. The modernisation of Britain's conventional forces will have to suffer as long as the costs associated with the Trident programme increase. The present government's policy has been one of level funding on defence since 1985–86, and this effectively means a decreasing commitment to conventional defence because of inflation (and the costs of defence equipment are increasing more quickly than the general rate of inflation). Britain's problems in this respect will become exacerbated with the decline in oil revenues and the possibility of economic growth rates remaining low. In these circumstances a crunch will come in the defence field; and as long as the commitment to nuclear expansion remains, cuts will have to be made in conventional strength. Either there will be a general erosion of Britain's conventional forces, or particular roles will be drastically diminished; the most likely to suffer are the surface navy and the British Army on the Rhine (BAOR). Such developments would have serious implications for Britain's political standing among its allies and its organisational representation in NATO's military hierarchy. Economic pressures will therefore compel agonising reappraisals on Britain's part in the years to come. Those who support a shift to a non-nuclear defence have faced up to this prospect. Something will have to go – conventional strength – under present policies, but it is not yet being faced up to in public.

HAS 'THE DETERRENT' DETERRED?

In any discussions of what is wrong with existing policy we must address the assertion, repeated like a litany, that 'nuclear weapons have kept the peace for forty years'. If this were clearly true it might seem a good reason for not changing anything. But there is less to the assertion than meets the eye.

We do not actually know what role British nuclear weapons have had in maintaining stability in Europe. And probably we will never know. We cannot know whether our nuclear strategy has 'worked' because we cannot know whether it has deterred the Soviet leaders from testing it. 'But it certainly has not failed' is the immediate reply of the supporters; 'We have not had a war'. But here again matters are not as simple as they first appear. It is tempting to exaggerate, as is done in Part II, the extent to which nuclear weapons as opposed to other factors have contributed to the relative stability of Europe since 1945. But nuclear weapons are by no means the only factor in the situation. War-weariness, unprecedented prosperity, settled nation-state boundaries, the clarity produced by two tightly-organised alliances, relative domestic tranquillity, the spreading belief (since the First World War) that war is not a way to settle conflicts, and a certain sense of the loss that would result from any massive breakdown in European security – all these factors together have decisively diminished the attractiveness and utility of major war. Europe has entered, albeit tentatively, a post-Clausewitzian era. If positive peace is not yet achievable across Europe, there has at least been almost absolute agreement that war is positively unacceptable.

The East–West line might therefore have remained stable since 1945 even in the absence of nuclear weapons. Their presence, on the other hand, has meant that the super powers might have blown each other, and the rest of us, off the face of the twentieth century. If nuclear deterrence is as stable as is suggested in Part II, why did the world slide towards the brink of catastrophe in the Cuban missile crisis of 1962? And this crisis was not essentially about Cuba; at its roots were the insecurities generated by the nuclear arms race, and particularly the fears felt in the Soviet Union about the growing US lead in strategic strike. The dynamics of the nuclear arms race have brought some caution to inter-state relations, but they have also brought novel fears and dangers. 'Nuclear stability' can easily be exaggerated. Historic political changes can and have taken place in the face of nuclear weapons. The Soviet take-over of Eastern Europe, for example, occurred at a time of US atomic monopoly, and China became communist. Nuclear weapons proved powerless against such changes.

We cannot 'prove' that nuclear deterrence has 'worked', but it is evident that it has not 'failed' in the sense that there has been a major war, or Western Europe has fallen to the Soviet Union. But its 'non-failure' has been at a heavy cost. It has depended upon catastrophic threats to civilised life in the northern hemisphere, and has produced pessimistic long-term expectations. There is good reason to believe that the postwar boundaries could have been maintained, and with more peaceful prospects, by a robust conventional deterrent on both sides. Given the destruction of the Second World War – evident above all to the Russians – it is likely that the threat of yet another devastating conventional war would by itself have produced a super power stand-off after 1945. Had that been the case, the stability we have enjoyed in the last forty years might by now have produced a more positive peace than that held together by the relentless pursuit of nuclear deterrence. The mega-logic of nuclear deterrence has institutionalised the Cold War and stimulated a process of competitive weapons innovation that ultimately represents a greater threat to the countries in the East–West confrontation than they do to each other. There can never be a mistake. A nuclear war would mean the end of Europe.

The answer to the question, 'Has nuclear deterrence worked?' has therefore both positive and negative aspects. We cannot prove that it has not worked; but neither can we prove that it has. War between the super powers has been avoided for forty years, despite their clashes of interest. There can be no doubt that nuclear weapons have imposed caution on decision-makers and demanded an extra degree of rationality; nuclear weapons do not make leaders good, but on issues of peace and war they do generally make them prudent. It is sometimes said that nuclear weapons have a 'crystal-ball' effect.[4] If leaders in the past had known the final outcomes of their warlike actions, it is doubtful whether they would have taken the same fateful decisions. World leaders since 1945 have been given a nightmare vision of where their actions might lead, as a result of looking into the crystal ball created by Hiroshima and hundreds of test explosions. Consequently, the importance of preventing all-out war has come to have a novel importance. But this should not lead to complacency, for crystal balls are fragile things. They can be shattered by accident; they can also be dropped by miscalculation, lost by complacency, or become clouded by having too many hands pawing over them.

Nuclear weapons are terrifying. And they do terrify. But four decades is not a long enough test from which to draw historic conclusions about their role, and we are too close. There is a yet more telling argument. Whatever the earlier role of nuclear weapons, the absence of nuclear war in the last forty years does not guarantee a nuclear war-free future for the next forty; and still less for ever. So even if one believes that nuclear weapons have 'worked' in the recent past, it does not follow that they will 'work' in this sense for evermore. The long-term future is surprisingly ignored by strategic commentators; they are generally content to aim at being six months ahead of the conventional wisdom. Deterrence theory in particular has exhibited a notably static character, with a marked absence of real forward thinking. This is the case despite the fact that the battlefields of strategic history are monuments to the attempts of nations to give yesterday's answers to tomorrow's questions. Fortunately, there are glimmers of change, as was made evident in Chapter 1. To a slowly increasing number of specialists, nuclear deterrence is now seen as 'the problem – not the solution'.[5]

At this stage in world history it is more rational that we agree to the logical proposition that nuclear weapons might not work for evermore than we argue over the unprovable assertion that they have worked in the past. It is therefore illogical to assert as in Part II, that the 'onus' is on the anti-nuclear critics 'to demonstrate' that their prescriptions are better than those of the supporters of nuclear deterrence. This cannot be 'demonstrated', any more than the pronuclear lobby can demonstrate that nuclear weapons will free us from cataclysmic war for the rest of history. If the onus rests anywhere, it must be on the supporters of the nuclear status quo, for every security system has broken down in the past, and no sin in strategy has been punished as implacably as that of resisting change.

It is impossible to calculate, objectively or statistically, the risks of nuclear war. Nobody actually knows how to think properly about this central issue of our time. As a result all we have are relatively informed and relatively uninformed guesses. Part I of this book is informed by a belief there are both negative and positive signs when thinking about the prospects of nuclear war. It happened that the risks in the first half of the 1980s were somewhat greater than in the previous decade. Starting in the mid-1970s we saw the development of a less sensible structure of nuclear strategy on top of foundations whose political and economic geology has been less predictable than formerly.[6] The increase in insecurity has not been dramatic but given the infinitely precious pattern of civilised life that would disappear in the event of nuclear war no increase in risk is acceptable. There have been some positive changes in super power relations since 1985, but we should not allow ourselves to become complacent because we seem to have survived the 'second Cold War'. For a decade or so it has been possible to ask a series of questions about international security which earlier would have been dismissed as far-fetched. The fact that we have been able to ask them is a clear indication of the insidious rise in the level of our insecurity.

- If Soviet hopes and power fail at home and abroad will it lead it to become more militant and edgy, and so likely to blunder into confrontation?
- Might resurgent American nationalism one day tempt it to take excessive risks, and push its rival into a corner?
- Will nuclear proliferation spread, and might a regional nuclear war draw in the super powers?
- Will the decline in the sense of international community lead to a rise in tension, and the emergence of 'crazy states'?
- Will the incapacity of many states create domestic disorder and so the conditions for intervention by external powers? Will it always be possible to contain Third World crises?
- In circumstances of nuclear parity and global conventional reach, will each super power always be willing to stand by and allow its rival to proceed with a particular intervention?
- Does talk of prevailing in nuclear war mean that the taboo against nuclear war will erode, and encourage decision-makers to be more aggressive in crises?
- Does planning for limited nuclear options make the fighting of one more likely, by giving a false sense of manageability?
- Despite the INF agreement, do not the shifts to more aggressive US doctrines – nuclear war-fighting, the Maritime Strategy, AirLand Battle, and so on – ensure a poor prospect for arms restraint, and an indefinite future of arms-racing and suspicion?
- Will the fear of nuclear war (or the expectation of Armageddon) be at some point self-fulfilling?
- Has the development of counterforce capabilities and anti-satellite (ASAT) weaponry made first strikes more attractive, and so reduced the prospects for crisis stability?
- Might NATO one day engineer a general nuclear war from what might be a limited conflict, because of its adherence to its nuclear 'first-use' posture?

- Is an 'accidental war' possible as a result of reinforcing super power alerts in a crisis, at a time when ASAT weaponry and accurate ballistic missiles with short flight-times will make military trigger-fingers itchy?
- Might the threat or promise of a strategic breakthrough (notably with Star Wars technology) provoke the weaker side to pre-empt, or tempt the stronger side to attack?

It is not inevitable that the future will give pessimistic answers to these questions, but they are worries now on the agenda. We have seen an unnecessary accumulation of destabilising weapons, over-militarised interpretations of super power relations, and mutual-threat inflation and suspicion. Arms races do not inevitably lead to war, but they do perpetuate cycles of mistrust and danger. The main risk is not of a nuclear bolt from the blue but of a 'nuclear Sarajevo'.[7] The 1987 INF agreement could be a very positive sign, but many questions remain. Will the super power thaw last? Is the agreement merely a gesture by two leaders anxious for a foreign policy success? Will it simply re-channel the nuclear arms race? Despite the agreement fundamentalist impulses and the nuclear infrastructure remain intact.

There is clearly a great deal to be done by those who want to reduce the nuclear threat. Britain must of course seek to impose heavy costs on those who would damage its interests, but it should do so in a manner that helps create those conditions of international security in which the use of force will be progressively reduced. The way in which a shift to a non-nuclear posture will help this is the subject of Chapter 4.

OPERATIONAL, MORAL AND INTERNATIONAL SECURITY ISSUES

Before explaining the advantages of a non-nuclear strategy, special attention should be given to three particular cirticisms of our existing posture.

(1) Contributing to NATO's pro-nuclear operational emphasis is a misuse of Britain's defence resources.
We cannot *defend* ourselves with nuclear weapons. This must never be forgotten. We can only defend ourselves with conventional forces. It is here therefore that Britain can make its optimum contribution to Western defence. As it is, we do not really have a defence policy; we

only have a deterrent posture which, however potentially destructive, cannot cope with one breakdown. Some of the greatest disasters of strategic history have been made by those who did not believe that their plans could fail.

NATO's posture remains heavily pro-nuclear, despite the widely understood need to strengthen the alliance's conventional military capabilities. This is a serious worry because inherent in the idea of nuclear deterrence is a recognition of the possibility, however remote, of nuclear use. We must face up to this prospect squarely, rather than pushing it into the background because we do not actually want to admit it as a real as opposed to a theoretical possibility. If nuclear war were to occur we would surely ask ourselves whether we could have done anything more to have prevented such a catastrophe. How would we justify our actions to our consciences, our god(s), history or a post-Third World War Nuremberg Trial? In the aftermath of millions of deaths the phrase flexible response will sound as sinister as 'final solution'. One thing is certain, if and when such a nightmare becomes reality, it will then be too late to say 'No'. As the missiles begin to land, it will be little comfort to tell ourselves that we had backed a nuclear deterrence theory that failed. The war to end all wars will be a go-as-you-planned scenario. More detailed criticisms of NATO's Flexible Response strategy will be discussed later, and in Part II. For the moment it is enough to note that nuclear weapons play a wholly disproportionate part, even granting a need for any of them. Flexible Response, as conceived since its adoption in 1967, is a thoroughly dangerous notion, since it is based on a hope that nuclear war can be fought and in some sense won. Instead of pushing our worst fears aside, those nuclear strategists who concede the finite possibility of nuclear war (and deterrence depends upon the belief in this possibility) must invest more effort and imagination into thinking about the operational dimensions of strategy. Wishful thinking is understandable, but it has now had too much rope.

Some in the peace movement assert that nuclear war will be an 'inevitable' product of the arms race, as John Baylis points out later. Such a notion forms no part of the present argument, however. On the contrary, a basic assumption in Part I is that we must believe that choices can be made which will affect events. In Part II it is suggested that those who tell people that war is inevitable encourage the preparation for it. But the opposite might also be the case. As the growth of the peace movement has shown, fear can energise people to try to take their destinies into their own hands. It is unlikely, for example, that we would now be waiting for the removal of cruise missiles from Western Europe but for the pro-arms control constituency built up by the peace movement in the early 1980s.

In contrast to the cosmic complacency of deterrence addicts, supporters of alternative defence schemes accept that nuclear war is a real possibility. If it comes, they generally believe that it will not be the result of a Soviet land-grab on the pattern of Nazi Germany, but will rather be a mixture of Soviet fear and loss of control in a crisis. They therefore argue that Western defence and foreign policies must give more emphasis in peacetime to reassuring the target of our nuclear weapons, and in wartime to operational strategies which offer some hope of being able to cope rationally with the breakdown of deterrence.

The starting-point for British thinking about defence must be that participation in a nuclear war would be the most irrational act in the nation's history. The idea of having a 'nuclear strategy' is therefore a contradiction in terms. Equally, NATO's present posture does not deserve to be dignified by the name 'strategy' because it could not cope with being employed. Under present arrangements, if deterrence does someday break down, we will leave the realm of strategic thinking and tumble headlong into a nightmare. With these thoughts in mind it is obvious in outline what Britain should do: it should make a bigger contribution to reducing the risk of war by helping to create the conditions for stable peace, while at the same time ensuring that its defence efforts help to raise the nuclear threshold and establish a more rational war-terminating strategy than present arrangements allow. A shift to a more robust conventional defence will help both these aims.

NATO's present abundance of nuclear weapons is largely justified as a compensation for the alliance's alleged weaknesses in conventional forces. The range of types and sizes of nuclear weapons has been said to be necessary in order to build a 'seamless web' of deterrence – an argument exploded by the INF agreement. Rather than going along with the alliance's nuclear addiction, Britain should use its resources, human and material, to produce a more effective conventional defence strategy, a more positive arms control policy, and a more enlightened picture of European security. At present Britain's nuclear posture, which threatens to destroy the nation in order to save it, does not represent the most sensible allocation of resources for the country into the indefinite future. It is both irrational and detracts from our ability to help remedy the weaknesses of NATO's pro-nuclear planning. A non-nuclear strategy would represent the optimum use for Britain's scarce defence potential.

As will be discussed in Chapter 5, Britain does not have the resources to make a substantial contribution in both the nuclear and non-nuclear fields. Choices have to be made. The choices made by the present Conservative government – the deployment of Trident and the continuation of other elements of the nuclear programme – mean that we are likely to see an erosion of our conventional forces. In future, the need for hard choices will almost certainly become more, not less, pressing. As *The Economist* put it when commenting on the 1987 Defence White Paper, 'Something has to give.'[8] Part I of this book argues that what should give are our costly, dangerous and immoral weapons of mass destruction.

(2) Weapons of mass destruction are neither right nor prudent.
Much has been written about the moral aspects of nuclear strategy, and rightly so. Both authors of this book agree that the nuclear problem offers no easy way out; it involves profound and inescapable moral dilemmas.

By the mid-1990s, with Trident and Tornado, Britain will have the capability of destroying 724 strategic targets in the Soviet Union.[9] With a full, as opposed to a SALT II-restricted load of warheads, Trident alone could have 896 warheads. This is a fourteen-fold increase on the maximum Polaris target potential. It is wrong that we are preparing, even in retaliation, to engage in a massacre of Russian people and other nationalities that is too inhuman for decent imaginations to contemplate. But nuclear deterrence dulls the imagination. It is the opium of the defence people. To make deterrence work, the threat to destroy the other's society has to be made 'credible', and this requires elaborate preparations – hardening thought processes as well as processing hardware – in order to ensure that the adversary believes that retaliation will take place. As in other aspects of life, the instrument might well shape the will to use it. What one worries about in this regard is not so much the lack of moral sensitivity on the part of the supporters of nuclear deterrence – disarmers have no monopoly of moral sensitivity – but their lack of imagination, and their apparent inability to accept that 'the deterrent', like other deterrents in the past, might one day fail. Such a breakdown is not inevitable; that is our opportunity. But it is possible; and that should shape our whole approach to the future of European security.

As well as supporting the continuation and improvement of British strategic nuclear systems, Mrs Thatcher has said that she is one of those who would rather be dead than red and that 'Of course' she would be prepared to give the order to fire Polaris missiles at Soviet cities in the event of a major Soviet attack on Britain.[10] Such a decision, some would argue, would be a war crime; all should be able to see that it would be tantamount to signing the death warrant of the British nation. A *kamikaze* British nuclear attack on Soviet cities, as a last-ditch effort to throw back a Soviet offensive, would provoke a massive counter-blow that would turn back the clock of British history to the dark ages. A *kamikaze* nuclear attack would not only be immoral, it would also be the height of stupidity.

Taking a less extreme position than the Prime Minister, John Baylis discusses the idea that in the event of a Soviet attack on Western Europe 'limited', perhaps 'demonstrative' nuclear strikes might re-establish peace and save millions of lives. Possibly. But realistically speaking, such an option places altogether too much faith in human rationality at a time when confusion and emotion will be heightened beyond experience. British feelings about such a demonstrative strike were expressed in the public outrage against Alexander Haig's suggestion along these lines in 1981.[11] Haig's attitude revealed the vocational failing of war-planners and other dramatic impresarios through the ages: the assumption that all would go right on the night. The theatre of war is no more able to guarantee smash hits than the theatre of make-believe.

The coming-together of war and make-believe was well illustrated a few years ago by General Hackett's bestseller, *The Third World War*. This book, written by a civilised and sophisticated soldier of great learning, implicitly assumes that nuclear war can be a rational instrument of policy, for it produces a winner (the West) and at acceptable costs. The fairy story told by the General does not promote the message that a Third World War might be an uncontrollable nightmare, but instead argues that if NATO takes remedial action the coming war with Soviet Russia can be *controlled* and *won*, if not actually deterred.[12] This piece of future history was intended by its author as a cautionary tale, of course, but it does reveal the extent to which the minds of supporters of nuclear strategy are gripped both by the military mind-sets of the past and a futuristic faith in rationality. Forty years of pervasive pro-nuclear attitudes and planning predispose us, in the event of war in Europe, to precipitate that very catastrophe we most want to avoid.

John Baylis agrees that his fellow deterrers are on shaky moral ground[13] in arguing that whereas nuclear use would be 'morally repugnant', nuclear deterrence is 'morally acceptable'; he accepts that even if a leader has no real intention of using these weapons, operational procedures in a crisis 'might inexorably' lead to their being used in practice. But the dangers are even worse than is suggested. We are not only threatened by the prospect of Britain's cosmic bluff failing, leading us to slide 'unintentionally' into nuclear war. Worse still, in some circumstances we may be threatened by the possibility that our Prime Minister will think it rational to order a nuclear strike against the Soviet Union. The earlier words of Mrs Thatcher make this danger plain. When we contemplate such possibilities, unlike some potential war criminals in the past, we do not have the excuse of not knowing where our plans might take us. We all should know that executing our nuclear threat would be a crime against humanity.

What has been labelled the 'just deterrent'[14] is an extremely dangerous idea. It can justify just about anything. As long as Britain possesses nuclear weapons, the British community is conniving in a defence posture whose implementation would stand shamefully alongside the worst war crimes in recorded history. There is no conceivable issue between Britain and the Soviet Union – including occupation – that could justify such a threat or its execution. Nuclear city-busting, involving the killing and maiming of millions of innocents, represents a complete rejection of all the values for which we are supposed to stand. If a nuclear holocaust were to occur, it would be no consolation to know, as is suggested in Part II,[15] that the 'major moral responsibility' for it would rest with the other side, 'the aggressor'. Such an argument sounds suspiciously like blowing up the world to save it.

It will be argued below that we have serious reasons for worrying about the long-term effects of deterrence ideology on international security. These arguments refute the suggestion in Part II that even if the non-nuclear case has the high ground in terms of the morality of intentions, nuclear deterrers re-possess it in the more important matter of the morality of consequences. This is not so. In the 1980s the case against a pro-nuclear strategy has become strategic as well as ethical. A typical debate on these matters in the 1950s and 1960s posed an ethics of intentions against an ethics of consequences. As Joseph S. Nye has pointed out: 'A theologian would argue that it was wrong to threaten the destruction of innocent lives, and a strategist would reply that the deterrent effect of the threat had saved millions of innocent lives.' But recently a new strand has been added: 'Anti-nuclear consequentialists attack the strategists on their own grounds. They argue that nuclear deterrence is bound to fail some day because all human systems are fallible. As long as there is a possibility of catastrophic failure, the consequences of nuclear deterrence will be immoral.'[16]

Faith in the perpetual peace promised by nuclear deterrence has declined remarkably in the last ten years. In the West there has been a defection on the Right (evident in the support given to President Reagan's Star Wars idea), as well as on the Left, where the hugely-expanded anti-nuclear movements in many countries have been protesting for some years. Meanwhile, in the Soviet bloc, we have witnessed the 'new thinking' of Mikhail Gorbachev, which includes declaratory criticisms of nuclear deterrence, unilateral initiatives in support of arms restraint, a call to remove all nuclear weapons from the face of the earth by the year 2000, and an ostensible commitment to base peace on a more stable political footing. There is a wind of change in thinking about security. Confidence in salvation through offensive nuclear overkill is waning. Among other things, this means that nuclear weapons are no longer the 'political cement' they once were in the Western alliance.[17] If the super power thaw develops, then the anti-nuclear wind of change could by the late 1980s become a far more powerful force than could have been imagined even in 1986.

(3) Nuclear deterrence institutionalises the Cold War.
As was suggested, it would not only be immoral, illegal and stupid for Britain to *use* nuclear weapons, but it is also unwise for us to continue to base our security on the *threat* of their use. This is because the technological, doctrinal and ideological infrastructure of nuclear deterrence institutionalises an anachronistic characterisation of the East–West conflict. The Cold War is brain-dead, though its muscles keep twitching because of the powerful nervous system built around nuclear deterrence. The military confronation and arms race now bears an irrational relationship to the state of political and economic relations between the blocs. The continuation of this irrational confrontation – which became grossly inflamed in the early 1980s – makes it difficult to see long-term East–West relations in sensible perspective. Not only does the nuclear addiction of the major powers institutionalise Cold War thinking, it also limits their ability to constrain the possibly dangerous drift of nuclear proliferation elsewhere.

Thus we continue to tie a nuclear fuse-wire between the European tinder-box and the instabilities of much of the rest of the world.

The fears and inter-reactions of both Western and Soviet leaders in the tense postwar years were understandable and justified, but the continuation of such thinking forty years later is anachronistic as well as dangerous. Nevertheless, powerful political, economic and military forces and ideas in both camps make it difficult to change. As will be discussed in the next chapter, the distortions of ethnocentrism, the policies shaped by political 'realism', the biases created by ideological fundamentalism, and the misplaced logic of strategic reductionism all contribute to patterns of behaviour that make progress towards a stable peace extremely difficult. In addition, entrenched military, industrial and bureaucratic interests contribute to maintaining the momentum of the cold war. Nor must we underestimate the fact that some of today's policymakers had their ideas frozen as well as shaped during that period. The obstacles to the evolution of a more stable peace are considerable, but there is room for manouvre. Since 1985 Mr Gorbachev has opened a door. The major Western leaders have been reluctant to respond, and by so doing have risked losing a major opportunity to refashion East–West relations.

Conflicts of interest exist between the Soviet Union and the Western world, and will continue. That should not mean that we need to talk and act as if we were ready, willing and able to exterminate each other's society at the flicker of a radar screen. Supporters of existing arrangements – favouring security based on fear rather than on a balance of defensive deterrence and reassurance – are unwilling to recognise the extent to which the infrastructure of nuclear deterrence heightens tension and undermines the prospects for a stable long-term political relationship. Existing arrangements promote a cycle of mistrust, mutual threat-inflation and arms competition. In the West we have consistently exaggerated Soviet strength since the late 1940s and have often misjudged its behaviour (though Soviet words and actions have not always helped).[18] We have set the 'enemy' status of the Soviet Union in concrete; war between us has been seen as more or less likely unless extensive military preparations were made. Rational suspicions, worst-case forecasting, inertia, vested interests, and simple Sovietology have led to a dangerous militarisation of our thinking about the Soviet Union. As George Kennan, the dean of US Soviet-watchers, has noted with regret over the years, US governments have acted as if the military balance, particularly its nuclear component, was the only serious determinant in US–Soviet relations.[19]

The comments above are not meant to suggest, of course, that the Soviet Union is a benevolent power, and that there are no major problems between East and West. This would be far from the truth. The Soviet Union is a super power, and exhibits all the characteristics of one: it wants the best weapons; it expects deference from neighbours; it interferes; and it demands the right to intervene in the affairs of distant countries. In addition, the Soviet Union has a 'strategic culture' which puts a high and expansive premium on security; it is xenophobic and suspicious; it conceives stability and strength (preferably preponderance) as synonymous; and it has a military tradition of over-insurance. Having said that, there have been significant changes in Soviet behaviour and outlooks over the years. The operational aspects of the ideology have been deradicalised, and the state has steadily if uncomfortably accommodated to the established international system. It must be remembered that it is over a generation ago, 1956, since Khrushchev revised the Leninist doctrine about inevitable war between the systems. Since that time Soviet leaders have regularly stressed that nuclear war could not be a reasonable instrument of policy. Mr Gorbachev has challenged some of the traditional outlooks of Soviet strategic culture in remarkable ways. Though it remains to be seen how permanent are the changes he has begun, his emphasis on common security is a cause for considerable optimism. In contrast, pessimism in recent times about the inevitability of conflict and war has come from the Right in the United States, with talk about the Soviet Union as an 'evil empire' and Armageddon. President Reagan and his strategic fundamentalist supporters have been at the fore in this. Despite the warning by John Baylis in Part II, it was not from the peace movement in the first half of the 1980s that we had to fear self-fulfilling prophesies: it was from the right-wing fundamentalists in the United States.

East–West relations have therefore become trapped in a vicious circle of over-militarised policies and perceptions, continuous weapons innovation, and the infrastructure and dynamics of nuclear deterrence. Together, these have produced strategic stability of a sort, but at the cost of any hopes of 'positive' or 'stable' peace as defined earlier. Unless we try to move towards such a goal, peace will remain the mere absence of war, unless it actually collapses into war. Order will rest on a mutual threat of annihilation. Under these conditions, the continuation of civilised life in the northern hemisphere will have to depend indefinitely on the strategic 'rationality' of the leaders of the powers, the non-invention of weaponry which might tempt somebody to imagine that a future war might be 'won', and a mite of good luck through all those crises and conflicts with which international politics will inevitably be strewn. There is no reason to suppose that we will be any luckier in these respects than our unlucky ancestors. All our futures will have to rest on a potentially catastrophic 'stability'. Rather than trusting our futures to more of the same, our aim should be to work towards a durable peace based upon a political relationship in which war is progressively ruled out as an instrument of policy. This is not just wishful thinking, as growing numbers of people recognise, both East and West. Events in the northern hemisphere point in that direction. This was observed by Bernard Brodie, one of the fathers of nuclear strategy, well over a decade ago.[20] It will be explained further in Chapters 3 and 5.

From operational, moral and security standpoints there is therefore much that is wrong with our established pro-nuclear policies. Above all, they are based on regressive thinking in a situation demanding foresight. Britain, of course, is no longer in the front rank of powers in world terms, but it is not insignificant. It could and should use its membership of NATO to do what it can to promote favourable change. Achieving a relationship with the Soviet Union in which peace and stability rest on political choice rather than cosmic fear will not be easy. At best it will take decades before people on both sides will be able to develop confidence in such a possibility. Mutual mistrust is profound. Nevertheless, there are glimmers of hope, and in any case the destructiveness of modern technology leaves us no alternative but to try to live together. War will never be a solution, while little comfort can be gained from resting our hopes about the future of civilised life on an infinite faith that nuclear deterrence will never fail. In these circumstances, the most hopeful way ahead consists of adjusting our military policies so that the message they give is one of reassurance rather than provocation, and of defence rather than offence. To deserve their name, our security policies need to be based less on calculations of destructive power and more on the desirability of creating the conditions for mutually acceptable behaviour.

Notes

1. Among the vast range of critical literature, see the Alternative Defence Commission, *Defence without the Bomb. The Report of the Alternative Defence Commission.* (London: Taylor & Francis, 1983); Nigel Blake and Kay Pole (eds), *Dangers of Deterrence. Philosophers on Nuclear Strategy* and *Objections to Nuclear Defence. Philosophers on Deterrence.* (London: Routledge & Kegan Paul, 1983 and 1984); Jeff McMahan, *British Nuclear Weapons. For and Against* (London: Junction Books, 1981); Robert Neild, *How to Make Up your Mind About the Bomb* (London: Andre Deutsch, 1981); Gwyn Prins (ed.) *Defended To Death* (Harmondsworth: Penguin Books, 1983).
2. Part II, p. 267.
3. *NATO Review*, 1985, No. 6, p. 31.
4. Joseph S. Nye, Jr, 'The Long-Term Future of Deterrence', p. 234 in Roman Kolkowicz (ed.), *The Logic of Nuclear Terror* (Boston: Allen & Unwin, 1987).
5. See, for example, Michael MccGwire, 'The Insidious dogma of Deterrence' *Bulletin of the Atomic Scientists*, Vol. 2 (10) December 1986, pp. 24–9.
6. The points below are from Ken Booth, 'Nuclear Deterrence and "World War III": How Will History Judge?' pp. 251–82 in Kolkowicz, (ed.) *The Logic of Nuclear Terror*, op. cit.
7. The phrase is Paul Bracken's: *The Command and Control of Nuclear Forces* (New Haven, Conn.: Yale University Press, 1983) p. 2.
8. *The Economist* 9 May 1987.
9. Ibid., 18 September 1982.
10. Ian Aitken, 'I would press Polaris button, says Thatcher', *Guardian*, 1 June 1983.
11. Part II, pp. 249–50 and 'Haig reveals NATO might fire first nuclear shot to warn Russia', *The Times*, 5 November 1981.
12. Sir John Hackett, *The Third World War: August 1985. A Future History* (London: Sidgwick & Jackson, 1978).
13. Part II, pp. 248–55.
14. Rev. Richard Harrries (ed.) *What Hope in an Armed World?* (London: Pickering & Inglis, 1982), p. 108, and his 'In search of a just deterrent', *The Times*, 1 March 1984. See also Donald A. Wells, 'How Much can the "Just War" Justify?', *The Journal of Philosophy*, Vol. 66 (23), December 1969, pp. 819–29.
15. Part II, p. 252.
16. Joseph S. Nye Jr, 'Ethics and the Nuclear Future', *The World Today*, Vol. 42 (Nos 8–9), August/September 1986, pp. 151–5.
17. Michael Clarke, *The Alternative Defence Debate: Non-Nuclear Defence Policies for Europe* ADIU Occasional Paper No. 3 (University of Sussex, ADIU, August 1985), p. 17.
18. This is discussed below, pp. 90–5, 221–8.
19. George F. Kennan, *The Nuclear Delusion: Soviet-American Relations in the Atomic Age* (London: Hamish Hamilton, 1984)
20. Bernard Brodie, *War and Politics* (London: Cassell 1973), pp. 274–275.

3 Towards a Stable Peace

In the longer term, both West Germany and the United States, in their different ways, will have a more decisive voice than Britain in shaping the future of European security. In the shorter term, though, Britain could play a key role in accelerating trends towards a more stable peace. Unlike West Germany, Britain is not divided nor on the front line, and so is not caught up with a rather absolutist concept of nuclear deterrence and forward defence. Unlike the United States, Britain lacks the capabilities and responsibilites of a super power. Britain therefore has more choice than these major allies; but unlike its smaller NATO partners, Britain has both significance and nuclear weapons. If Britain cannot renounce nuclear weapons, and therefore by example put more firmly on the international agenda both military confidence-building and a commitment to restructure East–West relations, what hope is there that countries with less geopolitical choice will take radical steps[1] towards a more stable peace?

As steps towards a stable peace, the record is not encouraging with respect to both British policy and multilateral arms control. The history of disarmament and arms control negotiations has been dominated by gamesmanship.[2] In the 1980s, the manipulation of public opinion has been a major objective. Although positive results might emerge from the INF agreement, it too will be seen as part of the same cynical pattern if it is merely followed by a channelling of the arms race, and no actual restraint. For Britain Mrs Thatcher's government went along with the super power INF deal, but like some other Western European governments, did so with no great enthusiasm. More to the point was the strong message Mrs Thatcher delivered to the Soviet leadership (and others) after the Reykjavik mini-summit. She told them to forget the talk about nuclear disarmament by 2000 since Britain would maintain its own weapons. This has been her firm position since that time. Greater restraint on arms, and a less nationalistic attitude to international security are essential if Britain is to make its contribution to a more stable peace.

A 'LEGITIMATE INTERNATIONAL ORDER'

A non-nuclear defence policy, as recommended here, should not be considered as an end in itself; it is, on the contrary, only a means to achieving the fundamental aims of policy. Strategy should always begin with the question: 'What is it all about?'[3] Only when we have identified the political aim we are trying to achieve does it make sense to discuss military strategy and tactics. The latter should not dominate attention: exponents of alternative defence must avoid merely becoming radical equivalents of the 'guns-and-ammo' brigade on the right. The whole point of alternative defence thinking is to prevent the outbreak of war, not look forward to testing it.

In the absence of a major crisis or calamity, international politics is not usually an area where attitudes on fundamental issues change quickly. We cannot therefore expect momentous developments within a short time-span in the way people think about international security. It is salutary to remember that it has taken over 25 years of debate to get Britain to the brink of contemplating nuclear disarmament, and that in 1985 the Soviet Union renewed the Warsaw Pact for another 30 years. Change is in the air but utopia is not just around the corner; nor can it be guaranteed. Nevertheless, travelling hopefully is not out of the question; nor is the possibility that attitudes will evolve more quickly than in the past. It is not inconceivable, for example, that countries in the East–West confrontation might manufacture a robust *détente* relationship over the next fifteen years. This relationship could contain some of the more constructive elements of the super power *détente* of the early 1970s. At its best, 1970s-style *détente* was reciprocal, sought to establish ground rules for behaviour, was mutually beneficial, produced concrete results, began to be institutionalised, and appeared for a while to give the participants the expectation of a more stable period of coexistence than anything that had existed since the Bolshevik Revolution. Against the background of the acrimonious super power relationship since the 1970s, it will obviously take time to recapture a similar commitment to *détente*, let alone a shared idea of constructive engagement. Both sides are short of trust, and the ballyhoo accompanying the 1987 INF agreement should not obscure that. It will take years for the participants to become predictably trustful about the intentions of the other. If the new relaxation of tensions were to last, with the super powers growing to understand that their enlightened self-interest lay in preserving and building upon their cooperative relationship, we could then look forward to the arrival over the following period of 10–15 years (by the end of the first decade of the next century) of a situation and process which has been variously called a 'legitimate international order',[4] or a 'security regime'.[5] Such an outcome should be the fundamental aim of Britain's non-nuclear strategy and its accompanying efforts to reform NATO strategy.

A legitimate international order requires that all the major powers agree on the permissible aims and methods of foreign policy. As a result, a condition of 'international security' will exist, namely one in which states have a justifiably high expectation that there will not be a major war, and that in the peace that prevails, their core values will not be under threat. If each major power is basically satisfied, this will ensure that none need express its dissatisfaction against the prevailing international order by a revolutionary foreign policy, as did Germany after the Treaty of Versailles. International security will therefore exist as a condition when the members of international society reach a common consent about the rules of behaviour between them, and about the practical implications of those rules. If states actually lived up to the spirit and letter of the United Nations Charter we would have a legitimate international order in the sense implied in the present discussion.

A notable example of a legitimate international order was the Concert of Europe after 1815.[6] Admittedly it did not last long – until the Crimean War of 1853 – but it did create many of the conditions required for that process of international security we all desire. The governments involved in the Concert placed a common value on moderation; they sought to prevent the attempts at domination that had characterised the Napoleonic era, at such a cost to all. They took a long view, recognising that they had an interest in restraint. Some treaties, for example, contained formal and mutual self-denying ordinances. The great powers, for a period, forswore unilateral advantages. Different political philosophies coexisted in the Concert; the restraint practised was not rooted in shared ideologies but in shared ideas about external conduct. Despite ideological differences there was a widespread recognition of the need for honest and full communication if effective cooperation was to be achieved. Differences between the powers were subordinated to a high degree of consensus; the fear of another period of bitter warfare, and the belief that war would provoke revolution greatly strengthened the commitment to cooperation. The attitudes just mentioned were assisted by the absence of some of the pressures which later raised fears and suspicion in European diplomacy: the impact of public opinion, the influence of economic interest groups, and the efforts of military establishments to increase national strength. The history of the Concert shows that international security is possible in a condition of interstate anarchy, but the history of Europe as a whole shows that these times have been rare.

In a world of nuclear overkill the need for international security has never been objectively greater. However, despite the absence of a major war in Europe for over forty years, and the general prudence with which the super powers have conducted themselves there, it is evident that a legitimate international order does not exist. There is a fear in both East and West that core values are under threat, and war is not entirely ruled out. In addition, although the postwar territorial status quo has been formalised, it is not universally regarded as having been permanently settled, as the German question shows. The heart of today's predicament, both in Europe and beyond, is whether the super powers are capable of creating a legitimate international order. The record is not encouraging, but there are positive signs: the confrontation which began over forty years ago, and which has shaped European security since then is changing, and in some cases changing fast. Across both parts of Europe, and within each super power, a struggle will take place in the years ahead between those groups which believe the Cold War is not obsolete, and those who know that it has already passed. The former dramatise the present in the language of the past, while the latter explain that we are living in a different story, and that a realistic view of the present is actually a good place from which to start our journey towards a stable peace.

'THE SOVIET THREAT'

We cannot predict the likelihood of a legitimate international order materialising within the thirty year time-span mentioned earlier. The character of super power relations today, over forty years after the common war against Hitler, is not entirely encouraging. But it is not entirely black. There are hopeful trends. Before these are discussed, it is necessary to make some general propositions about 'the Soviet threat', since this is seen in the West as the fundamental problem of European security.

One of the themes in the first part of this book is that much of our thinking about 'defence' rests on stale and inaccurate images of the Soviet Union. Western propaganda in the first half of the 1980s was employed to justify a confrontational posture which was wasteful and dangerous. A more relaxed attitude to the Soviet threat was both possible and desirable.[7] It is significant in this respect that Western Soviet specialists throughout the 1980s have been much less anxious about Soviet intentions and capabilities than the ideologically-derived interpretations of the Reagan and Thatcher governments. The need for a revised picture of the Soviet Union pre-dated the arrival of Mr Gorbachev. We can justify a more relaxed attitude on the basis of a 25- if not 30-year perspective on Soviet international behaviour. Having said that, Mr Gorbachev is probably the most hopeful Soviet leader we could have wished for, in terms of his approach to international security.

The great contribution of Mr Gorbachev so far has been that he has promised changes in the Soviet Union which nobody predicted were possible in so short a time, and he has gone as far as he conceivably could in disarming traditional Soviet obstructions to better relations; so far he always seems willing to take the extra step. That is one reason why he has opponents at home and sceptics abroad. In Part II supporters of alternative defence are taken to task for having views which are 'militarily suspect': but one can hardly respect the establishment presentation of 'the Soviet threat' with its crude Sovietology and hyperbolic figures about Soviet military strength. These are now challenged by such an august body as the military committee of the Western European Union.[8] Outside right-wing circles, and especially in the United States, it is difficult to find evidence for the 'widespread fear' of the Soviet Union postulated in Part II. On the contrary, there is a growing confidence among large sections of European opinion that the Cold War has long been over, except in the minds of some backward-looking elites in both super powers. As each year goes by, the idea that the Soviet Union will risk war for the dubious benefit of trying to control the nations of Western Europe becomes less and less imaginable. Furthermore, it became equally evident to the open-minded in the 1980s that the Soviet Union was economically weak and lacked the diplomatic clout to dominate international affairs. It had negative relations with a coalition of major power centres – the United States, China, Western Europe and Japan – while its record in the Third World was patchy and its future control of Eastern Europe was threatened by serious problems. The country Mr Gorbachev took over was a harassed socialist super power.

While there are differences of opinion in the two parts of this book regarding the level of fear about the Soviet Union, John Baylis does agree that it is 'extremely unlikely' that the Soviet Union wants war, and that the case for dialogue is 'overwhelming'.[9] While Part I is more relaxed about the Soviet Union, it should be stressed that its case is not based on what is later called a 'wholly benevolent' view of the Soviet Union.[10] Undoubtedly there are people in the peace movement who have such a view; but they are not prominent among those who support the search for alternative defence policies. Alternative defence is based on the assumption that some form of deterrent, albeit non-nuclear, is needed, since Soviet political culture is neither pacifist nor attractive. There are many aspects of Soviet life that we in the West do not like: Soviet ideology is not to liberal taste; there are clashes of interest between our states; Soviet propaganda has been long, loud and blatant; the huge Soviet military arsenal has shown little propensity for restraint, and it has us targeted; Soviet leaders have sometimes behaved in a dangerous manner; their diplomacy has sometimes been crude and untrustworthy; the Soviet Union has exhibited the typically expansive and interventionist ambitions of a super power; Soviet policy in Eastern Europe has been repressive; and Soviet leaders have consistently failed to recognise the extent to which their own behaviour has provoked Western fears, and so our rushing to the military, diplomatic and propaganda barricades. By virtue of its size and strength alone the Soviet Union represents a problem in European security.

The reasoned part of the continuing East–West conflict is historical, political and 'system-induced'; the latter refers to the almost inevitable confrontation resulting from there being two major power blocs in the world. But part of the conflict is also the result of exaggerated fear, and is irrational. It stems from a combination of ideological fundamentalism, the vested interests and parochial outlooks of threat-inflaters, and sheer ignorance. These exaggerations, present on both sides, were stoked once more by the mutual sabre-rattling and namecalling of the 1975–85 period. To the extent it is system-induced, the mistrust between the super powers cannot be entirely eliminated; but that does not mean that they cannot behave in such a way as to encourage a sufficient degree of trust to enable them to live together in a legitimate international order within the next thirty years.

The intentions and capabilities of the Soviet Union represent a challenge to the West at some levels, but not at others. More to the point, the conflicts of interest and outlook that do exist need not rule out the possibility of our societies being able to compete together without war. Despite the legacy of the past, the future is not entirely bleak both in terms of the evolution of the Soviet Union or of the super power relationship. On the Soviet side it is evident that their policymakers are not lacking in rationality; the operational aspects of their ideology have been de-radicalised; their use of military force has been limited and circumspect; and the Soviet people know full well the dangers of war and the need for coexistence. Since Stalin's time, although with frequent blips, the image of the Soviet Union has slowly changed in the West. Unfortunately, there are still many in the West whose minds are frozen in the late 1940s, just as in the Soviet Union there are those whose outlooks are dominated by the facts and legends of the period of revolution and foreign intervention. Under Gorbachev images and reality appear to have grown closer on both sides. Gorbachev and those who think like him appear to have a clearer view of the West than their predecessors and of the limitations on Soviet power; likewise, increasing numbers of people in the West are dissatisfied with Cold War images. More people in the West can see what has actually been evident for decades, namely that Soviet leaders are as anxious as we to avoid nuclear war, and that although they intend to compete with us, they primarily want to get their own society working more effectively. To achieve this they are looking towards more East–West cooperation and the winding-down of the arms race.

The changing character of Soviet society was evident before Gorbachev; the arguments here do not depend on him, though his reforms and approach have accelerated change and encouraged a more favourable image in the West. In particular, Gorbachev has introduced a new and welcome style into the Soviet approach to security. Since he came to power in 1985 almost all the initiatives aimed at furthering common security have come from the Soviet side.[11] The foot-dragging has been on the part of Western leaders. While Gorbachev remains somewhat vulnerable to the charge that his words have been more evident than his deeds, there is also evidence that he is a multilateralist who means it. He has shown a flexibility of approach to arms-control which would have been unthinkable in the days of Brezhnev; he has gone further in a short time than anybody in the West thought possible on the key issue of verification; he has taken unilateral actions, such as prolonging the nuclear-test moratorium; he has preached 'reasonable sufficiency' to his armed forces; and he has proposed talks on an enticing agenda of issues. President Gromyko and President Reagan, old and comfortable with their Cold War clichés, are probably equally bewildered by what has emerged from the Kremlin since 1985.

In addition to the promising changes in the Soviet Union, there have also been some hopeful developments in super power relations.

These were capped by the INF agreement of 1987. By the mid-1980s there was already some nostalgia for détente and serious arms control; people looked back to the first half of the 1970s (SALT I, the Basic Principles Agreement, and the Helsinki Final Act) which had seen an attempt to establish a framework and rules for living together while reducing the military risks. Even what had been called 'the new Cold War' in the early 1980s had never had the imminent expectation of war which had characterised the 1940s and 1950s, when conflict might have occurred as a deliberate act rather than being a catastrophic mistake; and apart from some right-wing ideologues in the United States who wanted to arms-race the Soviet Union into oblivion, and those diehards in the Soviet Union who wanted military strength at all cost, there has been a growing recognition of the common super power interest in saving money from the arms race. Despite the sabre-rattling, prudence has generally been demonstrated in the management of super power crises over the years; as difficult as that relationship sometimes was, they have had a common interest in stability and avoiding war. There have also been some fundamental shifts of attitude on both sides, notably Khrushchev's reversal of Lenin's idea about the inevitability of war between the systems, and the widespread (though certainly not universal) rejection of 'superiority' as a strategic goal in the United States. Such glimmers of a secular historical trend towards better super power relations do not guarantee peace, of course, but they do offer reason for believing that we are not doomed in a nuclear trap. A legitimate international order might yet evolve out of a perilous century of nationalism and ideology.

In time, one hopes that a web of inter-relationships, rules, institutions, and contacts will do for the East–West relationship – but without the prologue of disastrous wars – what the processes of European unity have done for the nations of Western Europe in the last forty years. In Western Europe deeply entrenched attitudes have changed, and old thinking about the role of force in their international relationships have been dramatically reversed. We could witness comparable changes in East–West relations. Movement can sometimes be dramatic. We have seen, for example, the transformation of Ronald Reagan, from the right-wing crusader whose behaviour threatened to match his 'evil empire' beliefs in the early 1980s, to the President who negotiated the first nuclear disarmament deal with the Soviet Union in 1987; and we have heard the 'Iron Lady' of the second Cold War won over to describe the leader in the

Kremlin as somebody who could be trusted and with whom the West could do business. For his part, Mr Gorbachev has transformed the language used by Soviet officials to describe the character of East–West relations; he has emphasised notions of common security and interdependence, and he promises to revolutionise traditional Soviet strategic culture by replacing over-insurance with sufficiency in procurement, and offensive doctrines by strictly defensive force postures. We cannot yet say how permanent any of these changes will be, or how far they will be allowed to go. We must always reserve the right to be cynical in those matters. In any case, progress in behaviour rarely can keep pace with declaratory changes. Talking the language of common security is one thing, but radically changing the outlooks and operating procedures of entrenched military and political bureaucracies is another matter entirely.

Even if there is further progress in super power relations, it will be slow, and there will undoubtedly be downs as well as ups. Mistakes will be made and international politics will toss into the arena a share of unpleasant surprises. Nevertheless, if a steady determination can be generated on both sides to build a stable relationship, it is not inconceivable that we can move towards a legitimate international order. There is only one certain obstacle, only one possibility which would cancel out this and all other possibilities. That is nuclear war. It is imperative therefore that we progressively reduce the risks of it, however small they may be. We cannot guarantee that a stable peace can be achieved between East and West, but have we any alternative but to try?

'PROCESS UTOPIANS'

One of the problems with deterrence theory is its static quality. It does not help us to think about the long-term future. Alternative defence thinking, in contrast, is concerned to identify future goals and reshape present attitudes and policies so that they might be achieved. While it is by no means a bad thing if we can daily abstain from the use of force in East–West relations, it is far preferable if we can shape a relationship so that the problem eventually disappears altogether. Unless we believe that this is the best of all possible worlds, and that nothing can go wrong – the operating belief of the pro-nuclear defence establishment – we need to identify long-term goals in order to shape short- and medium-term policies, and in order to mobilise political support behind them. In thinking about long-term goals, and ways of achieving them, Joseph Nye has offered a useful distinction between 'end-point utopians' and 'process utopians'.[12]

Most utopian visions, according to Nye, point to what are considered to be a better set of future conditions. Ideas about general and comprehensive disarmament or world government are of this type. History, in a sense, comes to a stop when these utopias are reached. The standpoint from which Part I has been written is that such radical end-points are not feasible in a foreseeable timescale. It is also far from self-evident that some of these visions are desirable. Might World Government be a global Big Brother? Furthermore, by giving undue attention to such distant and uncertain possibilities, we can distract ourselves from immediate predicaments and the very practical problem of how we get from here to utopia, since it cannot be done in one jump. It is easier to create a utopia in one's dreams than manufacture a structure of international security in a world characterised by the old habits of the game of nations.

The game of nations took centuries to evolve into its present form, and it will not disappear overnight. The most productive approach to our predicament – progressive yet pragmatic – is that of the process utopian. Nye has defined process utopias as benign or pacific trends, with the end-point being uncertain. The process utopian therefore takes modest, reformist steps in order to make a better world somewhat more probable for future generations. What exactly that better world will look like must be settled by those future generations, when the possibilities become clearer. For the time being we can only identify relatively short-term goals, say a generation ahead, while attending to the most important task of seeking to reduce the risks of nuclear war consistently over time. If, each year, we can lower the risk a little more than the previous year, we will in time wipe out the fear of nuclear war.

The next-generation utopia towards which the benign and pacific efforts outlined in Part I of this book are addressed is encapsulated in the idea of a legitimate international order discussed earlier. To many this might not be a compelling vision – compared, for example, with world government or complete disarmament – but it is the only 'utopia' realistically on the agenda. And even achieving that – something matching the hopes of the UN founders – would just about be a miracle within the next 30 years. If a predictable peace could emerge in that time-span, based on political attitudes rather than fear, then people could start thinking practically about what now seem dreams, such as radical disarmament or global institution-building.

Those who try to bring about a new world too quickly can easily become discouraged. In a limited fashion this happened in the Western peace movement following its failure to stop the deployment of cruise missiles and the marginalising of the nuclear-freeze campaign. One of the advantages of the process-utopian approach is that nobody expects heaven tomorrow, and that setbacks are taken for granted. Moreover, because movement towards a legitimate international order must be incremental and across a broad front, many different people can be involved. The long-term goal will not be achieved unless people believe it is possible, and so there has to be consciousness-raising, as well as changes in policies and institutions. The process-utopian approach is social, cultural and educational, as well as diplomatic and strategic. Process-utopian approaches can range from trying to negotiate crisis-prevention centres between the super powers, to encouraging cooperation through trade, to cultural and educational efforts which seek to reduce stereotyping. It is helpful simply to talk to friends, families and opponents about the international situation, with a view to encouraging them to adopt a wider perspective than simply that of the country in which they happen to have been born. Young people are important, before their political attitudes become rigidified, and in the super powers more than elsewhere. If the visceral anti-Sovietism of so much of US opinion could be moderated, together with the deep xenophobia of Soviet Russia, a major advance would have been made. Irrational mistrust is not the whole of the problem, but it is an aspect, and one we can all address.

At the British level much could be done to encourage more realistic analyses of East–West relations, and we could try to make government more accountable on the issue of nuclear weapons.[13] If we have so little control in our own domain – if secrecy is so complete and democratic involvement so minimal – what hope is there of wider control? At the super power-level crisis prevention is a priority. This involves, among other things, working through diplomacy and strategy to minimise the occurrence of dangerous situations and then to reduce the likelihood of miscalculations should such situations come about. This is a promising time to work on such ideas. There is a process of change going on in the Soviet Union, and we should take whatever steps are possible to encourage the favourable trends pointing towards moderate behaviour abroad and more respect for human rights at home. We must certainly seek to avoid actions that play into the hands of those in the Soviet Union favouring opposite ways of behaving. Since the accession to power of Mikhail Gorbachev we have seen a most sophisticated and flexible leader. Indeed, it is difficult to think of a General Secretary emerging from the political assault course of life in the CPSU whose views on international security could be as progressive, and in a liberal rather than a Marxist-Leninist sense. But the constraints on his efforts are enormous. Gorbachev cannot move too quickly or he will provoke the opposition of the many who fear change in the Soviet system. Consequently, we should not wait for the Soviet Union to reform its domestic politics in ways we find desirable before we try to improve our relationship. Over a long period the pattern of initiative and reciprocation between East and West will be asymmetrical. There will be times when the West may think it is giving up more than the Soviet Union, but it has the scope and security to do so. In the short term, however, on matters such as the nuclear test moratorium and ASAT testing, it has been the Soviet Union that has taken unilateral initiatives and the Reagan administration and its foreign supporters which have failed to reciprocate.

In order to achieve a stable peace, we need stable attitudes and stable policies. We cannot expect moderate and consistent behaviour from the Soviet Union if we do not act in a similar manner. This means that we must replace the confrontational posturing of the early 1980s with a consistent commitment to coexistence. What conclusions are Soviet policy-makers to draw about US policy when they face such pendulum swings as that of Jimmy Carter, from his initial cheerful commitment to *détente* to his later born-again containment posturing? Or, alternatively, the even more marked swing of Ronald Reagan from his deep anti-Soviet and anti-arms control instincts to the President who delivered deep cuts in US mistrust of the 'evil empire' and proposed doing the same in strategic armaments. The achievement of more stable attitudes on the part of Western leaders will to some extent, of course, depend upon Soviet behaviour, but in the past it has often been the case that the swings in fashionable US attitudes towards the Soviet Union have been as much a function of US domestic politics as of what was happening in the Soviet Union. Western Europeans, whose attitudes towards the Soviet Union have generally been more sanguine and stable – swinging to neither extremes of euphoria nor fear – and for whom *détente* never died, have some capability for playing honest broker between the super powers. Whether they will grasp the role, or whether the super powers give them the opportunity is another matter.

One of the most important lessons of the postwar period is that Western security is and will remain intimately tied up with the security of the Soviet Union. This means that we must accept the idea that increases in Soviet insecurity will not necessarily improve Western security. This apparently simple but rather radical idea has been slowly gaining support under the banner of 'common security'. In contrast to the prevailing security-through-strength ideology of the early Reagan presidency, the Palme Commission Report of 1982 gave political respectability to the notion of common security, arguing that states could no longer attain security at each other's expense but only through cooperative efforts. One implication of this is that Western policy-makers need to appreciate how and to what extent we ourselves are a 'threat', by better comprehending the psychological realities of Soviet policy-makers; then our decision-makers will be in a position to deal objectively rather than in a doctrinaire fashion with Soviet words and actions. If we do not better understand the Soviet side of any matter, we cannot claim to understand contemporary strategic 'reality'. It is not only on military matters where we need Soviet cooperation; we also need it in the management of apparently intractable political issues, notably the future of the two Germanies.

The pragmatic Soviet response to any sustained period of coexistence offered by the West would be one of reciprocation. This would require them to live up to the spirit of coexistence (as defined in the West) as well as to the Soviet-defined letter. If they did not do this – if there continued to be Czechoslovakias, Angolas, Afghanistans, Korean airliner incidents, and abuses of human rights – then Soviet policy-makers would play into the hands of Western hawks, as so often in the past. The phenomenon of Reaganism, which has been so costly and potentially dangerous for the Soviet Union, was not simply a facet of US domestic politics: it was also created by US images of Soviet policy in the 1970s. Successive Soviet leaders have signally failed to understand the extent to which their own behaviour has encouraged confrontational attitudes on the part of the West. To date Mr Gorbachev has shown signs of being the first Soviet leader with an understanding of how the Soviet Union appears in the eyes of others, and of the limitations within which the Soviet Union operates. For these reasons alone, he may prove to be its most successful leader. He has helped to project a more modern and moderate image of his country; this is not only valuable for his own diplomacy, but also for Western thinking. There is some evidence that Soviet analysts understand better than their Western counterparts that the greatest danger facing the world is not from the naked aggression of the other side, but from the insecurity trap created by the arms race. A more realistic image of the Soviet Union should help more of us in the West to appreciate that while relations will continue to be characterised by struggle, the real threat we face is not of a Soviet military breakout across the central front, but of the super power military confrontation collapsing through its own internal strategic and technological dynamics.

It is necessary, in order to avoid such an outcome, that stringent arms restraint is exercised. A predictably peaceful relationship cannot evolve as long as both super powers are obsessed by the balance or imbalance of their military confrontation. Armaments are necessary for all states at the present juncture of international politics, but their accumulation can sometimes detract from national security, instead of adding to it. The pattern of the postwar years has been that national strength merely provokes countervailing strength. This growing irrationality of the super power arms race has been admitted by an increasing number of former 'insiders', including Lord Zuckerman in a recent book.[14] He cites other famous scientific advisers who share his view. There is also some recognition from within the Soviet Union, made possible by *glasnost*, that weapons may be deployed through technological inertia rather than by political calculation.[15] The short term success of the INF agreement and the apparent seriousness of the commitment to deep cuts in strategic forces, should not lead us into unrealistic expectations about the immediate scope for super power denuclearisation. If a 50 per cent cut in strategic weapons was to be achieved, the level of nuclear arsenals would still be equivalent to those of the mid-1970s. Even if deep cuts then generated pressure for yet further reductions, we probably cannot in the foreseeable future create a framework of international security in which nuclear weapons could be 'disinvented' across the world, that is, scrapped globally and the knowledge lost. On the other hand, if we survive the first century of the nuclear age without nuclear use, we will probably have relegated them by that time to a merely symbolic role. As their use becomes progressively more unimaginable, so their disinventing will become both more conceivable but less urgent.

Although in the final analysis it is the super powers who have the capability to effect major changes in international affairs, other powers can have a significant role. For all its diminished status, for example, Britain could play an important role in helping to bring about those changes in policies and attitudes that will help to create a more reliable structure of international security. The old framework of ideas shaping Western attitudes to external affairs – the Cold War, the Soviet threat, the red menace, Warsaw Pact military predominance, the danger of war – have become less relevant to the daily preoccupations of governments and are becoming less saleable to their general publics. If we can change our behaviour to match what is evidently the reality of a more interdependent world, we will have made progress in managing what Stanley Hoffmann described as the central problem of international politics, namely, turning the traditional vicous circle of relations between states into a spiral of trust and peace. We can surely share Hoffmann's lack of illusions about it 'being achievable or achieved in the near future'; nevertheless, as he says, 'it is not necessary to hope in order to undertake, or to succeed in order to persevere'.[16] We need a new defence policy to reflect the changing realities and to shape future change in a benevolent direction. By embracing non-provocative defence, Britain can play a positive role in edging Europe away from the idea of order based on fear and towards the notion of peace through politics.

This process-utopian approach to international politics, the desirability of arms restraint, and the goal of a legitimate international order, are the background against which we should think about British efforts to promote a non-nuclear, non-provocative defence posture for NATO as a whole. What is being proposed in the rest of Part I (a non-nuclear strategy) is a realistic process-utopian approach towards a realisable mid-point utopia (a legitimate international order) within 30 years. It represents a convergence of the desirable and the feasible. The ideology of nuclear deterrence as it has developed is static and dangerous and relies indefinitely on cosmic good luck. The hope of lasting peace through multilateral arms control negotiations has achieved little, though it must not be cast aside. Some of the more radical ideas, such as world government or shifts to civilian resistance, are so far-reaching that no political leader would ever agree to them. Working unilaterally and multilaterally towards alternative defence schemes based on non-nuclear and non-provocative strategies and foreign policies is the only way forward.

Notes

1. The INF Treaty and deep cuts in START are steps in the right direction, but they are not 'radical'. They do not reflect a different conception of how East–West relations should be managed.
2. The standard reference for this is J. W. Spanier and J. L. Nogel, *The Politics of Disarmament: A Study in Soviet–American Gamesmanship* (New York: Praeger, 1962).
3. Bernard Brodie, *War and Politics* (London: Cassell, 1973), Chapter 1.
4. Henry Kissinger, *A World Restored–Metternich, Castlereagh and the Problems of Peace 1812–22* (Boston: Houghton Mifflin, 1957).
5. Robert Jervis, 'Cooperation Under the Security Dilemma', *World Politics* Vol. 30 (2), January 1978 pp. 167–214.
6. The points below are based on Kissinger, *A World Restored*, op. cit. and Jervis, 'Cooperation Under the Security Dilemma', op. cit., and Gordon A. Craig and Alexander L. George, *Force And Statecraft* (New York: OUP, 1983), Chapter 3, 'Balance of Power, 1815–1914: Three Experiments'.
7. This is elaborated in Ken Booth, 'New Challenges and Old Mindsets: Ten Rules for Empirical Realists', Chapter 3 in Carl Jacobsen (ed.), *The Uncertain Course* (Oxford: OUP for SIPRI, 1987).
8. *Guardian*, 25 November 1987.
9. Part II, p. 269.
10. Ibid.
11. Matthew Evangelista, 'The New Soviet Approach to Security', *World Policy Journal*, Fall 1986, pp. 561–99.
12. Joseph S. Nye, Jr, 'The Long-Term Future of Deterrence', in Roman Kolkowitz (ed.), *The Logic of Nuclear Terror* (Boston: Allen & Unwin, 1987), pp. 239–47.
13. See Hugh Miall, *Nuclear Weapons: Who's in Charge?* (London: Macmillan/Oxford Research Group, 1987) or Robert Dahl, *Controlling Nuclear Weapons* (Syracuse: Syracuse University Press, 1985).
14. Lord Zuckerman, *Star Wars in A Nuclear World* (London: William Kimber 1986), esp. Chapter 9.
15. *Guardian*, 21 November 1987.
16. Stanley Hoffmann, *Duties Beyond Borders* (Syracuse, NY: Syracuse University Press, 1981), p. 232.

4 Towards a Non-Provocative Defence Policy

Given the problems with nuclear strategy, and the implications of the evolving international and technological environment, it is a time to change NATO's military posture. But it is one thing to criticise existing policy; it is another altogether to replace it with something generally agreed to be better. Slogans are not enough, and in the 1980s anti-nuclear critics have been busy devising a now lengthy menu of non-nuclear alternatives. Their aim is non-provocative defence. Not surprisingly, as with nuclear deterrers, there are differences of opinion among alternative defence thinkers regarding the best mix of ingredients. Non-nuclear strategies are naturally susceptable to those ambiguities and inconsistencies to which any defence policy is heir. The aim in this chapter is to offer a non-nuclear package for Britain that is related to the threat, is militarily convincing, will contribute to arms restraint, offers stability in crises and promises de-escalation in the event of war. It should attract public support and be affordable. It builds on existing trends and could be put in place step by step.

The non-nuclear defence policy proposed below takes the best from various approaches, while offering some ideas of its own. Although it shares some common features with the non-nuclear strategy advocated in recent years by the Labour Party, it has a number of different emphases. In particular, it is both more pro-American and pro-European. These attitudes are more in line with the anti-nuclear wing of the Liberal Party.

There should be three main elements in Britain's future defence policy. First, a shift from the posture of indpendent nuclear deterrence to one based on conventional forces. Second, the adoption, in consultation with our allies, of a strategy of non-provocative defence to replace flexible response. And third, a continuing commitment to the North Atlantic Treaty, but with a more European than Atlanticist orientation. Such a package is realistic, starting from where we are, and reformist, along the lines discussed in the previous chapter.

THE PRINCIPLE OF NON-PROVOCATIVE DEFENCE

As has already been established, the objective of British external policy – the creation of a legitimate international order – involves moving towards a political relationship with the Soviet Union in which force will not be seen as a legitimate or necessary instrument of policy. The reformulation of the West's strategic posture must be a major element in this.

The principle of non-provocative defence is simple in theory, but more complex to establish in practice. As it was defined by the Alternative Defence Commission, the seed-bed of many ideas in this field, non-provocative defence means 'having a capacity to inflict heavy losses on any invading force, but at the most only a limited capacity to mount offensive operations in the opponent's territory.'[1] This approach has been labelled 'defensive deterrence', or (by German thinkers) a 'structural non-aggression capability'.[2] Non-provocative defence, by words and actions, attempts to loosen the insecurity trap caused by the threat-inflation and mutual suspicion which seem to be the inevitable products of the nuclear arms race. Non-provocative defence seeks to deter invasion by denying a potential aggressor the prospect of a cheap victory. The possible benefits of occupation would not be worth the cost.

A robust non-provocative defence is appropriate to deal with all Soviet threats except that of wiping Western Europe off the face of the earth. That threat, presumably, is only likely to arise if a Soviet leader comes to believe that we are about to wipe the Soviet Union off the face of the earth. However, by denuclearising our strategy, we will begin to show the Politburo that this is not our intention. Non-provocative defence is one of the foundations we must begin to put in place if we are to move towards a world in which force will no longer be seen as an acceptable or necessary instrument of policy, and for the creation of a lasting and legitimate system of international security.

A non-provocative defence policy is not simply a military reform; it also has a political component. Defence policy and foreign policy should move along parallel paths. In this respect there was something of a disjunction between the first and second reports of the ADC. The non-provocative defence posture which was recommended in the 1983 report was followed up by a second in 1987 which sought to devise a foreign policy to unfreeze the blocs.[3] Such 'dealignment' is a desirable long-term goal, but in the shorter term it is both unrealistic and, worse still, provocative to the Soviet Union. It is unrealistic because the Soviet Union as recently as 1985 renewed the Warsaw Pact for another 30 years, thereby underlining its intention to dominate Eastern Europe for the foreseeable future; furthermore, while the German problem remains as intractable as it is, speculation about dealignment is premature. Some unfreezing is desirable and possible, and has taken place (*détente* might have died between the super powers in the late 1970s, but it largely continued in intra-European affairs); but dealignment is not yet on the agenda. For the West to try and make it so, and in the near term, is provocative because its very aim threatens Soviet control of Eastern Europe, a primary foreign-policy priority. We all look forward to the day when the international politics of Europe are not characterised by the military and ideological confrontation between the blocs, and the restricted freedom of one half of the continent: but a 'healed' Europe is a distant prospect. It will only evolve in the course of time when the regimes in the East feel more confident about their security in all respects; this will enable the Soviet Union to begin to loosen the reins, and eventually retire its forces behind its own frontiers.

Worry is expressed in Part II about the threat of 'finlandisation' in Western Europe as a result of our deference to Soviet military strength. This exaggerates the military as opposed to the economic and political determinants of future European affairs. In any case, a more serious cause of instability in Europe in the next 20 years is likely to arise not from the finlandisation of the West, but from Soviet insecurity caused by the finlandisation or what might be called the yugoslavisatian of the East. Attempted defections from the 'socialist commonwealth' seem more likely in the years ahead than self-made Moscow puppets in the North Atlantic Treaty area.

For the moment we can only look forward to a winding-down of the Soviet presence in Eastern Europe when the Kremlin is confident about the stability and cooperation of the local regimes there. The latter requires a certain military and political reassurance on the part of the West, even at the cost of occasionally muting our demands – if not desires – for the freedom of the peoples of Eastern Europe. This should not be taken to imply that the West should completely abandon Eastern Europe to Soviet power, in the sense that it must never make its position on human rights clear, or that it should always refrain from speaking out against any unacceptable Soviet behaviour. However, progress on human rights and national independence in Eastern Europe must not be made a precondition by the West for undertaking other steps that will contribute to a safer world. A legitimate order does not necessarily depend on universal adherence to democracy, freedom, or human rights (though anyone with liberal instincts will believe that these will help). The first requirement is not democracy but moderate external behaviour. This argument is not based on cynical 'spheres of influence' thinking. It is based on the belief that the first human-rights priority for all Europeans is to avoid another war.

To be realistic and reformist about non-provocative defence it is necessary to accept Soviet hegemony in Eastern Europe for the time being while eschewing some of the more radical ideas about alternative defence, especially those advocating a shift to civilian resistance or reliance upon attrition by small groups. NATO strategy needs reforming, but small-is-beautiful goes too far. Aircraft remain essential in modern defence and main battle-tanks can be useful for counter-offensives on one's own territory. In addition, Warsaw Pact planners should not be able to think that every potential military target in their own territory will have a free ride. Arguing in favour of keeping some potential to strike back is likely to provoke objections from non-provocative defence purists, but a balance has to be struck between 'non-provocation' and 'military conviction'.

Quibbling over details of policy should not be allowed to obstruct the starting of processes that point in the right direction. The main features of the non-provocative posture which NATO should adopt over the next ten years are as follows:

(i) The complete withdrawal or scrapping of NATO's battlefield and theatre nuclear weapons
The 1987 INF Treaty has started this process, but there is invariably a hard road to travel in international politics between signature and success. We are not yet in the business of removing battlefield weapons, and even the INF agreement will have proved to be no more than a gesture if it simply rechannels the arms race, by one or both parties compensating for the removal of one category of weapons by developing or deploying more of different ones.

(ii) A nuclear no-first-use (NFU) declaration.
This should be an early step for NATO. Such a declaration would be a useful confidence-building measure and diplomatic signal to the Soviet Union, but equally important, it would be a vital step towards weaning NATO's operational doctrines away from an early resort to nuclear weapons.

(iii) The rejection of 'deep-strike' strategies such as FOFA (Follow on Forces Attack)
Deep-strike strategies are not only politically provocative; they are also unsatisfactory militarily. There are considerable problems involved in using both automated weapons and manned aircraft for long-range offensive purposes, and they also promote arms-racing and crisis-instability.[4] Retaliation and deep-strike doctrines should be replaced by an obviously defensive posture, though one that would include a designated counter-military target list in Eastern Europe. This list would be strictly limited, but all airfields in Eastern Europe would be legitimate targets for conventional attack.

(iv) The manufacturing of a network of confidence-building measures (CBMs).
In order to remove the fears (and temptations) of surprise-attack, mutual transparency should be energetically pursued. A forum exists for this in the Conference on Disarmament in Europe (CDE) in Stockholm; it also provides a microphone for non-super power voices. We should attempt to demonstrate by all means possible – including the details of field regulations, the character of exercises, the nature and siting of the weaponry deployed, and the type of doctrine adopted – that the Western aim is not to threaten the existence of the Warsaw Pact countries, but merely to create an effective conventional defence against attack.

(v) The pursuit of constructive engagement
Finally, we must remember the adage 'Fear the man who fears you' and pursue foreign and economic policies which do not increase Soviet insecurities. The greatest dangers in the postwar period have been when the Soviet Union has felt pushed into a corner, and that time is running out. We must recognise that we have a vested interest in Soviet security. This means, broadly speaking, promoting consistent attitudes of live-and-let live, constructive engagement rather than the hectoring and confrontation of recent years.

This package of non-provocative defence policies would, if successful, place East–West relations on a more permanent, stable and peaceful footing. Some of the ideas proposed go beyond anything likely to be in the files of the present major Western governments, for whom winning elections is more pressing than long-term speculation about international relations. However, with shifts of electoral fortunes, and benevolent trends in world affairs, it is not inconceivable that substantial progress in the direction of a more defensive deterrent posture could be in train by the end of the century.

Critics of the idea of non-provocative defence – notably the British government in the 1985 Defence White Paper – argue that it is not possible to make clear-cut distinctions between defensive and offensive weapons, and so they reject the notion. This criticism reduces the idea of non-provocative defence to absurdity. What matters is not whether individual weapons are 'offensive' or 'defensive' – an old and impossible conundrum – but whether the total posture looks provocative or otherwise. At present NATO's orientation is basically 'defensive' – as the government rightly stresses – but it does contain some enormously dangerous retaliatory and escalatory elements (especially if seen through the eyes of the adversary's defence planners – a mental exercise most Western policy-makers seem unwilling to try). NATO's posture – like that of the Warsaw Pact – is 'defensive' but intimidating. This need not be the case. It is undoubtedly possible to create defence policies that are clearly and without question designed for defence purposes only. They already exist. Several countries do not threaten their neighbours; they do not have dangerous retaliatory and escalatory doctrines and weapons; they are structurally incapable of aggression; and they do not provoke suspicions and threat-inflation among those who might challenge them. Nonetheless, they do have a robust defensive capacity: their forces threaten to put up the costs to any invader, their doctrines and equipment carry military conviction, and their governments speak from some strength. Sweden, Switzerland and Yugoslavia are three such countries whose defence policies are successfully non-provocative.[5] Their defensive deterrents have worked for far longer than 40 years in the first two cases, and for nearly 40 years in the latter case, including against a periodically hostile nuclear super power.

If non-provocative defence proceeds along parallel paths of political and military reassurance, then the criticisms made of it in Part II will be seen not to stand up. No Soviet leader or military planner could realistically expect a less provocative package than the one just proposed. Since between 1985 and 1987 Mr Gorbachev went further in his arms-control initiatives than anybody in the West forecast was possible for a Soviet leader, it is likely that in the Soviet political context he has now gone as far as is at present possible. The West has begun to respond, but more slowly and with more reluctance than many would like. While General Secretary Gorbachev stole President Reagan's clothes on the issue of the zero-option, he has quietened NATO's diplomatic thunder with his offers about conventional reductions and the defensive restructuring of the Warsaw Pact's posture. More than his Western counterparts, he is talking the language of alternative defence, though as ever actions speak louder than words. But actions will not come without more of a response from the West. If we successfully achieve the first round of de-escalation in the arms race, represented by the INF agreement, then a further and more significant winding-down of the political confrontation in Europe – and one with some promise of lasting – will require a further winding-down of the military confrontation. NATO is potentially well placed to proceed with denuclearisation.

FROM PRO-NUCLEAR TO NON-NUCLEAR

A complete move to conventional forces has been at the heart of the revived anti-nuclear campaign since the late 1970s. All nuclear weapons in Britain's arsenal should eventually be scrapped. Some dual-capable systems could be converted to conventional use.

Before the re-election of Mrs Thatcher's government in June 1987 there was some hope that Trident would not be deployed and that the money saved could be used to improve or at least maintain Britain's conventional forces. We now have to face the virtual certainty that by the time of the election of any party or coalition of parties committed to non-nuclear defence, Trident will be in place. As will be discussed later, the fact that enormous amounts of money have been spent on Trident is not sufficient justification for persevering with it. The 1964 precedent need not be repeated, and good money thrown after bad. By the time of the next election the choice between Trident and conventional forces will almost certainly seem starker than now; by then our conventional contribution to the alliance will be eroding. Mrs Thatcher may well leave it to the next occupant of Downing Street to face the serious political implications of that erosion in terms of inter-allied relations. How much better never to have spent the money on Trident in the first place.

In order to strengthen our conventional commitment, a logical step for Britain, though undoubtedly controversial, would be the reintroduction of conscription. National service would make a valuable contribution to the alliance in several important areas. It should help raise the nuclear threshold, stiffen the allies' ability to contain limited

Warsaw Pact aggressions, reduce dependence on 'warning time', increase Britain's manpower reserves, strengthen territorial defence at home, reduce defence costs, and send political signals to both adversaries and allies that Britain is serious about defence.[6] If conscription were reintroduced, as part of a shift to a non-nuclear strategy, it would not only strengthen deterrence (by invigorating the alliance and increasing its conventional credibility) but it would also contribute to a more rational strategy if war were to break out. Such a step by Britain would be all the more sensible in the light of the declining manpower which will be available for Western European armies in years ahead, as a result of demographic trends. There is also the probability of the erosion of US troop levels, as a result of US domestic politics.

Conscription would not be a revolutionary or costly step; all our Western European allies have national service, and they also spend less, per capita, on defence. Initially the expenses involved in organising national service would be high, but in time there should be a significant lowering of our defence spending, as the proportion of well-paid professionals to conscripts decreases, and as the need for maintaining dependents and the associated infrastructure in Germany declines. In any case, the costs involved in national service should be regarded as a small price to pay for freeing us of the nuclear burden. National service of a military or non-military nature is a democratic duty; and if properly organised – with a short term of service and without the trappings of militarism – it could have beneficial social advantages.

It may be that the reintroduction of conscription will remain too unpopular to be endorsed by any political party. If this is the case, defence planners will be faced by the need to operate on the basis of existing troop-levels, augmented by the better use of reserves. This would be costlier in monetary terms, and less symbolic than national service; but in political terms it is likely to remain more acceptable. However, the potential unpopularity of conscription should not be exaggerated, and it must be remembered as an *Economist* survey recently showed, that where conscription is employed in Western Europe it works fairly well and is fair, and it offers advantages not least in cost.[7] Despite such arguments in its favour, the reintroduction of conscription should not be regarded as a condition for movement towards a non-nuclear policy. Indeed, most anti-nuclear opinion is also anti-conscription.

Giving up nuclear weapons will not come easy to important

sections of British opinion. Nuclear deterrence has become an addiction in the minds of senior politicians, Ministry of Defence officials, and the hierarchy of the services. In the official mind, nuclear weapons have helped Britain hide our economic incapacity to be a first-rank military power, and they have served as a symbol (it was hoped) of our continuing significance in international affairs. It is hardly surprising therefore that kicking this dependence will prove to be very difficult for some to contemplate. More than anything, the possession of nuclear weapons by Britain in the last four decades has deterred the official mind from attacking the new realities of the postwar world.

The problem of how actually to get rid of nuclear weapons, once a British government has decided upon such a step, is not one which has attracted much attention either within the anti-nuclear movement or among the defence establishment. The problem has been a second-order issue for the peace movement, while the Ministry of Defence, used to bipartisanship in defence, has not been used to the pendulum-swings in policy which have characterised some other ministries of state. Reversing a policy which has evolved over forty years will be extremely difficult for a future British government, not only because of the opposition of major allies, but also because of the strong opposition from bureaucratic and other forces in Britain. The Oxford Research Group is one of the few bodies which has investigated this problem thoroughly.[8] Among the 'establishments' it identified which could be expected to exert strong pressures against a non-nuclear British government, it considered the following to be the most prominent:

- The Foreign Office would be particularly fraught because France would be left as the only European nuclear power.
- The Chiefs of Staff would be worried by the loss of the relationship with the US services.
- The nuclear establishment at Aldermaston would object to the loss of design teams and expertise.
- Various bodies within the Ministry of Defence would stress, from their own bureaucratic viewpoint, the costs, waste, dangers and difficulties of disposing of our nuclear capability.

Thus a British cabinet committed to nuclear disarmament would be confronted by major problems from its own officials, even before those of the allies had full say. However, in a further report, the Oxford Research Group concluded that the abolition of the independent deterrent over a five-year period of government was practicable, and that although it would be strongly opposed, it could be made acceptable to the military and our major allies.[9] When and if all the opposition can be overcome, other problems would arise. Should the nuclear disarmament process be verified, and if so by whom? And should the whole 'nuclear' infrastructure be broken up (including, for example, nuclear-powered submarines)? Deciding to 'get rid of' nuclear weapons is only half the story. Actually implementing such a policy will be a long and difficult task. But the main point is to start the wind-down, and show others that steps can be safely taken out of the nuclear labyrinth.

FROM FLEXIBLE RESPONSE TO DEFENSIVE DETERRENCE

Space forbids an extensive discussion of the doctrinal applications of defensive deterrence. Tactics, in any event, are largely the business of military professionals; whether we are talking about defending a ridge or stopping a tank column in conditions of nuclear or conventional war, we need the expertise of the insider. However, when it comes to establishing the principles on which defence should be based, the last word in a democratic society should be that of the civilian.

If we think of a ten- to fifteen-year time-scale, then substantial progress could be made towards a non-provocative defence for NATO. Fundamental change must be brought about slowly. Since the move must carry military conviction in the eyes of one's own armed forces, as well as the adversary's, what is being proposed is an evolution of existing conventional strategy rather than one of the more radical territorial defence schemes proposed in recent years.

When it was adopted in 1967, 'Flexible Response' was intended to improve NATO strategy in a variety of ways: it was supposed to be a climb-down from massive retaliation, to offer more rational options, to raise the nuclear threshold, and to provide the possibility for graduated reactions to aggressive moves. As things are, NATO will have to 'go nuclear' within a few days, and many uncertainties still exist about the actual process of nuclear release. The promise of a more rational posture through Flexible Response has not been fulfilled. Indeed, the doctrine now attracts much criticism, even from supporters of a nuclear posture. Some of these criticisms are elaborated in Part II, as a preliminary to introducing ideas of alliance reform. The more radical critics of the doctrine want it replaced and not simply reformed, because they believe it to be heavily pro-nuclear, inflexible, escalatory and incredible.

The critique of Flexible Response in Part II does not go far enough, since its basic flaws are not addressed. On the contrary, some of its flaws are justified on deterrent grounds. Ambiguity and inflexibility are rationalised as military virtues. But if that is acceptable, what cannot be justified in the name of 'deterrence'? It is argued that were NATO's nuclear bluff to be called, it is possible to surrender. This is true. But what if the system takes over, as John Baylis admits it might? Are ambiguity and inflexibility desirable at the point when dozens of confused, desperate and emotional commanders are faced with the terrible choice: if I do not fire my nuclear weapons first, might there not even be an opportunity to contemplate firing them second? A cosmic bluff cannot be called a strategy. The reform of Flexible Response elaborated in Part II consists of a 'Conventional Defence Initiative' and an 'Extended Firebreak Strategy'. These ideas do represent improvements on what presently exists, but they are only marginal reforms; they do not address the fundamental problem in NATO's posture.

A shift from pro-nuclear Flexible Response to a non-nuclear posture of defensive deterrence would obviously have profound implications for all aspects of NATO. It is clear that allied governments and their military are not yet ready to opt for such a fundamental change; but it is not only outsiders (alternative-defence thinkers) in Britain, West Germany and elsewhere who have been giving attention to non-nuclear strategies. NATO insiders have also examined methods of improving conventional defence, though in their case against the background of the present pro-nuclear doctrine. This is in the NATO tradition of seeing conventional and nuclear forces as complementary.

The Western allies have always believed that conventional forces were necessary, but they have invariably been thought as contributing to a phase in a nuclear strategy rather than offering an alternative means of defence.[10] Under the 'Lisbon goals' of 1952, which looked towards the creation of 96 divisions, it was expected that the conventional phase would be prolonged. The Lisbon figure has never been approached, and since that time both the size of NATO's conventional forces, and the length of time they might fight have been reduced. As the 1950s progressed, NATO's conventional forces were merely seen as a 'tripwire' or a 'plateglass window', to signify that the enemy had advanced too far. During periods when NATO's conventional forces have been relatively stronger, their task has been to impose a 'pause', to give the enemy time to reflect upon the accident or miscalculation which had led him to advance; the conventional pause would give the enemy some time to retreat before the US drew the nuclear sword.

Only in Robert McNamara's conception of 'flexible response' in the early 1960s was the idea of fighting a fully conventional war in Europe seriously considered. But this idea was unpopular with the European governments of the time. It seemed to increase the chances of highly destructive wars in Europe; it was thought that it would weaken deterrence by limiting (geographically and in terms of destructive power) the horror of war; it was argued that it would 'decouple' Europe from the US nuclear guarantee; it was seen to require the provision of greater resources, both men and money, than the Europeans of the time were willing to offer; and it seemed to be playing to Soviet strengths in conventional military power. In McNamara's doctrine of 'flexible response' nuclear weapons would inevitably remain in the background, but he believed that the provisioning of large and effective conventional forces would increase the chances that a US president would be able to avoid the decision to escalate. In the time so bought, he hoped, the crisis-managers would have the opportunity to resolve the conflict.

McNamara's conception of 'flexible response' was not implemented. Instead, the allies merely purloined his title. 'Flexible Response' was formally adopted in 1967, but it was a long way from McNamara's original idea. In the adopted compromised version the conventional component was marginally improved, but NATO remained heavily committed to an early reliance on the large numbers of tactical nuclear weapons that had been piling up since the mid-1950s, and the strategic nuclear threat in the background. After 1967 there was a strong feeling within the alliance that things had improved, but what NATO had adopted was what some have felicitously called 'flexible escalation' rather than pure 'flexible response'. NATO was still not organised to fight a prolonged conventional war; it would have to escalate or risk defeat. As John Garnett put it: 'the flexibility implied by the phrase "flexible response" does not relate to the decision of whether or not to escalate, but only to the timing of the escalation. The relevant question of not *whether* to escalate, but *when* to escalate.'[11] In 1969 the British Defence Secretary, Denis

Healey, said that the pause between a Soviet attack and the need for escalation would be a matter of days not weeks. Nearly twenty years later, there is no confidence in a longer duration for the conventional pause. Senator Sam Nunn, an American friend of NATO, has likened the alliance's nuclear/conventional posture to a Marx Brothers sketch: confronted by a group of thugs one of the Brothers put a gun to his own head and said: 'You take one more step and I'll pull the trigger'.[12]

Since NATO remains committed to a pro-nuclear strategy, little can be expected from within the organisation by way of ideas about movement towards a basically non-nuclear strategy. Nevertheless, some attention has been given to the tactics and weaponry necessary to strengthen the alliance's conventional potential, and this is likely to increase as a result of the prominence which the INF agreement will give to the military balance at this level. Earlier impetus to such thinking was the call in September 1982 by General Bernard Rogers, the Supreme Allied Commander at the time, for a stronger conventional defence in order to reduce the alliance's reliance on nuclear weapons.[13] SACEUR's public disclosure that more attention was being given to such matters was an indication of the need felt by insiders to respond to the concerns being loudly expressed in the early 1980s in the streets and elsewhere by outsiders, especially the peace movement. It also reflected a growing concern within the organisation about its reliance on battlefield nuclear weapons, and the growing sense of uncertainty about nuclear strategy in general. Despite the concern of such as General Rogers, NATO's strategy remains heavily pro-nuclear. It need not, with a real political will to change it. Were that to occur, one wonders what NATO planners could devise if they were told that Western defence was to be non-nuclear at the end of five years. No doubt it would concentrate wonderfully the minds of tacticians, logisticians and armaments manufacturers.

For several years there has been a consensus within the defence community that weapon development has enhanced the prospects of defensive forces against those on the offence. A range of new weapons offer, among their features, real-time reconnaisance, computerised command and control systems and missiles with a high-kill probability. This means that tasks formerly performed by aircraft can be performed by missiles, and that tanks and other targets can be effectively destroyed by conventional weapons. Modern systems greatly augment the firepower available to defensive forces, and so assist in increasing the entry price of invasion. The new weapons are also relatively cheaper than the offensive systems which they are designed to counter, as will be discussed later. These trends are all the more significant given the technological and economic superiority of the NATO countries over the Warsaw Pact.

The main characteristic of the conventional battlefield in the years ahead will be the progressive vulnerability of the tanks and aircraft on which any massive offensive would rely.[14] Tactical aircraft will become more vulnerable against sophisticated air defences, and their costs will mean fewer such aircraft in national inventories. Meanwhile, developments in area weapons such as minelets could degrade the air threat by destroying the airfields on which they depend. In addition, such weapons can help to canalise the movement of tanks, and so enable the defence to bring indirect as well as direct fire to bear. Tanks will remain in the inventories of potential aggressors, but they have been losing some of their former advantages, and for the future various types of anti-tank weapons have far greater evolutionary potential than their targets. The scope for radically improving the speed, armour, or inconspicuousness of the tanks is limited. Furthermore, the extensive use of the latest anti-tank guided weapons and associated tactics, which improve the chances of infantry being able to fight tanks, has only seriously been underway in NATO since the late 1970s. The training, tactics, and technology of the defensive have much further to go.

Despite the problems facing aircraft and tanks, they will still be required for defensive forces. NATO should not require them for a deep-strike role. In addition to that role being provocative, the aircraft and tanks carrrying it out would be likely to suffer heavy losses. Interceptor aircraft, however, are essential for defensive purposes since without them the adversary would almost have a free ride. Similarly, some tanks are required for defensive purposes. Although they face increased threats, there are still some tasks for which they are specially suited. On the central front they remain necessary for counter-offensives on West German territory following any early successes by Warsaw Pact forces and the latter's adoption of a tactical defence posture.

In addition to the trends in technology, the defence also possesses several inherent strengths. On a chaotic future European battlefield the balance of advantage should favour the defender, since he will know where he is, he will be in a friendly country, and he will have the simpler task. The advantages accruing to the defence have been evident since the time of Napoleon, according to the doyen of British military thinking in the twentieth century, Basil H. Liddell Hart.[15] He argued that improvements in firepower, mobility and communications meant that progressively fewer men would be needed to hold a given piece of ground. Nevertheless, he insisted that aberrations were possible, as with the German breakthrough in 1940. The aggressor would succeed, he argued, if the defence was not properly manned, trained and equipped, and if the defensive forces were not organised around a suitable doctrine. This is an important warning to those who hope that conventional defence will be either a cheap or easy alternative.

There is some danger that improvements in NATO's convential posture will only stimulate a conventional arms race. This danger will be minimised if the changes can be seen to be non-provocative, if reassurance is given, and if arms control is seriously pursued. Arms restraint and confidence-building measures, possible by both unilateral and multilateral steps, are essential to prolonged security in Europe. Given Western suspicions of the size and offensive orientation of Soviet forces in Eastern Europe, Soviet concessions on conventional forces (and verification) would be a major breakthrough. Mr Gorbachev has made positive statements with respect to both conventional arms reduction and the reform of Warsaw Pact doctrine. It is up to the West to press him on this, by engaging in realistic talks, that is, negotiations which seek agreement on the basis of give-and-take, in contrast to monologues seeking to win propaganda points and justify the continuation of existing plans. If mutually satisfactory reductions can be achieved, the outcome will be a West with a greatly reduced sense of threat from the East. Success here would have a bigger impact on the general sense of security than even a deal on ICBMs. A 50 per cent cut in super power strategic systems would still leave enormous overkill and the framework of the balance of terror. On the other hand, mutual and balanced conventional force reductions, acceptably verified, could result in the erasure from the East–West agenda of aggression, military confrontation, intervention and war. When everybody's mind has caught up with this prospect, in terms of what to do next, the security landscape of Europe will have been revolutionised.

So far, the record of multilateral arms control negotiations has been decidedly poor, not least in the field of conventional forces in Europe. The Mutual and Balanced Force Reduction Talks, held in Vienna since 1973, have been impressive only by their immobilism. But there is now reason to believe that substantial progress will be possible in future, including, on the Soviet side, deep reductions that were not imaginable in the Brezhnev era. For their part the NATO allies will have a serious interest in exploring the Soviet Union's new flexibility, for financial reasons if nothing else. If the West does not act quickly, it may find that Mr Gorbachev will grab the initiative in the conventional arms reduction field, as he did on INF. There have been signs that he understands better than his right-wing opponents in the United States and Britain that arms control should be a fundamental aspect of defence policy in the modern world. This is something to which the present British government has only paid lip service. Arms control is an essential part of a sensible security policy because progress towards a legitimate international order requires mutual restraint and mutual confidence, and also a slower pace in weapon innovation. This is why a Comprehensive Test Ban Treaty (CTBT) is so important. It is probably the simplest and certainly one of the most far-reaching of steps now available in the field of multilateral arms restraint. It is also popular in the West, supported by the Soviet Union, and presents no serious problems in the matter of verification, since no militarily-significant violations are possible. Despite all this, the present British government has dragged its feet, following the Reagan administration, but as far as possible in its shadow. Britain's behaviour on the CTBT says much about the government's real as opposed to its rhetorical support for arms control. This is an area where Britain's interest in international security has been sacrificed to the etiquette of the special relationship and the pursuit of 'better' nuclear deterrents.

Clearly, in the light of 1987 election result, we cannot expect a British government to pursue the principle of non-provocative defence until the early 1990s at least. But this is not to say that particular elements in the idea are unacceptable. There is general agreement between the allies, for example, about improving the efficiency of NATO's conventional forces. Indeed, there has been considerable progress in this regard since the late 1970s. This has been a matter of money and equipment, but there has also been a willingness to consider operational reforms as a result of the criticisms which have been levelled against flexible response. No doubt Soviet defence planners have been more impressed by NATO's strengthening than have NATO doomsayers, who constantly exaggerate Warsaw Pact strengths while playing up NATO's vulnerabilities. In addition to what has already been achieved, a range of further proposals are on the agenda, which both insiders and outsiders agree would strengthen the conventional posture. The main ideas are: improving reinforcement procedures and troop deployment, increasing readiness, developing more standardisation and interoperability, more sheltering, better sustainability, and improved command and control arrangements. In some cases progress has already begun; further improvement awaits resources. But neither funds nor political backing will be substantially forthcoming while we continue to rely so heavily on nuclear weapons. The corollary of this is that as we improve the effectiveness of our conventional defence, and see that the balance is not as one-sided as the threat-inflaters have argued, it will be easier to reduce our dependence on nuclear weapons.

Achieving denuclearisation in NATO will be more difficult than agreeing on conventional reforms. Although the leaders of the super powers have both talked about the elimination of nuclear weapons – by means of defensive shields in the case of President Reagan, and disarmament in the case of General Secretary Gorbachev – few people believe that the complete elimination of nuclear weapons by the super powers will or can take place in the foreseeable future. One reason for this is that other countries have set their face against denuclearisation. The Conservative government's commitment to an 'independent deterrent' has been more than matched by its counterpart in Paris; and they, like NATO's present military and civilian representatives, can be expected to resist more denuclearisation than that achieved by the INF agreement.

NATO's pro-nuclear addiction has been evident in its opposition over the years to – among other things – an NFU agreement. Such a step would not involve getting rid of nuclear weapons but only seeks to minimise the risk of escalation from the conventional to the nuclear level in the event of war. There are considerable advantages to be gained from NATO agreeing to reciprocate the unilateral Soviet commitment to NFU. The chief benefit would be on NATO thinking: a NFU declaration would underline the important fact that while nuclear weapons can deter, they cannot sensibly be used for war-fighting. NFU would compel NATO tacticians to pay more attention to devising better non-nuclear options. Such a declaration would be a significant step in freeing the alliance from its pro-nuclear habits and an important gesture of reassurance to the Soviet Union. Given the new flexibilty in Soviet arms control policy under Gorbachev, it would be unwise to miss such an opportunity.

The idea that Mr Gorbachev is a man with whom the West can do business has been underlined by the INF agreement. This agreement also constitutes an explicit recognition of the uselessness of nuclear weapons once fighting begins and the previous exaggeration of arguments about the 'seamless web' of deterrence. But even many supporters of these weapons had been doubtful of their military value. They had justified them more on political grounds, to show that the United States remained 'coupled' to Western Europe and that NATO could push through a tough decision. These aims were achieved, though at some political cost. We will soon look back on the history of the INF issue as another expensive, acrimonious and unnecessary distraction in the story of NATO.

The INF agreement might be a first step towards denuclearisation since it promises to eliminate a category of nuclear weapons. Clearly it will prove difficult for NATO to take the next step and accept the elimination of the next category of nuclear weapons 'downwards' in terms of range, namely battlefield nuclear systems. For one thing, whereas the deployment of US ground-based missiles of intermediate range represented a historical aberration in NATO's strategy, the deployment of battlefield systems has been integral since the mid-1950s and has been intimately tied to the official belief in an overwhelming Warsaw Pact conventional superiority. Strong opposition can be expected to any radical denuclearisation at this level. It will therefore be necessary to move slowly towards the elimination of these weapons, whose numbers and location would make them very dangerous at the onset of any war in Europe. Since many are situated near the front line, the temptation to commanders will be to use them or risk losing them. Following an NFU declaration, and finding that the sky has not fallen down, the next logical step would be for allied governments to work for a mutual NATO/WTO withdrawal of battlefield nuclear weapons on the lines of the Nuclear Weapon Free Zone (NWFZ) on both sides of the Inner German Border (IGB) agreed between the West German SPD and the East German SED (and presumably endorsed by the Soviet Union) at the end of 1986. This agreement looked towards removing nuclear weapons from 150 km on either side of the IGB. Again, like an NFU declaration, such an agreement would both contribute to a better atmosphere in East–West relations, and force NATO planners to think more constructively in a non-nuclear direction. Opposition within NATO to denuclearisation is and will be considerable, as the super power INF agreement showed. The defeat of the SPD in West Germany in January 1987, and that of the Labour Party in Britain five months later did not help. But electoral fortunes can change, and more positive super power relations can help ensure this. If the momentum generated by the INF agreement can be maintained, succeeding steps should become easier, as people learn that the sky is not kept up by nuclear overkill. Changing people's minds is always a long haul, of course.

If the process of denuclearisation proceeds along the lines indicated – an INF withdrawal, a NFU commitment, and the pulling-back and eventual scrapping of battlefield nuclear weapons – NATO will gradually adjust its doctrine to what should already be an accepted reality of the age, namely that we cannot fight with weapons of mass destruction in the pursuit of civilised political goals. This, and the need to work towards the eradication of the use of any military force in East–West relations, is the reason why the alliance should move to a completely non-nuclear defence strategy. At present the NATO old guard, who think of its role in the Cold War rather than in the future, are so worried about showing any 'weakness' that they neglect the long-term thinking that has been more characteristic of the alternative defence community. Some of the ideas that have been put forward from within the latter have been very radical, such as non-violent civilian resistance. The optimum way ahead, however, is not the propounding of drastic moves that are unlikely to attract public support, but rather a gradual reshaping of what exists in the light of the principles of non-provocative defence.

The tactical and other details of a non-nuclear defence for NATO will have to be worked out in consultation with military planners over the 10–15 years envisaged as the time in which the political foundations of a legitimate international order can be put in place. Inevitably, the elaboration of this doctrine will be a dynamic problem, since the answers will alter alongside the changing character of the threat and the developing capabilities of weapons. However, for the foreseeable future the convergence of the desirable and the feasible in a non-nuclear NATO strategy would seem to lie in the adoption of a layered defence.[16] This, like several other schemes proposed in recent years, would consist of three zones stretching back from the IGB: a foward defence zone, a strategic defence zone, and a strategic rear zone.

(1) The Forward Defence Zone
The concept of forward defence has always been a problem for the alliance because of the interplay of military and political considerations.

For military reasons West Germany wants its defence to be as far forward as possible, so that as little fighting as necessary takes place on its territory. For political reasons, however, West Germans have traditionally wanted to minimise developments which appeared to create a sense of permanence about the IGB. But West Germany cannot have it both ways: it cannot have both a serious forward defence and at the same time be over-sensitive about the physical reality of the border. Since the latter clearly is a fact of life for the indefinite future, it would appear sensible to go along with the military implications of this.

It would obviously be desirable that as little fighting as possible takes place on West German territory. Consequently, forward defence should be taken seriously in any non-nuclear scheme. As much attrition of hostile forces as possible should take place close to the IGB. A formidable forward zone of about 60 km should achieve this.

The forward defence zone would be a showcase for the 'automated battlefield'.[17] It would be saturated with sensors, underground communications, positions for cover, numerous anti-tank obstacles, and 'landscaping' wherever possible to frustrate the offence. All this would be backed by the appropriate weaponry deployed in the hands of some combination of anti-armour infantry and 'militia-guerrilla' networks. The appropriate weaponry for the close-in battle has appeared in various NATO force-enhancement initiatives. Defence in this zone would be relatively static.

It is vital that NATO blunt the initial attack. In previous wars breakthroughs have been exploited by first echelon forces, not those following on. It is therefore more important to maximise the impenetrability of the foward defence zone rather than diverting resources to attacking follow-on forces. On the ground of military priority, let alone political non-provocation, forward defence should be given sustained attention. Much can be done to persuade a potential attacker that a quick victory is not possible. For symbolic reasons this forward zone should be manned by troops from all the major allies.

(2) The Strategic Defence Zone
In this zone, which would extend back to about 150 km from the IGB, NATO's mobile units would operate. They should be deployed in a more dispersed fashion than at present. Whereas the aim in the first zone was to provide a barrier, the aim in the second is to provide a dynamic defence to deal with any breakthroughs. Such a defence

requires tactical depth. Fortunately, many parts of the North German plain are well-suited to defensive operations, despite the general flatness of the terrain. There is a complex pattern of urban sprawl, agricultural land and settlements, uplands, forests, and bogs, all of which can be used to canalise and contain the movement of hostile forces.

In dealing with Warsaw Pact penetrations into this zone, NATO requires both light forces and heavy firepower, and infantry and armoured divisions. Main battle tanks are indispensible since they will be necessary for both strictly defensive purposes and also for local counter-attacks. Some parts of the zone, across likely axes of attack, should replicate the automated battlefield of the forward defence zone. Elsewhere, the best-possible use should be made of modern technology. Developments in real-time target acquisition, together with the evolution of terminally-guided smart (conventional) submunitions and mines should enable NATO forces to conduct effective short-range missile attacks on those Warsaw Pact forces that penetrate the first zone of defence.

(3) The Strategic Reserve Zone
In this zone reserve army and air units would be kept back, waiting for deployment. They would be sheltered from attack to the greatest extent affordable. This means not only physical sheltering but also dispersal, in order to make many low-value targets rather than relatively fewer high-value ones.

As in the strategic defence zone, one of the most difficult problems facing NATO is that of finding the right balance between dispersal for the sake of security, and concentration in order to defend. This is not just a battlefield problem; it also has important implications for crisis-stability. The more concentrated NATO forces are, the greater will be the Soviet temptation in a crisis to pre-empt, perhaps with nuclear weapons. This will especially be the case if NATO forces adopt conventional deep-strike strategies, as was recommended by the Report of the European Security Study (ESECS).[18] In a severe crisis, or at the outset of a conventional war, Soviet trigger fingers would be itchy. They might interpret various signals on NATO's part as preparation for a massive missile attack, and so get their blow in first. Alternatively, they might not believe that the missiles launched in a deep-strike attack against them were conventionally armed. Unwilling to wait to find out, they might then launch their own nuclear weapons first.

The aim of the layered defence outlined above is to convince Soviet defence planners and political leaders that a cheap and quick victory on their part would be impossible. In Soviet contingency planning, surprise must be an essential ingredient since nobody in the twentieth century would choose a long war. For this reason some Western analysts have assumed that if the Soviet Union was planning to attack, there would not be a full mobilisation of Warsaw Pact forces; the latter would be a month-long process and should be obvious to NATO intelligence. Instead Soviet planners would rely on combat-ready divisions already in place in Eastern Europe. Mobilisation might then begin under the guise of manoeuvres. However much or however little warning time NATO has, the history of war gives strong hints that the signs might be misread; or that it might prove difficult to generate the political will to act decisively; and there will always be the inhibiting thought that a hasty move on NATO's part might turn a false crisis into a real one. With these possibilities, there is much to be said for a NATO posture that is in-place and ready, and inherently non-provocative.

The recommended layered-defence posture for NATO starts from where we are and moves in a non-nuclear and non-provocative direction. It represents a mixture of realism and reform, and contains elements that are not out of line with the thinking of some forward-looking commanders.[19] Such a posture cannot accurately be described, as it is in Part II, as 'exceedingly weak as a deterrent', especially if US forces stay in Europe in substantial (if not present-day) numbers. Under the conditions projected above, Warsaw Pact forces would have to contemplate attacking massive NATO forces, comprising an array of the most sophisticated military equipment in the world; they would be fighting on hostile territory against a united group of nations determined to defend the independence of their lands. And for what objectives would the Soviet leaders undertake such an act of folly, especially in the light of their existing problems in holding on to Eastern Europe? The risks they would face in such an undertaking are enormous, both militarily and in the long term politically. What would be the response of the United States to such an attack, as its troops were being killed? What strains would such a war create in Eastern Europe, and what opportunities, with Soviet military strength greatly overstretched? Soviet leaders know that war can be the midwife of revolution.

The prospect of any quick conventional victory in Europe is decreasing, while long conventional wars between industrialised nations today can hardly be contemplated. A conventional war in Europe would fall short of the absolute nightmare of nuclear war, but it would be an unprecedented disaster. If this is recognised, as it appears increasingly to be, then robust conventional forces will be seen to constitute a credible deterrent. Defensive conventional deterrence has worked for forty years for Yugoslavia. After 1948, following its defection from the Soviet camp, Yugoslavia represented a highly provocative symbol of independence from Stalin's Soviet Union. Its policies threatened not only the integrity of the Soviet Union's postwar empire, but also its claim to unquestioned ideological authority in the socialist world. Not surprisingly, intense pressure was exerted by Moscow. Nevertheless, small and isolated Yugoslavia survived; the Soviet Union did not invade, or blackmail Tito into submission. In comparison with Yugoslavia, a non-nuclear Britain would be more powerful, more inaccessible, and less of a threat. NATO as a whole, of course, would be even more indigestible. Nor need Western Europe as a whole fear 'finlandisation'. Realistically speaking, Yugoslavia and Finland today represent the very worst outcomes for a non-nuclear Britain; but since Britain will remain part of a vital Western European grouping of nations, tied by interest and sentiment to the United States, there is every reason to suppose that it would do significantly better, both in terms of military security and political independence. Defensive deterrents can work (Yugoslavia), as can conventional defence (Afghanistan).

FROM AN ATLANTICIST TO A MORE EUROPEAN NATO

The preservation of NATO will require its members to work out a new relationship to that which was established under the pressures of the Cold War in the 1950s. Some change has already taken place, and more is inevitable as the alliance, one of the most successful in history, approaches its fortieth anniversary. The key to the future will be the relationship which evolves between the United States and Western Europe. Will the allies struggle to stay as much the same as possible, or will they move to a more mature relationship? Will new patterns emerge through discord or collaboration? However it comes, change is likely to be more in the air in NATO's future than any time hitherto.

Some supporters of a non-nuclear strategy for Britain entirely reject the North Atlantic alliance. In their opinion it merely perpetuates an international order which fosters arms competition, the maintenance of tension, the cultivation of suspicion, and the continuation (by legitimising the Soviet pressure in Eastern Europe) of the repression of nations and human rights in Eastern Europe in the name of 'stability'. Nevertheless, a significant proportion of non-nuclear supporters, including the Labour Party, do at least conditionally accept continued British membership of NATO, albeit as a disagreeable necessity.

While some of the criticisms of NATO contain some truth, they are not the whole story. There is also a positive side to membership. Furthermore, as the argument in Part I insists, realistic reformers have to begin from where they are, and for the foreseeable future Europe has no alternative but to live with the results of the Second World War and under the shadow of the super powers. Even were NATO to be disbanded overnight, and US forces pulled out, most if not all Soviet interests in controlling Eastern Europe would remain. Soviet military might would loom in the East, and a degree of tension and suspicion would continue between the two systems, and repression in Eastern Europe would not cease. Against this possibility, there is little virtue in Britain becoming isolationist and neutralist. Geography, history and interest give it a commitment to uphold the security of the liberal democratic states of Western Europe as a whole. The West will be stronger collectively than individually; as a major middle power Britain has a responsibility to help the security of smaller European states; a divided Western Europe would be more likely to defer to a militant Soviet Union than if the states of the region acted collectively; an integrated alliance offers the prospect of rationalising defence efforts; NATO gives West Germany a role and sets limits to its policies; NATO helps set a framework for the discussion of *détente*, arms control, and confidence- and security-building measures; for Britain it is prudent that forward defence lies as far east as possible; a coherent alliance helps to draw those sharp lines which are desirable for deterrent purposes; and NATO helps keep the United States in Europe, which lessens even further the small risks of a Soviet attack or nuclear blackmail. NATO should therefore be maintained, but reformed. Change is in any case bound to occur in the years ahead. The most sensitive issue will be that of the future of Western European–United States relations.

A US military commitment to Western Europe is important for the indefinite future. It is likely to remain a serious commitment, despite some scaremongering on both sides of the Atlantic. The United

States is tied to Western Europe by culture, history and interest. It is to the advantage of both pillars of the alliance that the tie continues, but it is also to their mutual advantage that the relationship evolves into a different pattern to that established in the years of postwar reconstruction and Cold War.

For the reasons just mentioned, it is desirable that Britain remain in NATO but tries to reform it, but the question quickly arises of whether a non-nuclear Britain could remain a member of an integrated nuclear alliance if it proved impossible to persuade the allies to begin to shift in a non-nuclear direction. This is a difficult problem, and one which has led to much discussion within the anti-nuclear movement. Should an ultimatum be given, with Britain threatening to leave if particular reforms are not started by a particular time? Or should Britain stay in, indefinitely, trying to bring about change? The best way to deal with this difficult issue at the moment – at least several years before it becomes a concrete issue – is to leave it alone, and not make a decision in principle. It is not good tactics for a member of a well-established alliance to begin a process of negotiation by issuing an ultimatum. The most sensible starting-point is to assume that the alliance will survive, that Britain will remain a member of it, and that changes can be brought about by consultation and compromise.

Alongside staying in the alliance and attempting to denuclearise its strategy, Britain should continue the process, begun in the mid-1980s, of trying to give more explicit recognition to the separate interests of the European and American partners. To propose some distancing of the partners should not be regarded as 'anti-American'. Indeed, what is being proposed is believed to be in the interests of the United States, and working with the United States must be an essential part of any policy aimed at achieving a legitimate international order. Being critical of aspects of the Reagan administration's approach to foreign affairs is not synonymous with being anti-American, though the administration consistently labels it as such. For Western Europeans the most important relationship is with the American people, not with particular administrations; and in this regard, whatever we think of whoever is in the White House, there is plenty of cause to project a great fund of goodwill across the Atlantic. American democracy, for all its faults, remains a free and creative force in a world sadly lacking in both. For these and other reasons, it should be no part of the prescriptions of alternative defence thinkers to declare moral neutrality in the East–West confrontation. Whether we like it or not (and the Gorbachev phenomenon is giving us more reasons to be positive), we have no alternative but to try to live with the Soviet Union. Making a reality of this means that we need to recognise that we (the Western nations) are also a part of the problem of international insecurity. The Soviet commitment to communism does not make it an omnipresent devil in international politics, any more than the Western commitment to democracy makes us always behave like angels.

It will not be easy to win over some Americans to the non-nuclear security arrangements envisaged in the first part of this book. But the task is not impossible, for there is evidence that popular American attitudes during the 1980s have been less anti-Soviet, less pro-nuclear, less interventionist, and more pro-NATO than those of the Reagan administration.[20] This might not mean much, given the rhetorical and other extremes of this administration, but it does suggest a more sophisticated American public on security matters than the one usually portrayed by Europeans. Alternative defence in Britain and Western Europe in general will not advance far if it does not strengthen its ties to liberal elements in the United States. There will be no significant progress towards a legitimate international order unless the most progressive American people are behind it.

In contemplating the future of British policy towards the United States it is time we recognised how much this relationship has changed over the years. Too many people in Britain still have an anachronistic image of the 'special relationship', fixed at the time of the common struggle in the war against Hitler and in the building of a secure democratic world during the Cold War. But the 'special relationship' is not what it was, though there is an understandable unwillingness on the part of British opinion to admit how much things have changed in the last quarter of a century.

In the early postwar years, the relationship could justifiably be called 'special'.[21] In the Second World War Britain had been the closest ally of the United States, and for part of the war bore the brunt of the fighting. It earned its place as one of the Big Three. Britain's elevated role continued after 1945, in part because it took on the role of the USA's most dependable ally and main forward base. It also developed nuclear weapons, as both a symbol of its elevated position and as a means of hiding the reality of its diminished economic and military power. Gradually, Britain's residual great-power status and aspirations disappeared in the years between the Suez Crisis of 1956 and the withdrawal of troops from East of

Suez in the second half of the 1960s. Meanwhile, the United States had begun to develop a series of other 'special' relationships, notably with West Germany, Japan, Israel, and Saudi Arabia. As a result, the 'special' quality of the Anglo-American relationship is now talked about much more in London than in Washington. In the 1980s the chemistry between Ronald Reagan and Margaret Thatcher helped to delay the evaporation of the remaining elements of the relationship.

Without doubt, both Britain and the United States still benefit from their close relationship; the cultural and historic ties remain strong. But traditional Atlanticists exaggerate what might be lost because they exaggerate the cosiness of what exists at present. Britain has actually less to lose from trying to change the terms of the relationship than its nostalgic supporters would allow. What Britain gains from the relationship is mostly in the area of defence and intelligence. What the United States gains are the military and intelligence advantages offered by 'Airstrip One' – a secure advanced base – and a loyal ally in international affairs. What Britain loses is a degree of independence and a continuing distraction from facing the fact that it is a regional European power. A degree of political deterrence is one of the prices Britain has to pay for US help in staying in the nuclear weapons business. To act more creatively on European, East–West, and Third World issues Britain has to free itself from this deference. In future, Britain should remain a good ally of the United States, but that should not be synonymous with being in all circumstances an uncritical one.

Without doubt, any attempt by a future British government to implement the policies advocated in this part of the book will create a crisis in Anglo-American relations. If handled carefully, it could be one that will move the special relationship to a new phase, rather than one that will end in recrimination. In facing this difficult period it is important to keep two points firmly in mind. First, it will be vital to stress that the proposed changes will be in the interests of the United States, as well as ourselves. It is not in the US interest to be over-committed or to become dragged into a nuclear war over Europe, for example. We can expect, in any case, that US policy in the years ahead will be undergoing a process of retrenchment in its commitments. Let us help them to do it, with support and consultation, rather than wait until it happens as a result of a unilateral US decision. Second, when it comes to the point of changing our nuclear posture, it will be helpful that the British government concerned attempts to consult with the White House quietly, with no playing to the gallery. Nobody except the Soviet Union would gain from any British government being tempted to engage in anti-Americanism, which in turn would only provoke US anti-Europeanism and unilateralism.

The Reagan administration has shown itself to be utterly unsympathetic to any prospect of British moves in a non-nuclear direction. Indeed, several of the administration's most prominent spokesmen lost no opportunity in 1986–87 to involve themselves in British affairs, and tell British voters on radio, on TV and in the press, of their preferences. We are so used to this that we let it pass. Even NATO's SACEUR took the platform. Were members of the British government (or armed forces) to have a similar high profile in condemning the policies of one of the political parties in the next US election, there would be a justifiable outcry in that country. But it is not only the Reagan administration that is unsympathetic. All the indicators suggest that even if a Democratic administration were to secure power in the 1988 US elections, the course of US–British relations would not be smooth for any British government which began to change some of the basic assumptions of Western defence. The reception given to Neil Kinnock's explanations of Labour's defence policy from senior Democrats at the end of 1986 was instructive in this regard.[22] Nevertheless, it is not inconceivable that a more responsive group could come to occupy the White House, especially if further progress occurs in super power *détente* and denuclearisation. The proposals being advanced in Part I would be acceptable to the liberal wing of the Democratic Party, for example.[23] Furthermore, it is one thing for the US or any other government to oppose a proposed change of policy by a foreign power; once that policy has been put in place, pragmatic adjustments will be made. We should not be deterred by fear of criticism. In the event much will depend upon how well a British government committed to a non-nuclear policy finesses the revised relationship. It will have to be done slowly and with as much consultation as possible. Throughout the process the British government will have to demonstrate to the United States and its other allies that it is serious about defence, by actions as well as words, that it is committed to NATO, that it is taking practical steps to prevent nuclear proliferation, and that it is attempting to bring about reforms in Western defence that will enhance European security and so reduce the risk of the United States being dragged into a nuclear war for the sake of its allies. It would also have to be explained that we cannot maintain existing conventional commitments because of financial constraints. Finally, we should try and educate sceptical Americans that what is being proposed is in the best interests of their country, as well as Britain and the other countries of Europe.

The issue of US troop withdrawals from Europe will be an early barometer of US feelings following the election of a British government committed to winding-down its nuclear defence policy. By the time of the next British election, of course, this issue might already be creating waves across the Atlantic. It will be diplomatic to help the United States to do what it will in any case do one day. With regard to nuclear disarmament there are two interesting dimensions to the troop withdrawal issue. First, there is the general argument heard in the United States that Western Europeans are not doing enough for their own defence; and second, there is the concern many Americans will feel about the prospect of having their troops in Europe operate, in the first instance, according to NFU and NWFZ agreements, and then in the longer term according to the principles of non-provocative defence. Together, the points are likely to encourage some withdrawals and discourage complete denuclearisation, at least in the near term.

The idea of a non-nuclear Britain has already provoked a counter-attack from US policy-making circles. As was mentioned above, the Labour Party's defence proposals were criticised through the autumn of 1986 and in the early part of 1987 by Reagan administration officials (notably Casper Weinberger and Richard Perle), the SACEUR General Bernard Rogers, and also senior Democrats. These critics asserted that a non-nuclear Britain would directly lead to a rundown of the US commitment to Europe and the breakup of NATO. This over-reaction had several motives. In part it was scaremongering, to undermine support for the Labour Party, and to get it to change its mind. But it also represented genuine worries on the part of the pro-nuclear establishment.

US political circles are reappraising, and in the years ahead will continue to reappraise, their country's relationship with Western Europe. There have been plenty of warning signs for the Europeans, both of an immediate and more distant kind. Of the latter, the most familiar trends have been the demographic and economic shifts within the United States to the south and west, and the relative decline of the influence of the European-orientated east coast establishment. This suggests, if it continues, that Europe will get less attention and sympathy from the United States in the decades ahead. Immediate warning signs of this have already been evident in various examples of US unilateralism in the 1980s, notably the lack of consultation over the Star Wars announcement in 1983 and the proposals discussed with the Soviet Union at the Reykjavik summit in 1986. Both these US commitments had enormous implications for NATO strategy, yet the allies were ignored. For their part, the Western Europeans have frequently been confused, as well as ignored, by the Reagan White House. It would be a mistake to assume that these problems are temporary, the product of a unique set of personalities and issues. They are a sign of our times.

US policy-makers have their own set of complaints against the Western Europeans, and in a period when they are confronted by a heavy burden of global responsibilities and economic worries. Tension is in the air. It is likely therefore that Washington will discuss the future of US–Western European relations not only in terms of interests furthered, but increasingly in terms of unfair burden-sharing, over-commitment, and weak allied support for US problems out of the NATO area. The trends in US–Western European relations point in the direction of stormy seas ahead. The shipwreck of the North Atlantic Alliance is not inevitable, but there can be no doubt that captain and crew are due for a severe shaking, and that some of its cargo of ideas will be lost overboard. Whatever Britain does or does not do in the nuclear field in the next ten years, we can expect a reappraisal of the US commitment to Western Europe and a run-down of its troops at present deployed there. Western Europe must accept that it will happen one day. It is almost inconceivable, for example, that one-third of a million US troops will be on the central front in fifty years' time, nearly a century after the ending of Hitler's war. The question is not whether a big pullout will take place, but how and when. Will it be in thirty years, twenty, ten – or even less?

When the time comes for the US withdrawal, the Washington administration of the day will use whatever excuse it finds most handy. It may use British moves towards nuclear disarmament, if there have been any: but that would be a convenient excuse, not the fundamental cause. Since a wind-down of the US troop commitment at some point in the decades ahead is inevitable, it is preferable that Western Europeans begin to face up to the prospect, welcome it rather than allow it to be a focus of disagreement, take compensating steps, and create an atmosphere in which the process of withdrawal is neither abrupt nor, in the medium-term future, total. Western Europeans will have more influence on the United States if they welcome and seek to help the United States to do what it will do anyway, than if they bicker, appear obstructionist and seem always to want something for nothing.

Recognising that US troop-withdrawals are inevitable in the foreseeable future, the preferred method and time-scale is for a step-by-step reduction to something like 100 000 over a period of 10–15 years. The end of the century is a suitably prominent target. These withdrawals should take place with mutual though not necessarily exactly-balanced Soviet withdrawals. If a stable international order could then consolidate over the following fifteen years, it becomes conceivable that by about 2010 both super powers could remove all their troops from Europe. The combination of non-provocative defence and a more sensible relationship with the Soviet Union might have created conditions in Eastern Europe such that Moscow felt confident enough to pull its own troops back within its borders.

While a significant number of US troops remain on the central front, the risk of a Soviet attack on Western Europe is virtually nil, particularly if NATO undertakes defensive reforms which will eliminate any Soviet hopes of a quick victory. With no US troops on the ground in Europe – but perhaps a residual air-and-sea commitment to NATO – the risks of a Soviet attack would increase somewhat in theory, since it might be calculated in Moscow that the costs of aggression might be less. But what would be the benefits of such an attack? Following a substantial US withdrawal, the Soviet Union would have much less incentive to strike westwards, since its own position in Eastern Europe would appear to be under decreasing challenge. It would be erroneous, in any case, to assume that Soviet policy-makers would welcome a complete US withdrawal. There are two powerful factors leading them to favour the opposite. First, the continuing US involvement in European security helps limit the threat (to the Soviet Union) of Germany going its own way, politically and militarily. And second, the presence of US troops in Western Europe help to legitimise the 'presence' of Soviet troops in the East.

In the short term any threat of a complete US troop-withdrawal as a result of Britain going non-nuclear should not be taken seriously. Some wind-down in the foreseeable future is inevitable, but the United States cannot again become isolationist in the historic sense of the word; it is too enmeshed in the international economic and political system. Real isolationism would represent a radical change in the self-image the United States has as a super power and the leader of the free world. It would also shatter the image of the United States held by third parties. Were the United States to scuttle or sulk into fortress America, then some countries in Europe and elsewhere might begin to look more towards the Soviet Union, especially if, under Gorbachev, revitalisation and democratisation in that country make real progress. A US withdrawal out of petulance would be contrary to US interests in Western Europe and further afield. No rational US leader would carry out such a move (though brandishing the threat of it might be thought useful for alliance discipline). Furthermore, there is evidence that the US public is more committed to Europe than are policy-makers in Washington; an opinion poll early in 1987 showed that 62 per cent of Americans wanted to maintain their present level of effort in NATO.[24] Despite the warning signs, therefore, interest and sentiment should tie the United States to Europe and only an ill-considered assessment of interests could completely break that tie. There is nothing sacred, however, about the level of the US commitment. On the contrary, a slow wind-down could have a healthy effect on European unity, Soviet feelings of insecurity, American attitudes to Europe, and the prospects for a stable peace in Europe.

Despite the propaganda which accompanies super power disarmament talks, complete nuclear renunciation is not a serious possibility in the next half-century – if then. The world will continue to have to live under the nuclear shadow. Whatever becomes of NATO, the United States will keep its own independent nuclear deterrent, to foreclose any temptation the Soviet Union might have of carrying out a direct nuclear attack against the American homeland. Although nuclear weapons will not be disinvented in the foreseeable future, the shadow they throw need not be as dark or as pervasive as it has become. Whereas they were once thought essential for European security, US nuclear weapons are now no longer necessary for that purpose. Initially, there is no doubt that most Americans will be worried by the idea that their forces in Western Europe will not have nuclear weapons *in situ*. But this idea should become more acceptable as it is made clear to them that nuclear systems are utterly irrational for battlefield purposes. That nuclear weapons are worse than useless for 'defence' was actually made evident by successive American decision-makers during the Cold War: whenever a crisis threatened to erupt into fighting, the White House looked to the country's conventional forces for flexibility. In deterrent terms, a little nuclear overkill goes a very long way, but in terms of practical military flexibility only too much conventional strength is really enough.

As will be seen in Chapter 5, it is in the interests of the United States as well as Western Europe that US troops stay committed, on the ground, in large numbers. As long as this is the case, any Soviet leader will understand that if Warsaw Pact forces move westwards, not only will thousands of US military personnel be killed, but also many of the women and children who live alongside them. No even half-sane Soviet leader could contemplate such a possibility. There are no gains in Western Europe that could justify the risk. Anyone with a knowledge of history understands that it is not necessary to obliterate New York City in order to provoke the United States into war. This has been clear since the sinking of the *Maine*.

Rather than the prospect of having their troops in Western Europe operate without nuclear weapons *in situ*, most Americans in the near term will be more agitated about the economic burden of defending Europe. When the burden-sharing issue arises the European allies must remind the United States that the imbalance is not as much as is widely imagined, that the Pentagon believes that savings from any substantial pull-out from Europe are not likely for almost a decade (unless the troops concerned are demobbed[25]) and that European security remains a vital American interest. Some Americans clearly exaggerate their contribution to NATO in comparison with that of their European allies. Sir Geoffrey Howe, the British Foreign Secretary, reminded US critics in 1984 that the European allies provided 90 per cent of the manpower deployed in Europe in peacetime, 95 per cent of the divisions, 85 per cent of the tanks, 95 per cent of the artillery, and 80 per cent of the combat aircraft.[26] And whereas the United States pays a higher proportion of its GDP on defence than its European allies, the latter (with the exception of Britain) bear the hidden social and other costs that are entailed in conscription. US complaints about the lack of European support for out-of-area problems are also sometimes exaggerated, in view of the limited interests and resources which the allies have in relation to some issues. Certainly there have been occasions when honest differences of opinion have been present about what should be done, but in others common action has been possible, as was shown by the dispatch of allied ships to the Gulf in the second half of 1987.

Although the Western Europeans have more of a case than many Americans would allow, the latter do have some cause for complaint and many Europeans underestimate the strength of US feelings on this issue and therefore of the need to be seen to be giving more support. Whether or not the US complaints are justified, they have to be addressed. As a result of the non-nuclear strategy being advocated in Part I, Britain could make a more effective contribution to allied defence than will be the case under the present government's policies, especially as the growing commitment to Trident bites into the potential effectiveness of our conventional forces. Britain's optimum contribution to European security lies in improving NATO's conventional posture rather than in piling up further nuclear overkill, and in championing arms restraint and reciprocal security rather than in perpetuating the over-militarised confrontation left over by the Cold War.

Britain should encourage the United States to remain committed to the defence of Western Europe, in its own interests as well as our own. In this respect, Britain should try to help trans-Atlantic relations on issues other than defence, since the problems that exist in US–Western European relations are by no means confined to the Soviet threat. Encouraging fellow Europeans to be more sympathetic over trade would be helpful, for example. As part of the effort to work towards a more mature trans-Atlantic relationship we should envisage the two-thirds cut in US troops discussed earlier. As a result of this process NATO would move substantially towards a conventional posture manned overwhelmingly by Europeans. A large US force – 100 000 men – would remain in Europe. The long-term role and size of this force would then depend upon the allies' confidence in the evolving prospects for European security.

The isolationism of the United States in the interwar period and the mega-commitment of the US governments to Europe during the Cold War were both aberrations in US–European relations. A more appropriate and mature long-term relationship will avoid both these extremes. A continued US military commitment but nuclear decoupling is the appropriate strategic character of such a relationship, and political equality. Those in the West whose minds are dominated by the fears and habits of the Cold War – marked by US dominance and Western European deference – find it difficult to contemplate change. They want everything to stay comfortably the same. This is not an option: NATO is facing a new sort of crisis. Political, economic, and military interactions between the United States and Western Europe have and will continue to change. Adjustments will be difficult, but even more threatening to NATO in the decades ahead will be the efforts of those allies who want everything to stay the same. It cannot. If NATO does not evolve in 10–15 years, it may be extinct in twenty.

For NATO to survive its present and future structural pressures, it is necessary that the United States and Western Europe (Canada always falls between the cracks in this argument) move to the more mature relationship pointed to above. The early postwar framework of US dominance and European deference is decreasingly acceptable to Europeans, and cannot remain as the basis of the relationship for the indefinite future. The trans-Atlantic partnership was difficult enough sometimes in the past, when the pressures were not so great: trying to stand still is now a recipe for a breakup. The partners are less clear about what they want. The Americans are never sure whether they prefer the Europeans to bear more of the budgetary burden in order to save dollars, or whether they want matters to continue as they are, because dependence helps maintain US primacy. The Europeans for their part do not know whether they most dislike a strong US leader, who is prone to act unilaterally, or a weak one, who ineffectively tries hard. In short, both partners create problems, whatever they do. We need a friendly but different relationship.

Ideally, the new trans-Atlantic relationship must be based on a more equal partnership. This involves problems for all, of course. It means that the Europeans must take more responsibility for their own defence and foreign policy, while the United States must accommodate to the change. Change can be painful. Even so, if those on all sides are clear about their objectives and are willing to make an equal partnership work, then the alliance ought to survive. Strong ties of interest and sentiment should see the allies through this difficult time. If the ties are not strong enough to see them through a period of sensible change, it is unlikely that they will prove strong enough to see them through an attempt in the decades ahead to preserve an anachronistic framework.

For the Europeans the main problem about the idea of a more equal partnership is that of generating the necessary political will and economic resources to sustain unity and independence. The reasons why these are desirable objectives have become apparent to a growing number of Europeans. We rely too much for our security on the United States. Washington lays down the agenda and makes the key decisions. We sometimes have different interests in and ideas about what is happening in the world outside Europe. We do not share America's characterisation of the Soviet threat. We are frequently not confident about the White House's ability to make the best decisions, and are confused by its behaviour. And we are concerned that the decision for nuclear war in Europe rests so much in Washington's hands. For one reason or another, therefore, Western Europeans have found it difficult to identify with important elements of US policy. Nevertheless, we have often gone along with that policy because of our perceived security dependence. Traditional

Atlanticists, for example, have been so preoccupied with the need to maximise coupling across the Atlantic that they have ignored the importance of decoupling the risks of a crisis on the central front from the global struggle against the Soviet Union waged by the Reagan administration. This struggle was wasteful of Western resources, potentially dangerous, distracting from the real issues of the day, and it has not been helpful to Third World development or world-order building – the most effective barriers to Soviet influence. A more independent Europe would feel freer to give its democratic partner the advice it needs on such questions, if not the advice it always wants.

Achieving a more independent European pillar in NATO will be a difficult and halting process. The aim should be to create a sufficient degree of coordination of policies among the major Western European governments that a distinct European voice can be heard and be effective; the result of this should be that the burdens of alliance and the privileges of policy-making can more equally be shared. An independent voice presupposes a willingness of the countries concerned to take more responsibility for their own defence. So far, the Western European allies have been reluctant to exert themselves to spend more on defence – as much as Britain for example – while Britain itself remains a major obstacle to progress as long as it is a nuclear dependant of the United States. As was mentioned earlier, the extent of the latter became more widely understood in October 1987 with the 'revelation' that Trident missiles were not actually being bought from the United States; instead, they were being leased from a common pool of missiles. Our vaunted 'independence' would therefore depend on the willingness of US governments to remain in the 'rent-a-rocket' business.

Even if the will for independence is generated, Western Europe lacks appropriate institutions for the development of defence and foreign policy coordination. These were never part of the remit of the EEC, the now-stodgy standard-bearer of European unity. Recent years have seen greater efforts on the part of the Community to coordinate common outlooks on foreign policy, and from time to time this has naturally had a security dimension. In the mid-1980s the recognition of the need for Europeans to articulate their common security interests more effectively led to a minor revival of the Western European Union. But while Europeans remain preoccupied with economic problems and continue to rely on the United States for defence, significant progress towards coordination might not be forthcoming until a major shock occurs. A US decision to withdraw some troops from Western Europe is the most easily-foreseeable event that will concentrate the minds of the European allies. Like a major earthquake in California, this shock has long been predicted, but unless things change, for the most part will be practically ignored until the tremors begin.

The United States will possibly find it as difficult to adjust to a more independent Europe as the Europeans will find it difficult to generate that unity. Although Americans have frequently in the past expressed support for the idea of an alliance of 'twin pillars', they will not find it comfortable having to deal with a group of countries that is less deferential on matters of European security, and much more critical of US policy elsewhere. Adjustment will be uncomfortable, but thoughtful Americans should appreciate the advantages of a more equal relationship. The United States faces a difficult period ahead, economically and otherwise, including the need to come to terms with a reduced standing in international affairs. The label 'super power' created and attached in the 1940s, needs redefining for the 1990s and beyond. Just like Britain, exactly a century earlier, the United States will have to come to terms with the reality that it no longer has the power to act independently across the globe, and that its influence in international politics henceforth will have to be exercised with and through regional partnerships.

The alliance will take a step towards becoming a more equal and healthy partnership when the United States begins to withdraw some troops and the Europeans begin to make some compensating efforts. At present the latter is less popular in Europe than is the former in the United States.[27] The one-third of a million US troops at present in Europe represent the most obvious sign of European dependence. The allies will not need to try to replace them all in the event of a reduction. The threat from the Warsaw Pact does not require it, as will be discussed in the next section. With only modest improvements on our part, a balance of conventional forces can be maintained sufficient to make us confident that no Soviet aggression is likely. Ideally, compensating efforts would involve Britain providing more troops for the central front, as a result of conscription, with the other allies increasing their spending on equipment to levels more in line with Britian's. Failing this ideal response, the allies could compensate for US troop-reductions by increasing the efficiency of defence spending, developing the quality of troops, adding to equipment-levels, and encouraging the rationalisation of defence industries. We are rich enough to do more, but so far we complacently will the ends but not the means.

A more distinctive and self-reliant Europe will not only improve self-respect, it will also secure the future of the alliance and trans-Atlantic relations. Such a change will be difficult, but there is no reason why significant strides should not be possible over a period of 10–15 years. In line with the argument in Part I it is to be hoped that the distinctive European voice that emerges is committed to the principles of non-provocative defence and building a more legitimate world order. In order that this be achieved, supporters of alternative defence in Britain must strengthen networks with those in Europe and the United States (and Eastern Europe and the Soviet Union) who share a similar vision.

It is therefore not a question of whether there will be a change in the Western alliance in the years ahead, but of the nature and speed of that change. In these circumstances a non-nuclear Britain must not be isolationist with respect to either Western Europe or the United States. Indeed the opposite should be the case. Unfortunately, the one party in Britain to have carried the non-nuclear banner periodically gives way to 'Little Englander' sentiments. Much would be lost if any future Labour government allowed itself to indulge in anti-American or anti-European behaviour. In the future history of Western European efforts to free the continent of the nuclear shadow, the British Labour Party, together with the SPD in West Germany, will play a pivotal part. Other socialist and liberal groupings in those countries and elsewhere will help. Final success will also have to include the support of liberals in the United States.

The vigorous defence-debating and fractured consensus seen in Britain in the early 1980s was also evident in West Germany and elsewhere. Defence today is not such an intense issue as it was then, but events can still revive anxieties about war, as happened in 1986 in the aftermath of the US raid on Libya and the disaster at Chernobyl. If US policy in the Gulf in 1988 or beyond results in some disaster, then Western European fears about US leadership will again become inflamed. For important sections of Western opinion, defence-related questions are no longer ignored; they are highly politicised issues.

There are powerful obstacles to both the Europeanising and the denuclearising of NATO, of course, and support is variable in different countries across Europe, but anti-nuclear forces are strong, and the British peace movement must build bridges towards them if

European security is to be reshaped. The crucial SPD is at present in some disarray, following its electoral defeat in January 1987. To date it has favoured withdrawal of cruise and Pershing II, supported NFU and NWFZ ideas, and includes members who are strong advocates of the principles of non-provocative defence. There are like-minded political groupings elsewhere. In the Low Countries and on the northern flank a range of anti-nuclear positions have been taken. Norway's stance against foreign bases and nuclear weapons has always been special within NATO. In Denmark there was strong opposition to the deployment of cruise and Pershing II in the early 1980s, with the Parliament voting down the government, while the right-of-centre government later announced that it was adopting a 'defensive defence' posture. The centre-right coalition in the Netherlands was badly split on cruise and Pershing II, as was evident in the delays about deployment; the issue was reopened in the light of the Reykjavik summit in November 1986. The Netherlands government also announced that it would scale down the nuclear tasks allocated to it by NATO. In Belgium the centre-coalition was also split over the INF deployment, while the socialist opposition was hostile. On the southern flanks of NATO there have been no significant anti-nuclear movements in Turkey, Portugal and Italy, but strong opposition to membership of the alliance has been shown in Spain and Greece. Standing outside the integrated military structure of the alliance since the mid-1960s has been France, where nuclear weapons and national *grandeur* are synonymous; more helpfully, France has always stood for the independence of European countries and *détente* with the Soviet Union. And finally, outside European NATO there is Canada, whose politics in the mid-1980s for once became interesting to the rest of the West. The Liberal opposition party, which is quite conservative in nature, has opposed the testing of cruise missiles over Canadian territory and has argued that their country be declared nuclear-free. A major surprise in 1987 was the gain in electoral ground by the NDP, whose platform promises to revolutionise the country's postwar security arrangements by withdrawing from NATO, pulling Canadian troops out of Europe, and requiring the removal of US military activities from Canada itself.

Support for the principle of non-provocative defence is alive in most countries of the Western alliance, but it has not reached a critical mass at the political level. The main task of those favouring alternative defence ideas is therefore to secure the election of parties committed to as many of its principles as possible – a more mature trans-Atlantic relationship, the rejection of strategies of retaliation in favour of those some Germans call 'structural non-aggression', *détente* with the Soviet Union, and a reformed military posture for NATO based on a combination of static and mobile forces, regulars and conscripts, simple landscaping and the latest technology. Non-provocative defence offers the only feasible escape from the nuclear shadow. A revised military and political posture on the part of NATO will alter the security environment in Europe, and establish the necessary if not sufficient foundations for a more stable peace.

THE MILITARY BALANCE

It takes two to make stable peace, of course, and whether a reformed NATO will bring it about will ultimately depend upon Soviet behaviour. Cautious optimism was expressed in Chapter 3 that the Soviet Union might embrace the idea of a legitimate international order; that is, without radically changing its domestic structure, it might accept certain restraints in its external behaviour. Nevertheless, many people in the West are sceptical about this prospect. They have an unshakeable 'enemy image' of the Soviet Union. This belief is fed in turn by a dogmatic belief in the existence of overwhelming Soviet military potential. It comes therefore as a surprise to many people to be told that the NATO countries outspend those of the Warsaw Pact on defence, have over 200 million more people, and generate a total GNP which is over twice the size. In addition, the military resources of the Soviet Union have to be stretched to counter the rising problems of China and Japan in the Far East.

Robert McNamara, the former US Secretary of Defense, has said that we have always exaggerated the Soviet military threat and that we are still doing it today.[28] This authoritative viewpoint has been endorsed in one way or another by many Soviet specialists and a growing number of military commentators. That said, we certainly have to pay attention to the Soviet Union in a military sense, for it has immense quantities of men and weapons, and it has us targeted: but the Cold War stereotype of a Soviet juggernaut threatening a puny NATO simply does not stand up to close examination. Western threat-inflation continues regardless, because of political inertia, bureaucratic in-fighting, budgetary politics, propaganda and the fact that the 'keepers of the threat', to use Michael MccGwire's phrase, happen to have been the conservative strategic fundamentalists who have dominated the US defence agenda since the mid-1970s. It goes without saying that Soviet threat-inflation of Western capabilities and intentions has been at least equally powerful.

Assessing the military balance is a complex and difficult business since it involves uncertain information and dynamic comparisons of doctrines and qualitative factors as well as numerical comparisons of troops and weapons. In one sense it is an impossible task, since the balance or imbalance can only be assessed in relation to one of an almost infinite number of specific scenarios. In these circumstances there is a temptation to simplify, and there can be no question that official Western spokesmen have often gone too far in this direction. Invariably we are given crude and static presentations of the balance of NATO/WTO forces, with no dynamic or qualitative indicators. Official presentations become no more than a simple numbers game. We should be very careful before taking at face value the British government's view, for example, that the Warsaw Pact has significant numerical advantages in all major aspects of conventional arms. Numbers do not necessarily add up to anything much. A comparison of the number of tanks possessed by each side is less relevant, for example, than a comparison of the number of tanks possessed by each *versus* the whole array of anti-tank weapons they might face.

A growing body of authoritative and sophisticated analyses have become available to the Western public which give a markedly different assessment of the military confrontation in Europe to that offered by official NATO sources.[29] Space does not allow full examination of their findings; but two broad themes emerge. First, the image of overwhelming Warsaw Pact strength does not stand up. In terms of many indicators – numbers, political reliability, training, military spending, readiness, 'tooth-to-tail' comparisons, quality of weaponry – NATO is shown to be in relatively good shape given the less extensive requirements of an alliance committed to a defensive posture. Both alliances have strengths and weaknesses in relation to their objectives. Second, when it comes to actual combat, the balance of forces suggests that the Soviet Union could not be confident about achieving a successful blitzkrieg. Surveillance probably rules out surprise and NATO conventional forces are better prepared to discharge their allocated defensive tasks than is generally thought. Overall, study after study in recent years has debunked the idea of overwhelming Warsaw Pact superiority. One of these studies, interestingly, has even questioned the validity of the familiar image of a massive Red Army in the late 1940s threatening an almost defenceless

Western Europe.[30] The legacy of this image, it is rightly argued, still shapes much of our official thinking.

There is good reason to believe that the Soviet Union does not possess, in the words of the old NATO refrain, 'too much military force than it needs for its own self-defence'. There is a rough parity overall, such that Soviet leaders are unlikely to conclude that victory is possible – even assuming that they have ambitions to match the risks involved. Once the more realistic appraisals of the military balance are accepted, we will cease to demand nuclear weapons to compensate for alleged conventional weaknesses; indeed we will then be able to go forward more comfortably with our alternative agenda.

AN ALTERNATIVE AGENDA

There is obviously much to be done, but defence policy is an area of public affairs where radical change is difficult. It is much easier to be conservative and confrontational (and to win points for 'hard-headed' thinking) than to work for international cooperation (and risk being thought a 'dreamer'); it is much easier to plan to survive tomorrow (by being 'realistic' within the narrow confines of conventional thinking) than to try to ensure that people a half-century from now will enjoy a passably civilised existence (by being a real realist). Supporters of alternative defence and supporters of pro-nuclear policy have different agendas and radically different time-scales.

Although everybody in the defence debate might agree on the aims identified earlier, namely a legitimate international order and stable peace, the thesis of Part I is that it is illogical to pursue these aims by present means. We need to change attitudes and policies, and denuclearisation must be at the cornerstone of that change. Nuclear weapons represent a bigger threat to civilised life in the countries of the northern hemisphere than do their political and other differences; the present number of nuclear weapons, together with the characterisitics and doctrines, constitute a major inhibition to progress towards a more stable East–West relationship. Nuclear weapons are a source as well as a symptom of mistrust. Today's levels of destructive power are irrationally disproportionate to the character of East–West political and other differences. The latter will not significantly ameliorate unless the level of mutual threat begins to move in a more rational direction.

Britain could play a major role in strengthening the prospects for long-term peace and security in Europe. In order to do this we have to show, in word and deed, the inter-relationship between security and denuclearisation. Before the 1987 general election, some of us thought about timetables for a programme of denuclearisation: what could or should a non-nuclear British government try to achieve in one parliament? As the tide of international events since the election has been running in favour of a would-be denuclearising government, the disappointment of the election result for the anti-nuclear cause is bound to be all the greater. The election put an end to any early hopes that Britain might contribute positively to the denuclearisation of European security; instead, the outlook for the next four or five years at least on East–West issues and arms control threatens to be a mixture of spoiling tactics and more-of-the-same.

Since we cannot expect to see a British government committed to denuclearisation until 1991–92 at the earliest, and perhaps not even then, there is little point now in trying to draw up timetables: who knows what the situation will be by then? The only certainty is that it will be different; it has been so much in flux recently, and plenty more change is promised. To take but one example: in the past Britain's attempt to maintain an independent nuclear deterrent was periodically outflanked by US and Soviet technological innovation. Who could ever have predicted that a British Prime Minister during the presidency of Ronald Reagan would start worrying that the future of our nuclear deterrent would be threatened by the prospect of super power nuclear disarmament?

Whether or not a Labour Party committed to non-nuclear defence wins power at the next now-distant general election, the nuclear issue will not go away. A mixture of international events and economic pressures will focus the public's attention on defence issues. But reformers must be patient. As argued earlier, it has taken NATO many years to evolve its particular pro-nuclear posture, and the East–West conflict even longer to reach its present levels of mistrust. Radical changes will not come quickly, and this is why Part I has adopted a 30-year perspective. But even to achieve results in this timescale, it is necessary to begin certain steps now. Without a sympathetic government we cannot take large ones, but that should not be allowed to induce apathy. We must not scorn small steps, for every small step should make the next one a little easier, as it becomes apparent that change is not leading to catastrophe but to a more stable security environment.

The agenda below does not attempt to be comprehensive; it

intends instead to establish some priorities for the next ten years, in order to establish the foundations for later progress. Those in Britain who support the various elements of alternative defence cannot act directly on some of the most important issues listed below; they must instead work as best they can to ensure that all the issues stay on the political agenda, that some adverse trends are reversed, that the level of the defence debate is raised, and that a critical mass of sympathetic opinion is built up, both at home and abroad. Those who are sympathetic to the aim of moving European security from an order based on the balance of terror to a stable peace based on political relationships might consider beginning with the following:

(1) Maintain nuclear arms control momentum. The progress of 1987 should not be squandered. The major priorities in this respect are:

- Encourage a START agreement (see below), press for a Comprehensive Test Ban Treaty, and strengthen the Non-Proliferation Treaty.
- Resist attempts to circumvent the INF Treaty via 'compensations', and to poison the atmosphere of relations by the early adoption of 'modernisation' plans.
- Prevent the weaponisation of space by insisting upon the narrow interpretation of the ABM Treaty.

(2) Reduce the threat represented by 'offensive' conventional forces in Europe. This is a critical area for progress because of its potential effect on mutual threat perception. The INF agreement has created a major precedent for intrusive arms control verification, and there is a strong expectation that the Soviet Union might come forward in 1988 with major conventional proposals. It is now two years since the Soviet Union first proposed new talks on conventional forces. These opportunities will not last if we do not respond positively, and explore what might be achieved. Consequently the NATO allies should:

- Clarify their own ideas so that they will be in a position to respond to new Soviet initiatives and test Gorbachev's words about reducing imbalances of forces.
- Identify the most threatening areas of Warsaw Pact capability, since the West needs reassuring as well as the Soviet Union, and this should be transmitted effectively to Moscow.
- Create machinery for NATO/WTO communication.
- Help create a more promising negotiating atmosphere by announcing a revision of NATO's deep-strike strategies.
- Be more active in discussions about CBMs.

(3) Deepen knowledge and widen horizons. These aims are desirable for all those campaigning and other groups who seek to give voice to alternative defence ideas. Although some of the obvious targets of protest have gone, there are always useful tasks for 'process-utopian' researchers and activists:

- Try to raise the level of interest, expertise and debate in Parliament by pointing to the importance and fabulous sums of money spent on defence. Press for less secrecy and more accountability on defence matters.
- Try to keep defence in the public eye and raise the level of debate by disseminating knowledge, critical arguments, and an awareness that feasible and desirable options are available.
- Counter threat-inflation by more accurate knowledge.
- Encourage friends, families and whoever is interested, to think of national decisions in terms of the problems of Europe (and the world) as a whole. Organisations should seek to develop contacts with Eastern Europe. Individuals should take the opportunity to visit it. Whenever possible personal diplomacy should be undertaken; what has been called 'détente from below' will have long-term benefits.
- Try to build a critical mass of support for alternative conceptions of security by strengthening ties with like-minded campaigning groups, research organisations and political parties in Britain, Western Europe, North America – and Eastern Europe.
- Conduct specific campaigns for morale purposes (in the event, for example, of a decision to deploy more F-111s to circumvent the INF agreement) but also broaden the perspective of protest to include issues that involve over-militarised ways of thinking (military intervention in Central America, for example).
- Try to broaden the party-political base which supports alternative defence by stressing that the national interest is being served. Ideas such as common security, denuclearisation, robust conventional defence and non-provocative strategies are too serious to be left to any single party.
- Support organisations committed to improving the level of education in this area of political life.

(4) Support initiatives creating non-provocative defence postures. It was shown in Chapter 1 that some attention is being given in the alliances to several ideas consonant with those of alternative defence thinking. Western governments should be encouraged to support

those developments which help create the foundations for a non-provocative posture:

- Support the denuclearisation of NATO in order to encourage members to think more about conventional strategy. Endorse proposals for a 'third zero' (the removal of battlefield nuclear weapons); press for a no-first-use declaration.
- Support the maintenance of conventional military strength since this is desirable in itself and a run-down will only help those who claim we 'need' better nuclear weapons to compensate for conventional weaknesses.
- Resist nuclear modernisation and compensations, and work to revise deep-strike strategies.
- Make clear to Soviet opinion-formers what we in the West regard as provocative in the WTO's posture, and that reassurance has to be a two-way activity.
- Support the idea of a nuclear-free zone on both sides of the IGB, and try to build support for zones in which 'offensive' forces will be removed or thinned out.
- Press the government to take decisions about procurement and tactics which strengthen non-provocative elements of NATO's posture.
- Keep the theory and advantages of non-provocative defence in the public eye.

(5) Freeze Trident. Trident will almost certainly be deployed to replace the Polaris system, now well into the last decade of its existence. The present government's commitment to Trident means that this system cannot have its former centrality in the activities of the anti-nuclear movement. But even now Trident is not entirely invulnerable: it faces threats both on cost grounds and from the developing prospects for super power nuclear 'deep-cuts'. Trident will remain a symbol of the basic issues involved, and in this regard should still be a target for criticism and counter-proposals:

- Trident's use as a means of circumventing the INF Treaty must be resisted.
- Pressure should be applied to secure a declaration from the government that it will deploy no more warheads on Trident than on Polaris (192). While the latter is significantly lower than Trident's capacity, to escalate Britain's nuclear destructive potential so massively at this time threatens to undermine at worst and complicate at best the super powers' difficult task of reducing

strategic weaponry. It is also illogical to increase Britain's 'deterrent' power so massively when the Soviet Union seems serious about a 50 per cent reduction of its own strategic forces and when the perception of the Soviet threat is in decline.

- Support should be built up behind the idea of putting Trident into the START negotiations. The government will refuse to consider this, but public pressure, together with possible pressure from the super powers, might make it easier for a later government to deal with Trident in this way.
- Alternative (conventional) uses for the various components of the Trident system should be proposed. This should do something to counter those who confuse the case for scrapping the system with the peripheral argument that enormous amounts of money have already been spent on it.
- Support a CTBT and START, as a way of putting pressure on Trident. At the same time expose those actions that seek to hinder these processes.
- Keep alive in the public mind the direct costs of Trident and its opportunity costs (for conventional forces, for example).
- Argue that Trident represents an absolute faith in nuclear deterrence that was never justified, is now outdated, and might become electorally unpopular. In short, work to delegitimise Trident in preparation for its eventual scrapping.

(6) Reduce dependence on the United States. While accepting and welcoming continued US interest in the security of Europe, the NATO allies should seek to develop a more mature post-Cold War relationship. Recognising that there are changing attitudes in the United States, and major budgetary problems, a reassessment (and diminution) of the level of US involvement in Western Europe is most likely. Britain should join with its allies to shape an evolving alliance:

- Reaffirm Britain's commitment to Western defence and friendship with the United States.
- Do not discourage some US troop withdrawals from Europe.
- Support the evolution of a more variegated NATO, whereby different states have different relationships towards NATO and within NATO. This already exists, and should be extended. For example, France's *de facto* involvement seems likely to increase while several countries on the southern flank may press for different basing arrangements for US forces. Against the background

of a more patchwork NATO, the idea should become more acceptable that a non-nuclear British government would renegotiate the deployment of nuclear systems on US bases in Britain.

- Encourage a more moderate and consistent US policy towards the Soviet Union.
- Strengthen the European pillar of NATO by encouraging defence cooperation in the non-nuclear field, but resist any tendencies both towards an anti-American Europe and a 'European bomb'.
- Rationalise burden-sharing within NATO, with a more equitable distribution of effort. By taking a bigger share of its own defence, European self-respect should be improved and less excuse given to the United States for criticism.
- Encourage the development of a more flexible NATO, allowing a redefining of relationships and membership requirements. A more flexible NATO will permit a more independent role for Britain.
- Strengthen the European commitment to nation-building and peaceful development in the Third World, by rebuilding international institutions, ameliorating North–South differences, discouraging military intervention, and seeking to reduce the super power confrontation.

(7) Plan for a non-nuclear government. If the Labour Party 'fudges' its position on nuclear issues somewhat, it may or may not rebound to its electoral advantage: but anti-nuclear sympathisers should not be aggrieved, since politics is the art of the possible and even if the party leadership moves somewhat to the right on defence, it is still likely to further denuclearisation and *détente* to a greater extent than the present government. Whatever route the party chooses, the following steps seem essential for its progress:

- The defence 'lessons' of 1987 must be pondered carefully, so that avoidable mistakes are not repeated.
- More expertise needs to be built up in Parliament to keep the government on its toes.
- Wherever possible, links should be built up with those in other parties, in order to help create the idea that anti-nuclear opinion is wider than one party.
- There should be less emphasis on unilateralism and more on nonnuclear defence, less focus on Britain and more on the international context, and less discussion about nuclear deterrence and more about common security.

- In its manifesto discussions, the Labour leadership should let it be known that it would be patient on nuclear issues. On Trident it should pledge to decommission the system as soon as was convenient in the circumstances of the day; this might involve delay if it would be helpful to put it 'on the table' in any talks that might be going on. If it were not thought helpful, and the chances are that it would merely complicate matters, we should reserve the sovereign right to act unilaterally on this matter. On other nuclear issues Britain should give time for consultation with allies, allowing them the opportunity to adjust to changing British realities. It would not be the aim to achieve every objective within the lifetime of a single parliament; scope should be given to explain the advantages of changes to sceptics at home and abroad. It could be announced to the US government, for example, that the status and use of US bases would be renegotiated over a set number of years (three to eight) depending on the circumstances.
- Supporters and members of the Labour Party should be encouraged to become expert in the theory and practice of alternative defence.
- The commitment to uphold the country's conventional forces should be fully advertised.
- Polaris, due to be withdrawn in 1994–97, is a problem that time will solve. Near the end of its existence, a non-nuclear government could give precise plans: when the boats will be recalled, the mechanisms for nuclear release deactivated, and the withdrawal of the systems from NATO completed. Dismantling could be organised under an international body, as part of the learning experience of living with denuclearisation.
- Holy Loch, likewise, should become less of an issue in the course of time because of the phasing-out of Poseidon by about 1990. It is possible if not probable that the Pentagon will press to keep the base for other nuclear purposes, such as supporting submarines armed with SLCMs. This should be resisted.

(8) Develop a 'philosophy of coexistence' with the Soviet Union. Mr Gorbachev, of course, has not changed the essential features of the Soviet Union that most worry Western opinion. While he has created opportunities for better East–West relations, the thesis of Part I does not rest on the continuation of his leadership; the policies proposed should be adopted even if a less flexible and less visionary leader were

to take his place. The policies proposed arise out of the needs of the situation; they are not dependent on personality. The Soviet Union (regardless of Gorbachev) is not the threat it was once thought to be. And to believe, as its Western critics do, that the Soviet Union cannot change (except perhaps for the worse) is implicit enemy-imaging of the worst kind. Our leaders for the most part transact policy on the basis of anachronistic ideas. They do not know what the Soviet Union is, or have a philosophy for dealing with it:

- We must calm the US temptation to engage in a global crusade against the Soviet Union, and help it to see the actual problems of the Third World; in so doing we will more effectively contribute to building a stable and just world order. As in East–West relations there is also a need in North–South and South–South relations to reduce the level of militarisation in foreign policy.
- We must reassure as well as deter the Soviet Union from attacking us, be ready to test Soviet proposals, and be in a position to present realistic initiatives to the Soviet Union designed to help them reassure us.
- Openness should be encouraged at all levels, from personal to high diplomacy, and from cultural contacts to military-to-military dialogue. We should stand in the forefront of those encouraging such developments, not in the background with the sceptics.
- In relations between the super powers we should promote conciliation and assist moves towards *détente*.
- We should build upon Marshal Shulman's invitation to develop a Western philosophy of coexistence with the Soviet Union.[31] With such a philosophy our actual policies will have a sense of direction and be consistent.

If the West does not define how we want our relationship to evolve in a realistic and long-term fashion, it is doubtful whether we will achieve it. Otherwise, our relations will blow hot or cold according to the vagaries of technological innovation and political and other developments. The combination of alternative defence proposals advocated in Part I offers both long-term objectives, rational strategies and an underlying philosophy. The prospects for a more stable peace rather than an order based on the infinite hope in the success of the nuclear balance of terror have never been better. Alternative defence will not only be sensible strategy, it may also be good party politics. When contemplating the international politics of the next half-century and beyond, we are unlikely to secure a legitimate international order as long as nuclear weapons retain their threatening centrality in East–West relations. There is therefore more to fear from more-of-the-same policies than from trying to strengthen the benevolent trends of a post-Cold War world. But many fear change more than they fear to stay the same. It is now necessary to address their worries.

Notes

1. Alternative Defence Commission, *Defence Without the Bomb* (London: Taylor & Francis, 1983), p. 9.
2. See, for example, Andreas von Bulow, 'Defensive Entanglement: An Alternative Strategy for NATO', pp. 112–51 in Andrew Pierre (ed.), *The Conventional Defense of Europe* (New York: Council on Foreign Relations, 1986).
3. Alternative Defence Commission, *The Politics of Alternative Defence. A Role for A Non-Nuclear Britain* (London: Paladin, 1987).
4. Frank Barnaby, *The Automated Battlefield* (London: Sidgwick and Jackson, 1986), pp. 154–62.
5. See, for example, Adam Roberts, *Nations in Arms* (London: Macmillan, 1986).
6. This argument is expanded in Ken Booth, 'Strategy and Conscription', pp. 154–90, in John Baylis (ed.), *Alternative Approaches to British Defence Policy* (London: Macmillan, 1983).
7. *The Economist*, 9 May 1987.
8. Scilla McLean, *Who Decides? Accountability and Nuclear Weapons Decision-Making in Britain* (Woodstock: Oxford Research Group, 1986).
9. Oxford Research Group, *Do It Yourself, Minister – Implementing a non-nuclear defence policy in a nuclear world* (Woodstock: Oxford Research Group, 1987).
10. See, for example, John Garnett, 'Limited "Conventional" War in the Nuclear Age', Chapter 5, in Michael Howard (ed.), *Restraints on War* (Oxford: Oxford University Press, 1979), and Kenneth Hunt, 'Alternative Conventional Force Postures', Chapter 8 in Kenneth Myers (ed.), *NATO: the next thirty years* (Boulder: Westview, 1980).
11. Garnett, 'Limited "Conventional" War', op. cit., p. 91.
12. Transcript, *Defending Europe* (London: Channel Four Inquiry, 28 September 1986), p. 5.
13. *Guardian*, 29 September 1982; *The Times*, 29 September 1982; *Time* 25 October 1982.
14. Barnaby, *The Automated Battlefield*, op.cit.; Kenneth Hunt, 'The Development of Concepts for Conventional Warfare in the 1970s and 1980s', Chapter 12 in Robert O'Neill and D.M. Horner (eds), *New Directions in Strategic Thinking* (London: Allen & Unwin, 1981).

15. B. H. Liddell Hart, 'The Ratio of Troops to Space', *RUSI Journal*, Vol. CV(618) May 1960, pp. 201–12.
16. The discussion below is based on a range of sources, notably: General Sir N. Bagnall, 'Concepts of Land/Air Operations in the Central Region: I', *RUSI Journal*, Vol. 129(3), September 1984, pp. 59–62; General Sir Hugh Beach, 'On Improving NATO Strategy', pp. 152–85 in A. Pierre, *The Conventional Defense of Europe* (New York: Council on Foreign Relations, 1986); Barnaby, *The Automated Battlefield*, F. Barnaby and E. Boeker, 'Defence Without Offence: Non-Nuclear Defence for Europe', *Peace Studies Papers*, No. 8 (University of Bradford: School of Peace Studies, 1982); von Bulow, 'Defensive Entanglement', op. cit.; General Leopold Chalupa, 'The Defence of Central Europe: Implications of Change', *RUSI Journal* Vol. 130(1), March 1985, pp. 13–17; Major T. Cross, 'Forward Defence – A Time for Change', *RUSI Journal* Vol. 130(2), June 1985, pp. 19–24; Report of the European Security Study (ESECS), *Strengthening Conventional Deterrence in Europe: Proposals for the 1980s* (New York: St Martin's, 1983) and *Strengthening Conventional Deterrence in Europe: A Program for the 1980s* (Boulder, Colorado: Westview 1985); W.W. Kaufmann, 'Non-Nuclear Deterrence', pp. 43–90 in J. D. Steinbrunner and L. V. Sigal, *Alliance Security and the No First Use Question* (Washington DC: Brookings Institution, 1983); W.P. Mako, *US Ground Forces and the Defence of Central Europe* (Washington DC: Brookings Institution, 1983); J.R.F. Tillson, 'The Forward Defense of Europe', *Military Review*, Vol. LXV(5), May 1981, pp. 66–76; Lutz Unterseher, 'Conventional Land Forces for Central Europe. A Military Threat Assessment', *Peace Research Report*, No. 15 (University of Bradford: School of Peace Studies, 1987); Union of Concerned Scientists, *No First Use: The Report of the Union of Concerned Scientists* (Cambridge, Mass.: UCS, 1983).
17. See Barnaby, *The Automated Battlefield*, op. cit.
18. ESECS, *Strengthening Conventional Deterrence*, op. cit.
19. Beach 'On Improving NATO Strategy' op. cit. pp. 176–9.
20. See below, pp. 179–80.
21. See John Baylis, *Anglo-American Defence Relations 1939–1984* (London: Macmillan, 1984, Second Edition).
22. *Observer* 23 November 1986.
23. As revealed, for example, in Sherle R. Schwenninger and Jerry W. Sanders, 'The Democrats And A New Grand Strategy', *World Policy Journal*, Vol. III(3), Summer 1986, pp. 369–418.
24. *The Economist*, 14 March 1987.
25. Ibid.
26. Sir Geoffrey Howe, 'The European Pillar', *Foreign Affairs* 63(2), Winter 1984–85, pp. 330–45.
27. *The Economist*, 26 September 1987.
28. See his comments in *The Listener*, 10 June 1982 and *Guardian*, 9 August 1982 and 29 September 1982.
29. See, *inter alia*, Carnegie Panel on US Security and the Future of Arms Control, *Challenges for US National Security: Assessing the Balance*

(New York: Carnegie Endowment for International Peace, 1981); Joshua M. Epstein, *Measuring Military Power: The Soviet Air Threat to Europe* (Princeton, N.J.: Princeton University Press, 1984); Matthew A. Evangelista, 'Stalin's Postwar Army Reappraised', *International Security*, Vol. 7(3), Winter 1982/83, pp. 110–38; F.O. Hampson, 'Groping for Technological Panaceas: The European Conventional Balance and Nuclear Stability', *International Security*, Vol. 8(3), Winter 1983/84, pp. 57–82; Kaufmann, 'Non-Nuclear Deterrence', op. cit.; Mako, *US Ground Forces*, op. cit.; J. Mersheimer, *Conventional Deterrence* (Ithaca: Cornell University Press, 1983); B.R. Posen, 'Measuring the European Conventional Balance: Coping with Complexity in Threat Assessment', *International Security*, Vol. 9(3), Winter 1984/85, pp. 47–88.
30. Evangelista, 'Stalin's Postwar Army Reappraised', op. cit.
31. Marshall D. Shulman, 'Towards a Western Philosophy of Coexistence', *Foreign Affairs*, October 1973.

5 Criticisms of a Non-Nuclear Defence Policy

The critics of a changed strategy, like the critics of Britain's established nuclear posture, package their anxieties in different ways. Some of the criticism of a non-nuclear strategy is emotional and ill-informed, and there has been scaremongering both about what is being proposed and what are likely to be the consequences. But the non-nuclear case has also come to be taken seriously. Both types of critical reaction are, in fact, an indication of this. The present chapter will discuss the most frequent criticisms which have been levelled against the denuclearisation of British defence policy.

WOULD IT BE HYPOCRITICAL FOR A NON-NUCLEAR BRITAIN TO REMAIN WITHIN NATO?

Bernard Williams, a moral philosopher sympathetic to the anti-nuclear cause, has argued that moral arguments are best kept out of the nuclear debate.[1] One sympathises with this, because moral values are personal and sensitive; nevertheless, the view of Anthony Kenny and others, that moral arguments cannot be excluded, is more persuasive.[2] To say this is not to condone moralising, that is, the self-righteous parading of one's own moral preferences. If we are to advance this debate we must all recognise that people can honestly come to different conclusions about moral questions in the complex world of international politics. In the end, the risks from moralising are likely to be less than the dangers that might arise from ignoring moral questions altogether.

It is incumbent upon a liberal democracy to agonise about the acceptability or otherwise of the goals of policy and about the means for achieving them. Indeed, these moral issues are objectively of more importance than defence economics, though we do not always appreciate it. The actual boundaries of our defence spending are established by what we *want* to afford as a community, not by what we can actually afford; and what we want to afford is affected by our sense of right and wrong, and what we believe should be defended and how. It is our sense of what is right and wrong that also gives us courage to face challenges, and to accept some risks rather than others. Ultimately strategy is a continuation of moral philosophy with an admixture of firepower.

The peace movement has been particularly sensitive to moral considerations. It has therefore been stung badly when it has been criticised itself on these grounds, such as the charge that it would be hypocritical for a non-nuclear Britain to 'hide under the umbrella' of somebody else's nuclear weapons. This familiar criticism has been taken rather more seriously than any charge of 'hypocrisy' should be in the power politics of a multinational system of states. International politics is not an arena for those who require that all actions be whiter than white. With this proviso in mind the following arguments suggest why it would be justifiable for a non-nuclear Britain to remain in an alliance which for some years to come, perhaps many years, will have a nuclear component.

(1) There is a role in alliances for nuclear pacifists
Civilised societies accept the right of individuals to be pacifists. While the latter sometimes attract hostile criticism, on the grounds that they are not good citizens, being 'free-riders' on the security provided by others, liberal societies recognise and accept that pacifists have a particular vision which we do not want to lose. By analogy, in a nuclear alliance, we should be willing to accept the idea of a 'nuclear pacifist' state. Furthermore, whether or not a non-nuclear Britain would remain in NATO is a matter of tactics as well as morality. It should be no part of a non-nuclear Britain's policy to keep its hands clean and be above the fray. In any case, a non-nuclear Britain, whether in or out of NATO, would continue to bear some of the risks of the nuclear age, while at the same time enjoying some of the cautioning effects of the balance of terror. The Chernobyl disaster in 1986 reminded us that in the nuclear age no land is an island.

Britain's aim should be to use what influence it has to move Europe in a less nuclear and more secure direction. Staying a member of NATO is a necessary part of this aim. A state cannot be criticised for being hypocritical if it tries to shift the alliance away from nuclear policies, if it does not profess standards contrary to its behaviour, or if it shows itself serious about its responsibilities towards to common defence in other ways. That is, a state cannot be criticised for hypocrisy if its words and actions are in accord, and if it seeks to change minds while not just sitting back and allowing others to bear all the burdens and take all the risks. The aim of a non-nuclear policy is not, as some critics glibly say, 'to try and ensure that more bombs drop on others', but rather to do whatever is in Britain's power to ensure that no nuclear bombs drop on anybody.

(2) There is no escape from the super power nuclear confrontation
At first sight, the morally consistent line for a non-nuclear Britain would seem to be a decision to pull out of NATO immediately, since not to do so would involve relying on others for the nuclear 'security' (and, it should be added, insecurity) one has given up oneself. But simple moral 'consistency' is invariably a hobgoblin in the fallen world of international politics. Nuclear weapons clearly do make governments act with more caution, and all European states, including neutral Sweden and Switzerland, receive some deterrent bonuses from the super power balance of terror. So, inevitably, would a non-nuclear Britain. The latter does not constitute 'hiding' under somebody else's nuclear 'umbrella', as it is sometimes put. In any case, 'umbrella' has always been a misleading analogy. It implies that something can offer protection when nuclear trouble rains from the skies. But as will be seen later, nuclear weapons can offer no defence in such circumstances. What we all live under in the northern hemisphere is the common cloud of an 'existential deterrent'.[3] No European state today has the option of completely escaping the shadows cast by that cloud, the threatening shadows as well as those that cool. Sweden and Switzerland are not berated for being hypocritical, because, like all European states since 1945, they have derived some benefit from the increased destructiveness of war – in the short run at least. Nor does anybody attack them for not taking up the nuclear option.

The moral course for Britain is to remain committed to the North Atlantic Treaty, as a nuclear pacifist, and attempt to change the policies of our allies. This point deals with those critics (see Part II) who argue that British denuclearisation is unlikely to have any significant effect on the Soviet Union. This is not the aim in the first instance. After denuclearising British defence policy the aim should be to persuade our allies to follow suit. It is only by reforming NATO in the direction of non-provocative defence that we can seriously hope to encourage Soviet approaches to security in Europe to accelerate further in a moderate direction. As it happens, the prospects for reciprocation look more hopeful from the Soviet Union of Mikhail Gorbachev than they do from the major NATO allies; but words still outnumber concrete results from Moscow, and it will be some time before we can know whether a more enlightened Soviet approach can outlast the personality of Gorbachev. The argument in favour of Britain giving a 'moral lead' is therefore of most relevance in relation to our allies, and simply opting out of Western defence is likely to minimise rather than increase Britain's influence in this respect. It is not hypocritical to pursue one's interests and beliefs in a rational and open manner.

(3) Morality is contextual
It is always easier for individuals to have absolutist principles than it is for governments operating in an international milieu without a universal morality. For governments moral principles and *raison d'état* knock sparks off each other, and the traditional moral guideline has been the idea of the 'lesser evil'.

In contemplating the lesser evil in any specific set of circumstances, the size, location, and power of the state concerned will be significant. What is acceptable or justifiable behaviour for a small country under the shadow of a hostile great power is different from what might be thought acceptable or justifiable behaviour for a great power. In international politics there is sometimes one set of principles for the weak and one for the strong. Thus it was justifiable for Denmark to surrender to Nazi Germany without fighting to the bitter end: this would not have been justifiable for the much more powerful Britain.

Since 1945 successive governments of the United States, the world's biggest power, have had little choice, realistically speaking, but to keep nuclear weapons as long as the Soviet Union and other states have possessed them, and more might. What else could they 'realistically' do? How could they renounce them? This is not to say that it is 'morally right' for the super powers to possess such weapons, and it is indeed their declared aim to eliminate them within a relatively short number of years. Despite the rhetoric of the leaders of the super powers, supporters of British nuclear disarmament must accept that the super power nuclear confrontation will shape the outlines of the international strategic landscape for many years to come. It is radically more difficult for the super powers to contemplate ridding themselves completely of nuclear weapons than it is even for Britain. Since nuclear weapons cannot be disinvented, or made 'impotent and obsolete' by any technological fix, it is presently inconceivable that the most powerful states will agree to destroy all their stocks. Opponents of nuclear weapons hope that changed political 'realities' in the years ahead, shaped by less provocative defence and foreign policies, will in time create an environment in which denuclearisation becomes an objective towards which all states will seriously work. The achievement of the legitimate international order envisaged in Chapter 3 is not synonymous with general nuclear disarmament. However, it is probably dependent on a situation in which super power nuclear stocks will be both relatively small and merely symbolic. They will be tokens of status rather than instruments of policy. Because we do not know how to get rid of the last few hundred nuclear weapons – were the super powers to shift to minimum deterrence – that is no reason for us to reject winding-down to those levels, and thereby emphasising the symbolic rather than strategic value of the weapons.

The fact that Britain's most powerful ally will continue to possess nuclear weapons should be the cause for neither moralising nor rejecting relations with the United States. Indeed, if a non-nuclear Britain retained an alliance relationship with the United States it might have a reassuring effect on the latter, and so discourage petulant behaviour. While accepting that we will have to live with a nuclear United States, Britain should not accept that the United States must have nuclear weapons in the numbers and with the characteristics and targeting strategies which they have today. Trends in recent years towards effective counterforce weaponry and a variety of war-fighting doctrines constitute a dangerous twist in the arms race, and should be reversed as soon as possible. As in other areas, the British government through the 1980s was unduly deferential to the priorities of the Reagan administration.

(4) What of the inconsistency and hypocrisy in the position of the critics?
In an international system where, as somebody once put it, nations have always acted like prostitutes or gangsters, depending on their power, we must all be careful before casting the first stone. Those defenders of present policy who argue that it is Britain's duty to share the nuclear burden with the United States, and that it would be hypocritical for a non-nuclear Britain to shelter under America's umbrella, do not always carry their vaunted love for consistency and burden-sharing into practice. If burden-sharing and moral consistency were such a priority, those critics should loudly denounce all our other NATO allies who fail to take a full share in nuclear deterrence; indeed, Britain should presumably help all our allies to acquire their own nuclear capabilities, in order to help share moral burdens more equitably and extend deterrence more credibly. That is the logic of the pro-nuclear case, but for some reason it is not argued.

In strategy, as in other areas of life, people should take care before casting the first stone. With this in mind, criticism of the anti-nuclear movement on the grounds of hypocrisy has not come well in the 1980s from the spokesmen of British and US governments which declare against non-proliferation, but which themselves proliferate and extol the advantages of nuclear weapons; which impose sanctions against some countries where martial law is declared, but not others; which condemn the human rights violations of selected governments, but not all; which denounce terrorism, but which allow their own agents to practise it; which denounce nuclear war as unthinkable yet practise nuclear strategies which have nuclear war-fighting as an integral element; and which berate terrorist states while selling them arms, and which hold themselves up as lawful while simultaneously breaking laws.

In the opinion of many anti-nuclear supporters, the very label 'multilateralist' has understandably become synonymous with hypocrisy. As a result of the arms-control and disarmament gamesmanship practised by successive governments, the label 'multilateralist' is widely seen as a cloak to cover the maintenance of status-quo thinking, and further escalation of nuclear arms competition. British governments have stressed the critical national importance of possessing an irreducible minimum deterrent, but at the same time they have occasionally offered the prospect at some time in the future of bargaining it away (presumably without expecting a zero–zero deal with the Soviet Union). The falsity of this position was exposed by Mrs Thatcher herself at the end of 1986, when she told Mr Gorbachev, in the wake of the apparent super power commitment to nuclear disarmament at Reykjavik, that Britain intended to stay in the nuclear business indefinitely. Typically, some pro-nuclear supporters argued that the deployment of Trident would give the British government more scope for arms control flexibility. Since the total number of deployable warheads in the Trident system would give Britain a capability for exceeding a 'minimum deterrent', this permits the possibility of future cuts. This sort of argument is yet another example of the conservative approach to arms control: the best way to reduce is to gather bargaining chips. In practice – with the exception of the INF agreement – it has never proved possible to get rid of the 'bargaining chips'.

There is undoubtedly a role for genuine multilateral approaches to arms control, whereby governments seek to work together to achieve more security at lower costs. Unfortunately, the 'multilateralism' we have seen in most of the postwar years has been either a cheat, domestic politics, pie-in-the-sky, gamesmanship, or merely cosmetic. The INF agreement, though welcome, is hardly an exception. It was first proposed by the Reagan administration with no expectation that the Soviet Union would respond positively. It was then a useful propaganda weapon during the 'new Cold War'. Agreement finally came as a result of a combination of circumstances – notably the arrival of Gorbachev and the political difficulties of President Reagan. The agreement came about despite the President, rather than because of him, and it remains to be seen whether it will merely rechannel the nuclear arms race. It is an achievement of the multilaterist approach, but hardly a triumph. The multilateralism of bargaining chips, negotiating from strength, and gamesmanship has not worked; it has produced no more security – and sometimes less – at higher costs. It is not one of the arguments of Part I to reject multilateralism out of hand, but rather to suggest how unilateral actions can promote genuine multilateral efforts.

WOULD THE RENUNCIATION OF NUCLEAR WEAPONS BY BRITAIN MAKE WAR MORE LIKELY?

Though agreement is difficult to achieve on moral questions, both supporters and critics of nuclear weapons agree on the paramount need of avoiding any kind of war in Europe. Much of the debate therefore revolves around the problem of risk-assessment, one of the many primitive areas in the theory and practice of statecraft.[4]

If Britain ceased to be a nuclear power, and successfully encouraged its allies to follow, supporters of the status quo argue that NATO would be shattered in the short term, while in the longer run the West would be opened up to nuclear blackmail. A power vacuum would be created which may well tempt Soviet strength. In short, the critics argue that the road to nuclear disarmament, though paved with good intentions, will lead to international instability and so, perhaps, to the abyss of war.

(1) The exaggerated fear of war

Pro-nuclear voices frighten public opinion and appeal to its deepest suspicions, by asserting that a non-nuclear posture on Britain's part will make nuclear war more conceivable. The public is naturally worried when official spokesmen use words like 'destabilise' and 'war'.

Exaggerated beliefs about the risk of war and about Soviet military adventurism are firmly established in Western official thinking and, as a result of repetition, in much of the public mind. It is well beyond the time that these exaggerated beliefs should be disregarded.

Changing attitudes on these matters will be difficult, however, since there are powerful factors at work in the opposite direction, including the vested interest of the defence establishment. But movement towards a more realistic assessment of the threat of war is occurring. Increasing numbers of open-minded people are coming to reject the notion that the Soviet leadership is simply waiting for a reduction in NATO's destructive power before striking westwards. The exaggerated fear of war from deliberate Soviet agression (*à la* Hitler) is the result of people's susceptibilities to weak arguments, a poor reading of history, an unwillingness to accept anything positive in international politics and the grip of four regressive mindsets. These points will be considered in turn.

Bernard Brodie, in the view of many the foremost American nuclear thinker, criticised those who started arguments in strategy with the phrase 'it is conceivable that'. He wrote that such phrases establish their own truth; the fact that somebody had conceived what follows is enough to establish it as 'conceivable'. But, he added, whether the argument that follows is worth a second thought is another matter entirely. Brodie criticised some of the exaggerations of the Soviet threat made by the Committee for the Present Danger in the 1970s in this way.[5] Although some of their arguments were scarcely worth a second thought, the members of the Committee came to have enormous political influence in the United States.

A similar riposte can be made to those who argue that it is 'conceivable' that the adoption of a non-nuclear policy by Britain will increase the probability of war in Europe. The idea is 'conceivable', but it is scarcely worth a second thought. Nevertheless, pro-nuclear supporters have effectively intruded the idea into the minds of the public at large. Experience is a better guide to the future than scaremongering. Let us not forget Stalin, with his taste for control and his crude view of power, and Khrushchev, with his ambitions and predisposition to take risks. Even these leaders over thirty years ago did not use the atomic monopoly they possessed to blackmail or attack Yugoslavia. Nor did they invade that country with their overwhelming conventional superiority after Tito had defected from the Soviet empire, and set up his regime as a challenge to Soviet authority in Eastern Europe and the communist world as a whole.

The breakaway of Yugolsavia represented a major threat to Soviet ideology and authority, yet both Stalin and Khrushchev refrained from using war to settle the issue. If that was the case with respect to Yugoslavia over thirty years ago, it is surely not conceivable in the very different world of today that the Soviet Russia of Mikhail Gorbachev would attempt to invade and occupy a non-nuclear but well-armed Western Europe. Conventional deterrence has 'worked' for Yugoslavia (present population approximately 23 million) for nearly forty years. It is not evident therefore why future Soviet leaders should think that the technologically more advanced NATO countries (population approximately 630 million, including the United States) is a more enticing target.

War (though not the threat of war for deterrent purposes) has virtually become obsolete as an instrument of politics in Europe. The exception to this is 'police action' within the 'socialist commonwealth', to enforce Soviet-defined orthodoxy in Eastern Europe. But even here, as several studies have made clear, force has increasingly become an action of the very last resort. This was confirmed by the Soviet restraint shown in the Polish crisis of 1980–81.

War as a reasonable instrument of politics between the industrialised powers is obsolete, though that does not mean it is impossible. It is obsolete as a reasonable instrument of policy, but the risk remains of the escalation of a crisis under the press of events, emotions and operational procedures. Nevertheless, the West's relationship with the Soviet Union has been dominated by the idea of a direct Soviet attack, the least likely scenario. The more likely scenario, that of a 'nuclear Sarajevo', cannot by its nature be 'deterred'. Unpredictable and unstable crises are outside the bounds of established deterence theory. These can only be avoided by reshaping political relationships and revising military postures in a non-provocative direction.

In Part II it is argued that the peace movement has been unduly alarmist about the prospects of war. This is true with some individuals. But by the same token, we should recognise the complacency of the defence community, and the way in which many nuclear deterrers have neglected the possible implications of the combination of acrimonious super power relations, nuclear war-fighting doctrines, offensive conventional strategies, counterforce weapons in extravagant profusion, and Star Wars. War remains functionally obsolete, but the prospect of the greatest powers of the day forgetting their Clausewitz and acting irrationally – something not unknown in international history – has been somewhat greater since the late 1970s than it was in the preceding twenty years.

Nobody can guarantee particular future outcomes, but for reasons advanced in the final chapter of Part I, there is reason to believe that a denuclearisation of Western strategy (of which Britain's nuclear renunciation would be an essential part) will be more conducive to a long-term and stable peace than the heavily pro-nuclear strategies and heavily militarised thinking of today. The incantation of nuclear deterrers, who say that any departure from what we have is likely to trigger off the catastrophe it was designed to prevent, has been described as a form of 'intellectual blackmail' by the Alternative Defence Commission; that is, it is an attempt to try to paralyse thinking about strategy outside the orthodox and official framework.[6] The blackmail has been resisted, and the outcome has been the proliferation in the 1980s of alternative defence thinking in Western Europe, the United States, and even Eastern Europe. Some of the schemes that have been devised promise to be both robust enough to maintain the irrationality of war – any war – between the major industrialised powers while at the same time contributing to the evolution of conditions that will place the prospects for European peace and security on a firmer political footing. The first step towards loosening the grip of the East–West insecurity trap involves more emphasis on mutual military reassurance and less on assertions of national strength.

Pro-nuclear strategists argue that it is conceivable that Britain's nuclear renunciation will lead to war. This argument is no more tenable than their belief that nuclear deterrence will continue to 'work' through all the forthcoming decades of technological change, international crises, and the growth and decline of states. No policy can be free of risks of nuclear war, or, it now seems, of its wintery possibilities, and that goes for non-participants in such a war as well as the belligerents. Indeed, in the light of the threats to the stability of nuclear deterrence arising from the shift to highly accurate weapons and the adoption of war-fighting doctrines, the Alternative Defence Commission justifiably argued that the burden of proof about risk-assessment ought to rest with those who seek forever to avoid war by means of the mutual threat of genocide.[7] What confidence can we have, through thick and thin, in good seasons and bad, that the balance of terror will always be attended by rationality and good luck? True security will only develop through changing political relationships.

(2) The grip of regressive mind-sets

The argument in Chapter 2 that the risks of super power war have grown somewhat in recent years needs to be understood in the context of a secular trend in European international politics against the institution of war. We must therefore be hopeful, as well as urgent, in our attempt to try to reverse the unhelpful policies and attitudes associated with the domination of the 'hawks' in Western affairs since the late 1970s.

The conclusion that the institution of war is declining in utility does not simply represent the dreams of the European peace movement. Here again it is useful to quote Bernard Brodie.[8]

> Nations that formerly thought it quite impossible to live together in a condition of expanding nuclear capabilities have now got considerably used to it.... We can predict over the longer term a much lesser inclination than in times past to take for granted the periodic recurrence of war.... We can predict also much greater earnestness about searching for alternatives to war ... that violence should continue indefinitely to take the specific institutional form known as war ... is now decidely questionable. This could be wishful thinking, but we are not obliged to deny important visible changes simply because they happen to be in a direction we like.

There are two reasons why more of us have not been willing to recognise this benign trend; one is long-term, the other relatively short-term.

The short-term reason for the tendency to worry about the risk of war in Europe was the occurrence of the 'second Cold War' in the first half of the 1980s. This unfortunate deterioration in super power relations, together with its associated arms competition, exacerbated and brought to the fore deep nationalistic mistrusts and old preconceptions about the 'game of nations'. This short-term problem has helped to feed a more profound reason why so many observers have not recognised Brodie's picture of the evolving character of international affairs. This is the fact that much of our thinking on these matters is in the grip of a set of backward-looking preconceptions about relations between states.

Four regressive mindsets sustain an over-conflictual image of the 'reality' of international politics.[9] The first is *ethnocentrism*. This distorting mechanism makes people unable to appreciate the fears of other nations, and the extent to which almost all nations see themselves as 'peaceful'. We see international politics too much as a struggle between Right and Wrong, and not enough as a tragedy or trap. Ethnocentrism magnifies international conflict. Second, *doctrinal realism* underestimates the multi-cultural context of international affairs, exaggerates the propensity for conflict, stresses the primacy of power, and generally forces relations between states into Hobbesian 'state of nature' images. Third, *ideological fundamentalism* propagates the most basic beliefs and doctrines in any society and so tends to heighten one's sense of 'friends' and 'enemies'. And finally, *strategic reductionism* tends to reduce all questions, including that of the likelihood of war, to a numbers game. Mechanistic thinking pushes out sophisticated analyses of international events.

When foreign and defence policies are in the grip of these mindsets we are in trouble. This has been the case since the late 1970s in the United States, and to some extent in Britain. The agenda for the defence debate has been set by strategic fundamentalists who have conceived the game of nations far too narrowly, and have advertised a Soviet readiness to attack westwards which has not been evident throughout the postwar period and is not evident today, except in self-defence.[10] Those who argue that the Soviet Union will attack wherever a point of weakness appears base their view on crude Cold-War sovietology, a reductionist view of international relations, and undiluted doctrinal realism. This viewpoint also makes the false assumption that a non-nuclear NATO would be weak.

Unquestioning support for the static ideology of nuclear deterrence frequently accompanies the mindsets just described. The prevalence of such outlooks has meant that constructive steps in East–West relations have been constantly undermined by the belief (based on fear rather than reason) that the risks of war will dramatically increase if there is any decrease in NATO's nuclear capability. Escaping from the grip of this approach is more difficult than simply changing weapons and strategy, for it requires people to change their minds and adjust their images about what constitutes 'reality' in international politics. The threat we face is not only made up of Soviet weapons: it is also in our heads.

The likely destructiveness of any war in Europe would be somewhat less if NATO began progressively to reduce its nuclear capability, and ultimately eliminated it altogether, leaving US strategic weapons only to deter direct attacks on its own homeland. Even after such radical denuclearisation the costs of any conventional war in Europe today would remain almost unthinkable. The Russians cannot but be aware of this. They know what happened to Leningrad and Berlin a half-century of conventional technology ago. And for what purpose might the Soviet Union attack? It is almost impossible to identify a realistic objective that would justify the risks of aggression under modern conditions. There is one, however. If the Soviet leadership at some time in the future came to believe that NATO was about to attack, then getting in the first blow themselves would be a likely response. The shift to a non-provocative posture on the part of NATO would eliminate this most likely (albeit remote) rational cause of another European war.

The way to avoid nuclear war is to avoid war, and this can be achieved by moving towards a posture of non-provocative defence allied to a policy of constructive engagement with the Soviet Union, including efforts to limit the occasions for dispute in the Third World. Change is underway in the Soviet Union and it should be encouraged by our efforts. A non-nuclear posture by Britain as a step in the reform of NATO would help this process. By showing that the arms race can be wound down, without disaster, Britain can help change perceptions about the meaning of security, the role of force, the likelihood of war, and the Soviet threat. If Britain can help to restructure images of the 'reality' of contemporary Europe, and so reduce the threat in our own heads, it will have gone some way towards reducing the physical threat we face. The way to reduce the risk of war in a post-Clausewitzian Europe is not by the confrontation and competitive arms-building of the first half of the 1980s but by adopting non-provocative military postures and political and economic measures aimed at permanent co-existence. Our policies must work back from the assumption that nuclear war must never be allowed to happen.

WOULD CONVENTIONAL DEFENCE BE MORE COSTLY?

No state should spend more on defence than is necessary to maintain national security in an effective manner. High defence budgets are not a virtue, though some sections of British and US opinion appear to regard conspicuous military spending as a symbol of manliness and status. Successive British governments since the war have sought to elevate the country's declining economic, political and military status by the symbolism of being a nuclear power. In hindsight it is not evident that this symbolism has done anything beneficial for the British people, economically, politically or militarily. What is evident is that Britain's standing in international affairs has steadily declined while our economy has not competed effectively with our main rivals. British policy-makers should by now have left behind all pretensions of having great-power military status. Nevertheless, over 40 years after the Second World War, our ability to develop as a vital and civilised medium power continues to be sacrificed: investment in education and science, the sponsoring of industrial training and development, the provision of better housing and social and health services, the commitment to overseas aid – these are some of the prices we have to pay for bearing NATO's heaviest defence burden after the United States.

It is desirable, whenever possible, to spend less on defence. In the short term though, a move by Britian to a conventional strategy might well cost more than is spent at present, and British spending is already high. In 1984 it was 5.5 per cent of Britain's GNP compared with 3.3 per cent for West Germany. Privately, our allies probably have an ambivalent feeling about such a disparity. On the one hand they are pleased that Britain is paying a disproportionate amount towards the costs of a the alliance, but on the other hand a reduction by Britain would help them justify a lowering of their own defence budgets.

In the event, a temporary increase in spending might be necessary for a non-nuclear Britain in order to terminate some of the obligations of the old system while establishing the foundations for the new; but it is hoped that additional costs could be avoided by improving efficiency, reducing wastage and by stretching out various programmes. There is plenty of scope for more efficiency in the field of research and development, for example, as was indicated in the 1987 white paper,[11] and there is always room to cut wastage. Without doubt, movement towards a non-nuclear policy would result in several confused and difficult years of adjustment for the armed forces, but the carry-on-sergeant alternative offered by present policy does not promise an easy time either; it offers only a steady and acrimonious cutback on resources as the nuclear component of our defence budget eats into the funds available for conventional forces. Although the non-nuclear alternative does not promise a dramatic or early reduction in our defence spending, we can look forward to reductions in the longer term as a result of the more relaxed international atmosphere it would help create. And if conscription were reintroduced we could undoubtedly expect to let our defence budgets fall to levels equivalent to those of our European allies. In the long term, therefore, a conventional defence strategy would not be more costly: in the long term it is the present combination of a pro-nuclear posture and a large and expensive all-volunteer force that is not affordable.

It is possible to identify two broad trends in defence economics. First, and most obvious, the cost of military equipment is continuing to rise. While general inflation has dropped, the inflation of major defence items remains between 6 and 10 per cent above it. As a result replacement costs have risen steeply. The Harrier cost four times its Hunter predecessor, and the Type-22 Frigate three times its Leander predecessor. Unless there is some radical deterioration in the international situation, military spending in Britain in the years ahead will be under great pressure. The steady rise in defence spending since the late 1970s – begun, incidentally, under a Labour government – has now levelled off; and because of inflation, level funding will mean less money for defence. For some time a major defence review has been forecast,[12] in which the government of the day will have to make a choice between the main roles now performed by British forces; alternatively, we will try to maintain all our main roles and the result will be underfunding all round, and a process of 'equal misery' for all the services. The latter is the guess of most observers. Meanwhile the nuclear deterrent force will be fully modernised. One widely-expected consequence of this is a significant reduction in the size of the Royal Navy's surface fleet, as was foreshadowed by the cuts recommended by Mr Nott in the year before the Falklands War. It is also possible that there could be an erosion of the British contribution to the central front. The latter in particular could have a significant effect on Britain's standing and bargaining power within the alliance.

Second, there is widespread recognition that technological advances are making defensive forces more cost-effective. Massively expensive weapons systems such as tanks, fighters and surface warships can now be disabled or destroyed by relatively cheap missiles. The cost of a main battle-tank may be in the region of $3 000 000; a sophisticated anti-tank guided missile may cost $30 000. Even if ten such missiles were to be procured for each potential target, the cost is still only a fraction of that faced by the offensive forces. In future, therefore, it promises to be cheaper as well as less risky to plan for defensive rather than offensive operations.

Under present policies one cost of nuclear modernisation is the further squeezing of our conventional forces, where problems are already evident. In May 1987 *The Economist* reported that the British army was the worst-equipped of the main armies of Europe, with some equipment in short supply and some obsolescent.[13] This was the case, it must be noted, before the financial commitment to Trident fully bites, and at the end of nearly a decade of increased spending. The future prospects for our conventional forces are bleak indeed.

Despite the pressures on defence spending, it ought to be possible to generate the wherewithal for improvements in our conventional forces: for who is not in favour of them, to raise the nuclear threshold? Improvements should be politically possible, since, as Michael Clarke has rightly argued, money has been found for strategic forces when it has been thought necessary.[14] This strengthening of conventional forces will be cheaper if the effort is concentrated on more obviously defensive systems. The weapons required for the deep-strike missions associated with FOFA and Air Land Battle will be more complex, will have to be numerous, and may not work. Concentrating upon robust defensive systems is both more sensible and more affordable. It is unlikely that the political will and public support for improving our conventional forces can be generated as long as we remain addicted to nuclear weapons and the belief that they effectively make conventional forces irrelevant.

The British government's decision to deploy the Trident system has attracted much criticism. Its price is extremely high (£9 265 000 000 at 1986–87 prices) but its level of public support is low. The opportunity costs of this system are significant. It has been estimated, for example, that if the pound were to fall 20 cents then the cost of the programme would increase by six-to-seven million pounds, the approximate cost of six new Type-2400 hunter-killer submarines, or the Boeing AWACS system.[15] While it is true that less and less can be saved from Trident as time and development goes on, this is not a sound argument for retaining the system if it is not believed to contribute to British security. If it were cancelled soon, then the savings could help pay for some of the improvements in conventional forces which the defence establishment thinks so critical. These include not only major items but also more mundane things such as increasing stocks or modernising APCs (Armoured Personnel Carriers). Cancelling Trident will not make a radical difference to our conventional strength, but it will help, and that is crucial in a period of level funding. The government defends Trident partly on the grounds of its cheapness – in terms of overall defence budget – but this obscures the important point that the majority of the expenditure will occur during the next half-decade, when pressures on defence spending will be much greater than in recent years, and that Trident will account for a considerable proportion – probably well over 10 per cent – of the equipment budget.[16] Since the equipment budget may have shrivelled, it could then be eating 20 per cent of it. In addition, Polaris will still be operating during these years, so its maintenance and running costs need to be added on. Even semi-independent deterrents do not come cheaply. Here as in other areas, the non-nuclear critics are showing the government that in the present economic climate radical choices have to be made.

As a result of the general election of 1987 we have to face the fact that the development and deployment of Trident will continue. Despite the occasional rumbles of some Tory discontent at the costs of the system, Mrs Thatcher is clearly wedded to this post-Polaris symbol of British power. As a result, Trident will be in place, perhaps well in place, before any party committed to a non-nuclear strategy could hope to be in Downing Street. At that point the cancellation of Trident will have to be justified largely on principle rather than on cost grounds: it ties us into a dangerous and immoral nuclear strategy; it will complicate super power arms control prospects; it threatens to make Britain subservient to the United States for several more decades (more so than with Polaris); and it is too large and sophisticated for Britain's needs, even granting the need for a nuclear strategy. In short, we should not throw good money after bad. Even the running costs of Trident will help contribute somewhat to an alternative defence strategy that in all ways is a more appropriate posture for Britain.

It is not only modern military equipment that is expensive; manpower is also a major burden. As was discussed earlier, conscription is one way of dealing with this problem. It offers many advantages. Countries with conscription, and similar or smaller populations, can put many more men in the field than Britain, and still spend a smaller proportion of their GNP on defence. British defence spending is trapped in a costly commitment to nuclear weapons, an attempt to remain in the front rank of producers of military technology, and the maintenance of a very expensive volunteer armed force (involving heavy attendant costs such as pensions and the support of dependants in West Germany). While conscription would be a logical step for a non-nuclear Britain, no political party is likely in the foreseeable future to include it on its election platform. Indeed, the possibility of the reintroduction of conscription as part of a non-nuclear strategy is sometimes raised by pro-nuclear opponents as a scare-tactic. In reality, the unpopularity of conscription is probably exaggerated. There are sections of public opinion who would strongly welcome such a move, and believe that the national benefits would be wider than simply in the defence field. Whatever the present state of public opinion on the subject, and the lack of party support, conscription is an option which will have to be looked at seriously in the next decade, as pressure grows on defence spending and as demographic trends continue to reduce the pool from which Western armed services can be filled.

Unless there are changes in Britain's economic prospects in the years ahead – and it is difficult to be optimistic with the end of North Sea oil in sight – defence policy will evermore increasingly become the creature of budgetary considerations. Since the late 1970s oil revenues have enabled the government of Margaret Thatcher to run down industry without the nation as a whole – the unemployed being the major exception – really feeling it. The pinch is yet to come for everyone else. When this occurs, the quickly-rising defence costs mean that the British economy will not be able to keep pace. This means we are on what the military establishment has called 'the road to absurdity', namely a situation in which we will have the wherewithal to procure only one hi-tech tank, fighter and warship; plus Trident, presumably, unless we change course. Against the background of these trends it is clear that economic factors will force radical changes in the years ahead. It is surely sensible now to expand the process of arms restraint. The Soviet Union seems ready. It would also be better to start the reform of our own defence efforts at once, and give some hope of sensible planning, rather than have change rapidly forced on us at some (inevitably inconvenient) point by economic necessity. If we were to review our course, and follow the non-nuclear programme suggested in Part I, we would not only be on the road to more security, we would also be on the road to spending less of our national wealth on military power.

WOULD BRITISH NUCLEAR DISARMAMENT WEAKEN IF NOT SHATTER NATO?

A central element in the criticism that a British decision to move to conventional defence would make war more likely is the argument that such a step would lead to the collapse of NATO, and thus the end of the stability which has characterised Europe since the late 1940s. At the outset this argument must be set alongside the possibility that even under present conditions NATO's demise might be a breakdown waiting to happen. NATO could become overstrained by the tension between a unilaterist United States and Europeans who are perceived there as assertive but unwilling to bear their full share of the allied defence burden. Many futures are conceivable, including the possibility that neither of the extreme outcomes just described will occur; this is because the interests which bind the allies together are strong enough to keep them together through all the ups and downs of the years ahead.

Without doubt, British nuclear disarmament would create tension within the alliance. A poll of allied governments at present would indicate disapproval of such a step (though a poll of Western European public opinion would show a mixed picture of support and disfavour). The attitudes of these governments might well have little to do with the nuclear issue as such: their opposition might have more to do with a suspicion that British nuclear disarmament represented the start of a slide out of its alliance commitments. To meet this fear, the Labour Party in 1986–87 stressed that a shift to a non-nuclear strategy would not mean the abandonment of Britain's NATO responsibilities; on the contrary, it argued that it offered the only way of maintaining the most important of them, namely a robust conventional contribution.

There would be allied disapproval of British nuclear disarmament, but in time the governments concerned would adjust to the new reality. The eventual outcome would very much depend upon when the change took place, who was in power at home and abroad, and the state of inter-allied relations at the time. Some British cabinets would be much better than others at seeing such a change through – their words would be more credible and tactful – and some allied governments would be more responsive than others. The coming to power of a critical mass of anti-nuclear governments would obviously change the picture considerably. The conjunction of a Labour government in Britain committed to denuclearisation and an SPD government in West Germany could be of decisive importance; and for that reason it is crucial for anti-nuclear opinion in Britain to develop the closest possible links with similar groups in West Germany. Furthermore, supporters of a nuclear freeze in the United States would be more sympathetic to British denuclearisation than the Reagan White House, whose recipe for the future has been to look backwards, and whose theory of security has equated stability with the crude accumulation of strength. The allied reaction to a non-nuclear Britain would be a problem, but its outcome is not a foregone conclusion.

Serious difficulties are likely to arise between future US administrations and any British government committed to a non-nuclear strategy. This was evident in the campaign conducted by Secretary of Defense Weinberger and other Reagan administration figures against the Labour Party's defence ideas in the autumn of 1986. Opposition, though perhaps not so strong, is always likely, but to suggest that the United States would suddenly 'pull out' of Western Europe and withdraw into 'Fortress America' as a result of a change in British strategy, is to imply that the United States is involved in Western European security solely out of sentiment. This is far from the truth. However disappointed any future US administration might be in a Britain committed to nuclear disarmament, the overriding consideration in White House thinking will be that Western Europe is a vital US political, economic, and military interest, as was argued in the last chapter. A United States that would contemplate allowing Western Europe to fall under any significant degree of Soviet control would be a United States with no pretension to play a leading role in world affairs. Although a reduction of the US commitment is conceivable, and indeed desirable, in a world as interdependent as today's, the notion of Fortress America is a contradiction in terms.

Although the Labour Party delivered President Reagan a decisive message about its non-nuclear thinking as early as 1984, the administration apparently did not become excited about the prospect until 1986, when it seemed possible that Labour might win power within the life of the second Reagan administration. Until then US officials had been wrestling with too many urgent preoccupations of their own to worry whether a future Labour government would carry out its election promises (threats?) to the letter. As opinion polls in Britain made it easier in 1986 to imagine the possibility of a Labour election victory, the administration's growing concern was evident in the heavy-handed criticisms by Caspar Weinberger and Richard Perle at the time of the Labour Party Conference in Blackpool in September. With some justification these US officials were in turn criticised for interfering in British domestic politics. The attacks abated. In part this was because American administrations have heard unilaterist noises from Labour when in opposition before, and the Reagan White House probably hoped that even were Labour to be elected, the new government would shelve or fudge its pre-election defence policies; it would 'come to its senses' – as the administration saw it – under the pressure of responsibility, including pressure from its allies. Such an outcome would avoid the need for more active US intervention in the matter. In the course of the winter of 1986–87 the administration became progressively less worried as Labour's standing in the public opinion polls declined. During the election campaign in June President Reagan made clear his strong preference for another Thatcher government, but with a Conservative victory looking most likely, his advisers probably warned him that non-involvement would be the most effective as well as the proper course of action for a President whose own reputation was in sharp decline.

With Mrs Thatcher's victory in June 1987, the White House could stop worrying for the time being about an ex-nuclear Britain, a prospect against which some contingency planning had presumably taken place in Washington. The possible outcome of such planning had for some time stimulated fears among anti-nuclear supporters in Britain that an unsympathetic US administration would exert strong pressure on any British government announcing its intention to renounce nuclear weapons and renegotiate US base rights. A warning to this effect had already been given by the US reaction – it is impossible not to think of it as an over-reaction – following the decision of the New Zealand Labour government of David Lange in 1984 that no nuclear-powered or nuclear-armed vessels or aircraft would be permitted in New Zealand waters or air space. The Reagan administration tried to teach New Zealand a lesson, and also show other allies what might happen if they behaved too independently on nuclear matters. Military and intelligence links were cut with New Zealand and, with Australia in support, the United States suspended New Zealand from the ANZUS Treaty. Mrs Thatcher's government joined in the criticism of New Zealand's independent policy and suspended visits by RN warships. Despite, or because of all this, the Lange government was comfortably re-elected in 1987, and in the election campaign even the opposition had altered its stance on nuclear issues in order to appeal to the voters. While an anti-nuclear Britain could also expect a difficult time from its allies, it might not receive the same treatment as New Zealand. Britain is, at the same time, both more powerful and important in a military sense than New Zealand, while the maintenance of NATO is of greater significance for the United States than ANZUS.

What, then, could a hostile US administration do against a British government committed to denuclearisation? For the 1987 general election the Oxford Research Group produced an interesting discussion of the issue, and presented it in the format of a civil service brief to a new anti-nuclear Prime Minister. What follows is a summary of the list of possible hostile US responses, and the flavour of the associated advice [17]:

- *Threatening to withdraw or withdrawing some US forces from Europe.* Some troop reductions are likely regardless of what Britain does. However, since withdrawals might be threatened to deter a non-nuclear strategy, it might be useful to try to pre-empt domestic and international criticism by warning of this possibility in advance, including the possibility that the United States might be looking for excuses. In any case, large reductions are probably unlikely since the troops are there for US national security reasons.
- *Intervening in the British political process.* Sophisticated campaigns might be mounted in the media, with coordination between opponents of a non-nuclear policy in the two countries. There might be an attempt to generate an atmosphere of crisis. These campaigns could be met by diplomatic responses and the positive presentation of the changes in the two countries. Covert actions to disrupt the policy should be anticipated, and an attempt to destabilise the government cannot be discounted.
- *Threatening the supply of highly-enriched uranium for submarines.* If this were done it would eventually prevent the deployment of British nuclear-powered submarines in NATO roles, and this might be something even a hostile administration would not want to consider. If there was an embargo, Britain has alternative sources of supply.
- *Withdrawing military cooperation.* British forces might be debarred from joint exercises. This is very unlikely, since it would be damaging to NATO's fighting ability.
- *Stopping military contracts.* An embargo is possible, but this would be unlikely as long as Britain stayed in NATO. An embargo would damage the effectiveness of NATO forces.
- *Cutting off intelligence cooperation.* This threat has been made before, and might be again. The prospect causes great anxiety in the intelligence community in Britain, since it values its cooperation with the United States most highly. However, intelligence traffic goes both ways and the UK possesses some essential

facilities; it is therefore unlikely that all cooperation would be stopped by the United States, since by so doing it would hurt its own interests. Furthermore, the possible loss should be set against the fact that other NATO countries manage without the same level of intelligence cooperation, and it is doubtful whether the loss would be critical for what would then be a non-nuclear British government.
- *Diplomatic counter-measures.* The United States could try to isolate Britain diplomatically and refuse to support its foreign policy. This possibility would be affected more by the general diplomatic relationship than by nuclear matters. Some influence might be lost with the United States, but this would not be of critical significance because one of the aims of the non-nuclear policy is to shift Britain towards adopting a new role as a European power.
- *Economic and financial pressure.* Direct economic or financial pressure is possible but unlikely. It would hurt US interests in Britain, it would be bureaucratically difficult in Washington, and financial counters are less of a problem in an era of floating exchange rates. Anti-American economic policies by Britain would be more likely to provoke reprisals.
- *Approach to negotiations with the USA.* If the US administration acted in a hostile fashion, Britain has a range of possible counter-measures, including the intelligence asset and the prospect of expelling a range of US bases and facilities. But a non-nuclear government would hope to avoid threats and counter-threats. The approach to negotiations should be flexible but firm, with changes in policy made neither abruptly nor without explanation. In the final outcome much will depend on the character of the consultation between the countries at the time.

In conclusion, the ORG argued that a non-nuclear policy would need 'delicate handling' and careful timing; but it could be made acceptable to a US administration.

One of the biggest difficulties involved in speculating about future US responses to British policy arises out of the volatility of US domestic politics and the difficulty of generalising about 'American' views about anything. It is difficult to speculate about American thinking four or five years ahead. By that time, troop-reductions in Europe might have taken place because of unilateral US decisions, perhaps arising out of 'get-tough' attitudes generated by the need to deal with the budget deficit. There might have been Soviet offers of substantial troop reductions, and some start may have been made. A successful follow-up to the INF agreement might have occurred on strategic and battlefield nuclear weapons. At least serious talks might be taking place. In these circumstances the United States would be in the forefront of denuclearisation, and this would radically alter what US public opinion would want. If Britain at that point is still following the out-dated Sovietology and pro-nuclear attitudes of the Thatcher years, Anglo-American relations might become as acrimonious as they threatened to be when President Reagan contemplated the prospect of having to deal with Prime Minster Kinnock – and vice versa. We cannot at such a time of unfolding possibilities in world affairs assume the continuation of recent attitudes, including an automatic American veto on a non-nuclear policy for Britain.

In addition to the volatility of opinion, there is always a problem in identifying 'American' thinking, be it the competing voices within the bureaucracy or the mixture of attitudes emanating from the heterogeneous public at large. Who knows what Americans will think? Which Americans are we talking about? Given such uncertainties it would be foolish to allow British policy to be vetoed by anything as unpredictable as 'American' thinking, especially as that country, even in policy circles, has not yet become adequately acquainted with the range and depth of the arguments in favour of a non-nuclear non-provocative defence posture. This is why it has been argued that Britain should move more slowly in its non-nuclear programme than was proposed by the Labour Party in 1986–87. It is important that more time is allowed for the shift in policy than the life of one Parliament, and it is vital that every opportunity be taken to engage US opinion, and that of the other allies, in a clear and detailed discussion about the interrelationship between denuclearisation and European security. As an independent sovereign state Britain should pursue its best interests, as it sees them, while consulting with the United States and trying to shape its ideas in a favourable direction. The latter aim is not destined to fail, for the argument in this part of the book is that what is good for Britain is also good for the United States.

Without reading too much into it, it is worth recording that a nationwide opinion poll in the United States in the mid-1980s showed that:[18] a large percentage (55%) believed nuclear war 'very' or 'somewhat' likely; a greater number of those polled (47%) believed that the United States was more likely to become involved in a nuclear war as a result of Third World countries getting nuclear weapons than as a result of a surprise Soviet attack (20%); more now believed that the biggest threat to the United States was the nuclear arms race with the Soviet Union (27%) rather than the Soviet Union itself (21%); the majority (62%) thought that the White House was not doing enough to reach an arms control agreement with the Soviet Union or about controlling the further spread of nuclear weapons (56%); an overwhelming majority of Americans (75%) wanted to maintain or increase existing levels of men and equipment deployed in Europe, though many believed (56%) that the United States was shouldering more than its fair share of the defence burden; and, finally, most of those polled (81%) did not believe that the United States should help defend its allies by threatening the use of nuclear weapons. Putting all this together – though recognising the limitations of one poll – it appears that US public opinion does not have nightmares about the Soviet nuclear threat, is concerned about nuclear proliferation, does want to curb the escalation of nuclear arsenals, is committed to defending Europe, and does want a conventional emphasis in NATO strategy. Various developments since the poll have encouraged these trends. If a future administration reflected such attitudes it should be somewhat sympathetic to the changes of direction favoured by a non-nuclear British government. This poll also suggests the important conclusion that on nuclear matters the silent majority in America has been significantly to the left of the Reagan White House; the American people underlined this point in the Congressional election in 1986. Again the gap was exposed between the President's personal popularity and the popular disapproval of many of his policies. Reagan's late conversion to arms control for domestic reasons is further proof of the potential importance of winning over US opinion. With a serious and prolonged presentation of the non-nuclear case, using friendly voices in the United States, we can hope to see the growth of a much more receptive audience.

To date, the coolness or even opposition of ostensible liberals in the United States to the advantages of alternative security arrangements has been disappointing. The strength of the opposition was evident in the criticism which Neil Kinnock received in November 1986 when he tried to explain Labour's thinking to US audiences. Senior Democrats warned him that his non-nuclear strategy would be 'catastrophic' for the Western alliance. They said it would end the 'special relationship' with the United States, force the United States to pull out all its troops from Britain and require Britain to withdraw its army from West Germany, where it stands under the US nuclear umbrella.[19] These were alarmist opinions. Some of this over-reaction was undoubtedly because of the novelty of the ideas with which the senior Democrats were confronted, and a natural caution towards change when established policies seem to have 'worked' for forty years. It has taken British opinion, after all, a generation to reach only the brink of contemplating nuclear disarmament; we cannot expect full and immediate support from abroad.

There are elements of US opinion that are sympathetic to denuclearisation. Some liberal Democratic administrations could easily accommodate a non-nuclear Britain. An administration committed to winding down the arms race, putting the relationship with the Soviet Union on a more relaxed footing, adopting a less interventionist posture in the Third World, and inerpreting international politics generally with less emphasis on the US–Soviet dimension and more on the local and regional dynamics – such an administration would give a very different reaction to the idea of a non-nuclear Britain than the Reagan administration, or even mainstream Democrats who have not had much opportunity to think about the idea and who have had to operate in recent years in an America dominated by a conservative climate. We might hope, as many Americans hope, that the next President will adopt the policies just described. In the 1980s the tone of US political life has been set by Reagan, and no American politician believed that he or she could be successful if outflanked on the right on issues such as defence and super power relations. In what looks like being a more relaxed super power relationship for the rest of the 1980s, it will be possible for the next President to seem both patriotic and less Cold War-ish. This will give alternative defence thinking a more helpful environment.

Added to the difficulty of speculating about future US opinion is the fact that much would depend on the way any change in British nuclear policy was packaged and handled.[20] It would be unfortunate, for example, if the White House's opposition to denuclearisation provoked the non-nuclear British government of the day to luxuriate in that anti-Americanism which is never far beneath the surface in some sections of British opinion. Anti-Americanism should form no part of the outlook of a Britain committed to a non-nuclear strategy. We want to remain a firm ally, and unless our shift to a non-nuclear posture is merely a moral gesture, one of our priorities should be attempting to persuade as many sections of US opinion as possible of the desirability of taking an alternative view of European security. A Britain committed to NATO and making exertions for defence should not attract complaint from a sensible US administration; the latter might have lost a nuclear ally, but it would be gaining a robust defensive friend. It is already clear that some US policy-makers – those who are aware of what is happening – have been anxious for some time about the impact of Britain's nuclear programme on its conventional forces.[21]

The strength of US opposition to a non-nuclear Britain would be ameliorated if by that time a stronger Western European identity in defence had been established; in such circumstances Britain would be seen merely as 'one of the Europeans' rather than as the one with whom the United States has a 'special relationship'. History is moving in this direction, though there are some in Britain who still cling to old ideas about our status and the 'special' quality of our relationship with the United States. This is one of the reasons why British governments have exerted themselves to maintain nuclear weapons. If British nuclear disarmament was carried out slowly and responsibly, then the United States could live with a non-nuclear Britain within NATO. But if the change were handled badly – with the diplomacy crudely done and a failure to strengthen words by acts – then the United States would undoubtedly see British nuclear disarmament in terms of the defection of an old and major ally. Whether or not the special relationship is what it was, Britain will remain a major partner of the United States, and one whose actions are given more significance than those of smaller and less dependable allies. British nuclear disarmament might be seen by some in Washington as the sinking of the unsinkable aircraft carrier. But this need not be the case. That is why it is important to move slowly, to avoid anti-Americanism, and to explain that what is being done is in US interests, as well as Europe's.

While the problem so far has been presented in terms of the risks to the American connection, some disadvantages of the American connection must also be brought into the equation. The dangers of being drawn into the US global confrontation with the Soviet Union were referred to earlier; disagreements have occurred between Europeans and the Reagan White House over US policy towards the Middle East, Central America and the Soviet Union in particular. To point this out is not to indulge in anti-Americanism, no does it indicate 'neutralism'. To disapprove of the policies of particular administrations does not make one 'anti-American', and supporters of a non-nuclear strategy should resist attracting such a reputation. We must stress that we are pro-American and are attempting to persuade the United States to do what is in its best interests, as well as our own. Loyal opposition should exist in alliances as well as democracies. In a truly democratic alliance committed to rational decision-making the most powerful member should not always get its way, and policy should not be made on the basis of loyalty tests (as has been the inclination of the Reagan administration). Differences of opinion should be seen as healthy and rational in a democratic alliance. When only one view is allowed (that of the strongest ally) NATO will have become a Western Warsaw Pact.

Under Ronald Reagan the United States spent and spent to accumulate more strength but – contrary to White House propaganda – it has not provided the foundation for more security or foreign policy success. US administration spokesmen have criticised Western Europeans for drifting towards 'neutralism' and 'pacifism' over the years; but in the 1980s Ronald Reagan on his own did more to encourage Western European 'anti-Americanism' than any words or gold from the Politburo. Britain should not lock itself into unwise US policies and strategies: but this will remain likely as long as Britain relies on the United States for essential aspects of its 'independent' deterrent. A continuing sense of military dependence is bad for British independence, British relations with other European countries, and rational decision-making in the Western alliance. We will feel freer to reduce this dependence when we have a more relaxed view of the threat, and together with our European allies, come to understand the security advantages of denuclearisation.

NATO will not necessarily 'shatter' (to use the word much favoured by the critics of non-nuclear strategy) if Britain rejects nuclear weapons. The alliance would obviously face a 'crisis'. But crises are not always unhelpful. They can clarify. They are moments of opportunity as well as danger. This was the case in the mid-1960s, when NATO emerged stronger as a result of the reassessments necessitated by the French withdrawal from the integrated military structure and the removal of US and NATO activities from its territory. A non-nuclear Britain would remain a member of NATO but would try to change the alliance's strategy from the inside. NATO might lose some cohesion, but unity at any price should not be the objective of alliance policy, any more than strength at any price should not be the objective of military policy: what matters is whether one's security interests are being furthered. Means are too often confused with ends in foreign and defence policy.

British security interests are not likely to be furthered if we always defer to the United States in the name of alliance unity. It may be that it will become clear at some point that NATO will never bend from its pro-nuclear stance. At that point, it might be thought necessary for a non-nuclear British government to follow the French line, and announce our intention of leaving the integrated military organisation and removing foreign bases. In these circumstances we would maintain an unequivocal commitment to the North Atlantic Treaty, and coordinate our military preparations with NATO, as France does. But loyalty to the Treaty should not imply an indefinite and unequivocal commitment to any particular strategy. In one important respect our policy should differ from that of France. Unlike France, Britain should not withdraw from the integrated military organisation only to continue pursuing nuclear deterrence. Leaving France as the only West European country in the nuclear club would be difficult for some members of the British establishment to contemplate. But the track record does not suggest that it is wise to put one's bets on the warhorse called 'Gallic Strategic Logic'. On two occasions this century it has promised much, but has fallen disastrously at the first ditch. Before the Great War the logic of the offensive led to the horrors of the Western Front. This in turn led to the logic of the defensive, whose outcome was the bitter collapse of 1940. It would be a sad day for the British if they allowed foolish pride to make them follow in the track of yet another example of unwise French logic, that of 'independent deterrence' in the nuclear age.

Those in Britain who worry that British nuclear disarmament would represent slippage *vis-à-vis* France in the international status table, also worry, more publicly, that if Britain dropped out of the game the Federal Republic of Germany might go nuclear itself. It is argued that this is especially likely if NATO collapsed.

States acquire nuclear weapons for a complex mixture of strategic and political considerations. Whether the FRG will take such a step depends on many factors, notably the general state of European security at the time, and the amount of German confidence in some US commitment to its defence. The latter is significant, and on its own is sufficient reason for the United States to keep some troops in Europe, even if NATO became non-nuclear.

Some British supporters of nuclear deterrence use the threat of a nuclear FRG as an argument against British nuclear disarmament.

But if, as deterrent supporters constantly reiterate, nuclear states will not attack other nuclear states, what better than have the major industrial power in central Europe going nuclear? Will this not guarantee that Soviet forces will never penetrate westwards? The arguments usually levelled against proliferation to the Third World – it is a collection of unstable regions, irresponsible leaders and weak economies – do not apply in the case of the FRG. There is another reason why British nuclear deterrers, according to their own principles, should not worry about the FRG going nuclear: a nuclear FRG would ensure that the Soviet Union would never allow the two Germanies to unite. Clear lines, always useful for deterrence, would continue to be drawn across European security problems, while the most troublesome of those problems in the twentieth century – that of coping with an over-large Germany – would be permanently solved by permanent division.

To British nuclear disarmers, the problem of Germany and nuclear weapons presents itself in a rather different form. The argument is frequently heard that the FRG does not want conventional deterrence; its geopolitical position, it is suggested, is such that it must place absolute reliance on nuclear deterrence. Even a conventional war would be catastrophic. This argument has some force, but the possibility of opposition from within the FRG to any shift from a nuclear strategy by NATO should not be allowed to dictate allied strategy. For one thing, an anti-nuclear SPD government might come to power, preferring to stress strong conventional forces and so able to live with a non-nuclear Britain doing a better job for conventional deterrence. Furthermore, governments in Bonn are well aware of the disadvantages of acquiring nuclear weapons; if Bonn wishes to pursue an eastern policy with some hope of success, it needs some cooperation from the Soviet Union, and that is not likely to be forthcoming if it is seen to have aspirations to becoming a mini-super power in a military as well as an economic sense.

While the reaction of West Germany would be of most significance, the responses of the other European members of NATO would play a part in shaping the future character of the alliance. Again, their response to a British decision to scrap nuclear weapons would partly depend on the way the British government packaged its policy. It is possible that the Western European governments in power at the time would disapprove of such a move by Britain, since it would leave the United States as the only nuclear power in NATO, and because it might be seen as yet further evidence of Britain opting out of

European affairs. Against that, Britain's 'independent' nuclear deterrent presently plays little part in the calculation of our European allies, while a British commitment to invest in conventional forces would be something they would support. Allied governments, though not large sections of public opinion, are likely to be less worried about the scrapping of Trident than about the implications of Britain rejecting the use of battlefield nuclear weapons on the central front. The government of Helmut Kohl in Bonn would oppose such a change, as it would oppose NFU – but governments change and opinions adjust. In a Europe in the aftermath of super power *détente*, there could be talk of a NWFZ on the lines of the 1986 SPD-SED agreement and NFU. In such circumstances the allied response to a British decision to put denuclearisation into effect would obviously be less hostile than that likely in the still-cool climate of the mid-1980s. In the field of foreign policy, Western imaginations have become rather inhibited, after nearly a decade of following the regressive international agenda laid down by the British and US leaders.

While critics of a non-nuclear strategy have naturally stressed the challenge it poses to NATO, let us not forget that the continuation of present policies also puts the future of the alliance to the test. Britain's commitment to Trident threatens a rundown in our conventional commitment, and when this occurs, it will send a more worrying signal to our allies than would the renunciation of Trident. A large reduction of our forces in BAOR, for example, will increase the difficulties of some of our allies in maintaining their own defence efforts.[22] From the point of view of alliance cohesion, it would therefore be clear that Britain has alternatives other than nuclear weapons if it wishes to show it is serious about defence and is committed to European affairs. A unilateral declaration could be made, for example, committing Britain to maintain a given force-level in Europe for twenty years, unless an international agreement changed the situation. Ideally, the renunciation of nuclear weapons should be used as an occasion for a major pro-European tilt in British political life. Unfortunately, while the Labour Party's defence proposals point in the right direction on nuclear issues, its attitudes to Europe have left much to be desired in recent years, in the opinion of both Western Europeans and British voters. If the worst came to the worst, and there was no sympathy in Western Europe for British denuclearisation, what measures could NATO take against Britain? Here again it is useful to summarise the Oxford Research Group's assessment:[23]

- *Removal of British officers from NATO commands.* This would be likely, but Britain is already over-represented for historical reasons. The British military would be concerned by such a change, but it should not affect a government seeking a new non-nuclear role.
- *Removal or isolation of British officials on political committees.* There are no mechanisms for this, and Britain can and should assert its rights to stay on them.
- *Diplomatic measures.* West Germany might be sufficiently troubled that it would seek to isolate Britain diplomatically (and militarily) by working with the United States and France.
- *Changes in deployment.* The loss of British bases might be met by a NATO decision to redeploy its nuclear forces, such as the F-111s.

The verdict of the ORG was that there would be 'sharp declarations' against a non-nuclear Britain but that NATO's most likely reaction would be 'to seek to keep Britain within the Alliance, and to adapt to the change'. The prospect of a non-nuclear Britain would be against the background of an already troubled alliance and there could be some support for Britain within several countries. When France expelled all US bases and NATO facilities (including NATO headquarters) from French territory, the alliance continued without serious hindrance. Britain is strategically vital to the alliance, and 'NATO would have little choice but to accept the new situation'.

NATO's future cohesion is threatened therefore by both continuity and change. The alliance has done a good job, but over the years the organisation has become overblown. It has been such a success in a world where alliances are normally characterised by impermanence, that it has become part of the problem of European security, as well as part of the solution. There is now a NATO mentality, and it carries disproportional weight. It has institutionalised an image of the threat (inflated), how it should be met (heavily pro-nuclear), and how it should be organised (with a tightly integrated alliance under US leadership). These outlooks need to be changed, but without undermining the basic collective framework. Naturally, the organisation and its supporters resist change, for they fear it. But if they fear it because they believe the alliance is fragile, there must be something fundamentally wrong in any case. As was argued in the last chapter: NATO cannot stay the same while its members evolve. Indeed, Chapter 4 insisted that NATO might face more strains from trying to stay the same than from changing strategically and politically.

Whatever happens, it will be a troubled alliance, but it will remain one with a considerable degree of legitimacy.

A British government committed to non-nuclear defence should present its new policy to the allies as an adjustment to a position more in keeping with Britain's power and status, and as a step towards reshaping a more secure Europe. Careful diplomacy will be necessary at every stage. Consultation and reaffirmations of commitment will be vital, and abrupt unilateral gestures should be avoided. The aim, as discussed earlier, is to encourage the super powers to restrain their own nuclear programmes and encourage the United States to adopt a more consistently relaxed attitude to the Soviet Union, to encourage NATO to adopt a no-first-use strategy, and to seek the withdrawal of all nuclear weapons from Europe. We want US forces to remain committed to, and stationed in Western Europe, at least for the immediate future; but there is nothing sacred about their ultimate size and character. These will depend on the way the European security system evolves. As we work towards the establishment of a legitimate international order in Europe, it is hoped that US forces will be progressively denuclearised, so that at the end of the process NATO's strategy will have been decoupled from the nuclear strategy of the United States. The latter will maintain what we hope will be a much-reduced strategic nuclear arsenal simply to deter direct attacks on its own homeland.

A British government committed to a non-nuclear posture is likely to face a difficult time in its relations with most allied governments, though this prognosis could change radically over 5–10 years if benevolent domestic and international trends interact. There would in any case be less opposition to the more purely British aspects of a change to a non-nuclear policy (notably the scrapping of Polaris and Trident) than there would be to those aspects that have more direct implications for NATO in general or the 'special relationship' with the United States (such as the removal of nuclear weapons from US bases in Britain). It was to meet this problem that the timescale outlined in Chapter 4 envisaged dealing with the more purely British aspects in the short term while allowing the bilateral and multilateral problems a longer period, in order to allow fuller public education, more inter-governmental discussion, and more opportunity for the allies to adjust to changing British realities.

In the final outcome, much depends upon who is in government in different countries at the time, the state of public opinion in allied nations, the effectiveness of the British government's diplomacy, the state of the Soviet Union, the character of international relations and so on. Favourable scenarios can be imagined in all these areas; but that would be wishful thinking. It is more rational to expect a rough but not irrational reaction, and to remember that France's independent line in the 1960s neither shattered NATO nor led the allies to treat it like a pariah. While it is important to consider the possible responses of the allies, a future non-nuclear British government should also ask itself whether the expected criticism of allied governments should be decisive in preventing Britain from pursuing a policy over ten years (or more) which it believes will put European security on a surer and cheaper footing. The political choice is between continued conformity to extended deterrence or far-reaching change. The reforms suggested in Part II do not alter any of the fundamental problems that confront us. Some critics of non-nuclear thinking, like Caspar Weinberger, made some rather extreme statements at the end of 1986, but those should just be regarded as the preliminary shots in a prolonged diplomatic skirmish. NATO will not shatter if a non-nuclear strategy is advanced, for the allies have more common interests keeping together than they have differences that will split them apart. And war will not be the outcome, for we and our adversaries have more common interests in not fighting than we have in rolling the deadly dice, whether nuclear or conventional. There will be opposition, but the future is there to be shaped, not passively accepted: Britain should be seeking to clarify a new reality, and not simply keeping alive images of the old.

CAN A NON-NUCLEAR STRATEGY BE SUCCESSFUL IN WAR?

Not only would a shift from a nuclear to a non-nuclear emphasis make war more likely, the critics argue, it would also disastrously weaken Britain in the event of war. They ask 'Who would want to command conventional forces against a nuclear enemy? Could conventional forces ultimately stop a determined nuclear enemy, willing to use its most destructive weapons? What is to stop the nuclear state wiping its non-nuclear enemy off the board?' These are important questions, and ones which give supporters of non-nuclear defence considerable worry.

Michael Clarke has pointed out that the argument that the possession of nuclear weapons will pose a deterrent against the first use of nuclear weapons by the other side is one of the most difficult to counter.[24] However well or however badly supporters of non-nuclear defence cope with such questions, it is important that this must be set against the almost complete failure of pro-nuclear strategists to persuade people that the idea of fighting a controlled nuclear war (as in the NATO strategy of Flexible Response) is anything other than the road to the end of civilised life in the northern hemisphere, if not beyond. During the 1987 election some critics of non-nuclear defence went on at great length about the difficulties conventional forces would face against a nuclear enemy: a non-nuclear strategy 'does not carry military conviction' it was asserted. Without doubt, there would be enormous problems in such a scenario, but the election campaign almost completely ignored the suicidal and irrational characteristics of Britain's present posture, which threatens to throw together on the battlefield two highly-armed nuclear adversaries. This was one of the several weaknesses of our established policy which were not taken up with sufficient vigour in what passed for a defence 'debate' in June 1987. Who would want to command troops with nuclear weapons on a battlefield against a nuclear-equipped enemy? The idea of fighting a nuclear war carries less military conviction than any idea in the history of Britain arms.

It goes without saying that there are obvious dangers for any non-nuclear state involved in a war against a nuclear power. Some of the restraints that exist under mutual deterrence would go, including the possibility of intra-war deterrence. The dropping of the atomic bombs against Japan in 1945 is brought forward by pro-nuclear advocates to clinch the argument. It is not a good analogy, however. We should not spend much time wondering whether the United States would have called off the war had Japan acquired atomic weapons: it would have been unthinkable after Pearl Harbor and all that followed the 'Day of Infamy' that a US president could have called off the invasion of Japan in the summer of 1945, ordered his forces home, and accepted a return to the *status quo ante*. Japan had to be defeated. What then would Japan have done if the United States had carried out a conventional invasion? Would Japan have replied with a *kamikaze* atomic strategy? If so, would it have been wise? This is an exact analogy with Britain's prospective position, if faced in war by the threat of an overwhelming Soviet conventional invasion following a Soviet country-hopping campaign across Europe. In such circumstances a *kamikaze* nuclear strike by Britain against the Soviet Union would be irrational; it would only guarantee a vengeful counter-strike.[25]

In addition to analogies, there is empirical evidence from several wars that non-nuclear forces are not at the military disadvantage they would appear to be when facing a nuclear opponent. On several occasions nuclear powers have fought non-nuclear adversaries and have restricted themselves to conventional weapons. Korea, Vietnam, and Afghanistan, not to mention the Falklands war, were special cases; but so are all wars. In the case of a future European war, in which a nuclear Soviet Union might be involved against a non-nuclear NATO, the Soviet Union would still have to take residual US nuclear power into account. Consequently any attack westwards would still be a cosmic gamble on their part, especially if they used nuclear weapons at the outset. As a non-nuclear country, Britain in this scenario would be less of a prime target. In any event, would there be any sense in lunatic nuclear destruction by the Soviet Union of territory and resources it presumably wished to occupy and exploit in Western Europe? The Soviet commitment to no-first-use of nuclear weapons indicates its concern about the dangers of escalation and the desirability of limiting damage, as well as its desire for favourable propaganda. The only reason why a Soviet leader might decide that he wanted to wipe Britain off the board of international politics would be the belief that we were about to wipe it off the board. One of the major themes of a non-provocative, non-nuclear posture is to reassure the Soviet Union that this is not the case.

There are risks in conducting a non-nuclear defence against an aggressive nuclear power, but these identifiable risks are somewhat smaller than the cosmic risks involved in hostilities between two nuclear powers. The risks involved in the shift to a non-nuclear strategy are thought acceptable by its supporters in order to help create a more secure Europe, one in which the use of force between the blocs becomes progressively less acceptable as an instrument of power. Fighting against a nuclear enemy would involve great risks and difficult choices, but they would be less than the perils of trying to fight a 'controlled' nuclear war. Going back to one of the original questions, it is obvious that nobody would like to command conventional forces against a nuclear enemy, but who would relish fighting with nuclear weapons against a nuclear enemy? Would we be self-deterred? Would we follow orders or standard procedures, and so bring about hell on earth? When would NATO use its tactical nuclear weapons, or Britain its independent ones? Once any war in Europe begins, the prospects are terrifying to decision-makers and their agents; they become more so when nuclear powers fight each other. Even in peacetime there appears to be much confusion about

NATO's nuclear intentions. Thus the balance of arguments on the issue of war-fighting is not tipped against the advocates of alternative defence. On the contrary, they are tipped against the supporters of Flexible Response, who believe that nuclear wars can probably be kept limited, but if they cannot, that a general nuclear war can in some circumstances be a rational instrument of policy. Once we leave the tidy theory of nuclear deterrence and imagine the practical nightmare of nuclear battles between nuclear powers, the dangers and irrationalities of what is presented as a nuclear *defence* policy become clear.

Clearly there can be no hiding from the dangers of fighting a nuclear adversary, but history gives some comfort, as does the widespread belief of almost all serious analysts that the actual risk of a Soviet attack is extremely low. Furthermore, a premise of the critics of non-nuclear defence conjures up scenarios in which Britain would be somehow standing alone against the Soviet Union. This is implausible. One cannot image a realistic Soviet invasion of Britain without a preliminary attack on Western Europe as a whole, with all this implies in terms of the heightened risk of mutual obliteration between the super powers. When we discuss war-fighting scenarios in Europe we must recognise that we are talking about highly improbable situations. The Soviet leaders know the risks of any war in Europe; they know the costs of empire; and they know the problems they face in making the existing socialist commonwealth work. War offers no answers. So, if we think of probabilities instead of theoretical possibilities when contemplating the risks of Soviet attack, we must conclude that they are extremely low. This being the case, the more we can emphasise to Soviet policy-makers that they cannot secure other than a terriby costly and risky conventional victory, the more it is likely that we will avoid nuclear war, since the most conceivable scenario for any Soviet nuclear attack on western Europe would be eruption of a conventional war. It is important therefore that we invest in a robust defence force for the foreseeable future. This should be the case whether or not NATO maintains a nuclear capability; we need to raise the nuclear threshold in order to free ourselves from a possibly fatal dependence on Flexible Response, based as it is on the idea that we should be prepared to fight the Soviet Union at every level, conventional and nuclear. We need conventional strength, but with our present pro-nuclear emphasis, our contribution to NATO's fighting forces will erode. As a result, the nuclear threshold will be lowered. At the early stage of a future war we may feel forced to escalate to nuclear weapons because of a lack of faith in the strength of our conventional forces. Thus we have the danger that a former Chief of the Defence Staff Lord Carver, has warned us about, namely that of risking piling a nuclear disaster upon a conventional defeat.[26]

The critics of non-nuclear defence sometimes argue that a nuclear aggressor would not even have to use its weapons against a non-nuclear enemy in war; the threat of 'nuclear blackmail' on its own would be sufficient to bring victory. The threat of blackmail would be high, it is argued, since the stakes would be high in any European war. This is a risk that must be recognised, but several points can be made in rebuttal. Most important, would the United States – could it – allow the Soviet Union to get away with such blackmail against European states? If it did then the USA's super power status and the future of international order would be on a very slippery slope indeed. Any Soviet leader would understand this, and would be self-deterred. The two most likely circumstances in which blackmail is conceivable are, first, to threaten Britain with nuclear attack if its troops which were still resisting Soviet forces on the continent refused to surrender, and second, to force Britain to surrender if Soviet troops had reached the Channel.[27] The risk of nuclear blackmail in such circumstances cannot be ignored, though it should be added that in several wars since 1945 the temptation to blackmail has either been resisted or has not worked. The ineffectiveness of blackmail in such circumstances is related to its lack of credibility.

In the dangerous circumstances just foreseen, we must also ask ourselves whether a Britain with an independent nuclear deterrent would be any better off than a non-nuclear Britain, with its troops falling back before Soviet forces on the continent. Would a British government in these circumstances use its independent nuclear weapons, whatever it has said in advance? Lord Carver, quoted in Part II,[28] is not the only person who cannot conceive that a British leader would ever fire its missiles at the Soviet Union if the United States did not. If we did use them, thereby committing national suicide to avoid occupation, would Britain be better off than fighting on with conventional forces, or surrendering? In the scenario under discussion, the Soviet forces would have already conquered Western Europe without using their nuclear weapons, and the Kremlin must presumably have decided that the risk of an independent British nuclear strike was either acceptable or improbable; perhaps because of their confidence in their BMD or strategic ASW capability against Britain's nuclear force. A blooded and bloodied Soviet leadership, which had coldly decided to risk an adventure against NATO as a whole, would not be deterred from threatening or invading a nuclear-armed Britain following a nuclear-age Dunkirk. After successfully crossing Western Europe, weakening British forces on the way, the Soviet leaders would presumably be confident of conventional victory over Britain. So why, at that point, should the Kremlin invite the risk of a British *kamikaze* nuclear attack by escalating to the nuclear level? Britain would have the choice of national suicide by striking first with nuclear weapons, conventional resistance, or surrender. In Part II, the suicide threat is described as 'not very intellectually convincing',[29] though it is an integral part of the independent/ Flexible Response posture that is being justified. The fact is that nuclear weapons offer no defence whatsoever in wars between nuclear powers.

Alternative defence offers several counter-strategies against the threat of use of nuclear weapons: continued non-nuclear resistance, territorial defence, civil defence, and civilian resistance are among the possibilities.[30] They each have problems, though none as cosmic as Flexible Response. Supporters of alternative defence are willing to accept the risks inherent in threatening to fight a conventional war against a nuclear adversary, confident that the risks are less than those posed by a posture based on the threat of a limited nuclear war. A shift to non-provocative defence would not only help to contain the risks if war breaks out in Europe, it should also help to reduce the risks of war breaking out in the first place. Avoiding war is the only truly reliable defence against the dangers discussed in this section.

WOULD A NON-NUCLEAR BRITAIN BE EXPOSED TO NUCLEAR BLACKMAIL?

A frequent but superficially-discussed charge against British nuclear disarmament is the argument that a non-nuclear Britain would be at risk to the threat of nuclear 'blackmail'. This is more likely, it is suggested, than the threat of nuclear war. Any ambitious state might be tempted by a nuclear monopoly to behave more aggressively, and the Soviet Union is just such an ambitious state. War against a non-nuclear Britain would not then be necessary since the nuclear power could ensure submission simply by threats.

The issue of nuclear blackmail is undoubtedly important. There are risks, and these are generally recognised and accepted by supporters of the non-nuclear case. In theory blackmail is a worrying threat;[31] but in practice the problem is not so daunting, and several weaknesses should be apparent in the arguments in the opening paragraph. Even so, we should accept that no strategy can guarantee success: had more advocates of nuclear deterrence recognised this over the years the world would already be on the way to being a safer place. All strategies have worst cases, and non-nuclear advocates must face up to the risk of nuclear blackmail in the same way that supporters of Flexible Response should face up to the dangers of a catastrophic nuclear war following an unsuccessful conventional defence.

The issue of blackmail, like others, ultimately involves a balance of risks. Do we prefer the risk of nuclear blackmail or the risks and burdens of nuclear weapons and Flexible Response? Before this question can be answered, we need to discuss how much risk of nuclear blackmail there would actually be. This is a question on which there has been a good deal of assertion, but not much analysis.[32] Closer inspection of this complex issue will reveal that there is less to the idea of nuclear blackmail than meets the eye.

(1) Nuclear blackmail is ambiguous and a bogey. Before we can say much about nuclear blackmail as a risk, we must know more clearly what it is, how it works, and whether it has been effective in the past. The critics of non-nuclear defence do not help here, for they are non-specific when they raise the bogey of nuclear blackmail. We must seek clarification elsewhere than from the government, the Ministry of Defence, NATO HQ, or other critics. Interestingly, very little systematic investigation has been made into the problem; this in itself is a significant indication of its lack of salience. Furthermore, what work has been done has generally tended to confirm the argument that nuclear blackmail is ambiguous in theory and uncertain in practice.[33] Under close examination at least some of the problems of nuclear blackmail disappear on touch.

Until we better understand what we are talking about, nuclear blackmail will remain at least as much a bogey as a real strategic problem. It will remain a bogey unless someone finds unambiguous evidence that nuclear blackmail has been employed and has been successful. This is not yet forthcoming. Meanwhile, the bogey of nuclear blackmail looms larger in the imaginations of British leaders – those with historical memories of directing international affairs – than it does in the minds of those in countries whose histories have been characterised by the need to make the best of adjusting to the power-realities of the time. Sweden worries less about 'finlandisation' than does Britain. It is one of the ironies of the nuclear age that those nations possessing nuclear weapons worry more about the threat of blackmail than do those nations who are considered to be potential victims. In the past it was the weak who were paranoid: now it is the ostensibly powerful.

The uncertainties surrounding nuclear blackmail are compounded by semantic difficulties; what we call 'nuclear blackmail' is not analogous to real 'blackmail', and it is often difficult to draw a precise distinction between nuclear blackmail and nuclear deterrence.[34] As commony unerstood, however, it is 'the threat to use nuclear weapons in order to coerce a country to act in a certain way desired by the blackmailer. The threat may be explicit or merely implicit'.[35] It is generally seen as similar to 'compellence', which Thomas Schelling twenty years ago showed was much more difficult to operationalise than deterrence.[36]

(2) *Nuclear blackmail is likely to be rare.* There is little reason to suppose that there would be an outbreak of Soviet attempts to coerce non-nuclear European countries in future, especially if the NATO framework were maintained; the latter would immediately confront the Soviet Union with the nuclear power of the United States which, as was argued earlier, will remain a fixture of the international scene for the indefinite future, even if US nuclear weapons are removed from Europe. Soviet leaders can have no illusions about the importance of Western Europe for the United States, and therefore of the importance for the latter of not allowing its super power adversary to 'get away with blackmail'. US nuclear forces removed from Europe would act as an 'existential deterrent' to nuclear blackmail.

Unless one takes a mechanistic view of Soviet behaviour – believing that their propensity to expansion or co-existence is in direct proportion to the rise and fall in military balances – it is not self-evident that a non-nuclear Britain, or even a denuclearised NATO, would tempt Soviet nuclear aggressiveness. A Western Europe with conventional deterrence would not be weaker than Finland or Yugoslavia, or as exposed, and these states have not succumbed to implict nuclear blackmail, nor, insofar as it is known, have they been subjected to explicit blackmail, though in Yugoslavia's case its behaviour after 1948 represented an extreme provocation to Soviet leaders. If such relatively small countries, without defence relations with the United States, did not find themselves subject to nuclear blackmail through all the tensions of the Cold War, it is difficult to understand why and how the Soviet Union in more ordered times might attempt such a tactic against Britain or Western Europe in general. One must concede the possibility of nuclear blackmail, but the earlier statement that it is 'likely to be rare' is more a concession to intellectual rigour than any expectation that it will actually take place.

(3) *The risks of nuclear blackmail should decrease.* Nuclear blackmail is likely to be less impressive in the future than even in the past, and is therefore not the 'very real possibility' which it is asserted to be in Part II. The more unused the tactic remains, and the more often non-nuclear states stand up to nuclear states (and even fight them when the occasion arises), the more difficult it will be for nuclear powers to make credible coercive nuclear threats. Nuclear blackmail is an idea that has atrophied since the Cold War.[37] The history of nuclear blackmail has been short. What has developed since 1945 has not been an Al Capone international system but rather a 'tradition' of non-blackmail, analogous to what Thomas Schelling called the 'tradition of non-use' of nuclear weapons;[38] or what Stanley Hoffmann has called 'primitive rules' and Joseph Nye has dubbed 'prudent practices'.[39] Rudimentary or short-lived as these practices, rules and traditions may be, they are nevertheless more impressive than the history of nuclear blackmail. If this were not the case, the history of the nuclear age would have been marked by a succession of milestones showing successful nuclear blackmailers and unsuccessful non-nuclear victims. These milestones do not exist.

In order that nuclear blackmail continues its unimpressive history it is imperative to resist the growth of nuclear war-fighting and war-winning postures and attitudes, since the credibility of nuclear assets as instruments of peace-time coercion could rise more or less in proportion to beliefs about their usability and utility in war. One of the most dangerous trends in world affairs since the mid-1970s has been the rise to prominence in US policy-making circles of strategic fundamentalists whose ideas could have the effect of conventionalising nuclear war.[40] If the ideas of these nuclear war-winners were to take hold, the international outlook would greatly darken. The corollary of conventionalising nuclear war is the employment of nuclear weapons in peacetime to achieve greater diplomatic leverage. While the grip of the strategic fundamentalists has been strong in the Reagan period, economic and political developments suggest that their influence, at least for the moment, may have peaked. But politics in the United States are volatile, and right-wing fundamentalism is a resilient force.

Nuclear blackmail by the established nuclear powers is a decreasing prospect. The critics recognise this by shifting the argument to the danger of reckless Third World gamblers who may acquire nuclear weapons. These 'crazy states', it is argued, will lack the inhibitions of the established nuclear powers. There is undoubtedly a finite risk of an aggressive Third World leader with a few nuclear weapons issuing nuclear threats against a non-nuclear Britain, but this is not a scenario that need detain us long. It is not obvious why such a leader should choose to achieve his aims this way if a leader like Ronald Reagan, with his simplistic view of international affairs, his fundamentalist beliefs, and his apparent faith in military power chose not to employ blackmail from a position of overwhelming nuclear monopoly against the 'demons' he perceived to be facing him in small countries like Libya, Iran or Nicaragua.

(4) *Nuclear blackmail is a one-shot strategy.* One of the strongest constraints against nuclear blackmail is self-imposed. This is because nuclear powers understand that if blatant nuclear intimidation were to be tried against a non-nuclear power, and if it proved to be successful, then the chief result would be the biggest rush to nuclear proliferation since the atomic bomb was invented. Soviet leaders know (as do their US counterparts in analogous situations) that they have much more to lose as a result of an onrush of new nuclear powers than they have to gain from trying to coerce one non-nuclear country. The super powers know that a world of many nuclear states would be an unstable tinder-box lying alongside their own immense powder-kegs.

At present the many non-nuclear states are relatively satisfied with their security arrangements. Their worries are about the conventional threat from their neighbours rather than nuclear blackmail. This attitude would change profoundly if, instead of its undistinguished history, nuclear blackmail were suddenly seen to work. Were the Soviet Union, some time in the future, to attempt to intimidate a neighbour or adversary with nuclear threats, then that country (and many others) might well feel the need to 'go nuclear' or at least attempt to find shelter under the umbrella of the United States. Neither of those outcomes would be desirable for the Soviet Union. It has long been clear that the Soviet Union has even more to fear from nuclear proliferation than has the United States, since the next enemy for most near-nuclear powers, after a particular regional power, is the Soviet Union. Some authority for this conclusion was given by Leonid Brezhnev, shortly before his death. In a conversation with a Western visitor he said, 'You must remember that every nuclear weapon in the world is either in the Soviet Union or aimed at the Soviet Union.'[42]

Relevant information about possible cases of nuclear blackmail is obscure, and the conclusions one might draw are uncertain. But even the ostensible cases underline the present argument. The examples sometimes brought forward are of the effect on the Soviet Union of the US nuclear monopoly in the background to the 1948 Berlin crisis, and the nuclear signalling in various crises with Communist China in the 1950s.[43] But these were deterrent rather than compellent threats, and so do not count in the argument. And even if they helped deter certain actions in the crises themselves they did not deter the Soviet Union or Communist China from subsequently acquiring nuclear weapons of their own; in fact they strengthened earlier decisions to acquire such a capability. Nevertheless the Soviet acquisition of nuclear weapons did not ensure the success of its challenge to Western rights in the later Berlin crises.[44] The short and hardly successful history of nuclear diplomacy does not offer critics of non-nuclear defence an impressive brief for their case.

Because it is in the interests of the United States, as well as the Soviet Union, to stem nuclear proliferation, a rational United States would not only refrain from engaging in nuclear blackmail itself, but would also let it be known that it would resist any such behaviour on the part of the Soviet Union. In the past the super powers have been adversary partners in controlling nuclear proliferation; for the same reason they should also be tacit partners in resisting any temptation to nuclear blackmail.

(5) Nuclear blackmail is neither easy nor cost free. In peacetime there are strong political constraints operating against nuclear blackmail, and these should induce caution in many circumstances. This historical evidence gives little confidence to potential blackmailers that they will be able to achieve their objectives easily or without costs.

Based on historical studies of the ostensible episodes of nuclear coercion – Iran, Korea, the Middle East, and so on – McGeorge Bundy, a man of some political experience as well as scholarship – has challenged the view that nuclear weapons are useful in times of peace for political coercion (other than simply for the direct deterrence of nuclear attacks on one's homeland).[45] In Bundy's words,

> Direct threats to use nuclear weapons have not been frequent in the nuclear age, and even indirect threats have become fewer as

the realities of existential deterrence have been recognised more and more widely. I do not think this is an accident. When sanity requires care, and when even the most bitter adversaries perceive each other as sane, threats to do something rash become unpersuasive; they simply lack credibility.

Here Bundy is referring to 'blackmail' between nuclear powers, but the 'existential deterrent' also extends over the allies of the super powers. Threats 'to do something rash' against these allies have also become unpersuasive. And even less rash threats can be counter-productive. Bundy referred to a 'clear (Soviet) reference' to the nuclear vulnerability of Japan, which led not to fear on the latter's part, but to 'a healthy reaction of unfrightened anger'. This refusal to be intimidated by a nuclear adversary has also been evident in more conflictual settings: by the North Vietnamese, the Afghans, and the Argentinians in deciding to fight nuclear enemies. The Vietnamese fought both nuclear China and the United States. Soviet control over Eastern Europe was established, it should be remembered, during the period of the US atomic monopoly. And over the years, plenty of smaller powers have not deferred to nuclear might. The latter has been irrelevant for the most part. Although no causal relationship is suggested, it is interesting to note that the pattern of recent decades shows declining super power pre-eminence in world affairs alongside the massive increase in their nuclear arsenals.

In addition to the more direct costs of nuclear blackmail (encouraging proliferation or inciting the anger of the target) there are more indirect costs. International opinion would be outraged, and this could impair the blackmailer's foreign policy elsewhere, through alignment and realignment. Of course, 'international opinion' is not a decisive force, and has often been ignored, but it is a factor a potential blackmailer would weigh in the balance. More specifically, the hostility of the other super power would be guaranteed. This might provoke a variety of unwelcome outcomes, such as an intensified arms race, the breakdown of contacts, or a major crisis. Blatant nuclear blackmail would be very costly for the aggressor, both politically and in terms of proliferation. On truly vital issues the Soviet Union might be willing to face the costs: but are relations with Britain ever likely to be in this category?

(6) Blackmail can be resisted. If nuclear blackmail were to take place against a nation without a nuclear retaliatory capability, the latter could take one of a combination of counter-actions. What could

be done in practice would depend critically on the scenario: what was chosen would be affected by the reputation of the threatener (is he prone to bluff?), the extent to which core values were involved, the circumstances of the time, and so on. Sometimes a threat could be ignored; at others a threatener's bluff could be called; and on occasions it might be sensible to defer, though it is very difficult to imagine scenarios in peacetime when a nuclear threat would be credible. These are a similar range of options to those facing states with minimal nuclear deterrents when facing nuclear giants.

Governments with strong wills will not easily bend before nuclear blackmail, since they will understand the costs for the threatener, as well as for themselves. Stalin understood this. He described nuclear weapons as something with which one frightened people with weak nerves.[46] And the record seems to suggest that nuclear threats can be avoided by other than nuclear means. As Bundy and others have pointed out, Sweden and Yugoslavia rely for deterrence not on nuclear weapons of their own but on a combination of 'substantial conventional strength, solid political self-confidence, and a calculation that the costs of both conventional and nuclear attack on them, in the judgement of any sane Soviet leadership, would greatly outweigh any possible advantage.'[47]

The United States will keep some nuclear weapons, whatever Britain does. British security would remain affected by the super power standoff, even if the old Anglo-Saxon partners did not remain formally allied (just as the threat of super power nuclear war plays a role in the security landscape of Yugoslavia and Sweden). Soviet leaders are not likely to believe that the United States would allow them to coerce into submission a country like Britain with which it has always had a special relationship; indeed, they would believe that US leaders would see it as a vital interest to prevent such an occurrence. And on issues less than coercion 'into submission' are Soviet nuclear threats likely to be credible? As it is, the reason why Britain has not been subject to blatant nuclear blackmail may not have been due to the country's independent nuclear power, but rather to the character of the US–Soviet relationship and Soviet beliefs that nuclear blackmail is likely to be ineffective. If the Soviet 'rocket-rattling' of 1956 is brought forward as an example of nuclear coercion, this merely proves that 'blackmail' threats, which are usually likely to be vague, are best ignored. The British government's reversal of policy during the Suez Crisis was the result of US financial pressure and a crack in the government's resolve partly brought on by domestic opposition, not Soviet rocket-rattling.

In order to reduce the risks of blackmail, states should seek to create a more peaceful security system in Europe (the carrot) but also (the stick) make it very plain to the super powers that nuclear blackmail will only be a one-shot weapon for them: if they use it, the price they will have to pay will be widespread proliferation and a much more insecure world. It is difficult to think of the gains which the Soviet Union might hope to achieve as a result of nuclear blackmail against a non-nuclear Britain, especially gains worth the risk of provoking the acquisition of nuclear weapons by all those states which are at present suspicious of Soviet foreign policy. Soviet nuclear blackmail against Britain would be the single most important spur to the acquisition of nuclear weapons by West Germany and Japan. Which Soviet leader or defence planner would undertake actions calculated to bring about such an eventuality?

The balance of risks

The discussion above suggests that there is less to nuclear blackmail than meets the eye. There is a risk, or course, but all strategies involve risk. Just as general nuclear war (followed by a nuclear winter) is a possible but not inevitable outcome of the nuclear balance of terror, so nuclear blackmail is not an inevitable outcome of nuclear disarmament; it is only a possible one. Since there is no way of accurately predicting the risks of nuclear war, in terms of likelihood, it may be more profitable to weigh the risks we face in terms of dangers. When faced by two terrible but unpredictable worst cases, it is sensible to choose the risk whose consequences are less catastrophic, and which still offers some hope of a continuation of politics. This choice also avoids our participation in a strategy based on the threat of a crime against humanity.

A good deal of what we have heard about nuclear blackmail is not so much the result of rational thinking but more a manifestation of irrational anti-Soviet fears bordering on paranoia. If nuclear blackmail is such a potentially effective instrument among Soviet foreign policy options, one wonders why it has not been employed regularly and unambiguously over the past forty years, since there have been several occasions when they needed extra leverage. For whatever reasons, non-nuclear states are not blackmailed. The possibility remains, of course, but for the most part the fears about blackmail we have in our own heads will give us more headaches than those created by Soviet strategy: what issues between Britain and the Soviet Union in the years ahead could possibly call for the activation of this uncertain instrument? A Western Europe robust in conventional military power, self-confident politically, and resolved in the defence of core interests, has little to fear from nuclear blackmail. It is a distant worst case, and as such not sufficiently important to justify the continuation of a nuclear posture which risks other and more dangerous worst cases.

Some argue that those who support a non-nuclear strategy for Britain have already succumbed to 'implicit' nuclear blackmail. The argument is that the very presence of Soviet nuclear weapons has frightened a significant proportion of the British population into submission. Whether or not this is the case with some individuals, the overwhelming majority of the peace movement are more concerned by the possibility of nuclear war than by the threat of Soviet nuclear blackmail or attack. War is the threat, not the Soviet Union. Supporters of non-nuclear defence are not cowed by the Soviet Union, and for the most part, and increasingly so, opponents of British nuclear weapons are also supporters of robust defence. Alternative defence does not derive from being 'soft on communism'. Indeed, the patriotism of the left in Britain has always been strong. It remains so. It is the fear of nuclear war and the implications of the arms race, not a fear of the Soviet Union, that has produced a determination to try to do something towards reshaping the European security system, and making it less dependent on nuclear weapons. The peace movement does not 'fear' Soviet nuclear weapons as much as do the proponents of a pro-nuclear policy. What the peace movement fears is the endless tightenng of the nuclear knot, and an eventual 'nuclear Sarajevo' as a result of the blind addiction of the powers to nuclear deterrence. It also fears living in a world of many nuclear states, an outcome in which past and present British policy is conniving. All these risks are greater than the risks of blackmail.

Given that the idea of nuclear blackmail is ambiguous, the mechanisms uncertain, the risk remote, the likelihood incalculable, the counteractions various, and the dangers exaggerated, we should therefore conclude that it is not sufficiently significant a factor to prevent Britain from moving towards a defence policy better suited to its resources and values, and more likely to contribute to conditions in which the European states will be able to live together in something like peace.

WOULD SOVIET RUSSIA RECIPROCATE?

Finally, it is necessary to address the criticism that Soviet Russia would not reciprocate if Britain attempted to set an example by renouncing nuclear weapons. This is an argument about which both the critics and supporters of a non-nuclear posture make too much.

'Reciprocation' implies a positive act; it implies that state A either gives something back to state B in return for some action on the part of the latter, or alternatively, that state A gives up something in response to state B having relinquished something. To expect the Soviet Union to 'reciprocate' in a substantial and positive way to British nuclear initiatives is to expect too much. The stress on balanced reciprocation reflects an American rather than a European preoccupation with 'balance' and numbers. This preoccupation grows from a fundamentalist and mechanistic outlook on security; one which believes that stability is based on technical rather than political factors. This outlook also reflects another rather American attitude, namely the equating of success with positive rather than negative happenings. This might be related to the vaunted impatience for results which is said to mark the American character.

If Britain did renounce nuclear weapons, impatience must be checked. There should be no expectation of any significant positive reciprocation on the part of the Soviet regime, though it would be surprising if the latter did not in fact reciprocate in various ways. A Prime Minister who took Britain out of the nuclear arms competition could expect some plaudits from Moscow rather in the way de Gaulle's nationalism and anti-Americanism was flattered by the Soviet Union in the 1960s. A Soviet commitment to remove a non-nuclear Britain from its nuclear targeting-list in the event of war has been discussed by Soviet officials, and there have been reaffirmations of a commitment to make 'equivalent reductions' in return for Britain scrapping Polaris.[48] Since these offers have been made by Soviet officials there will be some pressure to abide by them. Equivalent reductions would be a welcome and worthwhile response on the Soviet part, but they would be cosmetic insofar as they would not fundamentally change anything in the strategic picture. But little more could reasonaby be expected. If Britain scrapped 100 per cent of its SLBMs, then the Soviet Union could not reciprocate with the same percentage. On the other hand, if we preferred to express the number in specific terms – 64 missiles in the case of Polaris – the scrapping of an equivalent 64 missiles would be trivial given the size of the Soviet inventory. There is in fact a case for arguing that strict numerical reciprocation of this sort ought to be positively discouraged by a non-nuclear government, since the way of thinking it represents plays too much into the hands of those who make balance and strict reciprocation the condition for any attempt to restrain armaments.

Positive reciprocation should not therefore be expected or even demanded. On the other hand, what the supporters of a non-nuclear Britain should hope for, expect and encourage is that there would be no *negative* reciprocation on the part of the Soviet Union. That is, we should expect that Soviet external behaviour will not in any significant way get worse following British nuclear disarmament. Britain's positive step does not require an identical positive gesture from the Soviet Union in return, but it does require the Soviet Union to avoid taking any steps which might make Britain feel more insecure; these include increasing subversive or militant behaviour, experimenting in nuclear blackmail, or increasing rather than restraining weaponry. There is reason to suppose that the Soviet Union would avoid such steps. It has economic, strategic and political interests in rewarding those nations which seek to wind down the arms-race targeted at Moscow, and which contribute to inhibiting nuclear proliferation. If Soviet leaders did respond in a negative manner to a British non-nuclear initiative, they would be giving a very strong message to the hawks in the West and third-party opinion elsewhere, and so condemn themselves to the risks of proliferation and another generation of confrontation; if the latter were to occur it would have major implications for Soviet plans for internal development in the next few decades. To expect the Soviet leaders to do much more than avoid negative reciprocation is too much. The achievement of that would therefore be entirely satisfactory; anything more from the Soviet side would be a bonus.

What has been discussed so far has focused on Britain and the prospect of Soviet reciprocation. But this is partly to miss the point, as is done in Part II when it is asserted that the Soviet Union will not reciprocate. Positive reciprocation by the Soviet Union – substantial actions rather than words or limited gestures – will probably not come immediately. In the first instance the aim of a non-nuclear British policy should be to encourage our own *allies* to reciprocate, by moving from NATO's heavily pro-nuclear strategy of extended deterrence and flexible response, to a posture of non-provocative defence. We should not forget the Soviet Union – we should engage it in cooperative ventures where possible – but we should look towards significant positive steps from the Soviet Union only when the West as a whole is clear and united in its non-provocative posture. But let us not be too self-righteous and NATO-centric on this question of reciprocation. In the light of the various arms control initiatives made by the Soviet Union since 1985, not least the unilateral nuclear test ban moratorium and the May 1987 Warsaw Pact proposals, we might well conclude that it is NATO rather than the WTO which is presently proving the bigger obstacle to reciprocation.

If and when NATO as a whole contemplates moving towards a less pro-nuclear posture, we should not demand immediate and positive Soviet reciprocation as a condition, such as the withdrawal of its troops from Eastern Europe, or a radical reduction of its strategic arsenal, or fundamental reforms on human rights, or an unequivocal reorientation of its military doctrine from an offensive to a defensive posture. If any steps in these directions were to be taken by Moscow they would be welcome. But if they were not taken this should not be seen as evidence of a failure in our non-nuclear policy, as long as the Soviet Union did not reciprocate negatively, by behaving more aggressively. Since the latter behaviour would be counter-productive for Moscow, it would probably be avoided. If the Soviet leaders want a genuine and long-term relaxation of tension between the super powers, they will have to reciprocate at least negatively.

Any far-reaching reciprocation is unlikely until the Soviet Union becomes quite confident that military conflict between the systems is not a serious possibility. We are a long way from that, though let us not forget how far Soviet attitudes have evolved in the last seventy years, from Lenin's belief in the inevitable clash between the systems to Khrushchev's 1956 declaration that war is no longer 'fatalistically inevitable'. Nevertheless, in the light of the terrible history suffered by the Russian nation, old insecurities towards technologically more-advanced nations will obviously not be eradicated quickly. Unfortunately, the confrontational style of the Reagan administration has not helped what George F. Kennan called the 'mellowing' process in Soviet Russia. It might take thirty years of reassurance before Moscow feels confident enough about Soviet security to adopt a significantly relaxed military stance. In the meantime, if Soviet leaders wish to waste resources on military over-insurance, that is their economic and possibly political problem.

Even if the Soviet Union did begin to bluster in Europe, following a winding-down of NATO's nuclear destructive power, what actually would they do? Threats across the East–West divide are empty, because the use of force will continue to carry heavy and unpredictable risks. Any Soviet posturing in this respect can be ignored. What the West needs are strong nerves. Stalin is one model, in the face of the US atomic monopoly. And Tito – in a situation where force was more usable than across the East–West divide today – is another. The West has little to fear from Soviet bluster; it has strength, self-confidence and margin for manoeuvre.

There is a final reason why positive reciprocation should be de-emphasised, that is, why Britain should not demand exactly balanced Soviet cuts in direct return for the scrapping of Trident. Britain of course should try to encourage benevolent Soviet behaviour, but to demand symmetrical cuts as opposed to negative reciprocation would allow Soviet leaders to exercise a veto (by non-compliance) on what is best for British security. We should not allow an unrealistic expectation about the Soviet Union's ability to reciprocate to be a condition for our moving our own defence posture in a sensible non-nuclear direction. We should not regard our existing nuclear weapons as bargaining chips with the Soviet Union in this matter. While one understands the old adage in international politics that one should never give up something for nothing, the 'something' Britain should give up in this case is a cost rather than a benefit; it is a problem rather than a solution.

Notes

1. Bernard Williams, 'Morality, Scepticism and the Nuclear Arms Race', pp. 99–114 in Nigel Blake and Kay Pole (ed.), *Objections to Nuclear Defence* (London: Routledge & Kegan Paul, 1984).
2. Anthony Kenny, 'Better Dead than Red', pp. 12–27, ibid.
3. McGeorge Bundy, 'Existential Deterrence And Its Consequences', pp. 3–13 in Douglas Maclean (ed.) *The Security Gamble* (Totowa, N.J.: Rowman and Allanhead, 1984). According to Bundy, 'existential deterrence' is not based on strategic theory or declaratory policy. It occurs because of the existence of very large numbers of nuclear weapons which could be used against an opponent. This creates a powerful uncertainty, and is relatively unaffected by changes in arsenals or declared intentions.
4. See Ken Booth, 'New Challenges And Old Mindsets: Ten Rules for Empirical Realists', in Carl G. Jacobsen (ed.), *The Uncertain Course: New Weapons, Strategies, And Mind-Sets* (Oxford: Oxford University Press for SIPRI, 1987).

5. Bernard Brodie, 'The Development of Nuclear Strategy', *International Security*, Vol. 2 (4), Spring 1978, p. 83.
6. Alternative Defence Commission, *Defence Without the Bomb* (London: Taylor & Francis, 1983).
7. Ibid.
8. Bernard Brodie, *War and Politics*, pp. 274–5.
9. This is elaborated in Booth, 'New Challenges and Old Mindsets', op. cit.
10. This is elaborated in Ken Booth, 'Nuclear Deterrence and "World War III": How will History Judge?', pp. 251–82 in Roman Kolkowicz (ed.), *The Logic of Nuclear Terror* (Boston: Allen and Unwin, 1987).
11. *The Economist*, 9 May 1987.
12. See Malcolm Chalmers, *The 1987 Defence Budget: Time for Choice?* Peace and Research Report No. 17 (University of Bradford: School of Peace Studies, May 1987).
13. *The Economist*, 9 May 1987.
14. Michael Clarke, *The Alternative Defence Debate: Non-Nuclear Defence Policies for Europe* ADIU Occasional Paper No. 3 (University of Sussex, ADIU, August 1985), p. 53.
15. Figures quoted from the House of Commons Defence Committee, p. 2 in Colin McInnes, 'The UK Trident programme: Problems and Prospect', unpublished paper, presented at PSA Conference, Aberdeen, May 1987.
16. Ibid., p. 5.
17. Oxford Research Group, *Do It Yourself, Minister. Implementing a non-nuclear defence policy in a nuclear world* (Oxford Research Group: Woodstock, Oxon, 1987), pp. 81–4.
18. The poll was based on a nationwide sample, and was conducted by Abt Associates Cambridge, Mass. Reported in *New Society*, 25 October 1984.
19. *Observer*, 23 November 1986.
20. See *Defence and Security for Britain*, pp. 23–4.
21. Rober W. Komer, *Maritime Strategy or Coalition Defense?* (Cambridge, Mass.: Abt Books, 1984), p. 7.
22. A Senator in the Belgian Parliament, referring to British troops in Germany said: 'If the British go, the Belgians go.' Quoted by Frederick Bonnart, 'Troops are needed to maintain credibility', *The Times*, 14 December 1982.
23. Oxford Research Group, *Do It Yourself, Minister*, op. cit., pp. 2–26.
24. Clarke, *The Alternative Defence Debate*, op. cit., pp. 18–19.
25. This analogy is discussed in Ken Booth, 'Unilateralism; A Clausewitzian Reform?', pp. 68–70 in Nigel Blake and Kay Pole (eds), *Dangers of Deterrence* (London: Routledge & Kegan Paul, 1983).
26. Field Marshal Lord Carver, *A Policy for Peace* (London: Faber & Faber 1982).
27. Jeff McMahan, *British Nuclear Weapons, For and Against* (London: Junction Books, 1981), p. 41.
28. Below, p. 262.

29. below, p. 264.
30. McMahan, *British Nuclear Weapons*, op. cit., pp. 137–8.
31. Ibid.
32. An exception to this is a book which came out after this chapter was first written: Richard K. Betts, *Nuclear Blackmail and Nuclear Balance* (Washington D.C.: The Brookings Institution, 1987). It is a book about nuclear 'diplomacy' rather than 'blackmail' as more narrowly conceived in this chapter; in terms of the way blackmail is defined here, Betts's findings did not lead to the need for any revision in the argument as originally presented.
33. Ibid, pp. 40–7, 83–5, 137–8, 145–6, and McMahan's 'Nuclear blackmail', pp. 84–111 in Blake and Pole, *Dangers of Deterrence*; McGeorge Bundy, 'The unimpresive record of atomic diplomacy', pp. 42–54 in Gwyn Prins (ed.), *The Choice: Nuclear Weapons Versus Security* (London: Chatto and Windus, 1984); Betts, *Nuclear Blackmail and Nuclear Balance*, op. cit., p. 6.
34. McMahan, *British Nuclear Weapons*, p. 41, Betts, *Nuclear Blackmail*, op. cit., pp. 4, 6.
35. McMahan, *British Nuclear Weapons*, p. 41.
36. Thomas C. Schelling, *Arms and Influence* (New Haven: Yale University Press, 1966), pp. 69–91. Betts uses 'blackmail' to refer to threats which deter *or* compel, *Nuclear Blackmail*, op. cit., p. 4.
37. Betts has shown that nuclear threats were more prevalent in the first two decades of the postwar era than subsequently, and that those with a 'whiff of blackmail', as understood here, were the most ambiguous and least salient. However, he is not as confident that it will not return as is argued in this chapter: see, for example, Betts, *Nuclear Blackmail*, op. cit., p. 227.
38. Thomas C. Schelling, *The Strategy of Conflict* (Cambridge, Mass: Harvard University Press, 1960).
39. Stanley Hoffmann, *Primacy Or World Order* (New York: McGraw-Hill, 1987), p. 11 and Nye, 'Ethics and the nuclear future', *The World Today*, vol. 42 (8/9), August–September 1986, p. 153.
40. See Ken Booth, 'Nuclear Deterrence and the "World War III": How Will History Judge?', in Roman Kilkowicz (ed.), *The Logic of Nuclear Terror* (Boston: Allen & Unwin, 1987), pp. 251–82).
41. Quoted by Bundy, 'Existential Deterrence', op. cit., p. 11.
42. Quoted by Freeman Dyson, *Weapons and Hope* (New York: Harper & Row 1984), p. 284.
43. R. K. Betts, 'Elusive Equivalence: The Political and Military Meaning of the Nuclear Balance', in S. P. Huntington (ed.), *the Strategic Imperative: New Policies for American Security* (Cambridge, Mass: Ballinger, 1982).
44. Ibid.
45. Bundy, 'The unimpressive record of atomic diplomacy', op. cit. Betts gives some support to this thesis in relation to compellent threats, finding the evidence in relation to Korea only circumstantial and in relation to Indo-China and the offshore islands weak. See Betts, *Nuclear Blackmail*, op. cit., pp. 44, 48.

46. George F. Kennan, *The Nuclear Delusion: Soviet–American Relations in the Atomic Age* (London: Hamish Hamilton, 1984), p. 32.
47. Bundy, 'Existential Deterrence', p. 6; and Adam Roberts, *Nations in Arms* (London: Macmillan, 1986).
48. *Guardian*, 14 April 1986.

Conclusion

The Cold War might be over; we might have won it; and in Europe today we might have a high degree of order. But that is not enough. Although the peace we now enjoy is based on relatively settled political arrangements and growing economic interaction between East and West, it is also characterised by a concentration of sheer destructive power unprecedented in world history. Some of that military power will remain necessary for the foreseeable future, as a reminder of the futility of war between industrialised and interdependent societies; but a major part of it, the nuclear stockpile, has now become disfunctional. During the Cold War years the accumulation of nuclear weapons discouraged mistrustful ideological adversaries from undertaking incautious steps. Today, the continuing nuclear arms race perpetuates anachronistic ways of thinking, provides through fear the most likely cause of war between the blocs, and prohibits the evolution of a stable peace.

The arguments in the preceding chapters have suggested ways of changing the dangerous features of the European situation. A truly stable peace as defined in Chapter 1 is a long way off; however, we could achieve a legitimate international order in Europe within 15–30 years, as a stepping-stone. But whatever the timescale, we cannot hope to see real peace in practice unless we first believe it possible in theory. Image and reality are interdependent. We cannot simply wish war away; nor can we achieve real peace without first imagining that it can happen.

We are living in a period of slow but spectacular change in international affairs. The postwar era is visibly breaking up. The conventional wisdom that created and sustained those years still grips the minds of most policy-makers in most countries, but the gap is increasingly evident between what they say and what is really happening. To a growing number of people in the East and West of Europe, and in the super powers, the clichés of the era of black-and-white television (and politics) are no longer tenable.

Cold War thinking and behaviour is out of touch with a world of complex interdependence. In a post-Clausewitzian Europe the coexistence of the blocs is increasingly recognised as an imperative; the widespread public welcome to the INF agreement was a clear reflection of the general desire to live together rather than escalate dangerous and wasteful confrontations. The accumulation of nuclear overkill is coming to be widely seen, by experts as well as the public at large, as much as a problem as a solution in East–West relations. In the West extended deterrence is progressively criticised as having had its day, while strategies of so-called Flexible Response and limited nuclear options are believed to be both dangerous and incredible. The strength of the US nuclear guarantee to Europe appears to be decreasing. The loyalty of the allies to the defence of the West remains strong, but the shape of NATO is not so sacrosanct. Both super powers are experiencing an overstretch of their military and political power; they are decreasingly influential even in their own spheres. Countries are catching up economically, and in some areas overtaking the United States. Few countries even want to copy the Soviet Union. The West of Europe has become a stronger and more independent voice in economic and political affairs, if not in defence. The two Germanies try to coexist, even when super power relations become chilly. Regimentation in international affairs is decreasing and orientations are changing. The United States is less concerned with Europe than it was, while Western Europe is somewhat less Atlanticist. For growing numbers of people in both pillars of NATO the image of overwhelming Warsaw pact military superiority, encouraged by unbridled Soviet ambition, is no longer convincing; for them, as a result, the controlling nightmare of a Soviet military land-grab westwards is a thing of the past. The Soviet Union is itself changing; it is striving to emerge not just from Stalinism but from even deeper cultural and other habits. Its leaders understand that they cannot create even a moderately successful society without first winding down the enormous military burden they have carried since the war. The economies of both super powers are under strain, and who gets what in this changing international environment is more often determined by economic and political success than by military rankings. And in that respect a significant shift is taking place in the international political economy towards the Pacific basin. In sum, the first postwar era has virtually run its course. Nevertheless, although the Cold War might be brain-dead, its powerful muscles, as mentioned earlier, can still twitch dangerously. Official mindsets are naturally conservative and for some time the problems of today and tomorrow will be met by yesterday's answers. But rational policy in this changing environment requires alternative ways of thinking, to take advantage of the opportunities and to minimise the inevitable risks. Nowhere are alternative ways of thinking at a greater premium than in the always-critical area of security.

Alternative defence strategies seek ways by which Europe might emerge from these interesting times with more security. The policies offered in Part I have rejected the idea that we are doomed to more-of-the-same; but they have not been based on utopian expectations about the way nations behave. Unlike standard deterrence theory the proposals indicated a way forward: unlike some anti-nuclear thinking, the journey began in the actual world, not in the realms of wishful thinking. This mixture of realism and reform risks being criticised from the doctrinaire right on the ground that it is too radical, and from the doctrinaire left on the ground that it is too embedded in traditional power-political ways of looking at the world. Between these extremes there exists a growing body of sophisticated realists and pragmatic idealists who will recognise the outline of a defence policy which is both feasible and desirable, and which offers the best hope of achieving the end we all share, that of living passably free of the threat of being either dead or red.

It is hoped that the package of ideas put forward in Part I will appeal to that large group presently dissatisfied with the attitudes that inform British defence policy. Support for the package might be expected from individuals in the centre and right of the Labour Party, among many of the effectively disenfranchised Liberal and Social Democrat voters, and even among those Conservatives who favour a less nuclear and more independent posture. A non-nuclear and non-provocative defence policy should appeal to what may be the growing centre of British politics – in the election after next, if not the next. By the early 1990s, following more than a decade of 'conviction politics', Britain will be more than due for a move to the centre, and in defence terms the centre will undoubtedly be to the 'left' of the postwar consensus.

As the postwar era comes to an end, symbolised by the shabby decline and hollow public relations of Reaganism on the one hand, and the promise of Gorbachev and new thinking about common security on the other, the ideas and assumptions that characterised British defence policy from the Attlee years to those of Thatcher appear to be increasingly anachronistic. Significantly, in the 1987 general election, those who spoke for the government failed to offer any interesting ideas on the future of East–West relations. Their menu was the reheated gruel of old and simpler times. By the next election, short of some unpredictable developments in the international scene, this menu will be even less attractive to the British public, and as it was, more people voted against the government in

1987 than for it. If super power relaxation and arms restraint gather pace, and if demands on resources make defence spending more contentious, then the anti-Soviet instincts loudly and proudly proclaimed by the government through the 1980s will seem even more out of touch in the early 1990s. The logic of British security policy points towards a future strategy which is less nuclear and more conventional and a future diplomacy which is less deferential to the United States and more conscious of the interdependence of the whole of Europe.

RECIPROCAL SECURITY

Historically, the search for national security has often been self-defeating. The interplay between national mistrust and the action-reaction process of weapons-acquisition has resulted in greater national 'strength', but not necessarily greater national security. When one country has attempted to increase its security over another, by accumulating military power, the insecurity of the targeted country has grown. International security is clearly not enhanced if major powers feel edgy and vulnerable. The insecure in any society are never the easiest to handle.

Because we have the destructive power to wipe out the Soviet Union as an effective industrial society, and they have the destructive power to wipe out us, and because neither of us has a guaranteed defensive capability in sight, national security is no longer possible in the traditional sense. We cannot simply equate national strength measured in destructive power and national security. For the foreseeable future, feeling safe and being safe can only come through relationships characterised by mutual commitments between states to conduct their relationships without the threat or use of force. This condition might be described as one of common or reciprocal security.[1] It is a notion which is gaining ground in every country.

Reciprocal behaviour designates a relationship in which something is given by each of two parties; there is mutual and conscious interaction in a particular direction. Between individuals there is reciprocal friendship, and between countries there is reciprocal trade. Reciprocity (at least in the negative sense discussed in the last chapter) should also be the objective in the security policies of the major powers, since national security in the old sense is impossible. Reciprocity implies the mutual exchange of privileges, and in the late twentieth century the greatest privilege which nations can exchange is that of security – the fundamental right to exist, independently, and free of the risk of genocide or domination. The achievement of such a goal should place arms restraint, including denuclearisation, at the top of the agenda of European security problems.

Nuclear deterrence cannot promise a long-term answer to the management of European security affairs. It is an essentially static dogma. Indeed, by assuming that nuclear war is effectively impossible, it discourages serious efforts to sort out the very problems that some of us believe might actually bring about a nuclear war. Nuclear deterrence is supposed to discourage direct aggression, and invariably will, but it does so with an inevitable accompaniment of technological innovation and arms-racing which sustain, and from time-to-time increase to breaking-point, the very tension which might in a Sarajevo-like crisis bring about that catastrophic breakdown nobody wants. As practised, therefore, nuclear deterrence cobbles together short terms, but fails to provide – in fact obstructs – any long-term programme of peace and security. The way we have conducted the nuclear arms race actually reduces the prospects for turning a confrontation checked by permanent fear (and therefore permanent insecurity) into a stable peace. In order to change this, denuclearisation should be placed at the centre of East–West relations. If it is not, the nuclear confrontation will continue to exercise an irrational influence on everybody's ideas about what is important and what should be done.

Denuclearisation should not mean trying to achieve the complete elimination of nuclear weapons across the globe as an immediate objective. This latter prospect is so distant at this stage in international relations that it represents a distraction from what might usefully be achieved, namely, reducing the prominence of nuclear weapons in the super power relationship as an essential step towards placing that relationship on a more rational footing. The complete elimination of nuclear devices does not begin even to be a feasible goal until we have achieved a legitimate international order characterised by reciprocal security. Even then it might prove to be impossible. Nevertheless, our inability to remove the last few hundred missiles from the inventory of the super powers is not a sound argument for refusing to reduce their numbers such that they cease to be what is erroneously called 'war-fighting' instruments. The fewer they are, as long as they are invulnerable, the more merely symbolic they will become. Denuclearisation seeks to change the character and deployment of nuclear weapons, and the associated doctrines, in a decreasingly less threatening direction. For the foreseeable future we must accept the existence of mutual assured destruction between the super powers. Even if the INF agreement manages to stimulate progress in START, and results in deep cuts of 50 per cent, the number of nuclear warheads available to the super powers will still be greater than at the time of SALT I, when mutual assured destruction was codified, and almost everybody knew that there was more than enough overkill for unacceptable damage. The first major aim of denuclearisation is not the complete eradication of nuclear weapons, therefore, but the adoption of minimum deterrent strategies by the super powers, since these represent the least provocative nuclear postures presently achievable.

Arms restraint is necessary if we are to progress towards a legitimate international order, and there is no shortage of ideas on the agenda for winding down the nuclear confrontation. It is through progress here that we should ultimately judge the success of the INF agreement. The following proposals have been the most prominent: a comprehensive nuclear test ban; the adoption of a no-first-use nuclear posture (or at least a no-early-first-use as a preliminary step); a super power nuclear freeze as a step towards deep cuts; increased efforts to inhibit nuclear proliferation; the prevention of the growth of weapons competition in space; the exercising of unilateral and if possible, multilateral restraints in technological innovation (especially with destabilising systems such as MIRVs), the strengthening of conventional deterrence options to raise the nuclear threshold; the progressive withdrawal of battlefield nuclear weapons from the forward zones on the Central Front; the pursuit of confidence-building measures; the creation of both political and military fail-safe devices (crisis-control centres and effective command and control systems); and movement away from strategic doctrines involving pre-emption, launch-on-warning, decapitation strikes, and 'victory' towards doctrines where retaliation is a last step not a first step, is gradual rather than massive, and is based on what is considered sufficient for a 'minimum' deterrent rather than what is thought necessary for war-fighting. Progress in these areas would help transform East–West relations. By pushing the nuclear arms race from the centre stage, it would help us see more clearly what divides us and what has to be done in order to coexist with more safety.

There is much on the arms control agenda in addition to denuclearisation. Chemical and conventional weapons are troublesome in different degrees for different governments. Proposals are likely to proliferate, and if the apparent flexibility evident in the later stages of the INF talks was more than image-manipulation, then more positive results can be expected than anything hitherto. If the Soviet Union of Mr Gorbachev really wants to impress the West with its good intentions, he can do nothing better than reduce Soviet conventional force levels in Eastern Europe and especially those with an 'offensive' character (such as tanks and bridge-building equipment). Almost at a stroke he could do a great deal to disarm Western suspicion, without any diminution of Soviet security *vis-à-vis* NATO. The more acceptably 'defensive' the Warsaw Pact's posture is seen in the West, the less provocative it will be and so the less suspicious will be the subsequent relationship. As was indicated in Chapter 1, there are glimmers that the Soviet Union is well aware of this and may, for the first time, try to do something about it.

The earlier discussion pointed to some positive features on the security scene, and indicated more than a few signposts ahead. Nevertheless, progress in European security is bound to be slow because of the very complexity and importance of the issues, their interconnectedness and the depth of mutual mistrust between the actors. The INF agreement should not encourage incautious expectations. The weapons to be scrapped in that agreement are of marginal military significance and the global ban on launchers means that verification will be relatively simple. The next steps will be more taxing. Reaching agreements about what constitutes a 'fair balance' in the computation of relative conventional strength will be a mathematical as well as a political strain; and it will pose many verification problems. Not least of the problems facing the prospects for further arms rerstraint is that of linkage. This can subvert arms-control in two ways. On the one hand, as seems likely to happen in the ratification process of the INF Treaty, critics in the US Senate will want to tie their adherence to the agreement to 'acceptable' Soviet behaviour in areas such as the treatment of dissidents or Soviet withdrawal from Afghanistan. On the other hand, linkage can affect arms control negotiations in a less planned fashion. Events are periodically thrown up that subject super power relations to strain, as happened during SALT II, and these can have an intrusive and deleterious effect on the arms-control process. Even in the absence of such strains, in the background of talks about arms restraint the military–industrial complexes in both camps work to a different agenda; their slogans are 'modernisation', 'catching-up', 'keeping ahead', 'strength', 'deterrence'. Although a growing number of analysts in both East and West are rejecting old ways of looking at the problem of security, the old dogmas have a strong hold on those groups which control powerful sinews of state. This is as true in Britain as it is of other major military powers. Recent evidence does not suggest that the government of Mrs Thatcher will be in the forefront of those pressing for denuclearisation (such as the removal of battlefield nuclear weapons) or a slowing-down in the nuclear arms race (as would be achieved by the completion of a Comprehensive Test Ban Treaty). Unless there is a marked change of attitude, Britain will hinder rather than encourage further denuclearisation.

As is evident from the agenda of denuclearisation proposals listed earlier, a move by Britain to a non-nuclear strategy would comprise only one step towards what should be a less dangerous structure of East–West relations. But each step, however small, should be welcomed. Each step will make the next one easier and each country can do only a limited amount. Having said that, what Britain can do, both unilaterally and in consultation with others, could be significant because of its special position within the alliance. Nevertheless, we should not expect to achieve too much too quickly. Britain cannot itself hope to have much direct effect on the Soviet Union; our 'moral' lead in reducing the role of nuclear weapons in defence postures should therefore be concentrated upon persuading our allies of the desirability of reform. That in itself will be difficult enough, though over a time-scale of 15 years there is some reason for hope. In the years ahead the NATO old guard, brought up with Cold War dogma, will progressively retire. Somewhat more flexible minds should then be in position to deal with the new problems and opportunities of the second postwar era.

If, as recommended above, NATO shifts its emphasis towards the principles and policies of non-provocative defence, we can expect a satisfactory Soviet response in the area which most directly worries us, namely the military threat. The Soviet Union has shown under Gorbachev just how quickly and how far it is sometimes prepared to move, even unilaterally. Both Reagan and Thatcher have identified the present Soviet leader as somebody with whom the West can do business. Unfortunately his modern outlook and flexible approach might not last long. This is not to say that a return to the more conservative approach of his predecessors would be much more dangerous for us; but if we allowed this opportunity to put international security on a more positive footing to slip by, we would simply teach yet another group of Soviet leaders and opinion-formers that they cannot do business with the West. This is a likely consequence of the US government tying SDI and START, and of NATO pressing for compensations (or more euphemistically 'modernisation') in its nuclear systems in the aftermath of the INF agreement. Avoiding such messages being transmitted to the Gorbachev regime (and his domestic critics) requires positive action on our part within months, not years. His arms control proposals have been as far-reaching as any Westerner could have reasonably hoped, and thus further than any Westerner could have reasonably predicted. If the West fails to take advantage of the political window of opportunity opened up by Gorbachev, it could be many years before anything comparable presents itself. Before too long governments in the nuclear age should learn that they have more to gain from reaching out through favourable windows of opportunity than they have to fear from intruders bursting through windows of vulnerability.

In response to some of the hopes and benevolent trends discussed earlier, sceptics will say that each generation of 'liberals' in the West always believes that the Soviet Union is changing, and is thereby creating an opportunity to put our relationship on a predictably peaceful footing. Such hopes have been dashed, these sceptics argue, as often as they have arisen. The pattern will continue with Gorbachev, they insist. Without doubt there has been plenty of wishful thinking in the West but it does not follow that because unreasonable hopes were invested in (amazingly) Stalin and (more justifiably) Khrushchev, that we should not do serious business with Gorbachev. Significant changes are taking place within the USSR, not least in the reassessment of Soviet history. A regime willing to begin to face up to the ugly truth of its past is surely one in which it is rational to invest some hopes. Furthermore, it is not evident that the consequences of wishful thinking in the West have been in any degree worse than the consequences over the years of 'implicit enemy imaging' by Western hawks; and it is the latter who have dominated Western policy. As a result, we have never pursued a consistent and coherent policy of constructive engagement with the Soviet Union over any lengthy time-scale (say a decade) calculated to create a relationship of stable coexistence. We therefore do not know if *détente* will work, for it has never been tried properly. It took the protagonists many years to tie the knot of the East–West conflict, and it will take those who believe a safer relationship is possible many years to loosen it.

In addition to the factors just mentioned, change will be slow on the Western side because it is necessary to persuade establishment opinion of the value of different aims and methods in relation to the Soviet Union. It will be a difficult task to encourage our allies to begin a process of reducing the arms competition, the paranoia, the institutions of confrontation, and the militarisation of thinking which grew quite naturally out of the pressures and perceptions of the late 1940s. At the same time we should also try to encourage benevolent trends in the Soviet Union. In the first place this means moderate behaviour in its external behaviour (what was called 'negative reciprocation' in the previous chapter). Ultimately we naturally hope there will be more freedom within the Soviet Union, but we should not make fundamental changes in Soviet internal affairs either a requirement for a less confrontational posture on our part, or regard it as essential for a more stable relationship.

In his first years in office Mr Gorbachev has given abundant evidence that he is willing to act as a moderate member of the international community. Soviet actions in many regions of the world attest to this; one sign of the times has been the way he has signalled a new attitude to the United Nations. In the autumn of 1987 be proposed giving the UN a stronger role. He suggested extending the jurisdiction of the International Court, extending the Security Council's role in arms control verification, and creating a UN tribunal to investigate international terrorism. He later announced that the Soviet Union would pay all its outstanding debts to the UN. As a result of this initiative the Reagan administration was left as the UN's largest debtor; thus it is not only in arms restraint where the pace for better relations and a more orderly world is being set by Mr Gorbachev, and where Western leaders need to catch up.

Gorbachev may fall from power, falter or become preoccupied by domestic issues. He may fail to follow through what have so far largely been words. Even if these outcomes do materialise, the West has the power and should have the liberal instincts and confidence to pursue the logic of common security. Of the Western powers, Britain has most room for a major immediate step. A shift to a non-nuclear posture by Britain would help prime the pump of new security arrangements and would show – actions speaking louder than words – that arms restraint will not lead to disaster. Rather than continue the posture of the past forty years, which keep alive old fears, the adoption of the policies recommended in Part I of this book will help change the images we have of the 'realities' of the European security scene. At the present stage of history we are more frightened because we continue to amass military power to fight the Soviet Union than because of any clear belief that the Soviet Union will ever attack us. Before we can move towards more peaceful relations with the Soviet Union we need to live in greater peace with ourselves; this is extremely difficult for nuclear states. Whatever they do to the enemy, nuclear weapons undoubtedly frighten their possessors.

LIVING WITH SOVIET RUSSIA

Europe has not suffered a major war for over forty years, and prudential rules of behaviour have evolved. Even so, Europe remains some way from exhibiting the characteristics of a legitimate international order discussed in Chapter 3. There are governments and sections of opinion in both halves of the continent which believe their core values are under real threat; there are plenty of fears about unacceptable political intervention by the other side; war, though generally thought to be remote, is not entirely ruled out; and there are still doubts about the legitimacy of the Yalta framework. Germany, at the heart of the continent and, as so often in the last century, at the root of its insecurity problems, remains a divided nation. In terms of military technology, Europe exists in a post-Clausewitzian era – even 'conventional' war would not be rational – but politically speaking there are still sources of turmoil. Furthermore, it is doubtful whether Europe could exist over a long period as an island of order and peace while the world outside is rent by political discord and economic problems. Troubles have an instinct to hunt in packs.

A legitimate international order requires some reciprocity. For much of the last forty years reciprocity has led to insecurity – deliberately so – through a mixture of political confrontation and the belief that the surest way to peace is through the preparation for war. In a Europe emerging from the postwar era, reciprocity must be designed to produce reassurance rather than intimidation, and constructive engagement rather than fear. Reciprocity and reassurance are not entirely alien ideas in strategic life, even between adversaries. Both mutual assured destruction and arms-control grew out of the insight that the nuclear age had created interdependence in insecurity, and therefore the need for formal and tacit arrangements to create a situation of tolerable mutual security. If such ideas could germinate in the depths of the Cold War, several decades of living together and learning about our predicament ought to encourage further thoughts about the advantages and mechanics of reciprocity. Why should we undergo the dangers and waste of interdependence in insecurity when a more stable peace beckons? In order to pursue the latter objective with some hope of success, several shifts in attitude must take place:

First, before we can have a legitimate international order we must regard and treat the Soviet Union as a legitimate member of international society. This does not mean that we must shut our eyes to any militant behaviour outside its borders or ignore oppressive behaviour within. Rather, it means accepting that geography gives it legitimate interests in various sensitive regions such as the Middle East, that its power gives it certain expectations, and that its history may have taught it security habits that are not to our liking, but are not necessarily signs of hostility. We must not treat Soviet Russia, over seventy years after the revolution, as a virus or bandit in international society. Soviet leaders are naturally annoyed when we do. Significantly, Gorbachev raised this very issue in Washington in December 1987.[2] After being lectured by President Reagan about human rights and religion, the displeased Soviet leader retorted that his country was not in a courtroom, that the President was not a prosecutor and that he himself was not a defendant. How can Soviet leaders feel more secure until the West changes such attitudes?

Second, nuclear deterrence must be taken away from the centre of our thinking about European security and super power relations.[3] As was pointed out in earlier chapters, scepticism about pro-nuclear postures has grown significantly in recent years. Hardly anybody has been left unaffected; even the most committed supporters of nuclear deterrence now express some doubts, where previously there had been none. Overcoming forty years of nuclear dependence will not be easy, but there are hopeful signs that deterrence is being delegitimatised. President Reagan has played a part in this, through his justifications of Star Wars and in his pronouncements at Reykjavik. The 'double-zero' agreement represents another blow to established deterrence thinking. It flies in the face of dogmas such as 'coupling', 'guarantees', 'shared risks', the 'seamless web of deterrence', 'options' and 'flexibility'. The INF agreement could well spill over in people's perceptions, and lead to a wider recognition of the wasteful and dangerous irrelevance of nuclear overkill. When coexistence replaces deterrence as the central concern in East–West relations, we will be well on the path towards a legitimate international order.

Third, we must recognise that Western security does not grow in direct proportion to the rise of Soviet insecurity. The history of the postwar years suggests the opposite. The periods of greatest danger since the war have not been periods when the Soviet Union has felt relatively comfortable (the late 1950s or the early 1970s) but rather when the United States has been aggressively strong and the Soviet Union has felt pushed into a corner, fearing that time might be running out (the late 1940s, the early 1960s, and the early 1980s). It is not true, as White House spokesmen have claimed, that the confrontational strategy identified with President Reagan has made for a safer world. What made for at least the basis of a safer super power relationship in the latter part of the 1980s was not the confrontational posturing of the early Reagan years but the dawning realisation that it was wasteful and counter-productive.

Four, we should give much more attention to the development of political and military confidence-building measures in our relationship with the Soviet Union. We must not become obsessed by operational military strategy, taking actions that we think might give us an edge in war, yet only exacerbate relations in peacetime. We must assume that an absence of war, rather than war, is a more likely future in East–West relations. Together with learning to accept the Soviet Union's right to existence, we should also get away from the idea that nuclear war with the Soviet Union could ever, in any circumstances, be an acceptable instrument of policy.[4] We must therefore reject fundamentalist beliefs that see us in an eschatological conflict with an 'evil empire' and fatalistic beliefs that 'Armageddon' is inevitable.[5] When such beliefs in the United States have been associated with the weapons and doctrines for 'prevailing' in nuclear war (such as the development of highly accurate counterforce systems and ballistic missile defence) it is no wonder that Soviet policymakers have been anxious. Prevailing has been the thrust of US strategy in the Reagan years, though achievement has lagged far behind intentions. Prevailing is a dangerous strategic conceit, especially when allied with notions of inevitability: leaders may be tempted to think about pre-emption or preventive attack. Presumably 'evil empires' should be destroyed when windows of opportunity present themselves. It has not only been Soviet observers in the Reagan years who have feared that US strategy has largely been a rationalisation of extreme right-wing prejudice. It remains to be seen whether the next president(s) will have different instincts. But if they reject such thinking they should build reassurance into military planning as opposed to arms racing, intimidation, pre-emption or, in the extreme, preventive war thinking. Pre-emption, nuclear first-use, or preventive attack should be ruled out in planning and made improbable by technology. They are, to paraphrase Bismarck, like threatening to commit suicide in order to avoid death.

Five, in order to develop a relationship of reciprocal security with the Soviet Union we must be prepared to undertake unilateral as well as multilateral actions. Both tactics have their place. We must also have the nerve to take some risks, and to anticipate failures as well as successes. We have done this with policies of confrontation and arms competition in the past. We should now show that we can take tough decisions and stick with them when it comes to creating a security system based on politics rather than intimidation. In the 1970s we did not give *détente* a chance. The United States exaggerated the threat represented by Soviet behaviour, and defected too soon.

Finally, although we have learned a good deal since the late 1940s, we need to know much more about the Soviet Union. Britain does not set a good example in this respect. Nobody looking for insights into Soviet foreign or defence policy would ever think of listening to a House of Commons debate, for example. The situation is even worse in the United States. Swings of opinion about the Soviet Union take place not because of changes in the objective situation, but because of domestic politics and excessive subjectivity. To point to widespread ignorance is not to endorse any simple argument that the problems that have developed since the war, or even since 1917, have simply been the product of a lack of knowledge and understanding. Rather it represents common-sense advice that the better we understand Soviet society the more likely we will know how to behave constructively. Our strategies should have a human face rather than being the products of prejudice and irrational fears of the unknown. It is surely not a coincidence that Western Soviet specialists have been far more relaxed, on the whole, than have Western politicians about Soviet strategic intentions and capabilities over the years. To the regret of the experts, political power in the West in the 1980s has rested in the hands of congenital anti-Soviets; this has nourished the militarised attitudes of the Cold War, and has created more wasted years. The vaunted 'realism' of the extreme right has not been the result of empirical analysis; it is ideology-in-action. The partial steps by Margaret Thatcher and Ronald Reagan in the second half of the

1980s towards a more businesslike approach to the Soviet Union is welcome; but the depth of their conversion remains to be tested, and we do not know whether President Reagan will be replaced by an even less flexible fundamentalist. The continuing strength of anti-Soviet feeling was clearly evident in President Reagan's reassertion, during Gorbachev's visit to Washington, of his belief that the Soviet Union remained an 'evil empire'; even so, the treaty-signing President was himself attacked by right-wing critics on the grounds that his arms control policy showed him to be one of the Kremlin's 'useful idiots'.[6]

As has been stressed above, achieving reciprocal security requires us to change attitudes; it is not simply a matter of adjusting policies. The 'threat' is not simply Soviet intentions and capabilities; it is also in our own minds. We are frightened because we have nuclear weapons and we have nuclear weapons because we are frightened. It will therefore be difficult to shift the emphasis of our relations with the Soviet Union from the obsessive interest in the nuclear confrontation to the building blocks of coexistence, such as trade and diplomatic relations. In the last chapter it was argued that the Soviet Union might not always reciprocate in these areas as much as we hope (for example on human rights) but what matters most for us is that it does not reciprocate in any negative fashion. Positive peace will not break out on the day the INF agreement is ratified (if it is) or on the day Britain decides to cancel Trident. Peace is a process, not an event: and there will be both ups and downs. Process utopians understand this, and should not let setbacks deflect them. We are fortunate in that we have a considerable margin of safety in a post-Clausewitzian Europe; the likelihood of a coldly calculated war between NATO and the Soviet Union should be ruled out in the daily discourse of East–West security affairs. The livelihood of too many people are invested in thinking about the opposite course to allow this to happen easily.

If the Soviet flag were to fly over London within the next thirty years, or if Soviet missiles were to fly westwards, the chances are that the present Politburo would be even more surprised than us. The risk we face is one of a 'contingent' rather than 'intrinsic' Soviet decision for war.[7] An aggressive war against the West, soberly calculated, is unlikely to be an integral part of Soviet planning: an attack would be conceivable, though, in response to an overwhelming fear in a crisis that NATO was about to attack, or as a result of a contagious war in the Third World, or in the chaotic circumstances of a collapse of Soviet power in Eastern Europe. Scenarios can be envisaged where an edgy leadership, which in normal circumstances would entirely eschew the nuclear option, might be pressed to decide the opposite: 'it's now or never'; 'we've no choice'; 'we can't back down'.

Western defence establishments have prepared for the least likely contingency – a premeditated Soviet act of aggression – but they have ignored the more likely (though still remote) contingency of a 'nuclear Sarajevo'. In addition, while criticising anti-nuclear supporters for 'alarmism', these self-appointed 'realists' in the West – those who pride themselves on understanding man's gloomy past – seem least able to conceive a loss of rationality at tense moments. This is understandable. To do so would mean conceding that nuclear deterrence theory is least applicable when it is most needed. The chances of avoiding any collapse will be improved if we can continue to reverse some of the strategic and political fundamentalism of the last ten years, and instead shift towards strategies of long-term coexistence rather than confrontation. Reciprocal security seeks to minimise the occasions when any leader might persuade himself, or herself, that firing nuclear weapons is the rational thing to do. Those occasions will only occur when and if nuclear decision-makers decide either that they want to eradicate the other society, and feel confident enough to do it, or they feel frighteningly insecure, and believe that the only sensible move is to attack first. The deployment of Star Wars would place us on a slippery slope in both these directions.

Without doubt, some of the requirements for reciprocal security fly in the face of traditional Soviet strategic culture, which is unilateralist and mistrustful. But is also flies in the face of Western military ways of thinking. Against this there are progressive forces in both societies, as is evident in the growing support for common security. In the West we tend to think of the Soviet Union as inflexible, but leaving aside Gorbachev's 'new thinking', we have seen in the last thirty years the amendment of Soviet thinking about the inevitability of war, war as a continuation of politics (as a reasonable instrument, as opposed to a cause) and the value of the idea of superiority. Gorbachev's 'new thinking' challenges other traditional outlooks and is indeed a direct echo of Western thinking about common security.[8] Even if there were to be some regression on the Soviet side, there remain enough shared ideas about the imperatives of the nuclear age to justify perseverance towards coexistence on our part.

In the 1980s fundamentalist beliefs about the inevitability of clashes between the systems have come from the political right in the United States rather than the deradicalised Leninists in the Kremlin.

If traditional left-wing Soviet ideology on the inevitability of war between the systems changed in 1956, cannot traditional right-wing American ideology change over thirty years later? The international system is a trap or a potential tragedy, not an eschatological drama between Good and Evil. We should behave accordingly. This does not mean that we have to believe that the Soviet Union is a benevolent force in international politics, and it does not mean that we have to defer to Soviet power. As long as we maintain a robust defence, as discussed earlier, Soviet military power is effectively unusable. Having said that, the Soviet Union will continue to be a difficult country with which to deal. As in the past, by its words and actions, it will sometimes feed our worst fears. It is then that we need to keep our sights on our long-term objectives, and stick to a coherent and positive strategy of coexistence. It is important therefore to make the most of the opportunities that present themselves, such as the opening up of the situation as a result of Gorbachev's reconstruction, at home and abroad.

It has taken several generations (if not all the time since 1917) to get where we are now in East–West relations; so we should not expect a short or trouble-free ride towards a legitimate international order in Europe. On the contrary, we should expect some backwards steps. Though disappointing, the latter should not be allowed to cause a change of direction. Such a lack of persistence led to the decline of *détente* in the 1970s. No Soviet behaviour during that period in the fields of arms control, policy in the Third World or weapons modernisation was dangerously threatening or outside the then crude norms of coexistence. The West could have countered those Soviet actions which it thought needed countering by less costly and more successful methods than those chosen; we could, for example, have weaned Angola from its relationship with the Soviet Union by economic and diplomatic methods, and still not defected from *détente*. The laudable effort to engage the Soviet Union in cooperative ventures made by Nixon and Kissinger in the early 1970s floundered on their country's need for instant gratification, even in diplomacy. The long-term commitment essential for an effective 'western philosophy of coexistence'[9] was missing. Without consistency it is obviously impossible to achieve and sustain a successful relationship.

Success requires that both Western and Soviet societies adopt a mutual commitment to the restrained norms implied by a legitimate international order. We can be more hopeful now than in the early

1980s, but it is far from plain sailing ahead. Indeed, there is some danger in overselling the change in climate signalled by the INF agreement and the contribution of Gorbachev. This danger is directly comparable with the situation in 1972, when SALT 1 and *détente* was oversold. As the years following 1972 showed that the daily stuff of international politics had not much changed, and when events occurred that magnified the differences between the super powers, there was a backlash against *détente*. If faith in cooperation disappears, cost/benefit calculations change when governments come to make decisions concerning the speed and character of weapon innovation, whether or not to ratify arms control agreements, or whether to intervene militarily in regional conflicts.

Implicit enemy imaging needs to be replaced by an explicit commitment to live together and progressively reduce the risks of war. If we step back, we should see that there is more in common between East and West than we sometimes think. Not least is the mutual desire to avoid nuclear disaster. We also have in common the dilemmas of European security, the need to overcome economic difficulties, the problems of surviving in an unstable world, and trying to cope with Third World countries whose outlooks are sometimes more alien than those of our major ideological adversary.

We do not know if we can live in stable peace with the Soviet union. It has never been our goal, or theirs. But the parameters of the old relationships are changing fast. In any case, is there a rational alternative to working towards a legitimate international order? Either we do this, or we prepare to fight or we try to live indefinitely with a nuclear balance of terror. The latter is the choice of today's so-called realists. It involves a continuing risk of having one day to face that concatenation of events when history will take revenge on the absolute faith of those who believe that the unpredictable dynamics of the nuclear arms race can bring eternal peace.

WORLD ORDER BUILDING

British defence policy and the process of reciprocal security naturally must focus on Europe and the Soviet Union. We must begin from where we are: Europe is the most heavily-armed continent and the Soviet Union has us targeted. But a sensible defence policy will not obsessively focus on the 'threat'. Europe cannot remain a stable ship of peace and security if the seas all around are stormy.

The major powers in Europe at the start of the century could not live securely while the Balkans simmered. Today 'the Balkans' is a metaphor for the unstable politics of much of the Third World. The potential sources of future instability are numerous: economic collapse, nuclear proliferation, destabilising arms transfers, illegitimate political systems, and social and population pressures. Many countries find it difficult to cope. In a world where interdependence is likely to grow rather than the opposite, European security cannot be compartmentalised from Third World troubles. Building a more just and more stable world order is a matter of enlightened self-interest for the industrialised northern hemisphere.

When Europeans talk of 'forty years of peace' they are only talking about their patch of earth; they are ignoring the forty years of very different evidence across the globe as a whole. There it has been a period of instability and violence. Europe has so far been largely immune to this wider turmoil, though wars in the Middle East have hoisted storm warnings. The Middle East is the most dangerous point of contact between the wider world disorder and the so-far unexploded European arsenal. The image has sometimes been invoked of a tinderbox (Europe) and spark (Third World troubles). Attention obviously needs to be paid to the potential sparks, of which the Middle East is the most dangerous.

The subject of Third World dangers is too large to be dealt with here. Reducing them involves, among other things, encouraging nation-building and nuclear free zones and discouraging foreign military intervention. These steps in themselves could also have a major impact on the East–West arms race.[10] The promotion of such measures would contribute more to the stability of Europe – and so to British security – than the purchase of Trident. Again, the reaction of the British government to this dimension of the security problem through the 1980s, including the 1987 election campaign, has been negative. Its stress on the supreme national advantages of possessing an independent nuclear deterrent is calculated to encourage rather than stem nuclear proliferation, while its erosion of Britain's contribution to overseas development since 1979 weakens the cause of nation-building in the Third World. One can exaggerate the extent to which peace and security across the world are interdependent, but it would be an even graver mistake to ignore the image of the tinderbox and spark altogether, or to believe, in Chamberlain-like fashion, that we have little interest in far-away-countries-about-which-we-know-nothing. We have an interest in limiting conflicts and resolving crises not only for the sake of the locals, but also to contain the risks of escalation. A legitimate international offer cannot develop in Europe as long as the super powers are tempted to battle for unilateral advantage among the opportunities thrown up by the instabilities of the Third World. As long as these problems exist some degree of linkage is always likely. The struggle in the Third World was one of the reasons for the collapse of *détente* in the 1970s. Future problems there could undermine the present tentative steps to better super power relations.

It was said in the 1930s that 'wars don't start nowadays because people want them, but because the world order has failed.'[11] This was something of an exaggeration fifty years ago, since the dictators relished the prospect of victorious wars. But today it is different, certainly in the industrialised world, and in many cases beyond. Unfortunately, world order remains fragile, and the 1980s did nothing to strengthen it. Attitudes of every-man-for-himself have replaced internationalism. International organisations have lost drive, while ideas such as the 'New International Economic Order', or the deep seabed as the 'Common Heritage of Mankind' have disappeared from the political agenda. Neither the United States of Ronald Reagan nor the Britain of Margaret Thatcher have shown any evidence of sympathy towards the nations of the Third World. Essentially, the free enterprise attitudes that have informed their responses to domestic problems have been simply projected onto the wider stage. The collapse of Reaganism, with its narrowly self-interested approach to world affairs might open up opportunities for internationalism that the collapse of Brezhnevism in the Soviet Union created for arms control. Unless, of course, Reagan is succeeded by an even less globally-minded president.

International institutions have established a solid foothold in the international system. And while it may be unfashionable to say so, the principles of the United Nations remain a valid basis for the evolution of international security, especially where they effect the inter-related issues of peace-keeping, super power non-intervention and nation-building. Typical of the mood of the 1980s, the idea of a UN naval force in the Gulf in 1987 was not given the attention it deserved. Preoccupations with super power competition took precedence over world order building. Britain could make a much bigger contribution to the latter. British nuclear disarmament itself would do little directly to address the wider world problems, except in two respects. It would contribute somewhat to strengthening the nuclear non-proliferation regime and it ought to lead to a general downgrading of the image of the Soviet threat. The benefits of limiting nuclear proliferation are obvious. Downgrading the Soviet threat would help clarify the real issues in the Third World and so help the achievement of more successful policies. The Soviet Union is not the source of the problems in the Third World; nor has it been successful in relation to its aims and efforts. It is constrained, ideologically and economically, and opportunities for successful influence-building are not opening up across the globe. A more realistic image of Soviet Russia in the West would release our human and material resources for more effective policies both at home and abroad.

In order that Britain can pursue a more positive role in international affairs it first needs more independence from the United States. As was seen earlier, political independence is greatly constrained by defence dependence in general and nuclear dependence in particular. It could be that there will be US administrations with whom a British government committed to world order building could identify completely. But this will not always be the case; this was clearly evident in the way many Europeans could not identify with the new Cold War posturing of the Reagan administration in the Third World and elsewhere. In the years ahead we can expect US administrations to pursue policies in which Europe is less central in their concerns. So, the Western European allies (including Britain) will get the worst of both worlds if they do not create more independence for themselves; it will be very uncomfortable for them to be dependent on a United States which is less concerned about Europe. For Britain's part, it is surely not a coincidence that those political parties which have been least committed to a pro-nuclear defence posture have been the ones most critical of some of the simplistic visions and unsavoury activities of the Reagan administration. Nuclear dependence has helped create a psychological dependence.

British defence policy may have become regional, but its foreign policy should be global. In the latter respect, Britain's experience and expertise is a valuable asset which should not be ignored; what is lacking is an internationalist vision of security to replace the great power ambition of the past, and the slavish adherence of the present to the outlooks of the White House. The importance of world order building should not be overlooked even if Britain, for one reason or another, does not renounce nuclear weapons in the years ahead. As was just mentioned, British nuclear disarmament only addresses part of the problem of international security, so a failure to progress towards a non-nuclear posture after the next election (or the one after) should not be allowed to discourage other security-enhancing actions. Whether or not Britain does relinquish nuclear weapons in the next five to ten years, its government, by its words and actions, ought to help change perceptions of the Soviet threat, encourage more peaceful dynamics in the East–West competition, and stimulate benevolent processes towards the goal of international security. In each of these activities we need radically to change our expectation of war as a deliberate instrument of politics between industrialised nations, and address our limited human and material resources to strengthening those ideas, relationships, institutions, and processes which in both the short and long term will preserve those values we cherish. Progressively reducing the importance of force in relations between states is a crucial objective in all this.

LOSING A BURDEN, FINDING A ROLE

While accepting that our security cannot be entirely separated from that of the world at large, it is inevitable in the near future that the Soviet Union will remain at the centre of the problem. Europe is the world's most heavily-armed continent, and it is where the benefits of moving towards a legitimate international order will be most immediate. In the first instance there should be more security at less cost (the latter enabling us as individuals and societies to spend more of our resources on promoting other values); while in the longer term we should be able to look forward to human rights benefits across Europe (a Soviet Union which is relatively relaxed about its security is more likely to tolerate incremental moves towards a 'finlandised' Eastern Europe). The latter paranthetical point underlines the importance of our recognition that Soviet insecurity is not in our interests.

Nothing in the preceding arguments – that the Soviet threat has been exaggerated, that Soviet society is changing, that Soviet insecurity increases our insecurity, that the Soviet Union needs reassurance – should be interpreted as appeasement, as a step towards deferring to Soviet power, as a belief that the Soviet Union is benevolent, or as indicating a belief that there is moral equivalence between liberal Western democracy and authoritarian Soviet socialism. None of these latter propositions has informed the arguments in Part I of this book. The Soviet Union has the instincts of a great power, and sometimes exercises them brutally; and aspects of the Soviet political system are reprehensible. There is no reason to assume that Soviet Russia in the years ahead will cease to be a 'problem' for the West. The present argument is not that Soviet Russia may become a state to be 'trusted' in the sense of one only wanting to show goodwill ('live-and-let-live') to the outside world. No major state can be trusted in that sense. The present argument only asks that we 'trust' Soviet leaders to know their best interests on the broadest questions of war and peace with the West.

The Soviet Union's external behaviour has rarely been as threatening as many of us have imagined, nor has the West's been as enlightened. Whatever the differences in our domestic societies, the differences in our respective behaviour in world affairs is not sufficient cause to bring about a war that would rid the Northern Hemisphere of cities. The Soviet Union will remain a fact of life, and the aim of British policy should be to coexist with it with as much security as possible and at the lowest cost, so that we can attend to all the other important objectives in life. The desirability and feasibility of living with Soviet Russia was the conclusion many of us reached well before Mr Gorbachev came to power. The argument in Part I does not depend on the changes in the international scene which he has encouraged. Alternative defence thinking predated him, and will remain valid even if he is soon toppled from power. However, he must be given prominence because his new thinking makes it easier to move forward. In contrast, in the minds of NATO's 'keepers of the threat', Gorbachev is too good to be true, and they will not be sorry if he falls. If he does soon fall it may be because he is unsuccessful in foreign policy; and that in part will be because of the lack of Western responsiveness. If Gorbachev fell in this way it would represent a self-fulfilling prophecy on the part of Western ideological realists. Their response would be one of self-congratulation: they would pride themselves on having not been 'taken in'. But even if Gorbachev *were* to fall, the desirability of the policies recommended here would not cease, nor would their achievement become impossible. Success would simply be more difficult, and take longer. This is therefore a most propitious time for major initiatives on Britain's part. We could not hope to have a more favourable leadership in the Soviet Union, one apparently uniquely committed to a notion of common security and unprecedentedly willing to compromise. Progress will not be easy, but if we do not take advantage of this moment, will we ever?

If evolution beckons with the Soviet Union it is being forced upon us by changes in the relationship between the United States and Western Europe. The United States is not the super power it was. It cannot police the world; its budget is in deficit; it has a trade imbalance; the dollar no longer demands complete loyalty; its military power is overstretched; and its political leadership has come to lack authority. It is sensible therefore for Western European countries to reduce US dominance in matters affecting their security. This is not because of any 'anti-American' animus – it is simply because Western Europeans should be in a better position than their major ally to know their own best interests. Logically this requires that the Western European states coordinate their policies more effectively; new pressures might in any case make this a higher priority than in the past. This particularly ought to be the case for Britain, as the transatlantic 'special relationship' becomes threadbare with geopolitical age. As the United States becomes less important in the world, so the world will become less important to the United States. This could well mean that the United States will be less willing than hitherto to risk its own cities in order to deter possible attacks on those of its partners. When we look back we may see that Reykjavik and the INF agreement were as significant for extended deterrence as were the first withdrawals from Vietnam for the strategy of containment. Psychologically, nuclear disengagement has begun; it remains to be seen how far it can go, and how quickly.

Whether or not the British government likes it – and that of Mrs Thatcher does not – denuclearisation in one form or another is likely to remain on the international agenda. It will either come from developments within Britain (economic pressures or governmental change) or outside (further super power arms reduction agreements for example) or a combination of both. The image of Britannia clutching Trident is outdated, as well as costly. The balance of political, economic, strategic and moral arguments favour Britain's shifting its contribution to Western defence from nuclear to conventional forces, and then trying to change NATO strategy from a pronuclear to a non-nuclear direction. This objective involves the reshaping of our own and then allied images about the role of force, the utility of nuclear weapons, and the nature of the East–West conflict. The adoption of a non-nuclear posture by Britain, allied to a policy committed to the notion of non-provocative defence and reciprocal security, would be a step in the right direction towards the achievement of our most fundamental goals: more security, more prosperity, and more confidence that our way of life can be preserved.

Dean Acheson's famous remark about Britain having lost an empire but not yet having found a role has rankled for so long with so many members of the British foreign policy establishment because it is true. But before Britain can pursue a settled role in world affairs it first needs to define its vision. What we have lived with for several decades now is a static approach to the future, based on the assumption of an indefinite military and political confrontation with the Soviet Union and unending nuclear stand-off. The five chapters above have offered an alternative to this static approach, combining a vision and a role, and realism and reform. In international relations we are constantly confronted by cross-roads, and no road we can take is entirely risk-free; even so, some routes enable us to travel more hopefully than others. The hopeful direction indicated in Part I of this book looks towards the evolution of a legitimate international order over the next fifteen to thirty years.

The first plateau towards a stable peace is still a distant goal, and reaching it is not guaranteed. It will not be regarded as a glittering utopia in some radical minds, but its achievement would nevertheless be remarkable. Not only do we face all the systemic problems of international politics, but we also face future decades of manifold anxieties. We cannot now predict the pattern of future economic, demographic, social, ideological, technological and political problems; but if the past is any guide, we cannot assume an easy journey. What disasters might occur? what realignments? which states might collapse? with all the problems we are likely to face, a more stable international security system is as necessary as it is problematic. Forty years ago the Cold War seemed perfectly rational to the participants. In most respects it was. Conflicts of interest still exist between the two systems, but several decades of small decisions, moulded by Cold War fears and outlooks have now produced an irrational confrontation. The tyranny of short-term vigilance tightened the Cold War trap; only long-term vision will begin to undo it.

If we were to achieve the goal of a legitimate international order within thirty years, then a truly stable peace would then be on the agenda. Indeed, objectives long dreamed of but not now feasible would become realistically conceivable: the 'healing' of our continent, massive nuclear disarmament, peaceful change, defensive-only military postures across the globe. These are matters for the future. But even the first plateau will not be reached without a change of vision and considerable effort. International security, unlike Topsy, will not just grow of its own accord. Britain could make a positive contribution to creating a legitimate international order by helping to change – to make more accurate – prevailing images of international 'reality'. The denuclearisation of East–West relations would be a major contribution to this process. Britain has scope to act. By giving priority to notions of non-provocative defence and common security, and by scrapping the Trident programme and taking the lead in denuclearisation, Britain could lose a moral, economic and military burden and finally find a brave new role.

Notes

1. I coined the phrase 'reciprocal security' as an alternative to 'common security' since the latter, as popularised by the Palme Commission, unwisely does not propose unilateral action by any country, and because 'common' has more passive connotations than 'reciprocal'. The Palme Commission defined 'common security' as 'a commitment to joint survival rather than a threat of mutual destruction' (p. 92). Palme Commission, *Common Security. A Programme for Disarmament* (London: Pan Books, 1984), p. ix.
2. *Newsweek*, 21 December 1987.
3. The dominance of nuclear weapons in super power relations is well brought out in George F. Kennan, *The Nuclear Delusion. Soviet–American Relations in the Atomic Age* (London: Hamish Hamilton, 1984).
4. This is one of the themes in Kennan, ibid.
5. See, for example, Richard N. Ostling, 'Armageddon and the End Times', *Time*, 5 November 1984. Such beliefs are deeply held in the fundamentalist right in the United States, and will survive the Reagan presidency.
6. *Newsweek*, 21 December 1987.
7. Dan Smith, 'The Crisis of Atlanticism', p. 234 in Baylis, *Alternative Approaches to British Defence Policy* (London: Macmillan, 1983).
8. See, for example, Matthew Evangelista 'The New Soviet Approach to Security', *World Policy Journal*, Autumn 1986, pp. 561–97.
9. The phrase is from Marshall D. Shulman, 'Towards a Western Philosophy of Coexistence', *Foreign Affairs*, October 1973.
10. See Randall Forsberg, 'Confining the Military to Defense as a Route to Disarmament', *World Policy Journal*, Winter 1984, pp. 285–318; and 'Parallel Cuts in Nuclear and Conventional Forces', *Bulletin of the Atomic Scientists*, Vol. 41(7), August 1985, pp. 152–6.
11. Quoted by Samuel Hynes, *The Auden Generation* (London: Faber & Faber, 1976), p. 102.

Part II
Alliance Reform
John Baylis

7 Nuclear Deterrence and the Preservation of Peace

> Be careful above all things not to let go of the atomic weapon until you are sure, and more than sure, that other means of preserving peace are in your hands.
>
> Winston Churchill, Address to a Joint Session of the US Congress, January 1952

There can be no doubt that the 1980s have witnessed a great deal of intense debate in Britain and throughout Western Europe about the role of nuclear weapons in Western strategy. The outcome of the 1987 British election has taken some of the steam out of the debate but the role of nuclear weapons remains a lively political issue. Such debates are not new of course. Throughout its history the North Atlantic Alliance has faced periodic waves of criticism of its strategy. What does seem new about the contemporary debate is that coherent alternative strategies have been proposed in recent years and the political consensus on defence in many Western European countries has begun to break down. Such a debate on issues of vital importance, after a period of neglect, is to be welcomed. Although some of the debate has often been overly emotional and sometimes ill-informed it has nevertheless produced important critiques of contemporary strategy and forced defence planners to think through the justifications for their policies.[1] In particular, when such eminent figures as the former American Secretary of Defense, Robert McNamara, and the former British Chief of the Defence Staff, Lord Carver, produce studies taking issue with many of the conventional wisdoms and orthodoxies of current Western strategic planning, it is clear that a major and important debate is underway not only in the public domain but in the defence establishment itself.[2]

In general this recent debate has tended to focus on two main schools of thought: those who believe that there is little wrong with existing alliance nuclear strategy; and those who argue that the prevailing Flexible Response strategy is immoral and imprudent and who advocate a radical non-nuclear strategy as an alternative for the Western Alliance (and for Britain). In the 1987 British General Election, the Conservative Party favoured the first of these schools of thought, while the Labour Party supported the second. Despite it's eventual acceptance of a British nuclear deterrent the SDP–Liberal Alliance contained supporters of both schools of thought.

Ken Booth has argued in the first part of this book (and elswehere) that the second school of thought favouring a non-nuclear strategy represents 'an idea whose time has come'.[3] He may be right although the defeat of the Labour Party in the 1987 Election suggests that a non-nuclear Britain is some way off. It is clearly possible to debate whether support for the non-nuclear alternative is or is not gathering momentum, but a much more important question is whether it *deserves* support and especially whether it would *actually* work. The argument presented in the pages which follow accepts that there are flaws and deficiencies in existing national and alliance defence policies but suggests that there are even more dangers and weaknesses associated with a non-nuclear strategy which its supporters have yet to deal with in a convincing way. The contention, however, is that the choice is not only between a 'nuclear-biased' and a 'nuclear-free' defence policy, that is between what we have now and unilateralism. The argument which follows suggests that what is needed is a reform of existing strategy and the adoption of a more rational, prudent defence policy which reflects the middle ground in the debate. The proposal is not for an airy-fairy compromise but a well-thought out, coherent, realistic and credible defence policy which is not complacent about the dangers of nuclear war but which recognises the difficulties of providing an effective deterrent and defence posture against a nuclear-armed opponent without possessing nuclear weapons oneself. It is not suggested that such reform is easy to achieve. Neither should it be forgotten (as it seems to be in Part I) that some improvements have already been made in NATO strategy in recent years in the right direction. The argument here, however is that more still needs to be done and that the 1987 Double Zero Agreement on short- and medium-range missiles based in Europe provides an opportunity for reform.

Before the case for the third alternative can be established, initially we need to consider the arguments for and against the status quo and a non-nuclear defence policy.

HAS NUCLEAR DETERRENCE KEPT THE PEACE

One of the most difficult arguments which the 'peace movement' and supporters of a non-nuclear defence policy have to deal with, is the often-expressed assertion by the establishment that the existing strategy based upon nuclear deterrence, whatever else one might say about it, has kept the peace since 1945. In order to make their case for change it is essential that the critics confront the contention that nuclear deterrence and the alliance strategy of Flexible Response have contributed in an important sense to the relative stability and absence of war in Europe during the second half of the twentieth century. Usually the challenge to this argument takes two forms. Firstly, that it cannot be proved that nuclear weapons have kept the peace. And secondly, that even if nuclear weapons have contributed to this end in the past, the present situation is more dangerous than ever before and the chances of nuclear deterrence breaking down in the future are very great.

Those who argue that it cannot be proved definitively that nuclear weapons have helped to maintain stability in Europe are obviously right. Equally, those who argue that it cannot be disproved either are also correct. This, however, is not the end of the matter. It is not a simple matter which can be proved or disproved. We can go a little further than this. Some arguments are, after all, better than others. Europe is a continent which has constantly been at war throughout its history. There have been two terrible wars this century with the loss of millions of lives. Since 1945 there has been no conflict in Europe while in the rest of the world well over a hundred bloody wars have been fought with a huge cost in human suffering. As one survey put it 'Post-war Europe's freedom from war has been a unique phenomenon'.[4] The explanation as to why no large scale war has occurred in Europe since 1945, given the history of conflict on the continent, the continuing sources of hostility between European states and the ubiquity of war elsewhere, must lie in the fact that 'there is an ingredient which is present today but was absent in 1914 and 1939, and is, certainly absent today outside the North Atlantic.'[5] That ingredient is without doubt the existence of nuclear weapons and a deterrent policy which warns a potential enemy of the truly horrendous consequences of aggression. This is not to argue that the existence of nuclear weapons has been the only factor contributing to more than forty years of peace in Europe. As Ken Booth has argued in Part I there are a number of factors which have contributed to peace. Nor is it to argue that the consequences of the deterrent policy have been ideal. There is no doubt that mistrust and dangers have resulted from such a policy. Nevertheless, it seems beyond all reasonable doubt that nuclear weapons, appalling as they are (indeed because they are so appalling) have contributed in no small way to the absence of either conventional or nuclear wars in Europe. It may be unpalatable that peace has been maintained through the threat of nuclear retaliation but this does seem to have been an important contributory factor. Those who want to sweep away the existing system of security must think long and hard about the enormous benefits of having been lucky enough to live in an era of relative peace (with all its imperfections) without having to face the horrors of war. The onus therefore is very much on them to demonstrate that what they recommend is likely to lead to a better and safer world.

There are those in the 'peace movement' who argue that it cannot be any worse than living in the shadow of nuclear destruction. Some change is essential, they argue, if the world is not to destroy itself in the inevitable nuclear war which they foresee as the result of existing policies.[6] Without being complacent about the contemporary dangers, such arguments have two major flaws. Firstly, of course, the situation in Europe could be worse, much worse, than we have at present. Those who argue otherwise would seem to have little imagination. Unilateralism *could* destabilise the existing balance and help to unravel the existing European security system. If conflict did ever break out British unilateralism would not necessarily protect us from nuclear war, as will be argued later, and the kind of conventional war which could take place today with modern technology would be almost unrecognisable to those who fought in the Second World War.

The second argument is that nuclear war is inevitable if we carry on as we are. The contention is that the present arms race will inexorably lead to nuclear destruction. In fact very few things in life are inevitable and nuclear war is not one of them. This is not to argue that nuclear war is impossible in the future or that there are no dangers in the present situation with ever higher levels of armaments on both sides. War, however, if it were to take place would be more likely to be the result of political conflict and changes in the power relationship between East and West than the arms race itself.[7] No one can predict with accuracy that war is just around the corner if we carry on as we are. Indeed those who attempt to do so are not only guilty of playing on vulnerable people's emotions but are themselves in danger of helping to create a self-fulfilling prophecy. To tell people that war is inevitable is to help prepare people for war. It also helps to create a fatalism in people's minds when the unilateral 'solutions' which are promoted as the only possible solutions do not occur thus precluding the search for less radical, but more practical, measures to ease existing tensions of East–West relations.

This brings us to the argument of those who suggest that even if nuclear deterrence has helped to keep the peace in the past, there is no guarantee that it will in the future, and the future is likely to be more dangerous than the past. If war is not inevitable, it is at least more likely (so the argument goes) than five, ten or twenty years ago.

There is no denying that the first part of this argument is correct. There can be no absolute guarantee that the present system of nuclear deterrence will indefinitely keep the peace. No realistic system of security could possibly give such a guarantee whether it be Mutual Assured Destruction (MAD), non-provocative defensive deterrence or the Strategic Defence Initiative (SDI). There is no such thing as a risk-free strategy. Given that nuclear weapons cannot be disinvented or simply ignored the aim must be to produce a strategy which minimises as far as possible the risk of nuclear destruction, defeat or intimidation. The object must be to avoid the choice between suicide and capitulation, or the alternatives posed between being 'red or dead'.

IS NUCLEAR WAR MORE LIKELY IN THE FUTURE THAN IN THE PAST?

The question still remains, however, whether the world in which we live is a more dangerous place than ever before. Those who contend that it is, point to a whole host of strategic and military dangers which, they argue, make the 1980s less safe than the 1970s or ever before. These include the so-called shift to intimidation in US nuclear doctrine, the development of 'first-strike' strategies, and adherence to a 'first-use' posture by the West, the risks of accidental war, the development of war-fighting strategies, the illusion of being able to fight a 'limited' nuclear war, unstable battlefield nuclear doctrines, offensive developments in conventional doctrine, technical breakthroughs and the dangers of the arms race.

It cannot be denied that the contemporary world does continue to pose dangers. Potential conflict over resources, large nuclear arsenals, changes in strategic and tactical doctrines, instability in the Middle East and the Third World generally, and the emergence of particular kinds of new technology are all worrying developments.

Without being guilty of 'cosmic complacency', however, it is certainly possible to question whether the world is any less safe now (or is likely to become so in the future) than in the 1940s, 1950s, or early 1960s at the height of the first Cold War. Judgements about risk are extremely difficult to make.

If the early 1980s were characterised by a 'new Cold War' it must be remembered that in terms of tension and instability the first Cold War was even worse. The Berlin blockade, the Korean war, the continuing Berlin crises from 1958 to 1961, the Cuban Missile Crises, the Soviet intervention in Hungary and Czechoslovakia, all involved periods of great strain, verging at times on very real threats of war between East and West. It is true that new accurate weapons technologies, the development of war-fighting strategies by *both* the United States and the Soviet Union, the existence of thousands of 'usable' battlefield nuclear weapons, and the prospects of a new arms race in space, undoubtedly pose great dangers. But we sometimes forget that the 1950s was the period of 'massive retaliation' and unstable first-strike capabilities. In an era before invulnerable second strike capabilities were developed there was a built-in incentive to strike first in a crisis with all of the instability which this entailed in tense situations. Today with hardened missile silos and especially with invulnerable submarine-based missile systems, both sides know that they could not possibly hope to get away with a successful first strike against their opponent. That, in essence, is what helps to keep the peace. At present despite *some* first-strike capabilities, associated with the greater accuracy of missiles, a strong case can be made that there is relatively greater stability in the nuclear balance between East and West than there was in the 1950s when there were very real incentives to destroy an enemy first before being destroyed oneself. Despite the *potential* dangers of SDI (in providing protection for one side and not the other and the encouragement it will probably give to the arms race) that kind of instability does not exist today and seems unlikely to arise in the next ten or fifteen years. Just as important, the new Gorbachev era in the Soviet Union also offers opportunities for better political relations between East and West in the years to come. This is not to argue that the present situation is wholly safe. Neither is it to argue that we can be complacent about the real dangers and paradoxes inherent in nuclear deterrence. It is simply to argue that despite the large increase in the nuclear arms on both sides, the present situation is not necessarily more dangerous than in the past. Professor Freedman is right when he argues that 'neither new weapons nor variations on the theme of limited nuclear war make life unusually dangerous at the moment'.[8]

It has to be accepted that no system of security in the past has been able to keep the peace indefinitely. The present deterrence system is probably no exception. There is, therefore, an onus on all responsible politicians and defence analysts to constantly search for something better. In line with Churchill's remarks quoted at the beginning of this chapter they have to be particularly careful, however, to make sure not to substitute what we have for something much worse.

DEFENDING THE STATUS QUO

Just as the 'peace movement' has a difficulty in coping with the argument that nuclear deterrence does seem to have been successful since 1945 in helping to keep the peace, so supporters of the existing system of security are vulnerable to the criticism that they have little to offer by way of overcoming the mutual antagonism between the two military blocs. Supporters of non-provocative defence argue that their alternative strategies are designed to help usher in more peaceful, cooperative relationships between East and West which will transform the system of European security. In Part I Ken Booth argues that his ideas of defensive deterrence are part of a system of reciprocal security which will help to bring about a more stable peace and a more 'legitimate international order'. It will take time to achieve these changes in international relationships, he warns, but a new system is desirable and possible. The message is very appealing – indeed much more appealing than one which offers largely a continuation of the status quo.

The key question is whether it is realistic to expect a fundamental change in the sysem of European security in the foreseeable future (even in 'the Gorbachev era'). The present structure in Europe which has been in place since the mid 1950s reflects the realities of power more accurately than the system which prevailed in the first half of the twentieth century. If the present system of two armed alliance systems is to be replaced what is going to take its place? Talk of a new 'European home' by Gorbachev or a return to the kind of cooperative era which followed the Congress of Vienna are all very well but given the range of territorial disputes, revisionist claims, traditional suspicions, ideological differences and disparities in power which still remain in Europe (even if some of them are dormant) how can we be sure that if we dismantle the blocs, peace and harmony will prevail. The past history of Europe is not comforting in this respect.

Caution, however, should not be used as an excuse for doing nothing. What follows in this section of the book is not static but positive and forward looking. While the present system seems likely to prevail for some considerable time to come there is a strong case for seeking greater cooperation between states. There is a case, as will be argued later, for accepting the idea of reciprocal security and pursuing the objective of a more 'legitimate international order'. There is a great deal of opportunity for improving East–West relations as the Gorbachev era gives witness. We should keep an open mind on whether these cooperative ventures will one day give rise to a significant transformation of the prevailing system. We should be realistic, however, about the difficulties and dangers of breaking up the two blocs until we have something demonstrably better to put in their place. As Ken Booth has argued in Part I we are living in interesting times in which important changes in the structure of the postwar world seem to be occurring. We have a duty to respond positively to opportunities which exist to lower tension in Europe and East–West relations in general. But we have to be cautious. Despite its flaws the prevailing system of European security has contributed to over forty years of peace. No realistic alternative system of security has yet been devised which reflects the realities of power in Europe in the way the existing system does. We may be in a transitionary phase to a second postwar era. But equally we may not. And even those who say we are, can offer no clear picture of the kind of European security system which is likely to replace the present one. Slogans and utopias can raise false hopes and make little contribution to the complex task of achieving greater stability and security in Europe. The 'peace movements' and the other supporters of non-nuclear defence policies have no monopoly in wanting better East–West relations and a more 'legitimate international order'. These are objectives which all sensible people desire. The key question is how these can best be achieved while maintaining our essential security. The aim must be reassurance *and* effective deterrence. The arguments which follow suggest that in Part I too much emphasis is placed on reassurance and not enough on deterrence. The contention is that cautious evolutionary reform rather than radical reform is the best way to achieve an effective balance of both of these important elements of security.

Notes

1. See P. Williams. (ed.), *The Nuclear Debate* (London: Routledge and Kegan Paul, 1984).
2. See McGeorge Bundy, George F. Kennan, Robert S. McNamara and Gerard Smith, 'Nuclear Weapons and the Atlantic Alliance', *Foreign Affairs*, Spring 1982; and Field Marshal Lord Carver, *A Policy for Peace* (London: Faber and Faber, 1982).
3. See Ken Booth 'The Case for Non-nuclear Defence', in John Roper (ed.), *The Future of British Defence Policy* (London: Gower, 1985).
4. See *Diminishing the Nuclear Threat* (London: British Atlantic Committee Report, 1984), p. 15. The group which produced the Report under the chairmanship of Lord Cameron included Sir Hugh Beach, Sir Frank Cooper, Sir Douglas Dodds-Parker, General Sir Anthony Farrar-Hockley, Hugh Hanning, Brigadier Kenneth Hunt, Professor Sir Ronald Mason and Major General Christopher Popham.
5. Ibid.
6. These are the views particularly of people like E. P. Thompson. See his book *Exterminism and Cold War* (London: Verso, 1982).
7. See the arguments presented in G. Segal, E. Moreton, L. Freedman and J. Baylis, *Nuclear War and Nuclear Peace* (London: Macmillan, 1983).
8. See L. Freedman 'Europe Between the Super Powers' in G. Segal et al., ibid.

8 How Valid are the Criticisms of Nuclear Deterrence?

The argument presented so far suggests that nuclear deterrence probably has *helped* to keep the peace in Europe over the past forty-five years and, without being unduly complacent, there are no overwhelmingly strong reasons to suppose that it will not continue to work for some time to come. This is not to argue that we should not be searching for something better and safer. If a convincing case for the retention of *some* form of nuclear deterrence is to be made (at least until something demonstrably better is found) it is, however, necessary to go further and confront directly the criticisms which have been levelled against the British nuclear deterrent and NATO strategy by the 'peace movement' and supporters of a non-nuclear strategy. These criticisms often take the following form:

1. Nuclear deterrence is immoral.
2. Nuclear deterrence is dangerous.
3. Nuclear deterrence lacks credibility.
4. Nuclear deterrence encourages proliferation and is hypocritical.
5. Nuclear deterrence involves close relations with the United States which undermines British independence.
6. The Soviet threat to Western Europe has been exaggerated and nuclear deterrence helps to exacerbate the conflict between East and West. Unilateralism would set an example for better East–West relations.
7. Nuclear weapons are an extravagance and create unacceptable opportunity costs.
8. Nuclear weapons have not brought Britain the kind of prestige and influence claimed for them.
9. Nuclear weapons have not proved useful in lesser contingencies.

Each of these criticisms will now be looked at in some detail.

MORALITY AND NUCLEAR DETERRENCE

Most members of the 'peace movement', disparate as it is, would accept the view that 'the possession of nuclear weapons by Britain represents a power of indiscriminate "mass destruction" which is immoral both to threaten and/or use.' According to Ken Booth:

> The use of nuclear weapons would violate the 'just war' principles of proportionality and discrimination; and it is wrong to threaten that which it would be grossly immoral to do.[1]

According to this view there can be no justification whatsoever for launching nuclear weapons against an opponent. There is no conceivable issue which is worth either the mass destruction of an enemy with nuclear weapons or the risk of initiating a series of events which could lead to a 'nuclear winter' and perhaps the end of civilisation as we know it.

Put like this the argument appears almost incontestable. And yet deeper questioning reveals the complexity of the moral arguments about nuclear deterrence. Even the argument about the use of nuclear weapons (as opposed to the threat to use them) is not as straight forward as it appears.

The moral argument against actually launching British Polaris, Trident or other Western missiles against Soviet (or any other) cities is a very strong one. There are those, however, who would argue that there are conceivable circumstances in which nuclear weapons could justifiably be used in a limited, perhaps demonstrative, way to bring a war, started by misjudgment or miscalculation, to an end. The use of nuclear weapons, some would argue, would force the enemy to pause and think long and hard about the fateful consequences of continuing with the war. If the end result were the re-establishment of peace through a negotiated settlement and, as a consequence, thousands, perhaps millions, of lives were saved then such a policy could conceivably be justified on moral grounds. This was the conclusion which a British Atlantic Committee Report, *Diminishing the Nuclear Threat*, came to in 1984.[2] The Report was written by a group of people who were very much aware of the dangers of nuclear weapons and who were particularly concerned with reducing the threat of nuclear war. Nevertheless, they argued that if war did break out by accident 'it would be necessary to make it unmistakably clear that it had to be stopped and that the Soviet Union had misread or miscalculated the situation.'[3] In their view the West should:

> reserve the right to use the nuclear weapon in a strictly limited role, with the purpose not of fighting a war but of conveying to the

Soviet Union that it had embarked on a course of action which would not be tolerated.[4]

There is, at least, a case here that firing a nuclear weapon into an uninhabited area which might contribute to a peaceful settlement of a war, begun by accident or miscalculation, could be defended on moral grounds. There is, however, admittedly a problem with this argument which the authors of the BAC Report, partially (but not entirely) recognise.[5] What if such use of nuclear weapons provokes reciprocal action which leads to further nuclear escalation with all of the consequences which this involves? Opponents would argue that, given the risks, such demonstrative use of nuclear weapons could never be justified on moral (or any other) grounds. And they have a case. It is not enough to argue, as the BAC Report does, that such demonstrative use has to be of a limited kind. The consequences would be unforeseen and the risks very high. As such, action of this sort must be morally questionable.

But what of the other moral arguments put forward by supporters of a non-nuclear strategy? For most members of the 'peace movement' there can be no distinction, in moral terms between the *threat* to use nuclear weapons and their *actual use*. Such a view however, is open to debate. There is a strong argument that, while the use of nuclear weapons is morally repugnant, nevertheless a strategy of nuclear deterrence, which threatens their use, is morally acceptable. According to this view, nuclear deterrence is justifiable to the extent that it helps to achieve morally important values, like keeping the peace and maintaining security. To those who take this position what matters above all else is the consequence of the actions and the intentions which govern the actions. If the end result is peace, then the fact that millions of lives are threatened with nuclear incineration is regrettable, but morally acceptable.[6]

The implication of this line of argument is that states can justifiably bluff with nuclear weapons in order to keep the peace but if that bluff is ever called they should either give in or at least refrain from doing what they had previously threatened they would do. Nuclear deterrence therefore is acceptable in moral terms as long as one intends (in private at least) never to use such weapons in practice and as long as they are never used as a result of one's strategy.

This is a view which should not be dismissed on moral grounds. There is a perfectly respectable line of moral thinking which accepts that if the end result achieves the greater good, then the means to achieve that good are morally justifiable. A strong moral case, for example, can be made for shooting a hijacker who threatens to blow up a jumbo jet with hundreds of people on board. Shooting anyone may be morally indefensible to those who hold an 'absolutist' moral code. For many people, however, saving hundreds of innocent lives is a greater moral value.

While there clearly is some strength in this argument as far as it goes, there is nevertheless a nagging problem for those who sincerely hold this moral position. Although nuclear deterrence may be a bluff it does involve the establishment of a military system containing a whole spectrum of nuclear capabilities which are designed to convince an opponent that these weapons will in fact be used under certain circumstances.[7] Even if there is an *intention* never to use them, such a military system may involve capabilities and operational procedures which in a crisis, or conflict situation, might inexorably lead in practice to the use of nuclear weapons. The existence of battlefield nuclear weapons in Europe, for example, poses serious problems in a future conflict of 'use-them or lose them.'[8] Given the risks then of being drawn 'willy-nilly' into a nuclear war as a result of the deployment and planning associated with such weapons, can any system of nuclear deterrence be justified morally? No, say members of the 'peace movement'. Supporters of the present strategy, on the other hand, would say that although there might be pressure to use nuclear weapons under certain circumstances the command and control procedures are such that nuclear weapons remain under firm political control. As such they would argue (and perhaps with justification) that the risks of sliding unintentionally into a nuclear war are not as great as the critics claim.

There is another argument sometimes used by supporters of nuclear deterrence which accepts that the use of nuclear weapons and indeed the threat to use such weapons *is* morally wrong but goes on to suggest that 'any weakening of nuclear deterrence to the point of jeopardising our security' is also morally objectionable.[9] According to this argument unilaterally giving up nuclear weapons by Britain poses the risk of creating a less stable international situation by undermining the NATO Alliance which could result in the greater likelihood of war and the loss of millions of lives. No one can prove such an outcome in advance but if it is sincerely believed that there is a distinct chance that this will occur it is possible to come to the conclusion, quite reasonably, that unilateralism is less morally acceptable than a strategy of nuclear deterrence which seems to have helped to keep the peace for the past forty-five years or so.

The argument presented here is that there is a moral dilemma which is inescapable and perhaps insoluble. There are surely no courses of action in the security field which are free of moral difficulty just as there are no strategies which are free of risk. For those who hold this position the main objective of any strategy and any defence policy should be to help maintain peace and to defend the values of that particular society. It may not be wholly satisfactory, supporters say, but the way to do this, in the kind of world in which we live, is through a system of nuclear deterrence – by threatening unacceptable costs to those thinking of aggression. It has to be accepted that such a policy involves wickedness. But for those who accept such a strategy, deficient as it is, there is no realistic alternative at present available which is likely to provide the kind of peace and security which has been achieved through nuclear deterrence. The major moral responsibility for war, would after all, lie with the aggressor.

These views of morality are undeniably rather complicated. Judgements on these matters are inevitably matters of choice based on personal values. The case made here is simply that the unilateralists do not hold the moral high ground as they frequently seem to claim. There are strong moral arguments, sincerely held, in favour of nuclear deterrence as well as against it. Those who argue that only the 'peace movement' is capable of moral rectitude on these matters are not only mistaken but surely are guilty of arrogance and perhaps moral blackmail.

NATO membership and morality

Another argument which needs to be discussed is whether those who argue for unilateral renunciation of nuclear weapons by Britain on moral grounds while accepting continued membership of a nuclear alliance like NATO are guilty of hypocrisy. There is surely a strong argument that this is the case. 'The morally consistent line for a non-nuclear Britain would be to pull out of NATO, since not to do so would involve relying on others for the nuclear protection one has adjured oneself.'[10] To argue that 'moral consistency is sometimes the hobgoblin of small minds' is hardly a sufficient rebuttal of this charge.[11] Neither is it convincing to argue that 'nobody in Britain berates Sweden or Switzerland for being "hypocritical" although their security is affected by the nuclear exertions of other countries, pre-eminently the United States.'[12] The security of Sweden and

Switzerland may well be enhanced by the system of nuclear deterrence but they have little choice in the matter. They are not members of NATO, Britain is. A unilateral Britain would be in a position to decide whether to continue membership of the nuclear alliance or not. Nor is it sufficient to say, as the Labour Leader Mr Kinnock, has done, that he would never call on US nuclear forces in defence of Britain. If the arguments against nuclear deterrence are predominantly moral then there is a strong moral case that withdrawal should take place. As the pro-unilateralist Alternative Defence Commission has argued in its Report *Defence Without the Bomb*:

> If ... unilateralism is based on a ... fundamental rejection of nuclear weapons [on moral grounds] – the view held by the Commission – the prima facie case for withdrawing from NATO is compelling, whatever the strengths of the tactical reasons for staying in.[13]

Some unilateralists clearly and honestly recognise this problem. There are others, however, who seem unaware of, or who choose to ignore, the moral dilemma involved in continuing membership of NATO. The Labour Party's pamphlet *Defence and Security for Britain* written in 1984, for example, advocated the cancellation of Trident, the phasing out of Polaris, the closure of American nuclear bases in Britain and the adoption of a non-nuclear defence policy. At the same time, the pamphlet argued that Britain should remain *firmly* committed to the North Atlantic Alliance. Britain's task within NATO under a Labour government, it was argued, would be to convince her allies that changes in Alliance strategy should take place away from the reliance on nuclear weapons towards defensive, conventional deterrence.[14] But what if the Alliance, as seems highly likely, refused to move in that direction? How long should Britain continue its membership of the Alliance? As the 1987 General Election campaign demonstrated, the Labour Party in Britain so far has been unable to grasp this sensitive political nettle and has refused to accept even the principle of withdrawal. It must be said that as a result the party has opened itself up to the charge of hypocrisy in its moral criticisms of the British nuclear deterrent and NATO strategy. Whether the Labour Party will change its position on this and other defence issues as a result of its review of policy after defeat in 1987 remains to be seen.

There are some members of the 'peace movement' and the Labour Party, who, recognising the moral difficulties of remaining indefinitely within a nuclear alliance, argue that Britain should make its willingness to remain a member of NATO *'conditional'* on the Alliance taking specific steps to disengage itself from reliance on a nuclear strategy. In their Report *Defence Without the Bomb*, the Alternative Defence Commission, advocates that the conditions proposed by Britain to its NATO allies should include:

1. The acceptance by NATO of a 'no-first-use' of nuclear weapons policy.
2. A phased, but total withdrawal of all battlefield nuclear weapons.
3. The removal of all US 'theatre' nuclear weapons.
4. The decoupling of NATO strategy from the US nuclear deterrent.[15]

As the Commission's Report noted such conditional membership of NATO 'must imply some kind of time scale for achieving the above goals if it is to have any force.'[16] As far as the Commission is concerned, although the time scale should not be too rigid 'Britain should tell its allies that it places a special importance on a "no-first-use" policy and that it will leave NATO *within a year* unless the Alliance adopts this policy as a signal of its commitment to move away from reliance on nuclear weapons.'[17] The Commission's Report follows this up by arguing for a definite time limit of *three years* for the removal of all American nuclear weapons from its territory and the removal of all short-range battlefield nuclear weapons and long-range theatre nuclear weapons from Europe within *three or four years*. Consistent with this time scale, the Report concludes that unless there has been substantial progress towards the adoption of a non-nuclear strategy *within three years* Britain 'should withdraw from the Alliance.'[18] Although it will be argued later that such a policy may well pose unacceptable risks to British and Alliance security, the proposals of the Alternative Defence Commission are without doubt morally consistent. As has already been argued this cannot be said for all supporters of a non-nuclear defence policy, especially those who fudge the moral difficulties of remaining dependent upon American and Alliance nuclear policy to maintain British security.

The question of a nuclear-free Britain in alliance with a nuclear United States raises another interesting question worthy of discussion. Supporters of a non-nuclear defence policy for Britain, like Ken Booth, would argue that 'morality is contextual.' What they mean by this is that 'what is acceptable or justifiable behaviour for a small country under the shadow of a hostile great power is likely to be very different from what is thought acceptable or justifiable behaviour for another great power in the system.'[19] According to this argument because one super power, the Soviet Union, has nuclear weapons the other super power, the United States, has little choice 'realistically speaking', but to keep her nuclear weapons. Britain on the other hand does have a choice and 'it is right', so the argument goes, that she should get rid of her nuclear weapons.[20] The contention seems to be that it is morally acceptable for the United States to retain her nuclear weapons because of the Soviet Union's nuclear weapons but it is not morally acceptable for Britain.

I must confess to finding this line of argument very strange indeed. If the independent British nuclear deterrent system is designed as a 'last resort' weapon to deter a nuclear attack on Britain by the Soviet Union (or any other nuclear power) in circumstances when the American nuclear guarantee may have been withdrawn or when the NATO Alliance, for whatever reason, has disintegrated, what conceivable difference can there be between Britain attempting to deter the Soviet Union and the United States attempting to deter the Soviet Union (apart from the difference in strength and capabilities)? If the United States has no choice then, as a 'last resort', it could be argued, Britain has no choice. If it is morally acceptable for the United States to retain nuclear weapons then it is no less morally acceptable for Britain to retain such weapons in a world in which the most likely opponent continues to possess nuclear weapons.

THE DANGERS OF NUCLEAR DETERRENCE

Just as important as questions of morality are questions of prudence. Critics of nuclear deterrence argue that the possession of an independent nuclear deterrent by Britain and the Flexible Response strategy of NATO with its heavy reliance on nuclear weapons, is extremely dangerous. In the words of Ken Booth, 'If nuclear deterrence were to fail, the consequences for Britain would be catastrophic almost beyond imagination. At worst it would mean the onset of the nuclear winter; at best the massacre of millions. In either case, a small overcrowded country such as Britain is peculiarly vulnerable to the effects of nuclear war.'[21] Similarly it is argued that NATO strategy, predicated on a first, indeed early, use of nuclear weapons together with the threat of deliberate escalation is extremely dangerous. Given the chances that any limited use of nuclear weapons is likely to get out of hand and lead to strategic nuclear war, means, the critics argue, that NATO is threatening to initiate a course of action which will lead to the complete annihilation of its own societies, as well as that of the eastern bloc – and perhaps of civilisation as we know it.

There are two arguments here which need to be looked at carefully and separately: firstly, the dangers posed for Britain by continuing with a nuclear policy, and secondly, the dangers of NATO's strategy of Flexible Response.

Those who argue that Britain's adherence to a nuclear deterrent strategy poses an unacceptable risk to the nation's security, point, in particular, to the added incentive it gives to the Soviet Union to target Britain with its nuclear weapons. Given Britain's own independent nuclear capability and the spectrum of American facilities in Britain, the critics argue, it is inevitable that the destruction of important nuclear-related targets in Britain must be a high priority in Soviet contingency planning. Thus any conflict, anywhere in the world, between the super powers, creates the risk that Britain would be dragged into a nuclear war even though her vital national interests were not at stake. Robin Cook and Dan Smith have articulated this argument quite well:

> In the event of ... a nuclear war the role of Polaris as an 'integral part of NATO's strategic nuclear force' would inevitably entrammel Britain in the exchange. Indeed mainland Britain provides a number of targets related to our strategic deterrent which no prudent Russian commander could leave out of his list of first-strike priorities – the Faslane base, the Rugby VLF communications station, and Fylingdales early warning station. Ironically, the retention of an 'independent' nuclear capability only serves to ensure that we are embroiled in any conflict between the Americans and the Soviet Union.[22]

For those who argue along those lines the best way to avoid such risks would be for Britain to adopt a non-nuclear policy. In such circumstances, there would be *relatively less reason* for the Soviet Union to target Britain. Indeed the Soviet leaders have said on numerous occasions that those states who remove nuclear weapons from their soil will not be the subject of nuclear attacks by the Soviet Union in the event of war.

This is obviously an argument which, on the surface, is highly appealing, especially to those sections of the population desperately worried about the growing dangers of nuclear war. Prudence seems to dictate the adoption of a non-nuclear policy. It is, however, an argument which is certainly open to questioning and rebuttal. Should Britain renounce nuclear weapons unilaterally, would she necessarily be any less at risk from nuclear destruction? Does living in a 'nuclear-free-zone' guarantee survival in a nuclear war? The answers to both questions are probably no. It could be argued that while Britain remains part of NATO with American intelligence and early-warning facilities, as well as advanced reinforcement bases for American troops she will continue to be a major target in Soviet contingency planning. There is a very strong case that the destruction of such vital targets in war, especially given Soviet military doctrine, could best be achieved by nuclear weapons, irrespective of what the Soviet leaders say in peacetime. As long as Britain remains in NATO therefore, even if she were to renounce nuclear weapons and close down American nuclear bases, there is a strong possibility that she would be involved in a nuclear war should it break out in Europe.

It is for this very reason that some members of the 'peace movement' advocate the withdrawal of Britain from NATO and the adoption of a non-nuclear neutralist stance similar to Sweden or Switzerland. The geographical, political and strategic importance of Britain is, however, different to Sweden or Switzerland. In these circumstances it is difficult to believe that neutralism is a realistic alternative for Britain. Even if it was, given the indiscriminate effects of nuclear weapons, it seems almost impossible to believe that a neutral Britain could emerge unscathed from a nuclear war on the continent. Nuclear weapons are after all no respecter of state boundaries or narrow channel divides. The Chernobyl disaster of 1986 is a vivid reminder of this.

Having said this, although a non-nuclear policy would not protect Britain from the effects of a nuclear fall-out or perhaps even a direct attack in the event of war in Europe, there is an argument which has to be acknowledged that, relatively speaking, Britain would be less likely to be an important nuclear target for the Soviet Union if she renounced nuclear weapons, closed down all American bases and other facilities in Britain. Whether the Alliance could survive such actions, however, is open to serious doubts. Whether a neutralist, non-nuclear Britain could effectively ensure the protection of the nation's national interests is also hard to believe. Even the Alternative Defence Commission's Report *Defence Without the Bomb* admits that:

> Neutralism is open to criticism on strategic grounds, since it is debatable how far any state, particularly a small one, can secure

itself against possible great-power attack, and in the nuclear age the ability to ensure non-involvement in war has become impossible. It is also open to criticism on political and moral grounds as a refusal to take responsibility for helping to tackle world problems or to stand by important principles.[23]

To return to the question, is Britain safer with an independent nuclear deterrent than without one? Clearly no definitive answer can be given. If one believes that the chances of nuclear deterrence breaking down are reasonably high and that in such circumstances Britain presents a priority target for the Soviet Union because of her nuclear weapons then, not only does British nuclear policy pose risks, but those risks are totally unacceptable. The counter to this would be that deterrence in practice is more stable than the critics say and that the very possession of nuclear weapons by Britain is designed to prevent the outbreak of war. (The credibility of the British deterrent will be dealt with in the next section.) The fact that Britain's nuclear submarines are invulnerable (and thus do not present targets for the Soviet Union) makes it less likely, so it is argued, that the Soviet leaders would take the severe risks to their homeland which a policy of aggression would involve. Nuclear weapons introduce great caution into relations between states who possess them.

Supporters of the British nuclear deterrent argue that although there are risks inherent in the possession of such weapons the dangers are not eliminated by the adoption of a non-nuclear policy. Whether Britain were to stay inside NATO or opt for neutrality the risk of being involved in a nuclear war would remain. Not only would such nuclear dangers still be present but the chances of war and the risks to British security would be much greater as a result of such a policy. According to those who accept the case for the British deterrent then the dangers lie more with unilateralism than with the possession of nuclear weapons.

The attempt to evaluate the balance of risk between these two alternative policies is far from easy. It is the present author's judgement that the dangers of the British nuclear deterrent have been somewhat exaggerated although they do undoubtedly exist. It is also the present author's view that the balance of danger lies more with a policy of unilateralism than with the existing nuclear strategy. In order to substantiate this judgement, however, further attention needs to be given to an analysis of the military and strategic effectiveness of a non-nuclear strategy and its likely impact on the

NATO Alliance. This assessment will be undertaken later in this study.[24]

Apart from the debate over the risks associated with a British nuclear deterrent there is also the question of the dangers posed by Alliance nuclear strategy. Critics of Flexible Response argue that, as it now stands, there is little flexibility in the strategy. The conviction that NATO is significantly inferior in conventional weapons has resulted in the threat to start a nuclear war to avoid conventional defeat. This is what Thomas Schelling has called 'the threat that leaves something to chance.'[25] Critics argue that if deterrence did fail, and there can be no guarantee that it won't at some point in the future, then the dangers of actually *doing* what NATO threatens to do, are unbelievably great. The Soviet Union might decide in a crisis that NATO would (as it says it would) use nuclear weapons early and as a result use nuclear weapons herself first in a pre-emptive attack. Or if a Soviet conventional invasion threatened to overrun NATO's battlefield nuclear weapons (as it probably would fairly quickly at present) there would be very strong pressure to use such weapons before they were lost. To critics, the notion that a limited nuclear exchange might take place before common sense prevailed and the Soviet leaders accepted a negotiated settlement, are fanciful in the extreme. Once the first nuclear weapons were used, the chances of an uncontrollable escalation to Armageddon would be very high indeed. Such a strategy which puts such a stress on the war-fighting role of nuclear weapons (in order to deter) poses the great risk that such weapons will be thought of as war-fighting weapons to be used, like any other weapons, if conflict does actually break out. That mentality might lead the Alliance to move across the all-important nuclear firebreak very quickly in the event of war, with all of the potentially disastrous consequences this would involve.

Supporters of Flexible Response would argue that the main objective is to prevent all wars – conventional and nuclear – from breaking out and that the emphasis on the early use of nuclear weapons, the ambiguity about whether nuclear war could be controlled, and the threat of nuclear holocaust is the best way of deterring an opponent who possesses a wide spectrum of conventional, theatre nuclear and strategic nuclear forces of his own. If the Soviet leaders recognise, so it is argued, that NATO would have little alternative but to use nuclear weapons when faced with a major Soviet invasion then they will desist from starting a series of events, in the first place, when they know such action is highly likely to lead to nuclear catastrophe for themselves (as well as for their opponents). In the past the West Germans in particular have been concerned to put the emphasis on nuclear weapons because the very danger, and indeed the horrific consequences, which they pose to everyone involved is, in their eyes, the best guarantee that no war, of any kind, will be fought on German soil.

There is also the powerful argument that only through the possession of, and the threat to use, nuclear weapons can one deter another state with nuclear weapons. According to this argument given the qualitative difference of nuclear and non-nuclear weapons, NATO could not hope to stand up to a nuclear Soviet Union in any crisis without nuclear forces of its own. The fact that NATO would know this and the Soviet Union would know it, would inevitably mean that any purely non-nuclear defence policy would be exceedingly weak as a deterrent.

Arguments such as these clearly cannot be dismissed out of hand. They provide very powerful support for the present strategy of Flexible Response. There are, however, *some* problems with the reasoning behind these arguments which must be acknowledged. The strategy does imply a certain rationality on the part of all leaders which may not always be present in crisis situations. Can leaders always be depended upon to act in a cool and rational manner in situations of intense confrontation? It also ignores the fact that deterrence could break down for reasons of accident, misjudgment, or miscalculation. The chances of this happening, it is true, are greatly exaggerated by some of the critics of Flexible Response. Nevertheless, they have a point, and if deterrence were to break down – what then? The more candid (and sensible) supporters of Flexible Response would say 'At that point we have a *choice*. Depending on our calculations we might well decide that a conventional defeat should not be compounded by a nuclear defeat. But in the meantime, let's use the uncertainty in Soviet minds which our deterrent policy creates to deter them. If our bluff is called we could always surrender at that point.' Again, this reasoning should not be dismissed out of hand, but it does have one major drawback. Even if the intention to carry out the threat made may not exist in the minds of the Western leaders (and obviously they would not say it does publicly if they believe in deterrence), there is still the problem that in trying to make the threat convincing by all of the military actions involved (including the adoption of a nuclear war-fighting strategy) the system itself might just take over in the confused and highly charged atmosphere of world crisis. Whether nuclear war is intended or not, its results would be just the same.

There is an argument that Flexible Response with its requirements for a spectrum of military capability and its emphasis in particular on nuclear weapons has helped to deter a conventionally superior and nuclear armed Soviet Union. In this sense the dangers have perhaps been exaggerated. Nevertheless, it must be admitted that the critics have a case. A strategy which emphasises nuclear escalation and which deploys nuclear weapons in such a way that there is a strong incentive to use them may work for the foreseeable future. But there is no guarantee that such a system of deterrence will work indefinitely and the dangers of catastrophe inherent in such a strategy must be worrying for all sensible people who have thought seriously about Flexible Response. Whether a non-nuclear defence policy for the Alliance is any less dangerous (or more dangerous in a different way), however, is a matter of debate and will be considered later, as well as other alternative reforms.

THE CREDIBILITY OF NUCLEAR DETERRENCE

The question of the dangers posed by the possession of an independent nuclear deterrent or a nuclear-biased Flexible Response strategy relates very closely to the question of credibility. Deterrent threats which are not believable for a potential opponent pose obvious risks.

Supporters of a non-nuclear defence policy for Britain put particular stress on the incredibility of British nuclear forces either as a deterrent 'held in trust' for Europe or as a 'last resort' deterrent to threats against Britain itself. The British government has on occasion justified the continuation and modernisation of its nuclear deterrent system on the grounds that not only will a 'second centre' of decision-making in NATO (which the British force represents) further complicate Soviet calculations, but also that the Polaris system is a European force.[26] The implication is that the Soviet Union would be *even more* inclined to believe that NATO will respond to aggression in Europe with nuclear weapons if part of the NATO strategic deterrent is itelf European-based. Those who question this justification argue that if it is unlikely that the United States will risk its cities for Europe then the same is true of Britain. While it could be argued that such a view is too stark – that extended deterrence does create uncertainties in the mind of an opponent which may well be valuable in helping to deter – nevertheless, it must be said that there is something in the argument. Given the consequences for Britain of launching her missiles, the threat to do so on behalf of other European states is not altogether convincing.

But what about the threat to launch her missiles to defend her own vital national security interests – to prevent either an invasion of, or nuclear attack upon, Britain? Once again supporters of a non-nuclear policy would argue that such a policy has no credibility. According to this view British leaders would know that if they ever did launch their missiles against the Soviet Union, retaliation would be inevitable and truly devastating. Britain could inflict large scale casualties on the Soviet Union but Soviet nuclear forces could wipe Britain 'off the face of the earth.' What is more, both British and Soviet leaders know this to be true. As such the *threat* to commit suicide is so irrational that no Soviet leader would be likely to take it seriously, so the argument goes.

Such a critique is not to be taken lightly, especially when it is supported by individuals like Field Marshal Lord Carver who has held the most senior military post in Britain. In his often-quoted speech to the House of Lords in December 1979 he claimed that as Chief of Defence Staff and, as such, the Government's most senior military adviser:

> I have never heard or read a scenario which I would consider it right or reasonable for the Prime Minister or Government of this country to order the firing of our independent strategic force at a time when the Americans were not prepared to fire theirs – certainly not before Russian nuclear weapons had landed on this country. And, again if they had already landed, would it be right and reasonable? All it would do would be to invite further retaliation.[27]

Supporters of a non-nuclear defence policy are fond of posing the Catch-22 question to the Prime Minister or any supporters of the nuclear deterrent, 'Would you ever press the button?' This is designed to show that if the answer is 'No', then the deterrent has no value and might just as well be scrapped. And if the answer is 'Yes', then the respondent must be either crazy or irresponsible, because such action would inevitably lead to the nuclear devastation of Britain. The implication is that the time has come for the men in white coats to come and take such supporters of the nuclear deterrent away, preferably in strait-jackets.!

It's a clever question. Whichever answer you give you lose. Prime Ministers, like Mrs Thatcher, who support the nuclear deterrent have no alternative but to answer 'Yes' in public, irrespective of any private doubts they may have. And any thinking person clearly would have doubts. The more important question, however, which the critics of nuclear deterrence rarely ask is whether the Soviet leaders, who presumably would be responsible in the first instance for contemplating a threat to Britain's vital interests, could ever guarantee with 100 per cent certainty that the British Prime Minister would not carry out the threat. In the confusion, tension and uncertainty of a world crisis could the Soviet leaders discount the possibility completely that Mrs Thatcher or her successors, faced with a threat to values defended at such great cost in the past, *just might* launch British missiles? The Soviet leaders would know that if they did invade or launch their missiles against Britain and Britain did respond the British nuclear forces, small as they are in comparison with Soviet forces, could nevertheless wreak unimaginable destruction on the Soviet Union, much greater than the devastation of the second world war. Given the relatively cautious behaviour of the Soviet leaders in world crises in the past forty years, would they ever take the risk? A strong argument can surely be made that even a 5 per cent chance of British nuclear retaliation would be enough to deter the Soviet Union given the horrendous consequences of getting it wrong.

Much the same paradox of threatening to commit suicide in order to keep the peace is inherent in the strategy of Flexible Response as it is presently constituted. Critics argue that the threat by NATO to start a nuclear war which could lead to a 'nuclear winter' and perhaps even the end of human life on this planet could not be believed by any sane and sensible person. To say that the Soviet Union is likely to take the threat seriously simply because NATO has no choice but to use nuclear weapons at an early stage of a conflict because of her conventional weaknesses, is less than convincing, so it is argued.

Supporters of Flexible Response would argue that providing NATO retains a spectrum of conventional, tactical, theatre and strategic nuclear capabilities sufficient to convince the Soviet Union that it cannot win a war against NATO at any of these levels (by any conceivable definition of victory) then the NATO deterrent will remain credible. Under these circumstances, so it is argued, the Soviet Union would never take the risk of testing NATO strategy to see if it was based on bluff. As NATO is a defensive Alliance it will inevitably be the other side which has to think through initially the consequences of its actions, weighing up the potential costs and gains, before adopting an adventurous policy in Europe. And faced with even a small chance of infinite destruction they would never take the risk.

In terms of rational logic, such a strategy, it must be admitted, may not be very intellectually convincing. There is a case, however, that it is nevertheless politically realistic – and this is what counts. States are usually very cautious indeed when faced with events that could lead to their destruction. The consequences of direct aggression against a nuclear armed opponent are so incalculable and potentially horrendous that few states would take the risk.

While the credibility of NATO strategy should not be underestimated the critics do have a point. A great deal depends on rational decision-makers who cannot always be guaranteed. And the consequences of deterrence breaking down as a result of accident, misjudgement, or miscalculation (even if exaggerated) has to be taken seriously. It is not sufficient for supporters of Flexible Response to argue that this is unlikely. Maybe so, but it could happen. And if it did, given the training, tactical planning and deployment of nuclear weapons, the chances of nuclear war in Europe would be very great. The Alliance, it is true, would have the choice of carrying out its threat or not if it was faced with conventional defeat. The pressures to use nuclear weapons at an early stage, however, could well prove almost irresistible. It may be, as supporters of Flexible Response argue, that even if nuclear weapons were used there would be a major incentive by both sides to avoid total destruction by limiting their nuclear exchanges. Certainly there would be a shared interest to do just that. Whether in practice this would be possible, however, at a time of carnage, unprecedented confusion and chaos in Europe must be doubtful. As most military analysts admit the chances of an uncontrollable escalation following the first use of nuclear weapons would be very great.

If this is accepted, while not dismissing the credibility of existing NATO strategy, there would seem to be a case for some reform. Whether a non-nuclear defence policy is the answer, however, is itself the matter of some dispute which will be dealt with later.

NUCLEAR DETERRENCE AND PROLIFERATION

Another argument against the British nuclear deterrent and NATO strategy is that it encourages other states to develop their own nuclear weapons.[28] According to this argument, when Britain modernises her nuclear deterrent by purchasing Trident missiles from the United States, the clear implication to other states is that Britain sees great utility in nuclear weapons. If that is the case then the conclusion these other states are likely to come to is that nuclear weapons may well be the answer to their own security problems.

Linked to this argument is the contention that Britain (and the West in general) is being hypocritical when, on the one hand, it urges Third World states to comply with the terms of the Non-Proliferation Treaty (NPT), and at the same time engages itself in vertical proliferation by modernising its strategic nuclear deterrent. Supporters of a non-nuclear defence policy argue that British unilateralism would avoid such hypocrisy and would encourage non-proliferation through example.

There is clearly some substance in the latter, if not the former, part of this argument. For Britain to urge other states not to acquire nuclear weapons while herself acquiring the most sophisticated nuclear system in the world must appear to many other non-nuclear states to be hypocritical self-interest. If we are being honest, that is what it is. Whether British unilateralism would prevent nuclear proliferation, however, is far from certain. States are more likely to decide whether to go nuclear or not on the basis of a whole host of domestic and regional factors. Can they afford it? Is there domestic support for such a policy? Are their neighbours acquiring nuclear weapons? Will their security be enhanced or diminished by a policy which might spark off a nuclear arms race in their region of the world? These are *some* of the calculations which countries like Brazil, Israel, Iraq, Argentina, South Africa, India, and Pakistan must make. What Britain does or does not do is irrelevant in this context. If Britain opted out of the nuclear weapons business it would certainly have no impact on the Soviet Union and very little on any other aspiring nuclear state. It would almost certainly be viewed as yet another example of Britain's post war decline from power – a decision taken largely on economic rather than moral grounds (however it was justified by the politicians of the day).

If Britain is unlikely to influence the process of future nuclear proliferation in any significant sense, there is a case that she should maintain her nuclear weapons in order to help deal with the consequences of that proliferation if, as seems likely, it does take place. The British nuclear deterrent force is after all designed not simply as a deterrent against the Soviet Union but against any nuclear (and perhaps not just nuclear) state threatening Britain's vital security interests. Who can tell what the world will be like five, ten, or twenty years from now? It does not take much imagination to foresee the possibility of reckless Third World countries with nuclear weapons engaging in various forms of blackmail. An independent deterrent may well have utility in this context in the future.

NUCLEAR DETERRENCE, THE UNITED STATES AND BRITISH INDEPENDENCE

Another argument often used against the British nuclear deterrent is that Britain has become so dependent upon the United States for the continuation of her nuclear force that she has lost her strategic independence as a result.[29]

Again there is something in this argument. The beginning of Britain's strategic dependence on the United States dates back to 1948 when American B29's were sent to Britain at the height of the Berlin crisis. At this stage Britain did not have nuclear weapons and she did not possess a long-range bomber capability of her own. Under a post war agreement, however, she received American Super Fortresses in the early 1950s which helped to fill the gap between the development of nuclear weapons (the first test took place in 1952) and the deployment of the V–bomber force in the mid 1950s. Even at that early stage there were leading political figures in Britain who were concerned about the growing dependence on the United States which these events implied. Harold Wilson, writing in 1952, for example, complained that more and more American aid was being voted on conditions which involved British acceptance of strategic decisions and control 'not even by Congress but by the Pentagon, HQ of the US Chiefs of Staff'.[30]

Despite such criticisms, throughout the 1950s and 1960s Britain became increasingly dependent on American strategic delivery vehicles and atomic energy information. Britain received some help with the abortive Blue Streak project and later agreements were signed providing Britain with American Thor and Polaris missiles. The Polaris, and more recently the Trident Agreements, in particular, have led to British dependence on the United States, not only for the missile itself, but also for a wide spectrum of other closely related information, materials and facilities to make the nuclear deterrent as a whole effective. These agreements have also been supplemented by the very important atomic energy information exchange agreements signed in 1958 and 1959 which have continued right up to the present day.

A strong case can be made that as a result of this special defence relationship Britain has 'tied herself to the American order of priorities in research, development and production and in some respects at least has become partially dependent on American satellite intelligence, navigation and radio communications systems.' As Andrew Pierre has argued, Britain has 'undoubtedly lost a measure of her strategic independence.' The recent Trident Agreements suggest that this is likely to be the case until well into the next century.[31]

To those who support a non-nuclear defence policy for Britain (and for others) this is a matter of regret. Britain's independence of action from the United States is significantly constrained as a result of this close nuclear (and economic) relationship. For many, matters were made worse by what they saw as the dangerous build-up of American military power and belligerent rhetoric of the Reagan administration in the early 1980s. In this sense, anti-Americanism is quite a powerful strand in the thinking of the non-nuclear lobby.

On several planes this argument can be questioned. In the first place it can be argued that Britain's dependence on the United States has been exaggerated. Britain may acquire a range of information and materials from the United States for her deterrent force but in the last resort Britain has the ability to fire her missiles totally independently if she ever wished to do so. This, British Governments argue, is the 'acid test' of independence. Secondly, a strong case can be made that the close defence (and economic) relationship with the US has, over-all, been more beneficial than disadvantageous to Britain during the post war period. Indeed this is one of the main reasons why British governments of the Left and Right have continuously maintained close relations with the United States, as the corner-stone of their foreign policy, from Ernest Bevin onwards. In terms of military assistance, economic aid and their major contribution to deterring war in Europe, the American connection can be regarded as being of great benefit to British security interests. Thirdly, despite the close ties, Britain has not been averse to criticising the United States at times. In the series of disputes between the United States and Europe which characterised the early 1980s, for example, Britain frequently expressed views critical of

American policies. This was the case over high American interest rates, steel imports, the Yamal pipeline, the intervention in Grenada and to a certain extent President Reagan's Strategic Defence Initiative.

All alliances circumscribe the behaviour of the member states to a greater or lesser extent. Britain, it is true, has been particularly closely tied to the United States for much of the postwar period. This, however, has not precluded disagreements and the 'special relationship' has after all been a matter of choice dictated by perceptions of Britain's vital interests.[32]

NUCLEAR DETERRENCE AND EAST–WEST TENSIONS

Critics of nuclear deterrent policies often point to the deleterious effects of such policies on East–West relations.[33] It is sometimes argued that the existence of two nuclear blocs in Europe has helped not only to freeze relations between both sides of the iron curtain but has helped to exacerbate and institutionalise the conflict between them. This is the result on the Western side, so the argument goes, of an exaggeration of the Soviet threat. The Soviet Union is portrayed as an 'evil empire' which can only be kept in check by a policy of military, especially nuclear, strength. In Ken Booth's words 'we have set the enemy status of the Soviet Union in concrete. . . . Rational suspicions, worst case forecasting, inertia, vested interests, and simple Sovietology have led to a dangerous militarisation of our thinking about the Soviet Union.'[34]

Those who argue that the Soviet threat has been exaggerated are not necessarily pro-Soviet fellow-travellers (although *some* may well be). Indeed many of them are highly critical of the Soviet system and would agree with one non-nuclear supporter, Robert Neild, that 'the Soviet Union has developed a beastly political system.'[35] Their argument, however, is that an analysis of Soviet behaviour since 1917 reveals that Soviet leaders have generally been very cautious in their use of force outside their borders. The main exceptions to this, it is suggested, have been in areas which Soviet leaders have regarded as largely within their own spheres of influence. They also tend to interpret the build-up of Soviet military strength during the 1960s and 1970s as resulting from attempts to catch up with the United States and to deal with the dangers of encirclement which conflict with the Western powers and the Chinese has brought about. Apart from the fear of war on two fronts, large military resources are necessary, from a Soviet perspective, to deal with potential instability in Eastern Europe. The implication of this view is that Soviet military policies are largely the result of feelings of national insecurity, traditional over-insurance and real political pressures. Far from wanting war with the West, the Soviet Union has its hands full simply keeping down a reluctant empire and deterring what they regard as hostile Western behaviour. For those who hold this view there is a 'margin for manoeuvre' in Western policies which allows the West to take some risks in trying to reverse the spiral of suspicion and mistrust.[36] To supporters of a non-nuclear defence policy a less hawkish response from the West, and especially the gesture of British unilateralism to demonstrate Western goodwill, could well make a significant contribution to breaking the cycle of mutual suspicion and ill-will.

Clearly there is something in this argument. It seems extremely unlikely that the Soviet Union does desire war. The memory of World War Two remains too strong in the Soviet consciousness. The Soviet Union also has genuine security problems which requires substantial military forces. The case for dialogue with the Soviet Union is overwhelming especially given Mr Gorbachev's fresh approach to relations with the West. This does not mean, however, that a wholly benevolent view of the Soviet Union can be taken even in the era of 'glasnost' and 'perestroika'. The history of Soviet foreign and defence policy may have been a cautious one in some respects, in terms of their desire to avoid war. Nevertheless, military force has been used to expand their territory and to maintain control over their spheres of influence and, as such, there is a threat which the West can do no other than take seriously. Apart from the fact that the Soviet Union is a super power, with a super power's interests and capabilities, it is also a state which continues to proclaim an ideology bent on transforming the international system into like-minded Soviet-style communist states. Those who suggest there is no Soviet threat tend to under-estimate the ideological component of Soviet foreign policy. The continuing ideological division between East and West, however, cannot be ignored. The ideological fervour of the Cold War era may have declined but serious ideological differences remain, even in the Gorbachev era. The West, it must be said, poses an ideological threat to the Soviet Union and the Soviet Union poses an ideological threat to Western values. Gorbachev seeks to return to pure Leninism not a transformation of the Soviet state into a Western style democracy. As such conflict remains inherent in the relationship between East and West. These fundamental ideological differences, as well as the frequent clashes of national interest between East and West, the continuing impressive Soviet all-round military capability and their penchant for resolving crises by force, all indicate that no responsible Western statesman can conclude that the Soviet Union is definitely not a threat now and will not become one in the foreseeable future. To conclude that there is no threat and to get it wrong could well be disastrous.[37] It may well be that the Soviet Union requires its massive military forces primarily for reasons of self-defence against numerous potential enemies and for political control of its empire in Eastern Europe. Intentions can, however, change quickly and the existence of powerful military forces does provide the Soviet leaders with the choice to use them for other reasons should circumstances change, opportunities emerge, or pressures prove unbearable. Mr Gorbachev has brought a new approach to East–West relations which requires a positive response from the West but there remain serious question marks about whether he will be able to bring about fundamental changes in the Soviet system. Neither is it certain that he will survive in power to introduce the important but, as yet limited, reforms which he seeks. The West's approach to the 'glasnost era' therefore, given the continuing military power of the Soviet Union, must be welcoming but cautious.

From Britain's point of view the most likely threat arises less from the possibility of direct Soviet aggression than from Soviet miscalculation or misjudgement arising out of conflicts in Europe or perhaps the Middle East. However one interprets Soviet behaviour in the past, it is clear (despite the present easing of tension) that a wide range of intractable conflicts between East and West still exist and could at some point in the future erupt into open hostilities. A strong argument can be made that the chances of misjudgement on the part of the Soviet Union are greater in circumstances in which Britain and her allies are not adequately defended.

There is also the threat of what has been called 'Finlandisation' and of nuclear blackmail. This question will be looked at in more detail later in the discussion of the inadequacies of a non-nuclear defence policy. It is sufficient for the moment to argue that one thing above all else which stands out about Soviet behaviour over the years is the ultra-sensitivity of the leadership towards neighbouring states who do not share their world view. The Soviet Union has intervened directly in Hungary, Czechoslovakia and Afghanistan in the past thirty years. More often, however, it has employed the use of force in a more indirect form of intimidation in an attempt to secure compliance with its line on major policy issues. Certainly this technique was used in the Berlin crises in the late 1950s and early 1960s, and against Poland in the early 1980s when the rise of Solidarity began to under-cut the legitimacy of the central role of the Communist party in that country. While 'Finlandisation' is not an altogether happy term, nevertheless to the extent that it implies the role of large armed forces to intimidate in order to secure acceptance of certain lines of policy, it does refer to a widespread fear in certain parts of Europe.[38] It is true that Gorbachev has been very critical of the Brezhnev doctrine and has intimated that the Soviet Union will allow Eastern European states greater independence. This may be so, but given the Soviet Union's strategic interest in the region, major instability in Eastern Europe could encourage the more conservative members of the Politburo and bring a change of mind. Neither should it be forgotten that, despite discussion of less offensive tactics, the Soviet Union remains a formidable military power. The failure of Western European states to defend themselves adequately against the impressive military power of the Soviet Union might not, it is true, result in a Soviet invasion. The awareness of inferiority together with military pressure from the Soviet Union might well, however, cause the Western European states to appease the Soviet Union in some future crisis. 'Finlandisation' might not be the end of the world (indeed in many respects life in Finland is better than in the Eastern European states). There are, however, self-imposed limitations on Finnish independence which the Western European states would not choose for themselves.

The fact that there is a potential Soviet threat which has to be met does not mean that such a threat should be exaggerated or that recognition of it precludes accommodation and coexistence between East and West especially in the Gorbachev era. There is something in the argument that worst-case forecasting and the preoccupation with Soviet capabilities has often been used as an excuse against searching in an imaginative way for measures to reduce tensions between East and West. It must also be admitted that the search for unilateral security through superiority favoured by some Western 'cold war warriors' is not only counter-productive but illusory. Much more concern with the impact of destabilising technologies on the perceptions of the other side is also necessary if mutual suspicions are to be dampened down and meaningful dialogue is to take place. Whether the renunciation by Britain of her nuclear weapons would significantly contribute to the process of reconciliation, however, is doubtful. As with nuclear proliferation in general, it seems highly unlikely that British unilateralism would have any impact whatsoever on the Soviet Union. It may be, as Ken Booth has observed, that the West does have some 'margin of safety.'[39] Already some unilateral gestures have been made by the West by reducing the number of battlefield nuclear weapons in Europe. There are probably opportunities for more gestures of this kind although there is a limit to how far this can be taken without reciprocation or mutually agreed reductions. It may also be that there is *some* room for manoeuvre with the British nuclear deterrent. There is a case that Britain might include Trident, with its vastly increased capability, in the arms control discussions between the United States and the Soviet Union. As will be argued later, major reductions by the super powers could allow Britain to decrease the number of warheads deployed on Trident (and still retain a potent nuclear deterrent system). Given that Britain's force is regarded as a minimum 'last resort' deterrent, however, the margin for manoeuvre, without destroying the credibility of the force, is limited.

THE COST OF NUCLEAR WEAPONS

A powerful argument against the British nuclear deterrent and especially against the proposed Trident system is that the costs are too high for a country with Britain's limited economic means. Not only is the Trident force an extravagance, it is argued, but it creates quite unacceptable opportunity costs. Such arguments are not confined to those on the Left supporting a non-nuclear defence policy but are to be heard across the whole political spectrum and even within the defence establishment itself.

For the critics, especially on the Left, the expenditure of around nine to ten billion pounds on nuclear weapons is a scandal. Given their views about nuclear weapons, this is money which is wasted when it could be spent on other, much more worthwhile projects, like kidney machines, hospital beds, roads, houses, schools, etc. At a time when unemployment is over the two and a half million mark, such resources, they suggest, could much more profitably be used in new investment opportunities designed to create jobs. When unemployment is an important political issue the slogan 'Jobs not Bombs' has an increasingly appealing ring about it.

There is another group of critics who argue that Britain cannot afford to stay in the nuclear business. This group, however, stresses the opportunity costs to Britain's defence system as a whole resulting from the ever increasing bill for Trident. Quite simply money spent on Trident is money which cannot be allocated to other badly needed conventional weapons. There are members of this lobby (some within the defence establishment itself) who argue that the deterioration of Britain's conventional forces is almost certain to occur in the late 1980s as a result of the 1980 and 1982 Trident decisions. Those who support this assessment point to the 1981 Defence Review when it was announced that 'something had to go,' even though the Government remained committed to a 3 per cent increase in real terms in defence spending.[40] In that Review cut-backs in the Royal Navy's surface fleet were announced. Since then the Falklands war has been fought and some of the cut-backs have been reinstated. If this is added to the Government's decision not to continue the 3 per cent real increases from 1986 (opting instead for level funding) and the requirement for peak spending on a number of conventional projects in the late 1980s when expenditure on Trident is increasing, then the chances of another Defence Review in which once again 'something will have to go' seems very high. That 'something' will almost certainly be conventional capabilities, so the critics argue. To back up this view they point to the high percentages of the research and development and new equipment budgets (16 and 20 per cent respectively) which will be taken up by the new nuclear weapons programme. They also point out that 3 to 5 per cent of the defence budget as a whole allocated to the new programme (over 15 to 20 years) will be on top of the 2 per cent which will have to be spent on Polaris to keep it going until the new Trident force is deployed.

The argument about costs is clearly an argument about priorities. Supporters of the British nuclear deterrent argue that the 'threats' to hospitals, education and roads have to be set against the threats to the nation's security. *All* defence spending (not just that on nuclear weapons) in a sense deprives the civilian sector of resources. The job of government, with its responsibilities for the nation's defences, so it is argued, is not to make a stark choice between 'guns and butter' but to decide on how much butter versus how many (and what kind of) guns. In making these political choices the Government's judgement has been that no other use of our resources could possibly contribute as much to our security and the deterrent strength of NATO as a whole. They would also argue that such security must take precedence over 'extra' spending on hospitals, education, etc.

As far as the opportunity costs within defence are concerned the Government's case has been that spending on the nuclear deterrent is better than spending on *extra* tanks, aircraft or ships.[41] According to the former Defence Secretary, Michael Heseltine, the opportunity cost argument has been exaggerated anyway. The average of 3 per cent per annum is a very small percentage of the overall defence budget. Governments of the Left and Right have been prepared to spend continuously at least 2 per cent of the defence budget on nuclear weapons over the post war period and often more. The Conservative Government's plans are little different and are modest in comparison with the 20 per cent of the defence budget which French Governments have been prepared to spend on their nuclear deterrent. Mr Heseltine's replacement as Secretary of State for Defence, George Younger, has also argued that the case for a new defence review is not proven.[42] Despite level funding, he and his predecessor have argued that careful management of the defence budget can avoid the cancellation of major conventional projects in the late 1980s.[43] There may have to be some adjustments here and there – cuts in numbers, projects stretched over a longer period – but there is enough flexibility in the defence budget to allow this to take place without major choices having to be made.

To come to a conclusion about whether Trident is too expensive or not is very difficult. If one believes, as Lord Carver and others believe, that Trident is a waste of money (for whatever reason) then it clearly is too expensive. If, on the other hand, one believes that nuclear weapons do help enhance the nation's security in a dangerous world, then the price is worth paying. Certainly the nation can afford nuclear weapons if it so wishes. This does not exhaust the argument, however, because there are those who would say that although nuclear weapons do have utility there must be a limit to how much is spent on them. Given the nation's economic and social problems together with the strong possibility that conventional forces will suffer in the longer term (despite what the Defence Minister says) it might have been more sensible to have purchased a cheaper system. By the time the next election comes however, the choice will be Trident or nothing. This is something which will be considered in more detail later.

NUCLEAR WEAPONS, POLITICAL PRESTIGE AND INFLUENCE

Opponents of the nuclear deterrent are usually at pains to point out that despite claims to the contrary, there is very little evidence that the possession of nuclear weapons has given Britain any particular prestige or special influence in world affairs. According to this view the claim that nuclear capabilities demonstrate impressive technological expertise and, as a result, put Britain in a different league to non-nuclear powers is regarded as not proven. Nor is the argument very convincing that Britain has been able to utilise her special nuclear relationship with the United States to achieve particular influence in Washington, or so it is argued.[44]

Those who hold this view usually point to Japan and Germany as two states who are generally regarded as more influential in world affairs as a result of their economic performance. Neither of them possess nuclear weapons. Indeed it is often argued that their non-nuclear status has prevented them from diverting resources into non-productive areas and has contributed in no small way to their respective post war economic miracles. In contrast Britain's attempt to stay in the nuclear business has drained vital resources away from the domestic economy and deflected Britain from coming to terms with its true position in the world as a medium-range power. According to this argument, nuclear weapons have not obscured Britain's decline. Indeed, they have helped to hasten it.

As far as influence in Washington is concerned, critics point to the Suez and Grenada crises as examples where Britain has been totally ignored by American administrations. At Suez the United States forced Britain to abandon the invasion in a humiliating manner as a result of economic blackmail. And in the case of Grenada, Britain's advice was not only disregarded but the Foreign Secretary, Geoffrey Howe, was put in a very embarrassing position in Parliament when the intervention took place twenty-four hours after he had told the House of Commons that the United States would act cautiously. So much for British influence in Washington, argue the nuclear opponents.[45]

Once again there is clearly something in these arguments. Although influence and prestige are difficult to assess, a strong case can be made that Britain's membership of the nuclear club has not prevented Britain from slipping down the international league table as a result of continuing economic difficulties. Neither is Britain at present any longer at the top table when major arms control discussions take place between the Soviet Union and the United States. She did not participate in any of the SALT negotiations or the INF talks and she is not at present participating in the Geneva negotiations.

On the other hand it should not be forgotten that Britain probably has been able to play an influential role in NATO's Nuclear Planning Group, as the only European nuclear power present in that forum. And there is some evidence that, although Britain is no longer a member of the top table arms control negotiations, she has nevertheless made some important contributions to the American negotiating position at various times as a result of the continuous process of consultations which have taken place.[46] A case can also be made that Britain's nuclear status is also of relevance in Western European politics. This is not so much because Britain would be unwilling to see France as the only nuclear power in Europe (although this would certainly be unwelcome to British Government ministers). Rather, Britain's nuclear capability together with that of France provides a potential nucleus of a European nuclear deterrent which might emerge at some point in the future. It is also of some political relevance in the important, but sensitive, triangular political relationship between Britain, France and West Germany. Certainly West German Governments with the restrictions which prevent them from developing nuclear weapons and their close ties with France seem to welcome the retention by Britain of its nuclear capability. West German leaders, like British leaders, appear to be reluctant to see a nuclear monopoly by France in Western Europe. In this respect nuclear weapons do appear to have *some* political utility for Britain.

It can also be argued that although the prestige and influence conferred by the possession of nuclear weapons should not be exaggerated, they have not been a source of great political embarrassment. Because Britain has been a nuclear power for over thirty years she has not been faced with the kind of difficulties which France and China had in trying to establish an effective nuclear weapons programme in the 1960s and 1970s when the weight of world opinion was very much opposed to further nuclear proliferation. Nor has Britain had to face the dilemma which countries like Israel, South Africa, India and Pakistan have had. The pressures both for and against nuclear weapons for these countries have been equally great and have tended to result in clandestine attempts to produce a nuclear capability without openly admitting it.

The overall conclusion seems to be that despite *some* political utility there is not an overwhelming case on the grounds of prestige and influence alone to maintain an independent nuclear deterrent. On the other hand, although the political benefits may not be very great, it must be said that nuclear weapons have not generated any undue political costs for Britain. On these grounds therefore there is no powerful case for giving up nuclear weapons unilaterally either.

THE UTILITY OF NUCLEAR WEAPONS IN LESSER CONTINGENCIES

Linked to the argument that nuclear weapons do not confer significant prestige or influence in today's world is the contention that in lesser, non-nuclear contingencies they are irrelevant.[47] According to this argument the most frequent conflicts that Britain has been involved in during the postwar period have been either conventional or guerrilla wars against non-nuclear opponents. In these conflicts in places like Malaya, Korea, Suez, Aden, Borneo, the Falklands, etc., nuclear weapons have played no part. Britain has been unable, so it is argued, to bring to bear her overwhelming nuclear power to achieve her political objectives. Where victories have been won they have been achieved by essentially non-nuclear capabilities and resources. Given that these are the most likely contingencies in the future, it is suggested that scarce defence resources could more wisely be spent on conventional and perhaps intervention capabilities. This need to improve conventional forces has been very much at the heart of the Labour Party's approach to defence policy in recent years.

Once again the argument is not without some merit. A case can certainly be made that if the 1981 Defence Review with its nuclear bias had been put into effect at the time of the Argentine invasion of the Falklands, the run down of Britain's surface fleet, and the poor state of the intervention capabilities would have made the task of retaking the islands seem almost impossible. The Government's December 1982 review of the Falkland's conflict and the modifications in defence policy which resulted seem, in some respects, to confirm this.

The counter to the general argument about the irrelevance of nuclear weapons in lesser contingencies, however, is that these are not the most serious threats facing British security. It can also be argued that no one has ever expected nuclear weapons to have utility in lesser contingencies. The major purpose of nuclear weapons is to deter, in the last resort, an attack on Britain itself by other nuclear states. The argument that nuclear weapons were irrelevant in such crises as the Malayan emergency therefore is something of a 'straw man' argument – easy to knock down but not really serious in terms of the central arguments.

It should also be noted that the argument that nuclear weapons are not relevant in lesser contingencies is itself open to dispute. Were nuclear weapons relevant in the Falklands dispute in the Spring and Summer of 1982? No, say the critics. The fact that Britain possessed such weapons did not deter the Argentinian invasion proves the point. But does it? Let us suppose that Argentina did (or will) have nuclear weapons. Would Britain have sent (or would she send in the future) a task force to the South Atlantic? Given the fanaticism of the Argentinian population on the issue of the Malvinas, the British Government would have had to (and may still have to) take any nuclear threats seriously. Whether Britain would have sent the task force, given its very great vulnerability, under such circumstances, must be doubtful. And if the Argentinian junta had possessed nuclear weapons and Britain had not (a situation which could arise in the future if Britain unilaterally disarmed) – would Britain have sent a large task force then (and would she in the future)? The answer is probably no. This is not to argue that Britain would have been likely to actually use nuclear weapons in the Falklands conflict or will do so in the future. What it does suggest, however, is that the absence of nuclear weapons on one side and their possession by the other in any conflict is part of the calculation which governments have to bear in mind when assessing the risks they are taking. In this sense, nuclear weapons do provide something of a backdrop in conflict situations which can indirectly influence the decisions being made. The lack of such weapons in *certain circumstances* could well influence choices and inhibit British options in defence of its interests. This may not be an overwhelming reason for possessing nuclear weapons. Indeed the precise circumstances in which they might be of value are difficult to forecast. And the precise utility of such weapons is also difficult to evaluate. However, in a world in which nuclear proliferation cannot be ruled out, the potential significance of a nuclear capability in lesser contingencies should not be completely ruled out either.

A SUMMARY OF THE ARGUMENTS

The arguments presented thus far are far from straightforward. *In general* the contention is that the range of criticisms levelled against the British nuclear deterrent and NATO strategy are not as convincing as supporters of a non-nuclear, non-provocative defence policy would have us believe. More specifically:

a. It has been suggested that, although it cannot be proved, a strong case can be made that nuclear deterrence *has* helped to keep the peace since the Second World War.

b. On the question of morality it has been argued that the feeling of moral superiority of many unilateralists is unjustified. It is suggested that in the nuclear age we face a moral dilemma which is inescapable and perhaps insoluble; there are no courses of action realistically available which are free from moral difficulty. It is also argued that those who recommend a renunciation by Britain of its nuclear weapons on moral grounds, but who are willing to remain indefinitely in the nuclear Alliance of NATO are themselves open to the criticism of hypocrisy.

c. The arguments about the risks of nuclear deterrence are partly accepted. There clearly are dangers and dilemmas arising from the possession of an independent nuclear deterrent and arguably even more so from an Alliance strategy which threatens the early use of nuclear weapons. Whether British unilateralism and non-nuclear strategy for the Alliance would be less dangerous, however, is a matter of some dispute and certainly not self-evident.

d. Just as there are some risks inherent in nuclear deterrence, so also, it is suggested, there are question-marks over the credibility of both the British deterrent and NATO's strategy of Flexible Response. The argument presented here, however, is that although there is a case that a strategy based on the threat of mutual suicide is not terribly intellectually convincing, it is nevertheless politically realistic in the sense that potential aggressors are highly unlikely ever to take the risks involved in starting a process which could lead to unimaginable self-destruction.

e. On the question of nuclear proliferation it is argued that although there *is* some hypocrisy about British support for the Non-proliferation Treaty while at the same time purchasing Trident missiles from the United States, there is no real evidence that a British decision to give up nuclear weapons would have any impact on potential nuclear powers. The reasons why states decide to acquire nuclear weapons would seem to be much more related to their own regional security problems and domestic political debates than to following Britain's moral lead.

f. It is accepted that Britain is to a large extent dependent on the United States for its nuclear deterrent force. It is suggested, however, that this dependence should not be exaggerated – the decision to fire Britain's nuclear weapons remains very much in the hands of British political leaders. It is also argued that dependence brings important security advantages as well as some disadvantages.

g. The argument that nuclear deterrence does help to 'set East–West tensions in concrete' does seem valid. It does not follow from this, however, that British unilateralism would assist in any meaningful way in breaking the deadlock. Indeed it has been suggested that there is no evidence that the renunciation of nuclear weapons by Britain would have a significant impact on the cycle of mistrust and suspicion between East and West.

h. Whether the expenditure of between nine and ten billion pounds on Trident is too much for a country like Britain to pay is a matter of some dispute. The argument presented above suggests that while the costs have often been exaggerated by the non-nuclear lobby, it is highly likely that Britain's conventional forces will be adversely affected by such a level of expenditure. This is a problem which cannot be ignored.

i. It is suggested that those who argue that nuclear weapons are of little value in lesser contingencies have largely missed the point. In the first place they are not intended for such purposes. Their main value lies in deterring the major contingencies. It is also suggested that even in non-nuclear conflicts they can have *some* value in terms of the diplomatic backdrop which they provide.

The overall conclusion would seem to add up to a qualified support for the British nuclear deterrent and for NATO's strategy of Flexible Response. The fact that existing policies are susceptible to some justifiable criticisms, however, on moral, strategic, political, and economic grounds does suggest that there is some room for improvement in both British and Alliance strategies. Threatening to launch missiles against Soviet cities does create moral difficulties for British politicians (and for the rest of us). There are also some problems with the credibility of such a threat. And the opportunity costs associated with Trident are, without doubt, worrying. The threat by NATO to use nuclear weapons at an early stage of a conflict, together with the emphasis on nuclear escalation in Alliance strategy, and the forward deployment of battlefield nuclear weapons, all pose problems of credibility and risk which undermines domestic support for the Alliance. All these problems suggest the need for some reform. But what kind of reform?

Notes

1. K. Booth 'The Case for Non-Nuclear Defence', in John Roper (ed.), *The Future of British Defence Policy* (London: Gower, 1985).
2. 'The Case for Non-Nuclear Defence', p. 20.
3. Ibid.
4. Ibid.
5. Ibid.
6. For a development of this argument see J. Baylis, 'Britain and the Bomb', in G. Segal et al., *Nuclear War and Nuclear Peace* op. cit., pp. 116–52.
7. This is particularly the case in the war-fighting modes of deterrence (sometimes called 'deterrence through denial').
8. Many short-range battlefield weapons are deployed within 60 or 70 miles of the inner-German border and in a crisis would be over-run, perhaps within hours or a few days, of conflict breaking out, the critics argue.
9. See the arguments in J. Baylis 'Britain and the Bomb', op. cit., pp. 130–33.
10. See the arguments presented in *Defence Without the Bomb: The Report of the Alternative Defence Commission* (London: Taylor and Francis, 1983), pp. 89 and 276.
11. K. Booth, 'The Case for Non-Nuclear Defence' op. cit., p. 41. Ken Booth's rejection of the hypocrisy criticism (on pp. 160–2) on the grounds that a State allows Pacifists to be members of Society, even though the State prepares to defend itself, is not accepted by this author. Membership of Alliances and States is rather different. Alliances are predominantly about security. One important member of an Alliance of 16 members which fundamentally rejects the whole basis of Alliance strategy, is different from one individual or a small number of individuals (in 50 million) who, as Pacifists, reject the defence policies of the State to which they belong. Nations have the choice of whether or not to belong to Alliances. Individuals do not have the same degree of choice.

12. Ibid.
13. *Defence Without the Bomb*: *The Report of the Alternative Defence Commission* (London: Taylor and Francis, 1983), p. 89.
14. *Defence and Security for Britain: Statement to Annual Conference 1984 by the NEC*, (London: Co-operative Press, 1984), p. 15. Ken Booth argues on p. 160 that to be consistent Britain should try to persuade all other non-nuclear members of the Alliance to acquire nuclear weapons. This author rejects this argument. There is no inconsistency in British policy on this matter. Although the Alliance does consist of non-nuclear states, those states accept the nature of NATO nuclear strategy. The difference is that a unilateralist Britain would not accept that strategy and therefore, in terms of moral consistency, should withdraw (if not in the short term then in the long term).
15. *Defence Without the Bomb*, op. cit., p. 89.
16. Ibid.
17. Ibid.
18. Ibid.
19. K. Booth, 'The Case for Non-Nuclear Defence', op. cit., p. 41.
20. Ibid.
21. Ibid.
22. See 'Memorandum submitted by Mr Robin F. Cook, MP together with Dan Smith, *Sixth Report to the Expenditure Committee. The Future of the United Kingdom's Nuclear Weapons Policy*', Session 1978–9, No. 348 (London: HMSO, 1979), p. 140.
23. *Defence Without the Bomb*, op. cit., p. 103.
24. See pp. 300–10.
25. T. C. Schelling, *The Strategy of Conflict* (Cambridge: Harvard University Press, 1960), pp. 187–204.
26. See *Defence Open Government Document 82/1*, Cmnd.8517.
27. See J. Baylis, 'Britain and the Bomb' op. cit., p. 125.
28. K. Booth, 'The Case for Non-Nuclear Defence' op. cit., p. 33.
29. Ibid. See also J. Baylis *Anglo-American Defence Relations 1939–84: The Special Relationship* (London: Macmillan, 1984).
30. H. Wilson, *In Place of Dollars* (London: Tribune Pamphlet, 1952).
31. Andrew Pierre, *Nuclear Politics: The British Experience with an Independent Strategic Force 1939–1970* (London: Oxford University Press, 1972), p. 316.
32. For an analysis of the advantages and disadvantages of the special relationship to Britain see J. Baylis, *Anglo–American Defence Relations*, op. cit., pp. 208–13.
33. K. Booth, op.cit., p. 33.
34. Ibid., p. 35.
35. Robert Neild, *How to make up your mind about the Bomb* (London: Andre Deutsch, 1981), p. 8.
36. K. Booth, op. cit., p. 53.
37. J. Baylis in 'Britain and the Bomb' op. cit., pp. 117–18.
38. See F. Bjol, 'Nordic Security', *Adelphi Paper 181* and Ulstein, 'Nordic Security', *Adelphi Paper 81*.
39. K. Booth, op. cit., p. 53.

40. See *The Way Forward*, Cmnd.8288.
41. Ibid.
42. *Sunday Times*, 12 January 1986.
43. See D. Greenwood 'Defence' in P. Cockles, (ed.), *Public Expenditure Policy 1985/86* (London: Macmillan, 1985).
44. See R. Neild, op. cit., pp. 89–124.
45. See J. Baylis, *Anglo–American Defence Relations*, op. cit., pp. 191–94.
46. During the SALT II and INF negotiations in particular.
47. See p. 69.

9 The Political Problems of Non-Nuclear Strategies

THE NATURE OF NON-NUCLEAR, NON-PROVOCATIVE STRATEGIES

Before we can discuss the problems of defensive deterrence we need to clarify what such a strategy would involve. Although there are a variety of non-nuclear prescriptions, many advocates support a defence policy based on the renunciation of all nuclear weapons by Britain and the closing down of all nuclear bases in Britain and, if possible, in Western Europe as a whole. Such a defence policy might also imply a move by Britain and the Alliance away from the concept of 'forward defence' in Western Europe and existing counter-offensive capabilities and tactics towards the idea of 'defence in depth' and the principles of territorial defence. According to one writer:

> Armed primarily with light weapons, soldiers would serve in their own localities, dispersing to fight and exploiting their knowledge of the terrain. They form no fronts and no rears, no concentrations to invite tactical nuclear attack. The whole country becomes a hedgehog, its prickles individually no more than pin pricks but cumulatively presenting all-round defence against any assailant.[1]

According to writers like Frank Barnaby, Egbert Boeker and Anders Boserup a non-provocative defence policy is one in which:

> The build-up, training, logistics and doctrine of the armed forces are such that they are seen in their totality to be unsuitable for offence but just sufficient for a credible defence without nuclear weapons.[2]

Supporters of such a defence policy emphasise the need to significantly reduce such offensive capabilities as tanks, long-range aircraft and long-range missiles. Instead most point to the availability of certain items of new technology which they argue have enhanced the defence. Advances in precision-guidance munitions, the availability of cheap short-range anti-tank and anti-air missiles, the new remotely piloted vehicles together with short-range tactical aircraft all make it possible, so the argument goes, to formulate a defence policy which relies on neither nuclear weapons nor offensive capabilities. The aim would be a war of attrition in which the price of victory to an opponent would be seen to be too high. Such a strategy, supporters argue, would be a strong deterrent, but if deterrence were to break down, it would also provide an effective (but not suicidal) defence.

There are some particularly radical proponents of a non-provocative, conventional defence policy for the Alliance, like the German writers Professor Carl von Weizsacker and Dr Horst Afheldt, who not only oppose 'forward defence' but who also wish to abandon weapon systems like the tank altogether. Afheldt's contention is that armed forces like those of NATO and the Warsaw Pact which are structured around armoured formations are inherently offensive. Certainly this is how they are perceived by the other side, and this encourages suspicion and international instability. Afheldt's solution is a defence made up of 'a network of small units of "techno-commandos" (about three to four men per square kilometer) deployed throughout West Germany in area defence.'[3] The strength of the system would derive from the men's local knowledge of the terrain and their ability to use light-weight weapons provided by Emerging Technology (ET) – especially homing guided missiles – to disrupt enemy armoured formations. 'Warsaw Pact tanks would have no line to break; they would be unable to make contact with any enemy concentrations, and instead would be gradually worn away in a battle of attrition.' Afheldt's contention is that by the time the Soviet Union had fought its way to the Rhine, it would have lost more than 50 per cent of all its formations. The capability to inflict such losses would be a great deterrent, Afheldt claims, because it would be 'the equivalent of losing its East European glacis at the same time.'[4]

Horst Afheldt's views represent one end of the spectrum amongst supporters of defensive deterrence. There are others, like Major-General Jochen Löser who are less doctrinaire and more pragmatic in their commitment to territorial defence. Recognising some of the political difficulties of completely abandoning 'forward defence,' Löser a former Bundeswehr officer, has proposed what he describes as 'wide-area territorial defence' which would involve a battle zone in the region of 80 to 100 kilometres deep (forward of the Weser–Lech line).[5] The idea of Löser's defence would be to use a range of pre-planned obstacles to funnel the advance of enemy armoured formations towards the prepared defensive positions. Similar to Afheldt, he advocates light, local forces with the new generation of highly accurate anti-tank missiles attacking the massed Soviet tank formations 'in a series of innumerable small battles.' Where he disagrees with Afheldt is over the need for some counter-attack capabilities. In Löser's defensive plans there would be a role for mobile brigades, which in traditional military terms could be used in a counter-offensive at the critical moment to throw the enemy back. Such capabilities would, nevertheless, be limited. For Löser, unlike Afheldt, the key operational objective would be annihilation, not attrition.

Interest in this form of defensive deterrence policy is not confined to Germany. The British 'Alternative Defence Commission' in its Report *Defence Without the Bomb*, recommends a defence capability sufficient 'to inflict heavy losses on any invading force, but at most only a limited capacity to mount offensive operations in the opponent's territory.'[6] Another closely associated British organisation, 'Just Defence', has proposed a 'non-provocative, non-nuclear defence of Western Europe' similar to that supported by Afheldt. Their defensive zone would be 50 kilometres deep and their forces would be mobile and lightly armed with the latest generation of 'fire-and-forget' anti-tank missiles. In their defence system there would be no room for the provocative weapons like tanks, long-range bombers or surface-to-air missiles with ranges in excess of 80 kilometres.[7]

The Labour Party in Britain also committed itself to a non-provocative conventional defence posture at its annual Conference in October 1986. Although the precise details of this strategy were not spelled out, the 'Statement on Defence' for the Conference made it clear that Labour envisaged a radical change in the weapons systems and the tactical doctrine of British forces on the Central Front in Germany. New long-range missiles were rejected as being too provocative and existing long-range nuclear bombers were to be reallocated to new roles. According to the statement:

> There is a need to restructure the air force away from offensive and towards defensive roles, as part of a process of abandoning NATO's current reliance on nuclear weapons and rejecting 'deep strike' and more offensive capabilities.[8]

It was also argued that the next Labour government would push for new military tactics for all NATO forces on the Central Front. This would involve giving greater attention to 'territorial defence.' Whether this involved a wholehearted commitment to the ideas of writers like Afheldt or whether territorial defence was to be part of a more orthodox conventional strategy proposed by Löser was not clear. Whether a Labour government would remain committed to the concept of 'forward defence' also remained unclear. Various statements by the Shadow Defence Minister, Denzil Davies, in television interviews in October 1986, however, suggested that he believed that 'forward defence' was outdated. Mr Davies argued that 'forward defence' had arisen for political reasons and made little military sense. Although he didn't spell it out, the implication of what he said was that a future Labour government would be less committed to the 'forward defence' concept.

An interesting approach to defensive deterrence is put forward by Ken Booth in Part I. He advocates a layered defence for NATO divided into three zones. The 'forward defence zone', of around 60 kilometres, would be 'a show case for the "automated battlefield"' backed up by a 'combination of anti-armour infantry and "militia-guerrilla" networks.' The 'strategic defence zone,' would stretch back to around 150 kilometres from the IGB and would contain mobile forces, including armoured divisions and short-range missiles capable of attacking Warsaw Pact forces which have penetrated the 'forward defence zone.' And the final layer, the 'strategic reserve zone,' would consist of reserve army and air units well dispersed and protected against Soviet attacks. Unlike many other supporters of defensive deterrence he accepts that aircraft are essential in modern defence and main battle tanks are of great value in counter-offensive attacks to retake lost territory. Although he rejects NATO's current deep strike strategy he does recognise that attacks on military targets in Warsaw Pact territory would be necessary in a future conflict. As he notes, however, some supporters of defensive deterrence would see such proposals as a violation of the basic principles of *non-provocative* defence. His justification is that 'a balance has to be struck between "non-provocation" and "military conviction".' He is not alone in this attempt to integrate alternative defence ideas into the existing NATO force posture. Such an approach is also characteristic of the work of a number of West German writers like Lutz Unterseher, Albrecht von Müller and Andreas von Bülow.[9]

ALLIANCE DIFFICULTIES

If Britain were to adopt a truly non-provocative, non-nuclear strategy it would require the cancellation of the 1980 and 1982 Trident

Agreements with the United States, the complete phasing out of Polaris and the destruction of all British nuclear weapons and related facilities in Britain and on the Continent. It would require the complete reorganisation of the army, navy and air force and the scrapping of most, if not all, Britain's tanks, long-range aircraft, nuclear submarines and some of the surface fleet. At least this would be the implications of a non-provocative defence policy. It would also require the closing down and removal of all American nuclear bases from Britain and the refusal of facilities to the United States for any weapon system which could be used for major counter-offensive operations. In effect this might well mean the closure of most American military bases in Britain, especially if the US decided to pull its remaining forces out. Clearly these revolutionary changes could not take place overnight. Most supporters of the strategy, however, would wish to see a significant movement by Britain and the Alliance towards a non-nuclear defence policy within the life-time (four or five years) of a new Parliament.

It is difficult to believe that such a radical departure from the kind of defence policy which Britain has maintained under both Labour and Conservative governments since 1945 could be carried out without severe political problems for Britain in the Western Alliance. The Labour Party's pamphlet *Defence: The Security for Britain* (published in 1984) says that 'such moves would inevitably result in changes in Britain's relationship with the United States.'[10] This is surely a gross understatement. Such a policy would not only significantly contradict the strategic and tactical doctrines accepted by all members of the Alliance but if carried out it would, in the eyes of many members, fundamentally undermine the ability of the Alliance to defend itself.[11]

For many supporters of defensive deterrence these are issues which are not worth discussing in any detail. Their reply takes the form of 'we believe such changes ... would be welcomed by intelligent people on both sides of the Atlantic.'[12] Or 'France closed down American bases, why not Britain.'[13] Or 'Norway and Denmark refuse to allow nuclear weapons on their soil. Britain could do the same without any undue repercussions in the Alliance.'[14] Such views hardly represent a serious argument given the political (and strategic) risks involved in such a policy. To suggest that those who do not agree with one's views are not 'intelligent' is hardly conducive to trying to convince one's allies of the need for such reform. Those who point to the French example ignore the continuing emphasis in

French defence policy on the Force Nucleaire Strategique and the Socialist President Mitterand's strong support for the deployment of cruise and Pershing II missiles in the early 1980s. Similarly the cases of Norway and Denmark are not as convincing or as clear cut as they first appear. Norway and Denmark have ruled out the deployment of nuclear weapons on their soil in *peacetime* – but they have said nothing about what might happen in a war situation. They also support current strategy. Nor can it be said that in terms of political significance Norway and Denmark are as important as Britain in the Alliance. This is not to suggest that Norway and Denmark are unimportant members of the Alliance. Norway, in particular, is of great significance in Alliance defence. However, they share accepted restraints on military deployments in their country which were adopted at an early stage in the Alliance's history. For Britain – with its central role in the formation of the Alliance, its important contribution to the development of Alliance nuclear strategy, its role in the Allied command structure, and its crucial support for the American reinforcement of the Alliance – to adopt a non-nuclear, non-provocative defence policy would be much, much more serious for the Alliance.

For those, like Ken Booth, who are sensitive to this problem much would depend on how the reforms were handled.[15] If they were done precipitously and insensitively then a crisis would be likely in the Alliance. However, if Britain emphasised its strong commitment to Alliance conventional defence, perhaps by spending more on defence (and even introducing conscription) then the likely outburst of protest might well be contained. Indeed, it is often argued that a Democratic President in the United States would give Britain a more sympathetic hearing in its attempt to move the Alliance in a non-nuclear direction. It could be added that governments might come to power in other Western European countries who are supportive of a non-nuclear defence policy.

Arguments such as these cannot be dismissed out of hand. It is conceivable that if Britain did agree to phase its unilateralist programme over a fairly long period, and if it was prepared to put more money into conventional defence, then given a more sympathetic government in power in the United States and other Western European states, there might not be a serious crisis in the Alliance. There are, however, so many 'ifs', in such a position. What seems *much* more likely is that an American government of whatever complexion would regard the defection of one of her major allies in Europe to the non-nuclear camp with very great alarm. What

Europeans sometimes forget is that in general the spectrum of politics in the United States is rather more conservative, further to the Right, than in Europe. There certainly are Democrats and distinguished defence analysts in the United States who favour less emphasis being placed on nuclear weapons in Western strategy. This should not, however, be confused with support for a totally non-nuclear, non-provocative defence policy. As Mr Kinnock found on his visit to the United States in December 1986, there is very little, if any, support for such a policy, even in Democratic circles in the United States.[16] Those advocating such a policy would be regarded very much on the radical fringe. What this means is that, unless there is a very significant shift in American domestic politics over the next couple of years, the chances of a sympathetic hearing for such radical reform in Washington must be very slim indeed. Many Americans (rightly or wrongly) already regard Western Europeans as 'free-riders' on American security policies. At least there is a strong conviction in Congress that the Western Europeans are not bearing their fair share of the defence burden.[17] To cancel the Anglo-American nuclear exchange agreements, the Trident agreement, to phase out Polaris, to close down American nuclear bases, and perhaps to make continuing membership of NATO conditional on the movement to a non-nuclear defence policy would surely be too much for the most persuasive Labour politicians, irrespective of how Britain's non-nuclear status was packaged. What if the American Government could not be persuaded that this was the best way forward and Britain went ahead with the implementation of such non-nuclear policies?

Given the preoccupations of the present American Government (especially with the budget deficit problem), the refusal by Britain to allow American use of key facilities to help defend Western Europe would run a severe risk of a reappraisal of US defence commitments in Europe. The American Government of the day would be likely to conclude that a crucial member of the Alliance – indeed its closest ally in Europe – was unwilling to share the risks of the Alliance and was actively undermining the pursuit of an effective deterrent and defence posture by the Alliance. Indeed, key members of the Reagan Administration went out of their way to express their grave misgivings with the non-nuclear policy of the Labour Party in October 1986. Defense Secretary Caspar Weinberger and Assistant Secretary of Defense Richard Perle both appeared on British television expressing their fear that the Alliance would be severely weakened by such policies. They also expressed the view that the implementation of Labour defence policies would make it very difficult for the American Administration to hold back demands for US troop withdrawals from Europe. According to the American Ambassador in Britain, Charles Price, these remarks were shared by the Administration as a whole.[18] There were also indications that Democratic Senators, like the influential Sam Nunn of Georgia, were also deeply worried about Labour's policies. Senator Nunn even went as far as to say that if Britain 'pulled up the rug, the Atlantic Alliance itself would start unravelling.' Given Senator Nunn's interest in the past in American troop withdrawals and his influential role in the Senate (as chairman of the Armed Services Committee), these warnings should not be lightly dismissed.

Given America's own interests in European security the withdrawal of *all* American forces may not be likely even in circumstances such as these. Nevertheless, the withdrawal of significant numbers of American forces and a refocusing of US attention elsewhere is certainly a possibility and this would be very serious for the Alliance.[19] If this were to happen the chances of the European allies being able to provide an effective conventional defence against the massive conventional forces of the Soviet Union would be negligible. In other words, policies designed to produce a non-nuclear, conventional defence strategy would pose the *great* risk of triggering political reactions in the United States which might undermine *even further* than at present the ability of the Alliance to defend itself conventionally. Significantly less American troops in Europe would also be a political signal to the Soviet Union that the United States was less interested in the fate of Western Europe than in the past – which might encourage Soviet probing. The question that supporters of a non-nuclear policy have to answer is whether they can provide a reasonably strong guarantee that the United States will not react in this manner. If they cannot do this, the policy, it would seem, poses grave risks.

There would be those who would argue that if the US did reduce its conventional commitment to European defence the Western European states themselves might fill the vacuum. They might. The chances are, however, that they would not. There are legal restrictions placed upon a significant increase in West German conventional forces (as well as the political impact which this would have on the Soviet Union).[20] And there are no signs that Western European states are as yet prepared to shoulder the economic and political costs involved. As will be argued later every effort should be made to encourage greater European cooperation. However the day when a unified European Defence Community can take over the responsibility for the defence of Western Europe still seems a long way away.[21]

Another political difficulty with the proposals for a non-nuclear defence policy is that this might appear to imply a movement away from 'forward defence' in West Germany to a system of 'defence-in-depth.'[22] In many respects 'defence-in-depth' is a sensible military concept and if it could be achieved NATO's defensive position would no doubt be improved. For most West Germans, however, such a concept is politically unacceptable. 'Defence-in-depth' implies giving up the defence of the inner German border and falling back to defensible positions to the rear. Given that a third of the West German population (approximately 20 million people) live within a 100 kilometre strip west of the GDR border and 42 million people live within 200 kilometres of the border (some 70 per cent of the West German labour force) it is clearly very difficult for any German government to give up the concept of 'forward defence.' As General Leopold Chalupa, the German Commander in Central Europe argued in May 1985:

> Forward defence is indispensable for political reasons.... [It] is politically unacceptable to tell the Germans 'we will fight for you, but in the worst case we will win the battle on the Rhine. Thirty per cent of your country may be destroyed and you might be dead, but you can be assured that we will win the battle for freedom.'[23]

Statements such as these clearly pose problems for the Labour Party's non-provocative defence posture. Labour's apparent rejection of 'forward defence' fails to understand the political symbolism of this concept. The Alliance has always had the problem of reconciling political and military realities. 'Forward Defence' is the only strategy acceptable to the West Germans. This is the constraint that military commanders and other NATO governments will have to continue to work with. The concept has a certain flexibility but it produces limitations on tactical planning which cannot be ignored. To say, as the Labour Party seems to be saying, that forward defence will have to go in the interests of military effectiveness and that the West Germans will have to accept this fact is not only diplomatically insensitive but politically unrealistic. A similar insensitivity to German thinking on 'forward defence' is seen in Part I of this book.

There will be those who would argue that not to pursue a policy of defensive deterrence on the grounds that the political repercussions in the Alliance are too great or the nuclear lobby too strong, are guilty of undue fatalism. It has been argued that at least it is worth the try of moving the Alliance in this direction. 'It might prove more successful than the pessimists argue. If not, then Britain can always withdraw.' This at least is an honest stand to take. The main objection to this position is that it tends to underestimate the very real dangers of significantly undermining the cohesion of the Alliance and it also underestimates the difficulties of a neutralist Britain (which might be the logical outcome) in looking after its own security in a dangerous world. For those who believe that the present policy is highly unstable and nuclear destruction is just around the corner, risks such as these may seem worth taking. To those, however, who see great value in remaining part of a like-minded Alliance – despite its deficiencies – these are risks which must be thought about very seriously given the potential political and therefore strategic consequences which might well follow from British unilateralism.

Will a non-nuclear policy work?

In part at least, the question of whether Britain should take the risks involved in pursuing a non-nuclear defence policy depends on an assessment of whether such a policy will work. This needs to be considered at two levels. Firstly, how would a non-nuclear Alliance, cope with threats from a nuclear state, like the Soviet Union? And secondly, could a non-nuclear alliance defence policy provide an *effective* defence against an opponent with a spectrum of offensive conventional, chemical and nuclear capabilities? The first of these questions will be dealt with here and the second in Chapter 10.

THE QUESTION OF NUCLEAR BLACKMAIL

A weak link in the non-nuclear case has always been the problem of coping with nuclear blackmail. Not surprisingly in the last year or so supporters of defensive deterrence have put a great deal of effort into trying to debunk what they describe as 'the myth of nuclear blackmail.'[24] One of the more intellectually interesting discussions of this 'myth' is presented by Ken Booth in the first part of this book.[25] He bases his contention that 'there is less to the idea that nuclear disarmament would lead to nuclear blackmail than meets the eye' on a number of key arguments. These need to be looked at carefully in turn.

1 'Nuclear blackmail is likely to be rare'

The argument here is that 'we need not assume an outbreak of Soviet attempts to coerce non-nuclear European countries in the future, especially if the NATO framework is maintained.'[26] This is because the United States will still retain nuclear weapons and the Soviet Union will recognise that Western Europe remains important to the United States. In response to this, it should be said that those worried about nuclear blackmail do not necessarily believe that there would be a rash of coercive threats as soon as nuclear disarmament took place. What they fear, and what this argument fails to confront, is an extreme crisis sometime in the future in which the Soviet Union attempts to coerce Western Europe, believing that the chances of a US response are very slim. The President, after all, in such circumstances would be faced with a stark and unenviable choice – to threaten to start a strategic nuclear war which would mean mutual suicide or to threaten to fight conventionally in Europe against a superior conventional *and nuclear* opponent (neither of which might appear credible). If the Soviet Union itself believed (as it might well) that in such a crisis the United States would be unlikely to unleash its nuclear forces or even, given its chances of defeat in Europe, to fight conventionally, then it might be tempted to initiate such a policy of nuclear blackmail. Such circumstances might be rare, but they are probably more likely to occur if the Alliance adopted a non-nuclear posture. Certainly, given the often brutal nature of world politics in which superior power often plays a central role, such circumstances could not be ruled out.

2 'The risks of nuclear blackmail should decrease'

According to this argument, the more nuclear blackmail remains unused and the more often non-nuclear states resist nuclear states (even to the point of fighting them), the more problematical it will be for nuclear states to utilise nuclear threats as an instrument of coercion.[27] To begin with, it does not follow that if nuclear threats are not used frequently they will automatically lose their effectiveness. Indeed it could be argued that quite the reverse is true. The use of nuclear threats only at times of great crisis might well emphasis the potency of such weapons which could well cause non-nuclear states to buckle under the threat of the catastrophic consequences which just might happen if they resist. The more that happens the more credible the threat becomes.

Another problem with the argument is that it encourages states to resist nuclear blackmail. This may be prudent for states in the war against terrorism but is it prudent in the context of conflict between nuclear and non-nuclear stress? It might work, as in the case of the Vietnamese, but equally it might not. By encouraging non-nuclear states to fight when they are subjected to nuclear blackmail, such a strategy poses serious risks of nuclear annihilation should the stakes be very high. Much depends on the circumstances in which the threats are made and the reputation for ruthlessness of the threatening state. Not all states, however, are likely to be able to summon up the collective resolve to resist threats of this kind given the knowledge of their inferiority and the potential consequences for their security. One only has to consider the late 1930s and the impact of military threats by Nazi Germany against weaker neighbours to illustrate this point.

3 'Nuclear blackmail is a one-shot strategy'

There is perhaps a little more in the argument that nuclear states are likely to weigh the advantages of successful nuclear blackmail against the disadvantages of nuclear proliferation which this would help to encourage.[28] Given the severe problems, especially for the Soviet Union, of more and more states acquiring nuclear weapons they would be very circumspect about using such threats, so the argument goes.

Once again this *might* well be so. But to base one's whole security policy on the expectation that the Soviet Union would *always* refrain from utilising such a powerful instrument of coercion because of a possible worry about nuclear proliferation would be the height of irresponsibility. The Soviet leaders might conclude either that further nuclear proliferation was not an inevitable consequence of their use of nuclear blackmail or that proliferation was likely to occur anyway and thus conclude that given the vital interests involved in a particular dispute, the advantages of successful nuclear blackmail outweighed the disadvantages. The Soviet Union has after all shown itself willing in the past to accept serious diplomatic difficulties and even long term security problems when an immediate crisis seemed to demand forceful action. It has also shown itself capable of miscalculating the consequences of its actions as well.[29] The argument therefore that nuclear blackmail is a 'one-shot strategy' must be regarded as unproven.

4 'Nuclear blackmail is neither easy nor cost free'

There is also a case to be made that 'in peacetime there are strong political constraints operating against nuclear blackmail, which should induce caution in many circumstances.'[30] In their critique of 'the myth of nuclear blackmail' Frank Barnaby and Egbert Boeker have argued that 'the Soviet Union would lose political credit by blackmailing Western Europe, not only internationally but also internally.'[31] On the domestic level, their contention is that there are so many references to peace and harmony in Soviet literature that 'the internal Soviet repercussions of nuclear blackmail should not be neglected.'[32]

It is true that there are political constraints against the use of nuclear blackmail. But then no one has ever argued that nuclear blackmail is necessarily easy or cost-free. But this clearly does not prevent its use. To argue that the Soviet Union would be unlikely to use such coercive threats against Western Europe because it would lose political credit abroad and there would be domestic repercussions seems naive in the extreme. Such considerations seem to have had little impact on Soviet actions in Hungary in 1956, Czechoslovakia in 1968 or Afghanistan in 1979. Nor did they prevent the Soviet Union from using military threats against Poland in the early 1980s.

5 'Nuclear blackmail can be resisted'

It may well be true that non-nuclear powers can resist nuclear blackmail. But as Ken Booth argues 'what could be done in practice would be very scenario dependent.'[33] Much depends, as he says, on the circumstances: the reputation of the threatener, whether vital interests are involved, the international environment at the time, the domestic difficulties of the country being threatened, the cohesion of the Alliance, etc. It may be that 'the threat could be ignored' or 'a threatener's bluff could be called.'[34] But, by implication, there clearly are circumstances when it would be necessary for a non-nuclear state to defer to nuclear threats. Even if one possesses nuclear weapons there might well be a case for surrender or compliance under certain circumstances. In situations, however, where both sides have nuclear weapons the consequences of initiating threats are incalculable and the restraints upon the potential blackmailer are very great given the consequences of getting it wrong. In circumstances, however, where a nuclear power confronts a non-nuclear power or non-nuclear bloc the calculations are easier for the blackmailer to make. The restraints are still present but they are much less.

The conclusion seems to be that although the idea of nuclear blackmail may be 'ambiguous, the mechanisms uncertain ... the likelihood incalculable, and the counteractions various', the risks are not as remote, or the dangers, as exaggerated, as the supporters of a non-nuclear defence policy would have us believe.[35] The arguments that nuclear blackmail will be rare, that it should decrease and that it is a 'one-shot strategy' may be little more than wishful thinking. Because nuclear blackmail will not be cost-free and because it can be resisted in certain circumstances does not mean it will not take place or that one does not have to worry about it. In this sense nuclear blackmail is not a myth but a very real possibility which defence planners have to guard against.

When confronted by the weaknesses of their argument about nuclear blackmail supporters of a non-nuclear defence policy fall back on the arguments that if a non-nuclear state is faced by nuclear blackmail it can always give in. 'The risks of blackmail, however, are preferable to accepting the risks and burdens of independent nuclear deterrence and flexible response'.[36] At this level the argument is about the balance of risk associated with particular strategies. Before we can make a judgment about the over-all balance of risk associated with different strategies it will be necessary to consider the military effectiveness of a non-nuclear defence policy. On the question of nuclear blackmail, however, the argument presented here is that such blackmail is more likely to occur in any conflict of interest between a nuclear Soviet Union (and Warsaw Pact) and a non-nuclear Britain and Western Europe than in a conflict in which both sides possess nuclear capabilities. Similarly the chances of successfully confronting nuclear blackmail would seem to be greater with nuclear weapons than without them. The risks of failure of a non-nuclear strategy are high. It would also seem to be the case that the risks of catastrophe are not noticeably less with a non-nuclear than with a nuclear deterrence policy. At the end of the day a nuclear state faced with nuclear threats has the same option to defer as a non-nuclear state has. In general then a strong case can be made that on the question of nuclear blackmail the balance of risk seems to be very much against a non-nuclear defence policy and indicates that great caution should be exercised in moving either Britain or the NATO Alliance in that particular direction.

Notes

1. See *Die Welt*, 3 December 1983 and *Defence Without the Bomb*, The Report of the Alternative Defence Commission (London: Taylor and Francis, 1983), op. cit., pp. 170–73 for the views of Horst Afheldt on defensive deterrence. See also H. Afheldt, 'Tactical Nuclear Weapons: and European Security' in SIPRI, *Tactical Nuclear Weapons: European Perspective* (London: Taylor and Francis, 1978).
2. F. Barnaby and E. Boeker, 'Defence Without Offence: Non-nuclear Defence for Europe'. *Peace Studies Papers* No. 8 (London: Housemans for the Bradford School of Peace Studies, 1982).
3. *Defence Without the Bomb*, op. cit., pp. 170–3.
4. Ibid.
5. Ibid., p. 173. Löser's books are *Weder Rotnoch Tot* (Munich: Gunter Olzog, 1981) and *Gegen den Dritten Wettkrieg* (Herford: Mittler, 1982). See also Jochen Löser, 'The Security Policy Options for Non-Communist Europe,' *Armada International*, 2/1982.
6. Ibid., pp. 7–12.
7. F. Barnaby and S. Windass, *What is Just Defence?* (Oxford: Just Defence, 1982).
8. Labour Party Conference, 'Statement on Defence', October, 1986.
9. For a useful summary of the ideas of Unterseher, Von Müller and Von Bülow see Jonathan Dean, 'Alternative Defence: Answer to NATO's Central Front Problem?, *International Affairs*, vol 64, no. 1., 1987/8.
10. *Defence and Security for Britain*, (Statement to Annual Conference 1984 by the National Executive Committee), p. 15.
11. Certainly the Labour Party's unilateralism has brought warnings from the US Assistant Secretary of the Defense, Richard Pearl, that such a policy could lead to the destruction of the Atlantic Security relationship. See *The Times*, 7 February 1986.
12. *Defence and Security for Britain*, op. cit., p. 15.
13. *Defence Without the Bomb*, op. cit., p. 95.
14. This is a view implied in the Labour Party's NEC document, *Defence and Security for Britain*, op. cit.
15. K. Booth, 'The Case for Non-nuclear Defence', op. cit., p. 44. See also Denis Healey, 'A Labour Britain, NATO and the Bomb,' *Foreign Affairs*, Spring 1987.
16. Those like Robert McNamara, who have been critical of NATO strategy would not go as far as supporting a non-nuclear, non-provocative defence policy.
17. See Simon Lunn, *Burden-Sharing in NATO* (London: Routledge, and Kegan Paul, 1983).
18. The American ambassador to Great Britain, Charles Price, warned in May 1986 that if a future Labour government went ahead with its pledge to remove American nuclear weapons from British soil then the United States would face pressure from the American people to shut down *all* its military bases in Britain. See *Sunday Times*, 'U.S. Warns Labour on Bases,' 4 May 1986.
19. Given the debate in American defence circles between supporters of

	continentalist and maritime strategies the debate could swing in favour of the maritime lobby advocating a more unilateral global role for the US focusing on the Pacific rather than Europe.
20.	Restrictions stemming from the Paris agreements of 1954 and the bargain struck on West German rearmament through the Western European Union.
21.	For the failure of the European Defence Community idea in the 1950s, see E. Fursdon, *The European Defence Community: A History* (London: Macmillan, 1980).
22.	*Defence Without the Bomb*, op. cit., pp. 170–73.
23.	See *Sueddeutsche Zietung*, 9 May 1985.
24.	See F. Barnaby and E. Boeker, 'Defence Without Offence', op. cit., pp. 32–5.
25.	See K. Booth, op. cit., pp. 49–52 and pp. 194–204 above. See also R. K. Betts, *Nuclear Blackmail and Nuclear Balance* (Washington: Brookings, 1987).
26.	Ibid., p. 49.
27.	Ibid., p. 50.
28.	Ibid.
29.	Soviet intervention into Afghanistan seems to be an example of this.
30.	K. Booth, op. cit., pp. 50–1.
31.	F. Barnaby and E. Boeker, op. cit., pp. 32–3.
32.	Ibid.
33.	K. Booth, op. cit., p. 51.
34.	Ibid.
35.	See p. 203.
36.	K. Booth, 'The Case for Non-nuclear Defence', op. cit., p. 49.

10 The Military Problems of Non-Nuclear Strategies

While there are doubts about the ability of a non-nuclear defence policy to cope with nuclear blackmail there are even greater problems about the military effectiveness of such a strategy. Indeed in part the two difficulties are related. If the strategy is seen to be militarily suspect (as will be suggested here) then the chances of nuclear blackmail being used (successfully) will be increased.

The military objective of a non-nuclear, non-provocative defence policy would be to wear an enemy down through a war of attrition. The aim would be to deny him an easy victory, to constantly harrass his forces, to utilise new technology to make the price of aggression too high by blunting his military capabilities. This, it is argued, would prove effective in deterrent and defence terms. There are, however, a number of military weaknesses to such a strategy which supporters seem either to play down or ignore.

THE DIFFICULTY OF DEALING WITH ARMOURED FORCES

The first problem with the kind of territorial defence advocated by Afheldt, Barnaby and Boeker is how such lightly armed, small military formations can in practice deal with a massive armoured blitzkrieg by a country with the kind of military resources possessed by the Soviet Union. Such a 'defence-in-depth' strategy puts a very heavy emphasis on the effectiveness of new technology. While recent experiences in the Arab–Israeli wars and the Falklands conflict indicate that new technology can be very potent, to put such total faith in anti-tank and anti-aircraft missiles would seem to be highly questionable. The Middle Eastern and Falklands battlefields are clearly very different in terms of terrain, weather and urban conurbations from the likely battlefields of Western Europe. All these things can make targeting very difficult – even with new technology. The consensus amongst military analysts seems to be, as Hew Strachan has pointed out, that 'the tank is more vulnerable than it was, but is not yet so vulnerable that a defence can afford to structure itself disproportionately around anti-tank weapons.'[1] The need for mobility against a range of offensive thrusts also indicates that the tank itself retains an important role in anti-tank operations.

The importance of the tank in counter-offensive operations has also been deliberately played down by most supporters of non-provocative defence. Because tanks are perceived as major instruments of offensive strategies, they must either have no place in a defensive strategy or their numbers must be severely constrained in order not to appear provocative to an opponent. The problem with this view is that tanks have a number of different roles one of which is to conduct the counter-offensive to recover ground lost and to disrupt enemy operations, which is an essential part of any *defence*. Most military manuals stress the importance of wresting the initiative from an opponent in effective defence operations. In the words of a 1981 American Army field manual:

> An offensive spirit must be inherent in the conduct of all *defensive* operations – it must be active defence, not a passive one. This is because offensive action, whatever form it takes, is the means by which the nation or a military force captures and holds the initiative, achieves results, and maintains freedom of action.[2]

Few military strategists would recommend the kind of negative tactical defensive tactics inherent in a non-provocative defence policy which emphasises a 'war of attrition' rather than a 'war of restoration'.

Major-General Löser and Ken Booth are two supporters of defensive deterrence who seem to recognise this problem. Löser has a place in his defence plans for mobile brigades which will be capable of counter-offensive operations.[3] Ken Booth also has a place for armoured divisions in his second layer of defence. The difficulty with both plans is that either this capability for the counter-attack will be too small to cope with the scale of operations required against many axes of a Soviet advance, or, if it is large enough to undertake effective counter-offensive operations, it may be perceived to be provocative by the Soviet Union.

THE DIFFICULTIES OF DEALING WITH NUCLEAR-ARMED FORCES

All of this so far assumes that the Warsaw Pact confines its operations to conventional forces only. But what if the Alliance as a whole had only conventional forces based on defensive deterrence principles while the Soviet Union retained a full spectrum of offensive conventional capabilities, nuclear and chemical weapons? How could NATO defend itself against such forces? Even if NATO as a whole retained a nuclear capability, Labour's defence policies might withdraw such weapons from British forces on the Central Front. If a non-nuclear BAOR stayed in its existing sector while NATO forces on either side were nuclear armed, there could well be a grave danger that, in the event of war, the Soviet Union would regard the British sector as very weak. Knowing that nuclear weapons would not be used against its forces the Warsaw Pact might well see this as the most fruitful avenue of advance. This being the case Labour's policies would seem to lead logically to the withdrawal of BAOR from its present role in Alliance defence. What role would it then play? Perhaps a role as part of the Alliance's mobile strategic reserve. But this could well still bring it into operations in various sectors where nuclear weapons were being used. Apart from this difficulty of what to do with BAOR if the Alliance as a whole retained its nuclear strategy there is also the problem of military commands in the Alliance. At present British officers hold key positions commanding NATO land, sea and air forces in various sectors, all of which have nuclear capabilities. A non-nuclear Britain would find it very difficult to go on providing officers for such positions. The result would be the loss of a great deal of military and political influence in the Alliance. It is difficult to see how the Labour Party's non-nuclear policies would allow it to stay in a nuclear alliance like NATO given the practical problems involved.

The importance of forward strike capabilities

Another military weakness with a non-provocative defence policy like that proposed by the Labour Party is that there is little or no provision for striking at the enemy's rear – his second and third echelons – as they are deployed to support and replace the main advances. Because long-range missiles and aircraft are potentially offensive weapons, supporters of defensive deterrence are reluctant to include them in their defensive plans. For most military observers, however, such ideological rigidity would rob the Alliance of one of the most important tactical objectives of any defence. To leave the enemy to build up his logistic support and communications without fear of being attacked, just because they were outside the territory of the defending armies, to most military strategists would appear ludicrous.⁴ Such proposals would leave the initiative entirely in the hands of the enemy and make the tasks of defending Western Europe almost impossible.

Ken Booth's proposals outlined in Part I partially recognises this problem. He accepts that some ability to attack beyond the IGB would be necessary. His proposals, however, are rather vague. He does not tell us how much 'shallow-strike' capability will be needed. He does not tell us what kind of capability will be required or how deep the strikes should be. Should they be restricted to 20, 50 or 100 kilometres into Warsaw Pact territory? How would we limit our capabilities so precisely to send just the right signal to the other side?

The attempt to achieve a non-provocative defence is a laudable objective. The dilemma, however, is clear. In leaning over backwards to signal one's non-aggressive intentions to a potential adversary there is a distinct danger of weakening one's defensive effort to the point where it is no longer effective. Sending the right political signals often seem to be more important than providing a military defence which will work against the armed forces which the potential enemy actually has. NATO in the past has always had a defensive military strategy and a limited counter-offensive potential but this has not prevented the Soviet Union from adopting an essentially offensive military strategy and providing itself with superior conventional forces which are arguably more than it requires for its own defence. If the argument is that the Soviet Union traditionally over insures, that it requires large conventional forces in part to control Eastern Europe, and that its offensive strategy is the result of its strategic culture and particularly its experiences in the Second World War, then it seems doubtful that it would radically alter its defence policy as a result of a move towards a non-provocative defence policy by NATO. The debates at present in the Soviet Union about defensive tactics have as yet had no impact on Soviet deployment or procurement.

The case being made here is not that NATO should ignore the consequences of its strategy on Soviet perceptions. There is a strong case for trying, as far as possible, not to be provocative. This must not be done, however, at the expense of effective defence. Nor is it being suggested that ideas like the militia-guerrilla network concepts should be rejected out of hand. Some of these defensive concepts may provide interesting options for improvements in NATO'S tactics provided they are seen as a *complement* (not an alternative) to existing mobile concepts. Also it is not being argued here that there is no room for new technology in conventional defence. New technology is certainly no panacea but it does seem likely to provide a useful supplement to the defence and may help to lessen the dependence on nuclear capabilities. What NATO requires is a sensitive mix of new and old technology which provides a sound defensive capability without being *unnecessarily* provocative to the Soviet Union. Some of the ideas inherent in the concept of defensive deterrence are worth thinking about. This is a theme which will be developed later.

The problem of morale

Apart from the tactical difficulties of dealing with massed armoured formations and providing a capability for recovering lost ground there is another weakness with the ideas of Afheldt, Barnaby and Boeker which needs to be considered. This is the problem of morale. The basic fighting unit in most of the non-nuclear proposals would be very small. Afheldt talks of three or four men covering an area of a square kilometre. A number of writers have questioned whether the individual soldiers in such small formations will be sufficiently motivated to cope with the magnitude of the task facing them.[5] Various studies of war have pointed to the importance of group solidarity in creating good morale.[6] The problem with small groups is that individual soldiers may well feel alone and isolated. Their individual responsibility would be very great and their chances of support would be decidedly limited. This feeling of isolation together with the commitment to indefinite combat, it is argued, could well have a very serious effect on the morale of the defending soldiers.

The weaknesses of territorial defence

Over the past few years these ideas of territorial defence have been subjected to a great deal of scrutiny by military experts who have attempted to assess the effectiveness of such 'alternative strategies'. With very few exceptions the consensus of opinion is that they simply *will not work*. In a debate on 'alternative strategies' which took place in the West German Bundestag Defence Committee in November and December 1983 the ideas of Professor Carl Friedrich von Weizsacker and Dr Afheldt on 'area defence' were discussed in some detail by a range of high ranking German military experts. Despite some differences of opinion on current NATO strategy amongst the German Generals, without exception, they found serious flaws in the Weizsacker/Afheldt proposals.[7]

The idea of territorial defence has also been sharply criticised by Field Marshal Lord Carver, the former British Chief of the General Staff, who in recent years has been a consistent critic of the British nuclear deterrent. Lord Carver is often quoted by the unilateralist lobby in Britain to give military respectability to its ideas. In practice although Lord Carver has supported the abandonment of the British nuclear deterrent and would like to see less emphasis placed on nuclear weapons, he nevertheless supports the presence of American nuclear bases in Britain and the retention of some nuclear weapons by the Alliance. Lord Carver believes that some reform of Alliance strategy is needed but he is not a supporter of the territorial defence school. In his book *A Policy for Peace* he argues that:

> The prospect of having to deal with these forms of defence is not likely to deter a country like the Soviet Union, which has massive military resources, not least of manpower and is insensitive to both domestic and international opinion about how they are used. Nor would such strategies provide forces that could quickly seal off and contain an invasion which had a limited aim or had resulted from some misunderstanding, an eventuality that is more likely than that of massive all-out invasion designed to overrun the whole of Europe.[8]

Lord Carver is one of the more radical military figures in Britain and not unsympathetic to the criticisms of the nuclear-bias in NATO strategy. His military critique of territorial defence therefore is all the more devastating.

Other conventional strategies

The concept of a non-provocative defence policy is not the only one put forward by supporters of conventional deterrence. A non-nuclear strategy could take other forms. There are those who argue that the Alliance should beef up its existing conventional forces, retaining largely the present mix of defensive and offensive weapons. Contingency plans should then reflect this particular conventional force structure. And there are those who favour a more offensive or retaliatory conventional posture designed to threaten Soviet control over Eastern Europe in the event of an attack upon Western Europe. According to Samuel Huntington, to be effective, deterrence has to move beyond the possibility of defense and include the probability of retaliation. Conventional deterrence requires not just an increase in conventional forces; it also requires a reconstitution of conventional strategy.[9] The key question is whether either of these conventional options would prove effective in military or deterrence terms without the backing of nuclear weapons?

In the case of an improved conventional defence along existing lines there is not only the problem of the additional financial resources to create such a capability but there is also the military problem of dealing with an opponent with an offensive strategy.[10] In his analysis of the 1973 Arab–Israeli war Saadia Amiel argues that 'without very clear offensive options, a merely passive or responsive defensive strategy, which is based on fire-power and fighting on friendly territory, cannot withstand an offensive strategy of an aggressor who possesses a relatively large, well prepared standing offensive force'.[11]

This is likely to be the case in central Europe. Should a Soviet offensive occupy part of West Germany in any future conflict NATO would then be faced with the problem of removing Warsaw Pact forces. Even with improved conventional forces this would prove difficult and the pressures for a cease-fire would be very great. As Huntington has argued, 'a Soviet invasion of West Germany that ended with the neutralization and/or demilitarization of all or part of that country would be a tremendous success from the Soviet point of view.'[12]

It might be argued that a more retaliatory conventional strategy would pose more political and military risks for the Soviet Union and as a result make invasion much less likely. This was the view put forward by the American Commission on Integrated Long-Term Strategy which produced its Report under the title, *Discriminate Deterrence* in early 1988. At present NATO's 'follow-on forces attack' (FOFA) strategy envisages NATO striking selectively at the aggressor's reinforcements. This strategy does not, however, imply any will or capacity to conquer or hold Warsaw Pact territory. The *Discriminate Deterrence* Report, however, recommended that plans should be made for Alliance 'ground forces to mount counter-offensives across the Nato–Warsaw Pact border' and for the development of a capacity to counter-attack 'deep into enemy territory'.

It must be said, however, that plans such as these would pose serious difficulties for a defensive alliance like NATO. As Sir Michael Howard, François de Rose and Karl Kaiser have rightly pointed out the adoption of such a strategy by the Alliance would 'demand a transformation of NATO forces of a kind which would be economically and politically unacceptable in Western Europe'.[13] It would destroy the popular consensus which depends on the Alliance being seen as strictly defensive in its purposes'. Those who recommend such offensive conventional strategies usually envisage such operations as being part of a wider nuclear strategy. Even if they were seen as the central component of a wholly non-nuclear conventional strategy, however, the same problem of acceptability would exist. Such a strategy would also suffer from the same difficulty which all purely conventional deterrent strategies face – how an alliance armed with only conventional forces can deal effectively in military terms with an opposing alliance armed with a wide spectrum not only of conventional forces but also nuclear and chemical weapons as well? Given the strategic parity between the super powers and the question marks over the credibility of the American nuclear guarantee to Western Europe, a nuclear-armed Warsaw Pact and a conventionally armed NATO would leave Western Europe at a severe military disadvantage.[14]

THE CASE OF YUGOSLAVIA

Those like Ken Booth who argue that robust conventional forces can constitute a credible deterrent often point to Yugoslavia's defiance of the Soviet Union from 1948 onwards. According to this view 'the defection of Yugoslavia from the Soviet camp represented a highly provocative symbol of independence from Stalin's Soviet Union. Its policies threatened not only the integrity of the Soviet Union's postwar empire, but also its claim to unquestioned ideological authority in the socialist world.' Despite the pressure, however, exerted by the Soviet Union to bring Yugoslavia back into the socialist commonwealth', Tito did not give in and Stalin did not invade. The reason for this, so we are told, was that Yugoslavia's military preparations, her reputation for tough resistance and her geography provided an effective deterrent to direct Soviet intervention. If small non-nuclear Yugoslavia can hold out against the might of the Soviet Union, why not the stronger states of Western Europe? This is the implicit question in Ken Booth's treatment of the subject in Part I.

The Yugoslavian case study, however, is very misleading. Provocative as Tito's behaviour was, Stalin almost certainly believed that Yugoslavia, given its geographical location, was of secondary strategic interest to the Soviet Union. Much more important Soviet security interests in 1947/8 were affected by events in Germany and Czechoslovakia and relations with the West. The fear of getting bogged down in a conflict against the partisans in the mountains of Yugoslavia may well have affected Stalin's judgement. But the relative unimportance of Yugoslavia, preoccupations elsewhere, as well as the tasks of domestic recovery and consolidation after the devastating effects of the Second World War must have weighed much more heavily on Stalin's mind.

An interesting parallel can be drawn with Afghanistan in 1979. The Afghan rebels had an even greater reputation for resistance than the Yugoslavian partisans over a much longer historical period. Also the terrain is even more rugged and difficult than Yugoslavia. And yet *this* non-nuclear defensive resistance did not deter the Soviet Union from intervening when it believed important security interests were at stake. Why, as Ken Booth suggests in Part I, should Yugoslavia be any more significant than Afghanistan?

What matters are questions of strategic interest. When, in the past the Soviet Union has perceived its security interests to be adversely affected, (as they seemed to be in East Berlin in 1953, Hungary in 1956, Czechoslovakia in 1968 and Afghanistan from 1979 onwards) it has been prepared to use force to achieve its objectives – irrespective of the conventional military capabilities of the states involved. In this sense Yugoslavia tells us very little about the defence of Western Europe.

In summary, the case being made is that conventional deterrence of whatever kind (without any nuclear backing) is unlikely to work. History would seem to confirm this conclusion. John Mearsheimer has undertaken a detailed study of twelve cases of conventional deterrence between 1938 and 1979.[15] In ten of these cases deterrence failed; in only two of the cases did deterrence work. As Samuel Huntington has argued 'this 83.3% failure rate for deterrence by conventional defense after 1938 contrasts rather markedly with the zero failure rate for deterrence by nuclear retaliation for a quarter century after 1945.'[16] This is not, however, to deny that improvements in conventional defence are necessary. They clearly are. Nor is it to suggest that defensive and non-provocative ideas should not be an important component of NATO's conventional strategy (especially *if* the Soviet Union itself eventually adopts a more defensive posture). The point is that conventional forces *alone* are unlikely to provide effective defence or deterrence for the NATO countries.

THE BALANCE OF RISK

The argument in the last two chapters suggests that the political and military weaknesses inherent in a non-nuclear defence policy for Britain and for the NATO Alliance are much more formidable than supporters of such a policy would have us believe. The crucial question is whether the risks associated with a non-nuclear policy are greater or less than those associated with a nuclear deterrent policy?

As has already been argued the concept of nuclear deterrence is not without risk and danger. The strategy of Flexible Response in particular abounds in illogicalities and paradoxes. As Lord Carver has argued:

> At the heart of the problem is the dilemma that if one wishes to deter war by the fear that nuclear weapons will be used, one has to appear to be prepared to use them in certain circumstances. But if one does, and the enemy answers back, as he has the capability to do and has clearly said he would, one is very much worse off than if one had not done so, if indeed one is there at all. To pose an unacceptable risk to the enemy automatically poses the same risk to oneself.[17]

As it presently stands the ball is likely to be very much in NATO's court. If deterrence were to break down the Alliance would be faced, as General Bernard Rogers, Supreme Commander of NATO forces, has confirmed, with the decision to go nuclear, with all of the potentially catastrophic consequences, possibly within a few days.

Dangerous as such a strategy probably is, it would be foolish to ignore the fact that even a small risk of unimaginable destruction has been, and is likely to remain, a powerful deterrent to aggression in Europe. Risks there are, but given the inherent caution of states faced with total annihilation, the risks would appear to be relatively small.

Given the political and military weaknesses of a non-nuclear non-provocative defence policy the risks of war would seem rather higher. A strategy which allows the opponent to make a careful calculation of the consequences of his actions and which does not threaten his complete destruction might, in certain circumstances, lead him to threaten, or to actually use force to achieve his political objectives. There will be risks to the aggressor, but the risks will be nowhere near as great as being involved in a nuclear war. Supporters of defensive deterrence would no doubt counter this by saying that the risks of war in general *may* be higher, but the chances of *nuclear* destruction will be lower.

The question then is how to balance a small risk of nuclear destruction against a much larger risk of nuclear blackmail and conventional war (with a continuing, arguably reduced, risk of nuclear attack). It would help a little if the risks could be quantified in some way but clearly this is not possible. At the end of the day it comes down to a matter of judgement. Both strategies, in various ways, pose risks. But the risk of moving from the present policy which has contributed significantly to peace in Europe for the past forty years, to one which is so radical that it poses a major risk of destabilising the present balance, is too great to take. The onus for proving that Europe will be a safer place if Britain and the Alliance adopted a non-nuclear strategy is on the shoulders of those seeking radical change.[18] So far it has been suggested here that their arguments have proved less than convincing.

Notes

1. H. Strachan, 'Conventional Defence in Europe,' *International Affairs*, Vol. 61, No. 1, Winter 1984/85, p. 33.
2. See Harry G. Summers, Jr., *On Strategy: a Critical Analysis of the Vietnam War* (Novato, CA: Presidio, 1982), p. 199. Quoted also in H. Strachan, ibid., pp. 32–3.
3. Löser, 'The Security Policy Options for Non-communist Europe,' op. cit.
4. SACEUR, Bernard Rogers, has made this point on numerous occasions.
5. See S L A Marshall, *Men Against Fire* (New York: William Morrow, 1947) and H. Strachen, op. cit., pp. 32–33.
6. Ibid.
7. See *Sueddeutsche Zeitung*, 1 December 1983.
8. Field Marshal Lord Carver, *A Policy for Peace* (London: Faber & Faber, 1986), pp. 100–1.
9. See Samuel P. Huntington, 'Conventional Deterrence and Conventional Retaliation in Europe', *International Security*, Vol. 8, No. 3, Winter 1983/4, p. 40. Huntington advocated a retaliatory conventional posture as an adjunct to the existing Flexible Response strategy.
10. Simply transferring the money spent at present by Britain (and France) to improvements in conventional forces would not be sufficient to provide a significant improvement in conventional defence.

11. Saadia Amiel, 'Deterrence by Conventional Forces', *Survival*, Vol. 20 (March–April 1978), p. 59.
12. Huntington, op. cit., p. 49.
13. For a critique of the Huntington thesis see John J. Mearsheimer, 'Nuclear Weapons and Deterrence in Europe,' *International Security*, Vol. 9, No. 3, Winter 1984–85, pp. 29–30. See also 'Battleground Europe' by Howard, de Rose and Kaiser in *The Times*, 10 February 1988.
14. Henry Kissinger commented in 1979 that 'it is absurd to base the strategy of the West on the credibility of the threat of mutual suicide.' See Henry A. Kissinger, 'The Future of NATO,' in Kenneth A. Myers, (ed.), *NATO: The Next Thirty Years* (Boulder, Colo: Westview Press, 1980), p. 7.
15. John J. Mearsheimer, *Conventional Deterrence* (Ithaca, N.Y.: Cornell University Press, 1983), pp. 19–20.
16. Huntington, op. cit., p. 38.
17. Lord Carver, op. cit.
18. Despite what he says, Ken Booth's proposals must be regarded as radical.

11 Towards a New Strategic Concept for NATO

To argue that the risks associated with a non-nuclear defence policy are relatively greater than those posed by current defence policies is not to argue for the status quo. Certainly there is room for improvement in both British defence policy and NATO strategy. The kind of changes which will be recommended below will not eradicate the risks of nuclear war completely. Nuclear weapons cannot be disinvented and risks of one kind or another are inevitable in the kind of nuclear world of which we are a part and from which there is no escape. What can be done however, is to shift British and Alliance strategy relatively away from their present nuclear biases towards a more credible conventional response. Nuclear weapons would still have a role in deterring nuclear threats but the emphasis would be very much on improving conventional capabilities.

THE FUTURE OF BRITISH DEFENCE POLICY

It has been argued earlier that there is a case for a British minimum nuclear deterrent.[1] The chances of the NATO Alliance collapsing and Britain finding herself totally alone in the world abandoned by the United States are rather slim. Nevertheless, as a 'last resort' weapon system against threats of nuclear and conventional attack, from whatever quarter, a British independent nuclear deterrent does seem to provide some insurance for an uncertain and possibly volatile future. As Lord Carver has argued 'one cannot forecast the future and safely assume that the present international structure will always remain. In an uncertain world, in which proliferation has perhaps increased Britain could find herself in conflict.'[2] Such conflict could involve other nuclear powers and Britain might not always have the support of the United States. Where Lord Carver is wrong is in his view that if Britain gave up her nuclear weapons now, she could easily get back into the nuclear business in the future if it was 'thought that nuclear weapons were essential to the nation's security.'[3] Getting back into the nuclear business would almost certainly not be easy, it would take time, and it might well be very expensive. The attempt might come too late. Maintaining some form of nuclear deterrent for these unlikely, but conceivable, contingencies when the life of the nation was at stake would seem to be a prudent course for defence planners.

If a strong case can be made for an independent nuclear deterrent the question arises whether Trident is the right choice. It has already been argued that Trident is a very expensive weapon system for a state with Britain's financial difficulties to afford. The Government's argument however, has always been that the choice is between affording Trident or nothing. Useful as this argument is for the domestic political debate it is nevertheless open to some questioning.

The Government and Ministry of Defence has in recent years insisted on a nuclear weapon system which:

a. must be submarine-based to be invulnerable
b. must involve a ballistic missile delivery system to penetrate enemy defences
c. must be capable of hitting Moscow, and if possible,
d. must be the best system available.

If these criteria are accepted as the essential prerequisites for an effective British deterrent then Trident probably is the best buy. While some form of submarine-based system probably is essential, however, there are some question marks over whether Trident missiles are the only system capable of penetrating enemy defences, over whether it is essential to be able to hit Moscow, and whether Britain does require the most sophisticated system in the world. A case can be made that a cheaper nuclear system could provide Britain with a minimum deterrent and release valuable resources for maintaining the effectiveness of Britain's conventional forces in the late 1980s, 1990s and beyond.

Ballistic missiles are undoubtedly the system best able to penetrate Soviet defences now and probably will remain so in the future. The question is whether Trident is the only system capable of doing this job. The alternatives to Trident at present are, it is true, very limited and not without their own difficulties. One option might be to negotiate with the French. This might involve purchasing French ballistic missiles. French nuclear forces are reasonably sophisticated and the French have a proven capability to produce ballistic missiles. Britain's warhead design, however, is significantly ahead of France's. Some form of Anglo–French agreement therefore might be possible. So far political difficulties have precluded such an arrangement. France has continued to stress her independent nuclear policy and much of Britain's expertise in warhead design is entangled with that of the United States. Such political problems, however, are not necessarily insoluble if the will existed in Britain and France to move in the direction of greater nuclear collaboration. Further detailed studies of the Anglo–French alternative would therefore seem to be worth undertaking.

Whether ballistic missiles are the only system of penetrating Soviet defences is also a matter of some dispute. Cruise missiles, with their ability to hug the ground, confuse enemy radars and their high degree of accuracy might also be capable of performing this function adequately, especially as new, faster versions are developed to replace the older, more vulnerable systems. Once again some form of submarine-launched cruise missile system could well have been an alternative to Trident worthy of serious consideration.

A strong case can also be made that although the 'Moscow criteria' may be desirable to reinforce deterrence it is not essential for a minimum nuclear deterrent force like that possessed by Britain. The ability to hit a range of cities apart from Moscow would surely be sufficient to cause Soviet leaders to act with very great caution. As such systems with a lesser capability than Trident could well prove effective deterrents even though they might not be capable of destroying Moscow. The threat that cities like Leningrad and Kiev might be lost together with major industrial facilities and millions of lives is likely to deter Soviet leaders in most conceivable contingencies.

Supporters of Trident would argue that its extra sophistication acts as a cushion in case there are major technological breakthroughs in ASW or ABM warfare. They point to the Strategic Defence Initiative (SDI) as a possible illustration of this. The point about SDI, however, is that if the concept is taken to its logical conclusion, *all* offensive nuclear systems (including Trident) would lose their effectiveness. Major defensive programmes by both the Soviet Union and the United States, if they proved technologically feasible, would change the whole bases of deterrence away from assured destruction. This is one of the reasons why Britain and France have been apprehensive about President Reagan's SDI programme. It could also be argued that ballistic missile defences might lead to greater emphasis being given to cruise missile technology. That alternative therefore might appear more attractive. There is another argument, however, put forward by supporters of Trident which is more difficult to deal with. Should the Soviet and American SDI research programmes discover that absolute defence is not technologically possible, which seems highly likely, there may be nevertheless an incentive to reinforce the existing deterrent situation based on Mutual Assured Destruction (MAD) by protecting retaliatory capabilities (MX silos) and providing some limited defence of cities. In that context, it is argued, the extra sophistication of Trident will be useful in ensuring a continued ability to threaten Soviet cities. This could well be the case. Nevertheless it could also be argued that if the SDI produces only limited defences there will be a powerful incentive by both the Soviet Union and the United States to negotiate an arms control agreement over space-based systems. Why spend the phenomenal sums involved for only limited results? Such reasoning after all has already been responsible for the ABM Agreement in 1972. If this occurred, other less capable systems than Trident might still have an effective deterrent role.

The argument presented here then is that Trident probably is the best system available but it may not be the only option. Other systems, with lesser capabilities (in terms of range, number of warheads and accuracy) are worthy of serious consideration. A loosening of the criteria poses some risks but it may be that alternatives to Trident do exist which would provide Britain with a very powerful military instrument capable of deterring the Soviet Union in most circumstances. The risks of a less capable (but still very potent) system have to be set against the risks associated with the possible weakening of Britain's conventional forces by purchasing Trident. The assessment of the risks involved also have to take into account the signals sent to our allies in NATO. The decline of Britain's conventional forces which seem likely to occur will make it difficult for Britain to take the lead in persuading our NATO allies that Alliance strategy should be reformed through putting less reliance on nuclear weapons.

If a cheaper, less capable system than Trident (but one which nevertheless provided a credible minimum deterrent) could be found as a result of a review of Britain's nuclear deterrent requirements, there *might* be a case for cancelling the Trident Agreement.[4] The Government could present this change of policy both as a contribution to arms control and as part of a more emphatic policy of trying to improve Britain's conventional forces and reform NATO strategy. For Britain the defence of the Homeland and Channel, the defence of the Central Front and Europe and the defence of the Eastern Atlantic are vital core security interests. As the Falklands War also demonstrated, intervention forces cannot be wholly ignored either. Expenditure on Trident could (and probably will) lead to a stretching out or even cancellation of key projects in each of the three services in the late 1980s and 1990s.[5] This would not only weaken Britain's vital conventional defences and those of the Alliance, but would signal Britain's continuing, indeed (in resource allocation terms) increasing, commitment to a nuclear-biased defence policy. Expenditure on an alternative nuclear-deterrent would not be cheap but it would release some resources (perhaps up to 5 billion pounds) for conventional weapon improvements and more importantly provide a political signal to the Alliance that the steps taken towards improving the Alliance's conventional defences as a whole should, in Britain's view, be taken much further.

There is, however, one major problem with this argument. By the time of the next election, probably in the early 1990s, a significant amount of money (up to four-fifths) will already have been spent or committed to the Trident system.[6] Should Trident be cancelled at this point or later there is no guarantee that any other nuclear deterrent system (based, for example, on submarine-launched cruise missiles) would be very much cheaper. If 7 to 8 billion pounds had already been spent or committed on Trident, and an alternative system would cost 5 or 6 billion pounds, there would be no saving. Indeed it would probably be more expensive. It may be the case that the Trident submarines already built could be fitted with cruise missiles rather than Trident missiles but there would undoubtedly be significant conversion costs associated with such an option and once again there is a question-mark over how much would be saved.[7] There would be a danger of ending up with an inferior deterrent system without making substantial savings.

This clearly poses a very difficult dilemma for those who wish to improve conventional forces and retain a viable British nuclear deterrent. Much would depend on the timing of the decision to cancel Trident. If the decision is taken in the next year or so, and a cheaper alternative, like sea-launched cruise missiles, were available, this might still be an option worth considering if only to signal to the Alliance Britain's interest in transferring resources relatively away from nuclear to conventional forces. Such a policy might also have value as part of a British contribution to a wider arms control agreement between East and West.

The fact has to be faced, however, that the choice facing any government in the 1990s will probably be Trident or nothing. If one accepts that there is some political and strategic value in possessing a British nuclear deterrent one may be forced to accept, however reluctantly, that Trident is the only answer. This in fact would be tantamount to accepting that some weakening would have to take place in Britain's conventional forces in the early 1990s and beyond.

Even if this was the Government's decision, however, it need not prevent Britain from backing a concerted drive to improve the Alliance's conventional forces particularly through greater European cooperation. There are clearly great difficulties to be overcome in the search for a European defence pillar within the Western Alliance. There are a range of existing institutions like the Western European Union (WEU), European Political Cooperation (EPC), the Eurogroup and the Independent European Programme Group (IEPG), with a range of different members and different, but overlapping, responsibilities. Individual Western European countries have different modernisation time scales for their weapons and problems of sovereignty preclude any undue weakening of national defence industries. There are, however, strong economic and political pressures towards greater collaboration between Western European states. Collaborative projects already make up 15 per cent of the UK equipment expenditure. Most of these collaborative projects are with Western European allies. There is no doubt that more could be done in this direction if Britain committed itself more positively to an improvement in European defence cooperation.

There is also a case for Britain encouraging institutional cooperation. In November 1984 the IEPG was strengthened when a ministerial meeting issued a directive stating that:

1. Military staffs must work more closely towards harmonisation of operational requirements and timescales.
2. That all significant projects are to be referred to ministers at the staff target stage.
3. That rationalisation of research and industrial resources is to be studied.
4. And that nations should exercise greater discipline in not

launching their own development proposals in competition with existing ones elsewhere, and should be ready to adopt others' equipment if it is already in production.

At the same time that this IEPG directive was being issued, moves were afoot to try and revitalise the WEU. In the future Foreign and Defence ministers of member states (West Germany, France, Italy, Britain and the Benelux countries) are to meet twice a year to discuss defence and arms control issues. On the whole, Britain has tended to support the IEPG initiatives more than the attempts to revitalise the WEU. In neither case, however, has Britain been very enthusiastic about taking European defence cooperation very much further forward. There is an ambivalence to the very concept of a European pillar of the Alliance (especially when it clashes with close Anglo–American defence collaboration) which produces caution and reluctance to undertake and pursue initiatives in this direction. The 'Westland Affair' in 1986 was a clear demonstration of this.

Without a single strong European defence framework there clearly are limits to how far European cooperation can be taken. At present, such a single European pillar is not possible. There is a strong case, however, for making the existing institutions work as well as possible. In this area at least despite an increasing interest in cooperation with France: Britain should be playing a greater role in the process than she has done in the past.

A strong case can also be made that a decision by the British Government to continue with a nuclear deterrent after the next election, even if it was Trident, need not prevent Britain from making an important contribution to arms control. The Conservative Government of Mrs Thatcher has been unwilling to enter into the arms control process with the United States and the Soviet Union on strategic nuclear arms. The Government's position has been that the British minimum nuclear deterrent will not be put into the arms control ring until drastic cuts have taken place in the strategic forces of the super powers. Given that Trident will represent at least an eight-fold increase in target coverage over the existing Polaris force, a case can be made that a more positive contribution to arms control could be made by Britain. It is true that the Conservative Government has not been as negative about arms control as some of its critics have suggested. In the field of chemical weapons, for example, Britain has made a number of contributions to try and break the deadlock. On the other hand, Britain certainly hasn't been as enthusiastic as she might have been. Military strength seems to have been a much more important component in the search for security than arms control.

The over-capacity of Trident should allow a future Government to be more flexible than in the past. Rather than waiting until after drastic cuts in super power arsenals have taken place, Britain could try and contribute to that process, for example through a willingness to trade cuts in the number of warheads planned for the Trident force. A more positive approach by Britain to arms control (at both the nuclear and conventional levels) would certainly be welcome – and could contribute to greater European, and therefore British, security.

The decision by the Government to continue with a minimum nuclear deterrent system, need not prevent it from championing changes in NATO strategy. The Government could still add its considerable weight to the various proposals for reform which have been supported in recent years by numerous eminent political and military figures in Britain, the United States and West Germany. In Britain these have included Dr David Owen, a former British Foreign Secretary; Sir Frank Cooper, a former Permanent Under Secretary in the Ministry of Defence; Sir Ronald Mason, a former Chief Scientific Adviser to the Ministry of Defence; General Sir Anthony Farrar-Hockley, Commander-in-Chief of NATO's forces in Northern Europe until 1982; and the late Lord Cameron, a former Chief of the Defence Staff.[8] In America, supporters of reform include Robert McNamara, a former Secretary of Defence; McGeorge Bundy, a former Special Assistant to the President for National Security Affairs; George Kennan, a former US Ambassador to the Soviet Union; and Gerard Smith, who was Chief of the US delegation to the Strategic Arms Limitation talks from 1966 to 1972.[9] And in West Germany Helmut Schmidt, the former Chancellor has also thrown his weight behind the campaign for reform.[10] Although there are some differences of opinion between these individuals over the exact nature reform should take, they all agree that a change in NATO strategy which de-emphasises nuclear weapons and puts more emphasis on conventional deterrence and defence is highly desirable. According to these 'Alliance Reformers' nuclear weapons will still have a role in NATO strategy, but much less than at present. In supporting this campaign by men who have had experience at the highest level of their respective political and military establishments, the British government, as a leading member of the Alliance, could be highly influential in moving NATO strategy in a more rational and prudent direction.

THE REFORM OF NATO STRATEGY

In a pamphlet entitled *Diminishing the Nuclear Threat*, written in 1984, a group of senior British military and political figures produced a major critique of current NATO strategy.[11] According to the authors the notion of defending Western Europe by 'controlled step-by-step escalation,' starting with conventional weapons and moving gradually up the scale from battlefield to strategic nuclear weapons, is 'impractical nonsense' and could not be achieved in a war which would be 'unpredictable and largely uncontrolled and chaotic.'[12] They are particularly critical of the present reliance on short-range battlefield nuclear weapons which they argue is 'illogical, dangerous and unlikely to be credible.'[13] What is needed, they suggest, are changes which will ease the 'appalling dilemma of having to decide whether to initiate an early exchange of nuclear weapons'.[14]

Most 'Alliance Reformers' would agree with this diagnosis of the current weaknesses of NATO strategy. The problem comes in trying to remedy these weaknesses.

Towards a true Flexible Response strategy

One solution often suggested would be to try to make the existing strategy work more effectively. During his period as Supreme Allied Commander Europe, General Bernard Rogers made no secret of his unease with the prevailing strategy. His approach, however, was not to abandon Flexible Response but to introduce improvements whenever possible, particularly in conventional defence, so that the strategy resembled more closely the original conception of Flexible Response proposed by Robert McNamara in 1962. In recent years considerable improvements have taken place in NATO's conventional capabilities and many contemporary 'Alliance Reformers' argue that this process can, and should, be continued. Dr James Thomson of the RAND Corporation is representative of this school of thought. He has advocated improvements in NATO's defence planning, especially in the weapons acquisition process and has urged the Alliance to focus on key areas of force improvement, such as preserving the survivability of air operations and increasing the operational reserves available to NATO. For Dr Thomson, however, given the constraints, these improvements are only likely to occur at the margins and they have to take place within the existing strategic concept. He expressed the view of many establishment 'Alliance Reformers' when he argued that:

> NATO's principal strategic problem is the declining credibility of nuclear escalation threats to deter Warsaw Pact conventional aggression. But political, technological, fiscal and manpower constraints foreclose strategic choices which would decisively alter this situation and sharply limit the range of realistic choice to quite modest changes in NATO's conventional defence posture.[15]

For Dr Thomson, as for General Rogers, 'there is no viable alternative to "Flexible Response"'.

According to this school of thought Flexible Response has been successful because of its vagueness. It represents a political compromise, as Jane Stromseth has shown, which means all things to all men.[16] Both those who want to emphasise nuclear weapons and those who want to downgrade such weapons can all agree that flexibilty of response, which provides a range of nuclear and non-nuclear options is the best way to deter an enemy who also possesses a range of nuclear and non-nuclear forces. Those who favour maintaining, and improving, the existing strategy point out that Flexible Response represents a delicate compromise which is deeply rooted in Alliance politics. NATO strategy is as it is because that is what is acceptable to all members of the Alliance. The only reform which is possible therefore, according to this view, is one which doesn't rock the Alliance's political boat and which occurs within the existing doctrinal framework.

This is a very powerful argument and one which those who wish to change Alliance strategy must confront. There are two questions in particular which have to be discussed. Firstly, whether a more flexible Flexible Response strategy is the best solution to the current weaknesses. And secondly, whether the assertion that there is no viable alternative is correct.

The movement to a more truly flexible Flexible Response strategy would seem, in some respects at least, to be an attractive option. It would help to de-emphasise the nuclear component of existing strategy to a certain extent and provide the Alliance with a greater range of options in the event of aggression. The main problem, however, is that the doctrinal legacy of the existing strategy is likely to colour attitudes, especially towards nuclear weapons, even if conventional forces are improved. Even a more flexible Flexible Response strategy would be likely to emphasise a stage-by-stage process of nuclear escalation in which nuclear weapons are perceived as having a war-fighting role. The nuclear dilemma therefore is not significantly changed by the kind of 'marginal' conventional improvements advocated by those like Dr Thomson. Indeed the ambiguity towards nuclear weapons is likely to remain if the strategic concept remains Flexible Response and this in turn will make the task of improving the Alliance's conventional forces more difficult. A new concept on the other hand could provide a clearer sense of direction. But is a new concept practical?

Dr Thomson is probably right when he argues that the chances of radical changes taking place (especially of the non-nuclear kind) are rather unrealistic because of the practical realities of Alliance politics.[17] If this is accepted (and it seems a realistic assumption in the light of what has occurred in the Alliance in the past) then the question which arises is whether *any* change of strategic concept is possible, even one which represents an evolutionary modification of existing ideas? The weakness with the status quo argument (in favour of Flexible Response) is that it asumes that because existing strategy reflects political realities no change is possible. Past experience does suggest that changing NATO strategy is not easy but the fact that important evolutionary changes have occurred in the 1950s and 1960s does show that when weaknesses become apparent the Alliance is capable of taking the decision to reform its strategy. Just as the adoption of Flexible Response became possible in the late 1960s so changes can be introduced in the late 1980s. The fact that there is widespread recognition of the deficiencies of Flexible Response and a rapidly changing international environment in the late 1980s makes reform at least a possibility. If evolutionary reform is possible (including the replacement of Flexible Response by a new strategy) what form might it take?

The 'no-first-use' solution

In a major article in the journal *Foreign Affairs* in the spring of 1982, the so-called American 'gang of four' led by Robert McNamara (who had been responsible for formulating the Flexible Response Strategy in the early 1960s) put forward proposals for a 'no-first-use' strategy for the Alliance. According to these four highly experienced Americans:

> The one clearly definable firebreak against the worldwide disaster of general nuclear war is the one which stands between all other

kinds of conflict and any use whatsoever of nuclear weapons. To keep that firebreak wide and strong is in the deepest interest of all mankind ... Given the appalling consequences of even the most limited use of nuclear weapons and the total impossibility for both sides of any guarantee against unlimited escalation, there must be the gravest doubt about the wisdom of a policy which asserts the effectiveness of any first use of nuclear weapons by either side.[18]

McNamara and his colleagues accept the fact that adequate, survivable, nuclear capabilities for appropriate retaliation to any kind of Soviet nuclear attack should be retained. Varied second strike forces would be a necessary part of deterrence. In their view, however, there is no need to match the Soviet Union missile for missile. All that would be needed is a 'minimum' force of a few tens or even hundreds of missiles rather than the thousands NATO possesses at present.

At the same time the American writers recognise that a move towards a 'no-first-use' policy would require 'a strengthened confidence in the adequacy of the conventional forces of the Alliance.'[19] This could be achieved they suggest without excessively high levels of effort. 'Precision-guided munitions, in technology and the visible weakening of the military solidarity of the Warsaw Pact, in politics, are only two examples of changes working to the advantage of the Alliance.'[20] They also argue that there has been a tendency, over the years to exaggerate Soviet conventional superiority and 'underestimate Soviet awareness of the enormous costs and risks of any form of aggression against NATO.'[21] In their view even if improving NATO's conventional forces did cost more than the 3 per cent real increase which the Alliance had accepted in the late 1970s and early 1980s, 'it would be the best bargain ever offered to the members of the Alliance.'[22]

These proposals put forward by McNamara and his colleagues have been severely criticised by supporters of existing Alliance strategy, particularly those in West Germany. Four highly respected German commentators responded to the American 'gang of four' in an article in the *Foreign Affairs* issue produced in the summer of 1982.[23] In their article Karl Kaiser, George Leber, Alois Mertes and Franz-Josef Schulze argue that the over-riding purpose of NATO strategy must be to prevent, not only nuclear war, but conventional war as well, from occurring. Their rejection of 'no-first-use' was largely based on the fear that such a policy would rob the present strategy of war prevention of one decisive characteristic. In their words:

One cannot help concluding that the Soviet Union would thereby be put in a position where it would, once again, calculate its risk and thus be able to wage war in Europe. It would no longer have to fear that nuclear weapons would inflict unacceptable damage to its own territory. We therefore fear that a credible renunciation of the first use of nuclear weapons would, once again, make war more probable.[24]

Linked to this is the argument that the American 'gang of four' had 'considerably underestimated the political and financial difficulties which stand in the way of establishing a conventional balance through increased armament by the West.'[25] For the German writers then a 'no-first-use' declaration – which would make war more likely than under the present strategy – is unacceptable. Also the pre-condition of increased conventional forces is something which is not likely to be achieved given the economic and political situation prevailing in the United States and Western Europe.

The rejection by the German 'gang of four' of the 'no-first-use' idea is not accompanied, however, by total support for the present strategy of Flexible Response. They go out of their way at the end of the article to argue that they 'share many of the concerns about the risks of nuclear war' contained in the article by McNamara and his colleagues.[26] Their suggestion, however, is that an energetic attempt should be made by the Alliance to 'reduce the *dependence on an early first use*' of nuclear weapons.[27] Such a 'no-early-use' policy, they argue, could be achieved both by a greater commitment to arms control measures by Western States and by measures to strengthen conventional forces within realistic defence budgets. These are proposals which this author supports.

Perhaps the most important objective of 'no-early-use' is to extend the firebreak or threshold between the use of conventional and nuclear weapons. In psychological terms the nuclear firebreak is clearly the most important rung in the escalation ladder. Once that division is crossed, most strategic analysts accept that there is a *very* grave danger of a slide into uncontrollable nuclear war. Anything therefore which emphasises the fundamental significance of the conventional-nuclear threshold is to be welcomed. Anything, which helps to extend this threshold – to allow NATO to continue operating at the conventional level when faced with conventional aggression rather than being forced to go nuclear – is of crucial importance in lessening the dangers and improving the credibility of NATO strategy.

This might be described as an 'Extended Firebreak' strategy to distinguish it from a 'no-first-use' strategy.

For the layman to evaluate this somewhat esoteric argument between these two sets of 'Alliance Reformers' is not an easy task. On the surface, the arguments by the McNamara group are, in some respects, more appealing. The merit in particular is that a declaration not to use nuclear weapons first in any conflict is a clear and simple position which everyone can understand. The problem with 'no-*early*-use' (or the Extended Firebreak idea) they say, is that it involves exceptions, and exceptions can easily become rules. 'What the Alliance needs today,' McNamara and his colleagues suggest, 'is not the refinement of its nuclear options, but a clear-cut decision to avoid them (nuclear weapons) as long as others do.'[28]

There is clearly some merit in this argument. To the present writer however, the argument is flawed. More complicated as it is, the argument for an Extended Firebreak strategy is much more sound. Superior arguments should not be rejected because they appear more complex. The security of the Western Alliance after all depends on such arguments. The onus, however, is on those supporting a change in NATO's strategic concept to put the arguments across to the general public as simply and clearly as possible.

Why is the case for 'no-first-use' flawed? What are the advantages of an Extended Firebreak strategy? How exactly does the Extended Firebreak notion differ from existing NATO strategy? These are questions which we must now consider.

The flaws in 'no-first-use'

For all its merits, the suggestion put forward by McNamara and his colleagues is weak particularly on the three main grounds indicated by the German 'gang of four'. Firstly, if NATO were to renounce the first use of nuclear weapons unilaterally that would be tantamount to saying to the Soviet Union 'if you invade us with conventional forces and you are on the verge of defeating us, we will not use nuclear weapons to prevent our own defeat. You need not worry on that score! You can calculate in advance that nuclear weapons with all of the uncertainties and dangers of escalation which at present you have to worry about, will not be used by us.' But why should the Alliance make such calculations easier for the Soviet Union or any potential aggressor in advance? It may be that when the time comes the Alliance would rather capitulate than 'heap a nuclear defeat on top of a conventional defeat.' But isn't it better to keep the choice of how NATO will respond to aggression open, to keep the Soviet Union guessing as to the likely, possibly devastating, consequences which would follow *their* aggression? Deterrence would seem to be better served through the alliance indicating that it just *might* use nuclear weapons rather than accept defeat by the Warsaw Pact armies.

Apart from weakening deterrence and perhaps making war in general more likely, the 'no-first-use' argument does have a further weakness. Even if NATO was able to build up its conventional forces to a level where the Alliance was confident of defending effectively, there would still be the problem of making Soviet calculations easier. The whole case is predicated, however, on the argument that this can be done relatively easily. Most writers on military affairs in the West these days would accept, without question, that a strengthening of NATO's conventional forces would be desirable. The crucial question, however, is: can it be done? Is it a realistic political option? Does the political will exist to spend these necessary resources? From the period of the Lisbon goals in 1952 onwards the Alliance has constantly tried to improve its conventional forces. From 1952 the Alliance has not had spectacular success in this respect. There clearly is a case for strong determined and courageous political leadership in Europe and in the Alliance as a whole to argue the merits of strengthening conventional forces. The problem is not one of resources. The Alliance *could* afford to improve its conventional forces if it so wished. What is lacking is the political will to do so. Even when the populations of Alliance states were wrestling publicly with the nuclear problem in the early 1980s, many Alliance members failed to live up even to the modest increase of 3 per cent real increases accepted in 1978. The emergence of strong and courageous leadership could not be ruled out, but to be realistic, the chances of the Alliance being willing to spend the kind of resources necessary to allow it to adopt a 'no-first-use' policy are not very great.

The third problem is the impact which such a policy would have on West Germany with its particular dependence on the American nuclear guarantee. Despite their concern with the exposed position of the Federal Republic of Germany, the American writers fail to think through adequately the impact of their proposals on German sensitivities. As Karl Kaiser and his colleagues rightly point out:

> The feeling of vulnerability to political blackmail as a result of the constant demonstration of superior military might, would be bound

to grow considerably if the nuclear protector of the Atlantic Alliance were to declare – as suggested by the four authors – that it would not use nuclear weapons in case of a conventional attack against Europe.[29]

It is clearly much more obvious to Europeans than Americans across the Atlantic – especially West Germans in their 'precarious position within a divided country' – that a Western European feeling of inferiority could, in certain circumstances, be exploited by Soviet political pressure. If this were to happen the 'no-first-use' proposals would have contributed to the further destabilisation of Central Europe and break-down in the cohesion of the Alliance. Also, if the feeling of vulnerability were to increase in West Germany as a result of what might well be interpreted as a significant weakening of the American nuclear guarantee, who knows in what direction West German security policy might move? It could conceivably lead to some form of accommodation with the Eastern bloc or even increased support for German nuclear weapons with the increased worry which this would cause for allies and potential adversaries alike.

THE ADVANTAGES OF AN EXTENDED FIREBREAK STRATEGY

An Extended Firebreak strategy is designed to avoid the disadvantages of both a 'no-first-use' strategy and the existing Flexible Response strategy which emphasises the early, first use of nuclear weapons in any conflict. The Extended Firebreak concept involves modest, realistic improvements in conventional forces which would allow the Alliance to say to the Soviet Union 'if you invade conventionally we have the capability to defend conventionally for a considerable period. We are, however, not ruling out the possibility that we *just might* use nuclear weapons first, especially to demonstrate our resolve to resist.' Such a strategy, it could be argued, provides an effective deterrent because it makes Soviet calculations difficult by not ruling out in advance the first-use of nuclear weapons by the Alliance. It is also more credible and less dangerous than threatening to use nuclear weapons at a very early stage of any future conflict. The ability to prolong the conventional battle would provide time for negotiations to occur and Soviet miscalculations (the most likely cause of conflict) to be resolved.

How does an Extended Firebreak strategy differ from the existing strategy of Flexible Response

The major contrast between the present version of Flexible Response and an Extended Firebreak strategy is in the attitude to the role of nuclear weapons in Alliance strategy. Despite attempts to improve conventional forces and to play down somewhat the role of nuclear weapons (especially battlefield nuclear weapons) in recent years, NATO still retains a strategy in which nuclear weapons play a major role. An Extended Firebreak strategy would be designed to move military thinking in the Alliance significantly away from scenarios about large scale nuclear war-fighting, most of which make no real sense. The idea would be to put nuclear weapons into reserve, on the 'back-burner' so to speak, as far as the Alliance is concerned. The radical (but realistic) nature of this change in attitudes should not be underestimated given the traditional nuclear bias within the Alliance. It would mean a major effort being put into conventional defence as the key component of NATO's over-all strategy, with nuclear weapons playing a 'minimum' deterrent role.

Two important questions arise from these recommendations. Firstly, how are conventional forces to be improved, even on a limited basis, given the traditional reluctance to do so? And secondly, what is meant by a 'minimum' deterrent role for nuclear weapons?

Can conventional forces be improved?

Despite the Soviet military build-up and the conventional superiority of the Warsaw Pact in Europe the disparity between the two alliances at the conventional level is often exaggerated. It has become something of a conventional wisdom that the Warsaw Pact enjoys an overwhelming advantage over NATO forces in Europe. Indeed, in order to sustain the sometimes wavering commitment to defence in Western Democratic states, NATO itself does a great deal to perpetuate this view. It is perhaps not surprising that this should be so. But in fostering the view (or perhaps one should say the myth) that NATO is hopelessly outgunned, there is a tendency for Western governments to become the victim of their own propaganda. If the balance of conventional forces is so unfavourable there is little chance of realistically bridging the gap. Hence an acceptance of the reliance on nuclear weapons to make up for what is presented as a major conventional imbalance.

In reality the balance of conventional forces is not as unfavourable as it is often portrayed to be. As a number of recent studies have shown, although NATO does not have the capability to win a conventional war, the balance is such that the Soviet Union could not be confident of being able to achieve a quick victory.[30] With not too much improvement the Alliance could provide itself with the wherewithal to turn any conflict in Europe into a lengthy war of attrition, where NATO's advantage in population and GNP could prove to be of great importance. And there are good reasons to believe that the Soviet Union would not want to get involved in a lengthy war of attrition. Apart from the tremendous costs of modern conventional wars the Soviet Army itself is not organised to fight a long, drawn out conflict. Soviet blitzkrieg tactics based on the Operational Manoeuvre Group (OMG) concept, are designed to achieve rapid penetration of NATO's forward defences and a quick sprint to NATO's rear to paralyse the command and control arrangements of the Alliance thus achieving a swift victory.[31] There is also the Soviet fear that the Sino-Soviet rift and Japanese hostility might lead to a war on two or more fronts. And the perennial problem of nationalism in Eastern Europe would also lead Soviet decision-makers to the conclusion that the reliability of Eastern European armies might also be suspect especially in a protracted conflict. To this must be added the Soviet recognition that if victory was not achieved quickly there would be the danger that nuclear weapons might be used with all of the implications that this would involve.

Such a view that the conventional balance is not as unfavourable for NATO as it is sometimes presented is clearly controversial and needs to be justified. Making an assessment of the Warsaw Pact-NATO balance is notoriously difficult. If the balance is considered in quantitative terms, the Warsaw Pact has a two to one advantage over NATO in divisions in Central Europe, a 2·5 to 1 advantage in tanks, a 2·8 to 1 advantage in artillery and a 1·1 to 1 advantage in over-all manpower.[32] Such a comparison, however, is highly misleading in a number of respects. Apart from questions of morale, leadership, training and reliability there are also qualitative differences in equipment – NATO artillery, for example, is generally believed to be better than Warsaw Pact artillery. There are also problems of comparing different categories of weapons like tanks and anti-tank missiles.

Many defence analysts prefer to compare capabilities through a system of weighing weapons in terms of mobility, survivability and firepower. The composite figure often used is known as Armoured

Division Equivalents (ADE).[33] Using this system for assessment the Warsaw Pact has an advantage of around 1·2 to 1. As John J. Mearsheimer has pointed out, figures such as these show, that NATO is not 'hopelessly outnumbered'.[34]

There is, of course, the crucial question of reinforcement which must also be considered. While it is reasonable to assume that it is unlikely that NATO will be taken by surprise there is the more dangerous problem of the timing of mobilisation. Will NATO governments have the political will to mobilise in time when they receive the intelligence reports that Warsaw Pact mobilisation is underway? This is clearly a question which cannot be answered in advance. All that can be said is that a swift response by NATO would almost certainly be crucial for any chances of success.[35] If NATO waited a week before responding to a Warsaw Pact mobilisation then the gap would be so great in the early stages of a war that NATO would probably lose. If, however, the Alliance mobilised within a couple of days of the Warsaw Pact, the balance of forces would probably reach 2 to 1 for a time but would then fall back to the pre-mobilization ratios. In such circumstances the Alliance would not be faced with the 3 to 1 or more advantage which the Soviet Union would probably need to achieve its victory.

Some critics would argue that even if NATO did mobilise in time the Warsaw Pact would be able to choose the moment and places to strike and would be capable of concentrating their resources in such a way as to create significant local superiority. They would then be able, so the argument goes, to punch a number of holes in NATO's defences which could be exploited by their Operational Manoeuvre Groups (OMGs).[36] This argument is not, however, as convincing as it first seems. Most military analysts would argue that in order to achieve a decisive military breakthrough the Soviet Union would have to operate on at least six to eight axes of advance.[37] If they did, however, concentrate on a multi-pronged attack of this scale they would be unlikely to produce a force ratio much in excess of 2·5 to 1 which would not be sufficient. However, if they concentrate on few axes (like the Fulda Gap, the Golingen Corridor and the Hof Corridor) they might be able to muster significantly superior forces, but it is doubtful they could achieve decisive breakthroughs on a sufficient scale to be confident of a decisive victory. In areas like the Fulda Gap and the other possible routes for advance the terrain is well-designed for defence and would canalise Warsaw Pact forces attempting to break-through. In many of these areas it would be difficult for the advancing forces to concentrate all their divisions at the point of attack. The nature of the terrain would force the Warsaw Pact to 'echelon' its forces, making them exceedingly vulnerable to destruction.

The conclusion would seem to be that although NATO cannot be complacent about its conventional forces and there is certainly a need to improve conventional capabilities further, it does not seem to be the case that NATO is hopelessly inferior to the Warsaw Pact. While there are a number of important deficiencies (which will be discussed later) over-all, the gap is not as wide as some of the pessimists and propagandists claim. With a concerted and unambiguous effort it would be possible to provide a conventional capability which produces sufficient confidence within the Alliance that the Warsaw Pact could be denied victory in any conventional campaign in Europe. This, together with the continuing nuclear capability in the background, would provide a powerful deterrent to aggression. This is not to argue that the task of improving NATO's conventional forces and bringing them up to the point where much less reliance can be placed on nuclear weapons will be easy given the economic and political restraints. Nevertheless, it is not beyond practical possibility for the Alliance to utilise new technology, to build up stores and ammunition stocks, to make better use of reserves, to rationalise its resources more effectively and other structural changes to make a significant move in this direction. This would be made somewhat easier if Alliance leaders collectively set themselves the target of extending the threshold publicly and explained to their electorates that a small extra price was worth the decreased dependency on nuclear weapons. The acceptance by NATO Ministers of a Report on Conventional Defence Improvements in May 1985 is a move in the right direction, but a more comprehensive initiative is required. If President Reagan can sell the Strategic Defence Initiative (SDI) to Western publics, with all of the costs involved, on the basis of the need to create a non-nuclear defence in space, it should not be beyond other Western leaders to make the case for strengthening non-nuclear forces on earth. The costs would be considerably less and the immediate (and long term) advantages are likely to be significantly greater. A Conventional Defence Initiative (CDI) is more important than a Strategic Defence Initiative (SDI).

One area in particular which does seem promising is that of new technology. As the British Atlantic Committee Report *Diminishing the Nuclear Threat* argues 'Technology now offers a genuine opportunity to reform strategy and reinforce deterrence.'[38] By acting as a 'force multiplier it can increasingly roll back the West's present over-dependence on nuclear weapons'.[39] Attention in particular at present is focused on the wide spectrum of electronics systems which are already available, and could increasingly assist the Alliance in its non-nuclear defensive tasks. These include 'remote sensing, surveillance and communication by space vehicles; tactical surveillance, precision-guided munitions, and electronic support and countermeasures in the air, land and maritime environments.[40] Clearly technologies such as these can be no panacea and there is little doubt that the Soviet Union will utilise its own Emerging Technology (ET). The West, however, has a significant lead in many of these areas and it seems sensible to utilise such technology if it can enable the Alliance to defend itself more effectively by conventional means. Conventional weapons can increasingly be used to replace nuclear weapons as a means to destroy certain targets.

It must be admitted, however, that there are problems with new technology which require serious consideration. Much of the new technology is American and given the existing imbalance in arms sales between the United States and Europe, a significant shift towards utilising this emerging technology will exacerbate the problem further. Already American pressure to make use of ET has met resistance from European governments and armament industries. The political and economic difficulties which this creates are not insoluble but they will have to be dealt with sensitively on both sides of the Atlantic.

Another problem arises from the application of the new technology. New techniques of target acquisition and precision-guidance over long distances makes it possible not only to substitute conventional for nuclear weapon systems but also to strike deep into the enemy's rear. A great deal of debate has taken place over the 'Follow on Forces Attack' (FOFA) plan advocated by General Rogers and adopted by NATO's defence planning council in November, 1984.[41] The idea behind FOFA is to attack troop concentrations, choke points, bridges and the main operating air force bases up to 300 kilometres into Eastern Europe. This 'deep strike' strategy is designed to hit second and third echelon Warsaw Pact forces in order to delay or prevent them from reaching the battlefield.

The criticisms against FOFA have taken two forms. Firstly, by concentrating on the second and third echelon forces there may be a tendency to deflect effort away from the all-important battle against the first echelon, especially the enemy Operational Manoeuvre Groups (OMGs) which are designed to exploit any breakthroughs in NATO lines in the early stages of a conflict. There is obviously a danger of this but as NATO authorities have pointed out, there is no intention of letting this happen.[42]

The second criticism is that FOFA is essentially an offensive concept and as such departs from the basic defensive orientation of the Alliance. In response to this, NATO officials have been at pains to point out that NATO has always had a capacity for disrupting enemy communications, lines of supply and follow-up forces in the rear. What is proposed with FOFA is simply to update this function with more effective technology.[43] Such an explanation seems perfectly reasonable. It does not make any military sense whatsoever for a defending army to avoid hitting enemy formations after an attack has started just because they are beyond the border one is trying to defend. It is important, however, that there should be some caution in the application of new technology in this counter-offensive role. NATO is a defensive organisation and if new technology resulted in a major shift in the balance towards counter-offensive operations that might appear particularly provocative to an opponent causing a new spiral in the conventional arms race. Such a shift might also cause dissention within the Alliance which might help to undermine the credibility of Alliance strategy. New technology therefore does have an important role to play in helping to raise the nuclear threshold but some care needs to be taken by the Alliance to make sure its application does not appear overly provocative or spark a major new dimension to the arms race.

Important as new technology is, there are other ways of strengthening NATO's conventional forces. Supplies of ammunition, vehicle stocks and spares have until recently been seriously neglected. Although NATO countries are supposed to possess war stocks which could last for thirty days at current expectations of attrition, in some vital respects they have only about seven days. Only the United States forces in Europe have taken the thirty day rule seriously. As a result of pressure from the American Senator Sam Nunn, the Alliance did try to remedy this deficiency in December 1984 when the Secretary General Lord Carrington, secured agreement from the NATO Defence Ministers to improve ammunition stocks to bring them up to the thirty day level. It was also agreed to spend four million pounds over the next six years on new aircraft shelters which would be needed for the large numbers of US combat aircraft which would cross the Atlantic in wartime. This is an important step forward but much more needs to be done if the ability to fight at the conventional level for thirty days is to become a reality.

Another measure urgently needed is the build-up of, and better equipment for, reserve forces. Many military and political figures have urged recently that much better use should be made by the Alliance of its reserve forces.[44] French reserves in particular need to be better equipped and there is a requirement for the build-up of British manpower reserves. In a speech in March 1985, the former German Chancellor Helmut Schmidt was particularly critical of Britain's renunciation of conscription in the late 1950s. He described Britain's lack of military service, unlike other Western European states as being 'hardly tolerable.'[45] There would be great domestic political difficulties for any British political party to advocate the return of conscription, but courageous political leadership might make a strong case that the price was worth paying to put less emphasis on nuclear weapons. For Britain to make such a gesture would greatly reinforce any commitment it might make to a reform of NATO strategy in the direction of strengthening conventional forces.

Linked to the better use of reserves is the question of operational tactics. There is no doubt that although forward defence is essential for political reasons it does cause serious military difficulties in the defence of the central front. As General Sir Nigel Bagnall told the German newspaper *Frankfurter Allgemeine* in November 1984:

> Stringing all brigades like pearls in the forward line; distributing them evenly along the East–West German border immaterially of whether a main assault was threatening there, could, like any Maginot thinking, only lead to disaster. The aggressor always has the advantage of determining the time and the point of concentration of an offensive. He always could concentrate a decisive, local superiority, thus creating the danger of a breakthrough through the defenders' front. And then the latter's forces would be squandered in the wrong places.[46]

The great need is for the Alliance to adopt a 'forward defence *in depth*' which puts even more emphasis than at present on mobility and flexibility in operational planning. General Bagnall himself has argued that 'one must be able to organise defence in depth, to operate flexibly and form one's own points of concentration; one should not want to clash with the enemy head-on but out-manoeuvre him, by hitting him in the flank or from the rear, and launching counter-attacks at his weak points.'[47] Arguments such as these are clearly politically sensitive in Germany but, if handled carefully, emphasising that 'forward defence in depth' will provide more effective military defence and thereby enhance deterrence, gradual reform of NATO's operational planning and tactics can occur. Indeed, it is already under way with the FOFA concept which itself helps provide greater defence in depth for the Alliance through operations further east.

It is almost certainly true that strengthening NATO's conventional forces will require more money to be spent by the members of the Alliance. Supporters of the status quo argue that realistically this is not likely to occur. NATO countries have after all not lived up to the 3 per cent real increase in defence spending agreed on in the late 1970s let alone the 4 per cent real increase which Bernard Rogers suggested would be needed to produce the level of conventional forces needed to put less reliance on nuclear weapons. This is a problem which reformers cannot skirt and it is not easy to resolve. To throw up one's hands and say it is not possible, however, is not good enough. Indeed there are some grounds for arguing that the task is not beyond the Alliance. Those who point to the failure to live up to the 3 per cent increase do the Alliance a disservice. In fact, with one or two exceptions, the Alliance came quite close to meeting that increase. If the Alliance could this time link a programme of increased spending to a deliberate and public campaign designed to reform NATO strategy in a non-nuclear *direction* it is not beyond the realms of possibility that this could catch the public imagination. SDI has after all been strongly promoted. Why not the same political investment in a CDI? In the 1970s, although the increased spending was designed to improve conventional forces in part, it was seen by the public to be linked to the modernisation of nuclear weapons. Linking it specifically to a programme which de-emphasised nuclear weapons and a new strategic concept, like the Extended Firebreak strategy, could well have more popular appeal. Given the prize it is certainly worth a try.

What is meant by a 'minimum' deterrent role for nuclear weapons in Alliance strategy?

The aim of strengthening Alliance conventional forces to put less emphasis on nuclear weapons is one which is widely accepted in NATO. Bernard Rogers, however, has argued on a number of occasions that what is required is an improvement of the *existing* strategy by achieving greater flexibility for 'Flexible Response.' NATO would then be able to fight for a longer period at the conventional level but the Alliance would still require a wide spectrum of battlefield, longer-range theatre and strategic nuclear weapons to convince an enemy that victory could not be achieved at any level of aggression. According to existing strategic doctrine preparations for conventional and nuclear war-fighting must be at the heart of deterrence. The logic behind this strategy is very clear. In order to convince your opponent that you intend to carry out your threats you must equip and deploy your nuclear and conventional forces and adopt tactical doctrines along credible war-fighting lines. You must match, or at least block, your opponent at every level.

It has already been argued, however, that the emphasis on nuclear war-fighting is exceedingly dangerous (given the incentive to think of nuclear weapons as being similar to any other weapons) and lacking in credibility (given the likelihood of escalation). Better conventional forces improve the situation somewhat by extending the period in which negotiations might take place. They do not alter the fact, however, that built into the strategy is the idea that a limited nuclear war might be possible. The notion that nuclear weapons can have an important war-fighting function may well condition attitudes to their use. Clearly, here we have a crucial dilemma. Detailed planning for nuclear war-fighting may well be useful for deterrent purposes but such planning and the mental conditioning which it helps create could be self-fulfilling if deterrence broke down.

Trying to avoid this important dilemma is far from easy and no solution is wholly satisfactory. It is suggested here that one way forward would be to adopt a new strategic concept ('Extended Firebreak') in place of Flexible Response which relegates nuclear weapons to a largely deterrent role. If it is accepted that the use of nuclear weapons poses unacceptable risks then extensive and elaborate nuclear war-fighting plans don't make a great deal of sense. The *main* purpose of nuclear weapons then should be seen as a deterrent against nuclear blackmail and nuclear attack by an opponent. A secondary but important function would be to deter any form of conventional aggression by posing the risk to any enemy that they just *might* be used (first) if the Alliance was facing conventional defeat. It might be a bluff but the enemy would never be sure in advance. If nuclear weapons were thought of in these minimum deterrent terms it would not be necessary for the Alliance to possess thousands of them to fulfil a wide spectrum of nuclear war-fighting tasks. It would be possible to drastically reduce the number of battlefield nuclear weapons (given the pressures either 'to use or lose them' in the early stages of a conflict) and perhaps to rely less heavily on theatre nuclear weapons if this strategy was accepted. The requirement for longer-range invulnerable theatre and strategic nuclear weapons would still exist and plans for their employment would be necessary. Thus a nuclear war-fighting component would not disappear from NATO strategy altogether. As long as the Alliance continues to need nuclear weapons against a nuclear armed opponent, operational contingency plans for their use will have to be made. The emphasis, however should be placed largely on their retaliatory function. Once this is done the Alliance would find that its requirements for nuclear weapons, which would still be fairly large and varied would nevertheless be much less extensive than they are at present with the large number of military targets assigned to them. Under the new strategy many of these would be targeted by new conventional weapon systems.

To allow the Alliance to move towards 'no-early-use' and a 'minimum' nuclear deterrent policy in Europe some strengthening of conventional forces would be essential. The question is, which comes first? What would be needed is a declaratory change in NATO strategy from Flexible Response to Extended Firebreak which would help to encourage a greater emphasis on an improved conventional response and a view of nuclear weapons as performing largely a deterrent role. It would also focus renewed attention on the importance of the conventional-nuclear 'Firebreak'. It would provide an unambiguous target.[48] As conventional forces were improved less emphasis could be placed on nuclear weapons. The declaration in advance, emphasising the need to move away from the present Flexible Response (or in reality 'flexible escalation') strategy, would be important. It would provide a sense of direction for the Alliance to move forward with the clear intention of putting less emphasis on nuclear weapons in the future.

It must be accepted that the proposals outlined here are not without flaws. They will be opposed by both supporters of the existing strategy and by the non-nuclear lobby. Various supporters of the present strategy in particular would argue that extensive reductions of battlefield nuclear weapons in particular would pose serious risks of defeat for the Alliance either in a massive conventional invasion or in a nuclear attack in which the Soviet Union itself used battlefield nuclear weapons. Given the weaknesses at this level, deterrence itself could be undermined. Nuclear inferiority might also lead to increased danger of intimidation. It is understandable that military planners, in particular, would require equivalent capability to an opponent at every level. And they have a point. Given that the Soviet Union has tended to think about deterrence in countervailing, war-fighting terms, a case can be made that the West has no alternative but to adopt a similar strategy. This apparent weakness, however, has to be set against the likely consequences of military commanders actually using battlefield nuclear weapons to stave off defeat, which is inherent in the existing strategy. The enormous risk of rapid and catastrophic escalation suggests that conventional defeat would be compounded by even worse nuclear defeat (in the sense that there can be no 'winners' in a nuclear war). Whether longer-range theatre nuclear weapons would be used would be a matter for *very* careful evaluation at the time. The nuclear component would be there to act as a deterrent but if deterrence broke down the existence of strengthened conventional forces and deliberate downgrading of nuclear war-fighting would go some way to extricate NATO decision-makers from the pressures inherent in present strategy to go nuclear quickly. The agonising question of whether to go nuclear might still have to be faced but the time for negotiations and cool calculation of the consequences would be greater than at present.

There is a body of strategic thinking in the West which argues that because the Soviet Union believes it can fight and win a nuclear war, the West must adopt not just a countervailing strategy, but a prevailing strategy – not simply planning to deny the Soviet Union victory, but planning to win a nuclear war against the Soviet Union. Colin S. Gray has argued that the United States should adopt, what he describes a 'true war-fighting, or "classical strategy",' which emphasises damage limitation to the United States and powerful offensive nuclear forces capable of achieving victory. In his study of *Nuclear Strategy and National Style*, he argues that American strategic superiority would not only enhance deterrence but it would also add weight to US diplomacy in the pursuit of wider foreign policy objectives.[49] For Gray the idea that nuclear weapons should be viewed as a minimum deterrent component of NATO strategy would no doubt be regarded as 'astrategic' because of the lack of operational criteria for such a concept.[50] There are, however, a number of flaws in Gray's analysis. It is not self-evident (and certainly not a 'fact') that the Soviet Union believes that it can win a nuclear war.[51]

There may be some military men in the Soviet Union who believe this, just as there are some in the West who believe that nuclear wars are winnable.[52] The stress on nuclear war-fighting in Soviet military literature in the past, however, can just as easily be explained in terms of the rhetorical requirements of ideology and military morale.[53] Just as President Reagan has said on a number of occasions that 'nuclear wars can never be won and should never be fought,' so similar statements have been made by Soviet leaders.[54] It is almost certainly just as clear to Soviet leaders, as it is to Western leaders, that past human disasters would pale into insignificance if a large scale nuclear war was ever fought. Gorbachev, in particular, has frequently warned against the dangers of nuclear war since he came to office in 1985. The problem is that strategies, like that proposed by Gray, which promote the idea that nuclear wars can be won in a meaningful sense of the term might well encourage policy makers and military commanders to believe that they can fight and win nuclear conflicts. Such thinking is highly dangerous. To base Western strategy on such assumptions (wrapped up in the guise of Soviet strategic culture to give them greater legitimacy) when there is no incontrovertible evidence that Soviet leaders do in fact think in this way, is somewhat irresponsible. It is also bad strategy.

Neither does Gray pursue the logic of his advocacy for strategic superiority through the pursuit of enhanced offensive and defensive capabilities in terms of the impact on the Soviet Union. Past evidence suggests that the Soviet Union would follow suit.[55] The resulting arms race in space and on earth would be expensive not only for the Soviet Union but also for the United States (with important repercussions for the economies of other Western economies), not to mention the increased tension and instability which would result between East and West. There is no evidence that security would be enhanced as a result of such a policy. Almost certainly the reverse would be true.[56]

To suggest also that it is 'astrategic' to view nuclear weapons in NATO strategy as largely retaliatory, minimum deterrent forces is also wide of the mark. There are obviously important operational questions regarding the numbers and uses of NATO's theatre nuclear weapons which the minimum deterrent posture will pose.[57] Clearly these operational issues cannot be ignored. It is true that general war could break out and that the Alliance has to think through, as carefully as possible in peacetime, how it would employ all of its forces in war. The most basic aim of strategy, however, is survival. The problem with the war-fighting emphasis is that nuclear weapons will simply be perceived as 'weapons like any other weapons' and the profound effects of their use together with the impossibility of guaranteeing that nuclear war would not escalate will be lost in the 'fog' of operational tactical planning. The minimum deterrent emphasis, however, alerts decision-makers and military commanders alike to the extreme dangers of using such weapons. As a result their use would not be almost automatic, as the war-fighting strategists suggest that it should be, at least in terms of deterrence rhetoric. The problem with deterrence rhetoric is that it has the habit of hardening into a specific 'mind-set' which could be self-fulfilling.

It is true that military critics and war-fighting strategists will need to be persuaded that the new (Extended Firebreak) strategy is less dangerous and more credible than existing doctrine. Many military commanders, however, are already aware of the paradoxes of nuclear deterrence and the consequences of the early release of nuclear weapons, and will not need much convincing.[58]

Non-nuclear critics, on the other hand, no doubt would point out that, however much 'Alliance Reformers' push nuclear weapons into the background, if deterrence broke down, the time would arrive *sooner or later* when the decision of whether or not to use nuclear weapons would have to be made. If nuclear weapons can probably never be used without catastrophe, then why have them at all, non-nuclear proponents argue. There is a certain logic and consistency here. But as I have tried to show earlier the task of deterring a nuclear armed opponent unfortunately does seem to require some nuclear capability of one's own. The challenge is to integrate nuclear weapons into Alliance strategy in such a way as to pose unacceptable risks to a potential opponent without posing unacceptable risks to ourselves. It is not an easy task. But with a conventionally biased Extended Firebreak strategy, with nuclear weapons held in reserve, the risks of aggression going terribly wrong are likely to be too high for an enemy. At the same time, without the built-in pressure to use nuclear weapons early, such a strategy would prove relatively less risky to ourselves than the one we have at present.

IS THE STRATEGIC DEFENCE INITIATIVE (SDI) THE LONG-TERM SOLUTION?

It has to be admitted that the kind of reform proposed here through a Conventional Defence Initiative (CDI) is far from ideal. Despite important changes in NATO planning and a change in NATO's strategic concept which would be involved, the system of nuclear deterrence based on the threat of retaliation would remain in place. NATO strategy would be relatively safer than at present but the danger of nuclear war would still exist and such a strategy could continue to pose ethical problems for certain sections of Western populations. For some of those who reject the non-nuclear alternative strategy but who remain uneasy about living indefinitely with the risks of Mutual Assured Destruction (MAD) the answer lies in President Reagan's Strategic Defence Initiative.[59]

In a speech to the American people on 23 March 1983 President Reagan took virtually everyone by surprise when he urged a move away from deterrence through retaliation to a new policy based on strategic defence. He put forward what he described as 'a vision of the future which offered new hope.' He asked the question:

> What if free people could live secure in the knowledge that their security did not rest upon the threat of instant retaliation to deter a Soviet attack; that we could intercept and destroy strategic ballistic missiles before they reached our own soil or that of our allies?[60]

In subsequent speeches the President and administration supporters of SDI have candidly pointed to the moral and strategic weaknesses of the present system of deterrence. In the election debate on the 21 October 1984, President Reagan agued that 'everything we can do to find something that would destroy weapons and not humans would be a great step forward . . .'[61] In criticisms of the status quo supporters of the SDI have come very close at times to the objections to nuclear deterrence put forward by the non-nuclear proponents. Colin Gray has questioned how long the system of reciprocated nuclear retaliatory threats could be expected to work satisfactorily. He concluded that it could not be expected to work indefinitely. From Gray's point of view there are 'no other alternative paths to greater security' than the SDI.[62] To reject the idea of strategic defence was, in his words, to 'endorse the seemingly endless competition in offensive arms.'[63]

To supporters of the SDI great benefits would arise not only from being able to protect one's own population through multi-layered strategic defence but also from the contribution such a system would make to the cause of nuclear disarmament. Indeed it has been argued that *only through* such a defensive system would very radical nuclear disarmament be possible. The ultimate aim of SDI, according to the President, would be the elimination of all nuclear weapons. In the meantime it is suggested that SDI could have a powerful effect on

Soviet calculations about the value or otherwise of offensive missiles. If the Soviet leaders came to believe that US offensive forces will fare considerably better against Soviet defences than will Soviet offensive forces against US defences, then they should be motivated to agree to negotiated reductions in offensive forces.

The case presented by the supporters of SDI is in many respects quite seductive. They are offering a largely non-nuclear, mainly space-based system of defence which will help the West (and indeed the world as a whole) to escape from the moral dilemmas and strategic paradoxes of the present system of nuclear deterrence. They accept that the process of transition from MAD to strategic defence has to be undertaken with care. Many of them also recognise that 'there is no way of knowing whether multi-tiered strategic defences capable of rendering ICBMs and SLBMs as obsolete as the horse cavalry will be technologically feasible.[64] What they are arguing for is the necessary investment in SDI to 'explore the possibility that the defence could resume a position of strategic pre-eminence'.[65]

Appealing as the arguments are they are not without their flaws. It is not unreasonable to seek a way out of the dangers and difficulties of the present system of nuclear deterrence. All those genuinely interested in East–West relations and questions of security should be interested in that task. Those recommending alternative strategies – whether non-nuclear, non-provocative conventional defence of SDI – have the responsibility, however, to think through questions of whether their proposed strategies will work and what the consequences for the stability of the existing military balance between East and West is likely to be.

Those who argue against the SDI point out that one of the biggest difficulties is likely to be the question of technology. As the former US Secretary of Defense Harold Brown has argued:

> If technology promised the certainty of a successful defence of the American population against strategic nuclear weapons, as even a high probability of over-all success, it is likely that policy-makers and defense analysts would agree that the United States should seek that objective.[66]

In fact, the consensus amongst scientists is that the technology available, and on the horizon does not 'offer even a *reasonable prospect* of a successful population defence.'[67] The problem is that if deterrence based upon retaliation is to be replaced by strategic defence the new technology would have to provide almost 100 per cent protection. Given the enormous destructive power of even a few nuclear warheads which leaked through the system nothing short of pefection would do, so the critics argue. Perfection, however, is unlikely to be available, not only because of the technology, but also because of the vulnerability to direct attack of the various components of a layered defence based in space. These difficulties, together with the costs (which could be as high as a trillion dollars) and the potential counter-measures which the Soviet Union might develop, have led a number of reputable commentators to argue that an alternative strategy based on the SDI concept is simply not feasible.[68]

Not only is the SDI criticised on grounds of feasibility, it is also opposed because of the uncertainty and instability which it is likely to create in Soviet–American relations. Contrary to Colin Gray's argument that the Soviet Union will be likely to accept drastic cuts in offensive missiles, there are those who argue that the most likely Soviet reaction would be to build up its offensive missile capabilities further together with other counter-measures to saturate such an American system.[69] The result would be a further twist to the arms race on earth and to the opening up of a new arena for competition in space. Further instability would be likely especially if the Soviet Union perceived the SDI as part of an American drive to achieve superiority and perhaps a first-strike capability over the Soviet Union. This could well be the Soviet interpretation given other developments in American defence policy in the 1980s – the development of the highly accurate MX and Trident II missiles and the odd references to 'prevailing' in various American defence documents.[70]

The critics of SDI do seem to have a strong case. Given the difficulties in the fields of science, technology, and engineering together with the costs, the opportunities for counter-measures and the dangers of instability in the transitional period the SDI does not appear to be a particularly attractive strategy. It is not altogether surprising therefore that opposition has arisen not only from the Soviet Union (which is to be expected) but also from various quarters in Europe. For many Europeans, apart from questions of feasibility and cost there are dangers that SDI would further 'decouple' the US strategic forces from Europe. If the new system only involved defence of US territory the fear would be that the US would be able to retreat behind its own defensive wall leaving Europe vulnerable to

Soviet nuclear threats. Associated with this is the fact that strategic defence would neutralise super power nuclear forces and make Europe more vulnerable to conventional attack. Europe would become the battleground with no effective nuclear weapons to ward off Russian conventional superiority.

There is also the impact which SDI would have on the British and French independent nuclear deterrents. If the Soviet Union developed its own system of active missile defence, which they would be likely to do, the British and French systems, developed at such great costs, would lose their viability. The ABM Treaty of 1972 played an important role in helping to maintain British and French deterrent forces. Super power strategic defence in the 1990s and beyond would increasingly bring them into question.

Not surprisingly Western European governments have been lukewarm about the SDI proposals even though American officials have gone out of their way to emphasise that SDI could cover Europe and that European companies might be able to participae in the technological developments involved. On a visit to the United States in December 1984 Prime Minister Margaret Thatcher secured from the American President agreement to four principles which the British Government regarded as essential for its support of SDI. These included:

1. The US and Western aim must not be to achieve superiority but to maintain balance taking account of Soviet developments.
2. That SDI-related deployment would, in view of treaty obligations, have to be a matter for negotiation.
3. The over-all aim must be to enhance, not undercut deterrence.
4. East–West negotiation should aim at achieving security with reduced levels of offensive systems on both sides.

Mrs Thatcher's conditional support was followed up by a speech by the Foreign Secretary, Sir Geoffrey Howe, at the Royal United Service Institute in London in March 1985 in which he seemed to pose serious question-marks about the SDI programme. He accepted that it would be wrong to rule out the possibility of achieving strategic defence on the grounds that the questions it raises are too difficult. He went on however, to say that:

> ... the fact that there are no easy answers, that the risks may outweigh the benefits, that science may not be able to provide a safer solution to the nuclear dilemma of the past forty years than

we have found already – all these points underline the importance of proceeding with the utmost deliberation.[71]

Despite attempts in subsequent speeches to play down any rifts with the US, the British Foreign Secretary was in effect expressing a warning to the United States (shared by a number of other Western European governments) that it must 'be careful above all things not to let go of the atomic weapon until they are sure, and more than sure, that other means of preserving peace are in their hands.[72]

On the surface, the positions of the United States and its European allies are not too dissimilar. As no one knows what the outcome of the research programme into SDI will be, there is merit in keeping an open mind and supporting the research programme especially as the Soviet Union is itself engaged in such research. Beneath the public statements, however, there are important differences. Within the American Administration there is some enthusiasm for the project. There is a belief in some quarters that the technology probably can be made to work over the next few decades and that solutions can be found to potential difficulties. The European governments, however, are far more sceptical and genuinely worried that the United States commitment to the project will cause them to slide from research to deployment without full regard for the implications. The failure of the mini-summit in Reykjavik in October 1986 did little to dispel European concerns.

These worries may or may not be justified. There is however, a very real danger that in focusing attention and large resources on SDI, the American Administration over the years will become deflected from the task of improving NATO's conventional forces. Western security would undoubtedly be weakened if priority were given to the great vision of a distant strategic defence while improvements in conventional forces which could make nuclear deterrence (as it exists) safer were neglected. Research into SDI is clearly needed given the dangers of being left behind. Despite the appeal of shifting from deterrence through retaliation to strategic defence, however, the strong reservations about the technological, strategic, and financial implications of an SDI programme suggest that very careful reflection is required before such a scheme is deployed – if indeed it does prove to be feasible at all. In a world in which (unsatisfactory as it may be) we are probably going to have to live with a system of nuclear deterrence for some considerable time to come, a strong case can be made that a Conventional Defence

Initiative (CDI) is likely to be a more fruitful policy than a Strategic Defense Initiative (SDI). Fortunately it appears that there will be much less attention given to strategic defences in the post-Reagan period.

THE IMPLICATIONS OF THE GLOBAL DOUBLE ZERO AGREEMENT

Of much more immediate importance than SDI is the Global 'Double Zero' agreement on intermediate range nuclear weapons finally concluded in December 1987 after six tempestuous years of negotiation. In many respects this agreement is a landmark, demonstrating after years of pessimism that important multilateral agreements, which actually reduce the levels of nuclear weapons, are possible.[73] Unilateralism is clearly not the only alternative to the arms race. Indeed if the unilateralist approach had been pursued the Soviet medium and short-range missiles would have remained and NATO would have got rid of its cruise and Pershing II missiles.

As one Whitehall official put it in July 1987 however the agreement has 'cosmic' implications for NATO strategy.[74] As we have seen Flexible Response puts particular emphasis on linking tactical, theatre and strategic nuclear forces in order to offset the Alliance's inadequacies at the conventional level. Under the 'Double Zero' agreement, however, both sides will scrap short and medium range missiles with ranges from 500–600 kilometres. This will still leave up to 4600 tactical nuclear warheads for use by fighter bomber planes, short-range missiles and artillery; 400 warheads on US strategic submarine-launched missiles assigned to SACEUR; nuclear armed cruise missiles on US warships in European waters; and British and French nuclear forces. This represents a sizeable force of nuclear weapons still available but the withdrawal of cruise and Pershing II missiles does significantly weaken the link between tactical and strategic nuclear weapons, upon which the credible threat of escalation is at present based.[75] The fear that this agreement would significantly undermine the deterrent effects of Flexible Response caused grave misgivings in the West German coalition Cabinet in the Summer of 1987.[76] German acceptance of the agreement was only grudgingly given, especially by right wing CDU/CSU politicians who openly expressed their concern that the existing strategy was being undermined. For them the withdrawal of short and medium range missiles weakened deterrence by removing important nuclear capabilities which were designed to couple US and European security and to help offset the imbalance between conventional forces on both sides of the East–West divide.[77] There was also a fear that the agreement might encourage a trend towards a denuclearised Europe by setting a precedent for zero solutions to other European security problems.

Worries such as these suggest that NATO planners and Western governments have some hard thinking to do. One way round the problem, which is already being considered, is for NATO to sustain its existing strategy by deploying new theatre nuclear weapons at sea and deploying more nuclear capable aircraft in Europe to fill the gap left by the departing cruise and Pershing II missiles.[78] This would at least have the benefit of helping to re-link tactical and strategic nuclear weapons so important in the existing Flexible Response strategy.[79] The main problem with the solution, however, is that it clearly breaks the spirit of the Double Zero agreement and as a result could well cause serious domestic opposition, even greater than that which followed the decision to deploy cruise and Pershing II missiles in the early 1980s. NATO would be viewed as giving up weapons with one hand and replacing them with another set of weapons. The euphoria over the arms control agreement would be undermined by accusations of hypocrisy. Such a response might also undermine the prospects for further arms control agreements between East and West.

Far better, given the weaknesses of the existing strategy would be to use the unique opportunity provided by the US–Soviet Accord to re-think NATO strategy. The logic of this major arms control agreement suggests the need for a change in the Alliance strategic concept away from Flexible Response towards something like the Extended Firebreak strategy advocated in this section of the book.[80] The Extended Firebreak concept fits in well with the main thrust of the Double Zero agreement which is to put less emphasis on nuclear weapons and more emphasis on conventional force improvement. NATO planners have already agreed that the INF Agreement requires much more emphasis to be given to conventional force improvement. The key question is how best to achieve this objective. The popularity of the arms control agreement, together with a change in NATO strategy would seem to present just the right opportunity for Western governments to argue that a price has to be paid if nuclear weapons are to be de-emphasised. In that context particularly with an emphasis on the need to reform NATO strategy Western electorates just might be prepared to spend the resources necessary to improve NATO's conventional forces to the required level. As this section of the book has tried to argue this need not be an unbearable economic and political burden. A conventional imbalance does exist but it is not as great as it is sometimes portrayed.

At present NATO strategy is in a state of some confusion. The Extended Firebreak idea would serve the purpose of encouraging the process of evolutionary change (which is the only practical option) by providing a new concept, with a clearer sense of direction and less ambiguity about the role of nuclear weapons in Western defence and deterrence policy. Such a strategy would avoid the weaknesses of both the existing nuclear-biased doctrine and the kind of nuclear-free alternative defence policy advocated in Part I of this book.

Notes

1. See Chapter 8.
2. Lord Carver, *A Policy for Peace* (London: Faber & Faber, 1982), p. 113.
3. Ibid.
4. There is a problem given the cancellation charges negotiated for Trident. A cheaper system plus the cancellation costs could add up to a figure close to the cost of Trident itself.
5. The case for a defence review is argued by David Greenwood in 'Defence', in P. Cockles, (ed.), *Public Expenditure Policy 1985-6* (London: Macmillan, 1985).
6. In May 1986 the Government ordered the first Trident submarine and agreed to pay cancellation charges to Vickers if the first Trident submarine was cancelled before the second boat was ordered. Under this agreement the company would be able to claim up to 125 per cent of the first contract value – just over 800 million pounds.
7. Trident submarines would be capable of taking quite large numbers of cruise missiles. See C. McInnes, *Trident: The Only Option?* (London: Brasseys, 1986).
8. See in particular, *Diminishing the Nuclear Threat* (London: BAC, 1984).
9. See McGeorge Bundy, et al., op. cit. *The Security Gamble* (Totowa, N. J.: Rowman Allanhead, 1984).
10. See H. Schmidt, *A Grand Strategy for the West* (New Haven: Yale University Press, 1985).
11. *Diminishing the Nuclear Threat*, op. cit.
12. Ibid., p. 11.
13. Ibid.
14. Ibid.

15. Dr James A. Thomson, 'Strategic Choices : Their Roles in NATO's Defence Planning and Force Modernization : Part 1', in *Power and Policy: Doctrine, the Alliance and Arms Control*, Part I, *Adelphi Papers* 205 (London: IISS, 1986), p. 18.
16. Jane Stromseth, *The Origins of Flexible Response* (London: Macmillan, 1988).
17. Dr James A. Thomson, 'Strategic Choices', op. cit., p. 35.
18. McGeorge Bundy, et al., op. cit.
19. Ibid.
20. Ibid.
21. Ibid.
22. Ibid.
23. K. Kaiser, G. Leber, A. Mertes, and F. J. Schulze, 'Nuclear Weapons and the Preservation of Peace, *Foreign Affairs*, Summer 1982.
24. Ibid.
25. Ibid.
26. Ibid.
27. Ibid.
28. McGeorge Bundy, et al., op. cit.
29. K. Kaiser, et al., op. cit.
30. In particular see John J. Mearsheimer, 'Why the Soviets Can't Win Quickly in Central Europe', *International Security*, Summer 1982, A. C. Enthoven and K. Wayne Smith, *How Much is Enough* (New York: Harper and Row, 1971), and M. Getler, 'Study Insists NATO Can Defend Itself', *Washington Post*, June 7, 1973.
31. See A. Ross Johnson et al., 'The Armies of the Warsaw Pact Northern Tier,' *Survival* Vol. 23, No. 4, July/August 1981.
32. See Robert L. Fischer, 'Defending the Central Front: The Balance of Forces,' *Adelphi Paper* No. 127 (London: IISS, 1976), James Blaker and Andrew Hamilton, *Assessing the NATO/Warsaw Pact Military Balance* (Washington, D. C.: Congressional Budget Office, Dec. 1977) and *Statement on Defence Estimates 1981* (London: HMSO, 1981).
33. For futher information about Armoured Defence Equivalents see Blacker and Hamilton, ibid.
34. J. Mearsheimer, op. cit. See also Jonathan Dean, *Watershed in Europe: Dismantling the East–West Military Confrontation*. (Massachusettes: Lexington, 1987), pp. 38–59.
35. For a discussion of the importance of mobilisation see J. Mearsheimer, op. cit.
36. See C. N. Donnelly, 'Tactical Problems Facing the Soviet Army: Recent Debates in the Soviet Military Press,' *International Defence Review*, Vol. II, No. 9, 1978 and J. Erickson, 'Soviet Breakthrough Operations: Resources and Restraints,' *Journal of the Royal United Services Institute*, Vol. 121, No. 3, September 1976.
37. See in particular J. Mearsheimer, op. cit. For a critical assessment of this argument see E. A. Cohen, 'Toward Better Net Assessment: Rethinking the European Conventional Balance,' *International Security*, Vol. 13, Summer 1988.
38. *Diminishing the Nuclear Threat*, op. cit., p. 11.

39. Ibid.
40. Ibid., p. 27.
41. See Bernard Rogers, 'Follow-on Forces Attack (FOFA): Myths and Realities,' *NATO Review* No. 6, December 1984.
42. Ibid.
43. Ibid.
44. See the various military contributions to J. Baylis (ed.), *Alternative Approaches to British Defence policy* (London: Macmillan, 1983).
45. The speech was given at the 'Institut Universitaire des Hautes Etudes Internationales.' See *Frankfurter Rundschau*, 9 March 1985.
46. *Frankfurter Allgemaine*, 10 November 1984.
47. Ibid.
48. Such a search for a new strategic concept is supported by the high-ranking group which produced *Diminishing the Nuclear Threat*, op. cit., p. 11.
49. Colin S. Gray, *Nuclear Strategy As A National Style*, (London: Hamilton Press, 1986), pp. 239–66. In this study Gray advocates what he calls a 'Damage Limitation for Deterrence and Coercion Strategy' or a 'Classical Strategy'.
50. Ibid., p. 169–71.
51. Ibid., pp. 70–71, 88, and 105.
52. For a debate about whether the Soviet Union believes it can win a nuclear war see R. Pipes, 'Why the Soviet Union Thinks it Can Fight and Win a Nuclear War,' *Commentary*, 64, No. 1, July 1977; B. Lambeth, 'How to Think About Soviet Military Doctrine' and R. Arnett, 'Soviet Attitudes Towards Nuclear War: Do They Really Think They Can Win?' in J. Baylis and G. Segal, *Soviet Strategy*, (London: Croom Helm, 1981).
53. See Arnett's critique of Profesor R. Pipes' article in J. Baylis and G. Segal, ibid., pp. 55–74.
54. By Malenkov, Khrushchev and more recently Gorbachev.
55. Gray's argument seems to be based on the assumption either that an arms race will bankrupt the Soviet Union or that the US will always win an arms race. Both assumptions are based upon pure speculation. The Soviet Union has proved itself in the past to be capable of catching up and matching US capabilities without 'bankrupting' its economy. It could also be argued that even if the Soviet Union did fall behind in the arms race that might make it even more dangerous.
56. One of Gray's criticisms of the Soviet Union is that it is not interested in 'stability' and has a unilateral view of security. Again this is a matter of dispute. In the aftermath of the Reykjavik 'mini-summit,' for example, Gorbachev developed various ideas of 'reciprocal' or 'common' security. Whether he believed what he said or not is impossible to prove. But no Soviet leader has made these kinds of statements before. There is therefore *some* hope for change in the attitudes towards security by the Soviet Union in the future. See M. Mandelbaum and S. Talbott, 'Reykjavik and Beyond,' *Foreign Affairs*, Winter 1986/7, p. 233.

57. This is also true of NATO strategy as it stands at present. It would also be true of Gray's enhanced war-fighting strategy.
58. The author's discussions with many military commanders suggests that this would be so. There is also the argument that nuclear inferiority at the theatre level would undermine Western resolve and wider foreign policy objectives. Once again this author finds such arguments highly debatable. One of the problems of Western strategy in recent years has been the fixation with equal numbers. If Western leaders emphasise that theatre nuclear sufficiency only requires a certain level of nuclear capability (that 'enough is enough' and explain their strategic arguments to their publics (and to the Soviet Union), there is no reason why foreign policies should be weakened or the West should feel intimidated. Perceptions of nuclear inferiority which allegedly give rise to political weakness are usually the result of hawkish rhetoric and scaremongering (and, as a result, may be self-fulfilling). As Robert Jervis has argued '... it takes two to make a successful act of intimidation, and the very improbability of the actual use of these weapons means that no one in Western Europe needs to be greatly intimidated by them, *unless he wishes to be*.' See *The Illogic of American Nuclear Strategy*, (Ithica: Cornell University Press, 1984), p. 164 (emphasis added).
59. See Dan Smith, 'The Crisis of Atlanticism,' in J. Baylis (ed.), *Alternative Approaches to British Defence Policy*, op. cit., pp. 219–38.
60. See R. Jastrow, *How to Make Nuclear Weapons Obsolete?* (Boston: Little, Brown and Company, 1985), and *The New York Times*, 24 March, 1983.
61. *The New York Times*, 22 March 1984.
62. K. Payne and C. Gray, 'Nuclear Policy and The Defensive Transition,' *Foreign Affairs*, Vol. 62, No. 4, Spring, 1984.
63. Ibid.
64. Ibid.
65. Ibid.
66. H. Brown, 'The Strategic Defensive Initiative: Defense Systems and the Strategic Debate,' *Survival*, March/April 1985.
67. Ibid.
68. See James R. Schlesinger, 'Rhetoric and Realities in the Star Wars Debate,' *International Security*, Vol. 10, No. 1, Summer 1985, and S. D. Drell and W. Panofsky, 'The Case Against Strategic Defense: Technical and Strategic Realties,' *Issues in Science and Technology*, Autumn 1984.
69. Ibid.
70. See D. M. Snow, *The Nuclear Future: Toward a Strategy of Uncertainty*, (Alabama: Alabama University Press, 1983).
71. Rt. Hon. Sir Geoffrey Howe, 'Defence and Security in the Nuclear Age,' *Journal of the Royal United Services Institute for Defence Studies*. June 1985. Also see T. Taylor, 'Britain's Response to the Strategic Defense Initiative,' *International Affairs*, Vol. 62, No. 2, Spring 1986.
72. Ibid. As such, he was reflecting Churchill's words quoted at the beginning of this section of the book.

73. It will be a landmark arms control agreement provided the systems which are being withdrawn are not replaced by new missiles based at sea. If that happens there will be no significant reductions in nuclear weapons, simply a change in deployment patterns.
74. See 'Hope of INF deal by the end of the Year', in *The Times*, 14 July 1987.
75. See Christoph Bertram, 'Europe's Security Dilemmas', *Foreign Affairs*, Summer 1987.
76. See *Frankfurter Rundschau*, 21 July 1987.
77. Initially the German government only agreed to accept the American proposals for an INF agreement provided the 72 Pershing I A missiles were not included. Difficulties within the German coalition between the CDU and FDP parties arose, however, when it appeared that this stipulation was the main obstacle holding up the 'Double Zero' agreement. Eventually the German government grudgingly accepted a compromise whereby the missiles would not be replaced at the end of their effective life. See *Der Spiegel*, 8 August 1987 and *Frankfurter Allgemeine* 12 August 1987.
78. This was proposed by the High Level Group in a military report produced in July 1987. See *The Sunday Times*, 2 August 1987.
79. This solution was also proposed by Christoph Bertram in his *Foreign Affairs* article written in the summer of 1987. op. cit.
80. Most defence specialists would agree that it would have been better to have started with either the more dangerous category of battlefield nuclear weapons or conventional forces. However, we have to start from where we are now with an INF agreement.

12 Towards a Broader Conception of Security

The arguments presented in this section of the book have attempted to suggest that the political and military weaknesses inherent in a non-nuclear defence policy, both for Britain and for the Western Alliance, are far greater than supporters of such a policy would have us believe. It has been argued that a non-nuclear strategy would be likely to create severe problems within the Atlantic Alliance. There are also very real doubts about whether it could cope with nuclear blackmail and whether it would prove militarily-effective against an opponent armed with the vast spectrum of conventional, tactical nuclear, theatre nuclear, strategic nuclear, and chemical forces. Given these weaknesses, it is suggested that there would be grave risks in moving from the present nuclear defence policy (which seems, at least, to have contributed to over forty years of peace) to such a radical, unproven, alternative non-nuclear strategy. Neither does SDI appear to provide a way out of the nuclear dilemma. At the same time it is accepted that nuclear deterrence itself is not without risks and that the NATO strategy of Flexible Response does abound in illogicalities and paradoxes. There may well be *greater* risks inherent in a non-nuclear posture but that does not absolve us from searching for better, more coherent, realistic, and credible alternative defence policies. It has been suggested that the choice is not simply between the present 'nuclear-biased' policies and the 'nuclear-free' policies of the unilateralists. Rather there are alternatives which, while not being complacent about nuclear war, nevertheless recognise the difficulties of providing effective defence and deterrence against nuclear armed opponents without possessing nuclear weapons oneself. For Britain this requires the maintenance of an independent minimum deterrent. If the choice is Trident or nothing, as it probably will be by the next election, then the Trident programme should continue with perhaps fewer warheads than is currently envisaged. Whatever choice is made there is certainly an argument for Britain playing a greater role in the arms control process.

A case can also be made for the reform of NATO strategy. Although NATO defence planners have emphasised conventional improvements in recent years it has been suggested that the Alliance remains ambivalent about the role of nuclear weapons in its strategy, especially about whether they can have a war-fighting as well as a purely deterrent role. It is argued therefore that what is required is a change in NATO's strategic concept away from Flexible Response (with its rather vague overtones) to an Extended Firebreak Strategy which would focus attention on the conventional/nuclear threshold and which would *emphasise* conventional defence within a total deterrence strategy. The new strategic concept would act as a catalyst designed to concentrate defence planners' and politicians' minds towards the needs for a more effective Conventional Defence Initiative (CDI) and the requirement to think about nuclear weapons in an essentially deterrent rather than a war-fighting role. It is accepted that such a change would not be easy and would not be without risks. It would, however, help to produce an Alliance strategy which was relatively more credible, less dangerous, and more capable of wider public support in Western countries.

THE POLITICAL ASPECTS OF SECURITY

Modifying NATO strategy is important, but it is clearly not sufficient on its own to enhance Western security. A new strategic concept can help but, as Ken Booth argues in Part I, there is a strong case for looking at security from a wider perspective than simply military strategy. Security is after all a subjective phenomenon. De Madariaga has argued that it involves 'a feeling of confidence which derives from the feeling that the order of things in which we live is stable.'[1] Security in this sense must be thought of in political as well as military terms. Western security is, after all, dependent as much on the political relationship between East and West as it is on the military balances between the Warsaw Pact and NATO. The easing of tension through *détente* is just as capable of increasing security in Europe as the procurement of nuclear weapons systems. Indeed sometimes more so. It has to be admitted, however, that security planners face a dilemma from which it is not easy to escape. Military strategy as presently conceived tends to focus on deterrence through the threat of punishment. Political strategies to achieve greater security on the other hand tend to focus on trying to achieve greater reassurance through arms control and confidence building measures. The two are not necessarily wholly incompatible but the problems of reconciling the two elements of security are never easy.

One of the problems of recent yeas is that confrontation between

East and West has tended to reinforce the unilateralist tendencies in both super powers. The focus has been on security through military strength. Both sides have at various times appeared to be searching for superiority over the other. The result has tended to be an acceleration of the arms race which has threatened to undermine the stability of mutual deterrence. This has contributed to mutual suspicion and feelings of greater insecurity rather than security. In the early 1980s it was the United States which felt insecure because of the build-up of Soviet heavy missiles. By the mid 1980s the American build-up of its military power and especially its commitment to SDI were provoking new anxieties in the Soviet Union.

The result of this process of action – and reaction – has been to reinforce what Robert Jervis has described as the 'security dilemma'.[2] That is to say the perception that an increase in security on one side has led directly to a decrease in security on the other side. Or to put it another way, that by concentrating on their own security needs, states tend automatically, and often unintentionally, to create insecurity for other states. Each state has a tendency to interpret its own measures as defensive, and the measures of others as essentially threatening. This tends to produce a confrontational and self-defeating view of security which has been very common in East–West relations over the past forty or so years.

There have been periods, however, in which both sides have recognised that they have common, as well as conflicting interests. There have been islands of *détente* in the 1950s, 1960s, and the 1970s, when the super powers have limited their adversarial relationship somewhat and searched for areas of cooperation to enhance their mutual security. During these periods, it was recognised that even ideological opponents and political rivals have a shared interest in survival in the nuclear age. This resulted in various arms control agreements and political understandings, which didn't solve the basic antagonism between East and West, but which helped to relax tensions and provide a political atmosphere in which international security was enhanced. This was the result of a broader conception of security on both sides.

THE NOTIONS OF 'COMMON,' 'COOPERATIVE' AND 'RECIPROCAL' SECURITY

There are those who argue that a wider view of security is necessary to *replace* the rather narrow prevailing concepts of national security.

The Report of the Independent Commission on Disarmament and Security Issues under the chairmanship of Olaf Palme, which was published in 1982, urged the adoption of principles of 'common security' by the super powers. According to the Palme Report because 'all nations would be united in destruction if nuclear war were to occur,' there must be a recognition that this 'interdependence means that nations must begin to organise their security policies in cooperation with one another.'[3] It is argued that the avoidance of war, particularly nuclear war, is a common responsibility which depends on mutual recognition of the need for peaceful relations, national restraint, and amelioration of the armaments competition. In the words of the report:

> Acceptance of common security as the organising principle for efforts to reduce the risk of war, limit arms, and move towards disarmament means, in principle, that cooperation will replace confrontation in resolving conflicts of interest.[4]

In practice, they argue, the pursuit of 'common security' must involve the adoption by East and West of six major principles. These include the principles that all nations have a legitimate right to security; that military force is not a legitimate instrument for resolving disputes between nations; that restraint is necessary in expressions of national policy; that security cannot be attained through military superiority; that reductions and qualitative limitations are necessary for 'common security'; and that 'linkages' between arms negotiations and political events should be avoided.

More recently the Defence Research Trust in Britain directed by Stan Windass has begun a Common Security Programme designed to encourage the adoption of what they describe as a 'Cooperative Security Policy.' Once agan the assumption underlying this policy is that there is an area of common interest between East and West which should be explored and exploited. The objectives of such a policy would be firstly, to prevent war by establishing that neither side is likely to initiate an attack; secondly, to control crises should they occur, to minimise escalation, and to restore stability; and thirdly, to reduce the level of military establishments in a way that enhances mutual security and stability. According to this programme, cooperative security involves the pursuit of confidence building, crisis control measures, and arms control based on certain principles:

1. Cooperative Security must take due account of the perceived interests of both sides.
2. Cooperative Security must progressively limit aspects of military activity or force posture which indicate offensive surprise attack potential.
3. All arrangements must include appropriate and adequate techniques to guard against deception.
4. Cooperative Security should allow for asymmetrical trade offers in the interests of common security.
5. There should be specific measures to deal with the problem of inadvertent war.[5]

Similar ideas to these are put forward in Part I. It is argued that what is required is a greater commitment to 'reciprocal security'. 'Reciprocal security' like 'common security' and 'cooperative security' suggests that there is no escape in the nuclear age from strategic interdependence. The emphasis is on restraint and reassurance rather than the narrow pursuit of national strength and self-interest. In particular it is argued that a change of attitude is required to achieve 'reciprocal security.' This necessitates a movement away from the moralising and self-righteousness which characterise East–West relations, an end to the mutual demonology and fixation with precise symmetry in the super power strategic relationship, and a greater emphasis on reassurance rather than intimidation in the strategic doctrines of both sides.

For some these ideas of 'common,' 'cooperative,' and 'reciprocal' security will be derided as simply 'pieties; and 'platitudes' which have little bearing on the harsh realities of international relations. It is true that these ideas are not beyond criticism. Olaf Palme's idea that the doctrine of 'common security' can somehow replace the doctrine of mutual deterrence, for example, does seem rather utopian. It is also the case that it is easy to recommend principles of 'reciprocal security' but much more difficult to have them accepted given the suspicions, conflicting interests, and differing perceptions about how to achieve security in Moscow and Washington. Whether we like it or not the military dimension of security is likely to remain dominant for the forseeable future.

This is not, however, to argue that the notions of 'common,' 'cooperative,' and 'reciprocal' security should be dismissed. Quite the reverse. This author, regards such broader conceptions of security as being of great importance. They may not be capable of providing a framework to *replace* mutual deterrence and it may be extremely hard to get the ideas accepted by the super powers given their inevitable suspicion of each other. Nevertheless the argument that security can be enhanced through a greater commitment to improved dialogue, arms control and wider cooperation between East and West is one which needs repeating time and time again. This is not to argue that the West has to drop its military guard (although it can be argued that a somewhat more relaxed attitude towards the military balance between East and West would help). Security does depend on having sufficient military power to deter war and to defend against attack. This involves a rough but stable balance of power in Europe. If a potential opponent has nuclear weapons it is difficult to believe that unilateral disarmament would enhance one's security. It is possible to bend over too far in the search for reassurance.

However, a willingness to accept that one's opponent has legitimate security interests of his own, and a recognition that one's own military policies can be perceived as very threatening to an opponent, are important in the wider search for security. This is not to argue that everything one's opponent does must be regarded as legitimate and understandable. Nor is it to argue that nothing should be done which will be perceived as threatening by one's opponent. Unsatisfactory as it may be there is no alternative at present to deterrence based upon threats. The argument here is that every effort should be made to get both sides to accept the ideas behind 'reciprocal security' – to accept the responsibilities of strategic interdependence. Everything should be done to persuade the hardliners that security through superiority is bound to be illusory. While military security must not be compromised, much greater attention needs to be given to policies which, as far as possible, will reassure the other side. This may involve hard-headed dialogue, but it does involve dialogue. It may involve tough bargaining to achieve greater cooperation, but it does involve cooperation. Above all it involves the acceptance of common as well as conflicting interests. Difficult as it is, the pursuit of a legitimate international order, described in Part I, is a worthy objective. Such an order, however, does not necessarily require a commitment to a non-nuclear strategy.

Modifications involved in NATO strategy nevertheless can help in this process especially by putting less emphasis on nuclear weapons and making sure defence plans are not overly provocative. A return to the ideals of the Harmel Report of 1967 which stressed the equal importance of *détente* and defence would be a step forward. As

Michael Howard has reminded us Deterrence and Reassurance ought to be the twin objectives of any security policy.[6] Thus, to be effective in enhancing security any new strategic concept for the Alliance must attempt to balance the requirements of deterrence and defence with the political efforts to reduce tension and build confidence between the two blocs. The Helsinki agreement of 1975 (altogether with the continuing Review process) and the Stockholm Accord of September 1986 are a small step forward but much more needs to be done. Progress in arms control negotiations in conventional forces, chemical weapons, battlefield and theatre nuclear forces, and strategic nuclear systems would help this process. So would some further movement towards banning nuclear tests. There is a strong case that Britain should be playing a more positive role in this area. Arms control, confidence building and crisis control measures are clearly no panacea but they can contribute to the wider improvements in the political relationships between East and West which are crucial for greater international security. The concept of reciprocal security does not provide a wholly new security framework but grafted on to a modified Alliance strategy could help to enhance European and international security while the search for a practical, realistic, improved security arrangement goes on.

AN AGENDA FOR THE FUTURE

Britain's support for the concept of 'reciprocal security' and the modification of existing Alliance strategy would involve certain distinct policies. These would include the following:

1. A more positive approach to Arms Control
   a. By being prepared to negotiate restrictions on the British strategic nuclear deterrent as part of the super power negotiations to achieve deep cuts in their strategic forces. Britain should continue to encourage the US to return to the limits of SALT II, to conclude a START agreement with the Soviet Union and to accept the narrow interpretation of the ABM Treaty.
   b. By encouraging the super powers to follow up the Double Zero Agreement with negotiations to reduce the number of battlefield nuclear weapons on both sides. A 'third zero' is probably not desirable, however, in the short term because of the dangers of encouraging a denuclearised Europe.
   c. By making every effort to follow up the reduction in shorter-

range nuclear weapons with an agreement to balance conventional forces at lower levels. Security will not be enhanced if nuclear weapons are reduced and Soviet conventional superiority remains. There may be room for trade-offs here between Western nuclear weapons and Soviet conventional (particularly tank) forces. In the meantime the Double Zero agreement will require improvements in NATO's conventional forces and some modernisation of a *reduced* battlefield nuclear force. Nuclear forces like other forces have to be modernised and a greater range for battlefield nuclear weapons would help stability.
   d. By giving every encouragement to attempts to extend the kinds of confidence building measures agreed to at the CDE Conference in Stockholm in 1986. Britain should also support the introduction of crisis reduction measures in Europe such as improved communication links and crisis control centres.
   e. By giving British support to a verifiable nuclear test ban treaty.
   f. By pursuing the idea of tank-free zones in Central Europe.
2. The acceptance of a broader concept of security which recognises some of the principles inherent in the 'common' 'cooperative' and 'reciprocal' security concepts. These include:
   a. A recognition that both sides have legitimate security interests.
   b. Efforts to limit aspects of military capability which are *overly* provocative.
   c. Efforts to limit military activity and a force posture which indicate offensive surprise attack potential.
   d. Efforts to guard against deception.
   e. A recognition that reassurance through arms control measures, confidence building measures and a continuing dialogue with the Soviet Union can have an important role to play in the pursuit of mutual security – as well as military capabilities.
   f. Encouragement of the new Soviet ideas of 'sufficiency' and defensive, as opposed to offensive, tactics.
3. In terms of British defence policy there is a case in the longer term for spending relatively less on nuclear weapons and more on conventional forces. The extra expenditure will not be sufficient to significantly improve conventional capabilities, but as part of a campaign to modify NATO strategy, it will represent an important signal to Alliance partners.

   a. Britain should give greater emphasis to developing a European defence identity. Britain can play an important role with Germany and France in linking the two pillars of the Atlantic Alliance more closely together.
   b. In terms of weapons procurement, Britain will still need to provide for home defence as well as to make contributions to the defence of the Central Front, and to the Eastern Atlantic. There will still be a need for some contribution to 'out of area' capabilities. If choices have to be made (as in 1981) although the Eastern Atlantic role will remain important, agonising as it is, Britain may need to change its contribution to the defence of this area to secure the necessary savings. This would involve *some* cuts in the surface fleet.[7]
   c. In terms of the defence of the Central Front, Britain will need to look carefully at new technology, new weapon systems, and new tactics in the future. Nuclear forces should be seen as largely retaliatory weapon systems and some consideration needs to be given to the ideas of defensive deterrence within a wider defensive and deterrent strategy.

4. British leaders should encourage a review of current NATO strategy stressing the need for evolutionary *not* revolutionary change especially in the context of the 1987 Double Zero Agreement. This should involve the adoption of what has been described as an Extended Firebreak strategy. The main features of this would be:
   a. Putting less stress on the early use of nuclear weapons and emphasising the importance of the crucial 'firebreak' between nuclear and conventional weapons. The new concept would recognise the difficulties and dangers of a policy which threatens deliberate escalation as part of a limited nuclear war strategy.
   b. A concerted effort to push for a more comprehensive Conventional Defence Initiative (CDI) – developing further some of the programmes already under way in NATO and developing new programmes. Part of this should involve greater European defence cooperation.
   c. Consideration of new tactics which combine some of the ideas of non-provocative defence with existing, traditional ideas of defence – maintaining vital capabilities for retaking territory and striking at the enemy's rear.
   d. Without declaring in advance a 'no-first-use' policy, an

approach to nuclear weapons which stresses their retaliatory (i.e. deterrent) role rather than their war-fighting role.
e. Concerted attempts to secure arms control agreements at every level bearing in mind the linkage between conventional, chemical, theatre, and battlefield nuclear weapons. This could involve some unilateral actions (such as those already undertaken with reductions in battlefield nuclear weapons) as well as multi-lateral negotiations.
f. A reassertion of the Harmel concept of the dual objectives of Alliance security – *détente* and defence.

There will be those who will argue that the 1987 INF agreement proves that Britain and the Alliance are already doing their best to implement some of these ideas. There is certainly something to be said for this view. After years of relative disinterest in arms control Mrs Thatcher did become an enthusiastic supporter of the super power agreement on reducing intermediate range nuclear forces. Since then, however, the mood has been one of great caution and in official circles there has been a concern to slow down the pace of the arms control process. The INF agreement has also created great uncertainty about the future of NATO strategy. There remains an ambivalence in the Alliance about the role of nuclear weapons and about arms control. The tendency to think in rather narrow terms about defence also remains evident. The argument presented here is that what is required is a clearer conceptual direction for future NATO strategy from the one we have at the moment to a broader philosophical approach to the whole question of security. Such reforms will not resolve the inherent dilemmas of security in the nuclear age. They are however, realistic and they seek to avoid the dangers of both a 'nuclear-biased' and a 'nuclear-free' defence strategy. Encouraging the momentum of the arms control process to achieve further balanced reductions in nuclear, chemical and conventional forces will also contribute to the creation of a more legitimate international order which we all desire.

Notes

1. S. De Madariaga, 'Current Problems and Progress in Disarmament', in *The Problem of Peace*, (Oxford: Oxford University Press, 1927), p. 140.
2. R. Jervis, *The Illogic of American Nuclear Strategy*, (Ithaca: Cornell University Press, 1984), p. 21.
3. Palme Commission, *Common Security. A programme for disarmament* (London: Pan, 1982), p. 6.
4. Ibid., pp. 7–8.
5. 'Cooperative Security Policy', a document produced by the Defence Research Trust, (London: 1986).
6. M. Howard, 'Reassurance and Deterrence', *Foreign Affairs*, Winter 1982/3.
7. This is based on the vulnerability of large surface ships demonstrated quite clearly during the Falklands War. Britain will clearly require a substantial, if slightly reduced fleet of naval ships for a range of military roles. Operations in the Falklands and in the Gulf in the summer and autumn of 1987 demonstrated the continuing value of such ships.

Index

ABM Treaty (1972) 13, 45, 146, 315, 344, 359
Accidental war 243, 249
ADC (Alternative Defence Commission) 49, 104, 165, 253–7, 286
ADE (Armoured Division Equivalents) 329–30
Afghanistan, Soviet intervention 7, 25, 33, 99, 125, 191, 200, 217, 271, 296, 308
Afheldt, Dr Horst 285–6, 300, 304
'Alliance reformers' 113, 237, 319, 320, 321–5, 335, 340
Alternative defence 3–6, 25, 45–61, 78, 88, 95, 127–8, 213, 245
 British 4, 8–10, 14, 25, 42–53, 103–52, 172, 203, 287
 organisations 48–51
 NATO 55, 113, 121, 141, 144–52, 192, 194, 212–3, 261, 287, 304
 Soviet Union 53–4, 92, 109, 233
 Warsaw Pact 56–7
 US 49, 50, 54, 147, 181–1
 Western Europe 50–3, 56, 147, 165
Anglo–French relations 314
Anti-American opinion 31, 127, 130, 140, 178, 181–3, 204, 234, 267
Anti-nuclear movement, the 9, 11, 14, 19, 20, 43, 48, 53, 58, 82, 110, 150, 161, 174, 176, 213, 267, 275
Anti-tank weapons 116, 143, 170, 284, 286, 300, 301, 329
Argentina 200, 265, 277, 278
Arms control 5, 12, 40, 83, 100, 109, 117, 134, 136, 206, 214, 324, 360
 British policy 60, 126, 145, 161, 172, 272, 276, 317–19, 353, 356–9, 362

Conventional arms reductions 117, 178–9, 359, 362
 Geneva negotiations 276
 MBFR 57, 117
 SALT I 29, 94, 216, 228, 276
 SALT II 7, 29, 33, 45, 53, 79, 217, 276, 359
 START 37, 146, 149, 216, 219, 359
 Soviet policy 93–4, 117–8, 145, 199, 205, 315, 356–9, 362
 Stockholm Accord (1986) 359
 US policy 32, 53, 126, 145, 180, 199, 217, 225, 315, 356–9, 362
 see also INF Treaty
Arms race
 Britain and 68–9, 130, 160, 218, 276, 278, 279, 312
 Conventional weapons 36, 39, 117, 125, 333, 339
 Europe 28, 47, 107, 166, 202
 INF Treaty 87, 162
 NATO strategy 248, 250, 264–6
 Super power 7, 72, 76–7, 94, 100, 104, 180, 200, 216, 224, 228, 243, 295, 339, 343
 unilateralism 24, 161, 346
ASAT Anti-satellite weaponry 67, 75, 76, 98
Atlanticism 10–11, 12, 58, 103, 125, 129, 138, 212
'Automated battlefield' 122, 287

Bagnall, General Sir Nigel 334
balance of power the 40, 100, 204, 329, 354, 358
'balance of risk' the 308–10
BAOR 20, 71, 186, 286, 302
Barnaby, Frank 284, 296, 300
Battlefield nuclear weapons 40, 52, 106, 115, 120, 134, 148, 179, 216, 218, 243, 244, 251, 254, 259, 272, 281, 320, 328, 336, 337, 338, 359, 360, 362

365

Berlin 56, 168, 199, 244, 266, 271, 308
BMD (Ballistic Missile Defence) 193, 223, 313–4, 315, 341
Boeker, Egbert 284, 296, 300
Boserup, Anders 284
Brezhnev, President Leonid 8, 33, 93, 118, 198, 230, 271
British Atlantic Committee 249, 250, 331
Britain
  Army 68, 71, 171, 288, 316
  defence policy 7–25, 59–61, 66–85, 87, 103–4, 118, 130, 156–8, 173, 176–8, 213, 228–31, 240, 273–4, 280, 312–19, 360
  defence spending 71, 110, 169–72, 272–4, 280, 289, 313, 316–7, 360
  democracy 14–25, 44, 70
  economy 44, 70, 111, 168, 173, 265, 272–5, 313
  foreign policy 16, 51, 231, 233, 235, 267
  General Election (1983) 8–10
  General Election (1987) 11, 14–22, 42, 43, 52, 66, 109, 118, 145, 172, 175, 176, 190, 213, 229, 239, 240
  Independent Nuclear Deterrent 7–25, 36, 44, 59, 66, 70, 103, 119, 134, 138, 145, 184, 186, 193, 229, 231, 240, 248, 256, 258, 262–7, 272–3, 278, 297, 305, 312–13, 344, 353
  NATO 4, 7, 67, 71, 87, 89, 101, 127, 151, 156–8, 169, 172–88, 193, 251–5, 257, 261, 270, 274, 284, 289, 302, 310, 312–34, 359, 361–2
  non-nuclear strategy 4, 88–9, 103–53, 156–68, 169, 174–205, 218, 220, 232, 240, 278–81, 284, 310
  non-nuclear, US response to, 176–82
  nuclear testing 13, 360
  SDI 344

Brodie, Bernard 85, 163, 166
Brown, Harold 342
Brzezinski, Zbigniew 47
Bülow, Andreas Von 287
Bundy, McGeorge 46, 199, 200, 201, 319
Burt, Richard 32

Canada 136, 141
Carrington, Lord 333
Carter, President Jimmy 33, 47, 98
Carver, Field Marshal Lord 59, 193, 239, 262, 274, 305, 309, 312
CBMs (Confidence Building Measures) 57, 87, 107, 117, 126, 146, 216, 223, 354, 356, 359, 360
CDE (Conference on Disarmament in Europe, Stockholm) 107, 360
Central Front, the 36, 116, 132, 138–9, 170, 186, 216, 286, 302, 316, 361
Centre of Peace and Conflict Research, University of Copenhagen 50
Chalupa, General Leopold 292
Chemical weapons 13, 41, 43, 56, 216, 293, 302, 307, 353, 359, 362
Chernobyl 40, 67, 140, 157, 257
China 73, 91, 142, 199, 200, 268, 276, 329
Churchill, Sir Winston 239, 245
Clarke, Michael 171, 189
Clausewitz, Karl von ('post-Clausewitzian era') 72, 164, 168, 211, 221, 225
CND (Campaign for Nuclear Disarmament) 6, 11, 17, 47, 48, 51
Coexistence, philosophy of 151, 152, 168, 219, 227
Cold War, the 3, 10, 14, 16, 22, 41, 42, 45, 46, 73, 82, 83, 90, 91, 93, 101, 121, 125, 127, 128, 134, 136, 142, 196–7, 211–12, 218, 222, 224, 235, 244, 269
'New Cold War' 7, 31, 44, 75, 94, 162, 166, 231, 243

Index

Committee for the present danger 32, 43, 163
'Common security' 3, 14, 25, 49, 51, 93, 95, 99, 147, 150, 213, 220, 226, 232, 355–6, 357, 360
Conscription 109, 110, 135, 139, 169, 172, 173, 289, 324
Conservative Party, the 11–17, 59, 176, 213, 239, 288
  defence policy 10, 213
CTBT (Comprehensive Test Ban Treaty) 13, 41, 46, 118, 146, 149, 216, 218
Conventional Defence Initiative (CDI) 113, 312, 331, 335, 340, 346, 354, 361
Conventional disparity, NATO–WPT 30, 41, 328–9, 348, 360
Conventional forces
  Britain 9, 12–13, 17, 20, 23, 25, 68, 71, 78–9, 103, 109, 136, 151, 168–72, 173, 182, 186–90, 253, 273, 277, 280, 286, 289, 305–6, 312–17, 334
  doctrine 40, 41, 76, 125, 139, 147, 148, 164, 171, 185, 189, 191, 193, 201, 216, 234, 243, 285, 303, 320, 324, 353–4
  NATO 68, 78, 109–19, 125, 136, 143, 146, 169–70, 203, 259, 263, 285, 289, 291, 302, 312, 316–17, 321, 323, 326–7, 329, 330–1, 335, 345, 347–8, 360
  Soviet and Warsaw Pact 43, 55, 58, 114, 117, 133, 142, 143, 146, 185, 217, 259, 261, 268, 270, 285, 291, 293, 301–3, 321, 323, 328–9, 330–1, 344, 360
  US 52, 110, 130, 133, 134, 136, 139, 149, 291, 324, 332–3, 335
  War 37, 73, 107, 114, 116, 117, 123, 124, 125, 167, 185, 192, 221, 242, 310, 323, 336
  West German 291
Cook, Robin 256
Cooper, Sir Frank 319
Cooperative security 355–7, 360
Crisis control measures 356, 359, 360

Crisis stability 5, 25, 28, 67, 75, 97, 107, 123
Cuba 29, 30, 38, 72, 244
Czechoslovakia 99, 244, 271, 291, 308

Davies, Denzil 287
'Dealignment' 104, 105
Deep cuts 70, 98, 118, 148, 216, 359
Deep strike strategies 12, 107, 116, 123, 146, 148, 171, 286, 287, 332
'Defence in depth' strategies 284, 292, 300, 334, 335
Defence Research Trust 356
Defence Review (1981) 273, 277
Defence White Paper 79, 169
'Defensive deterrence' 5, 6, 12, 83, 104, 112, 113, 125, 213, 243, 284, 287, 288, 292, 293, 301, 302, 304, 309, 361
Denmark 141, 159, 288, 289
Denuclearisation 5, 12, 14, 23, 25–6, 37, 39, 41–2, 51, 61, 69, 88, 100, 104, 109, 119–20, 130–1, 140, 145, 147–8, 150, 156, 158, 160, 165, 167, 174, 177, 178, 181, 215, 216, 218, 234, 236, 359
Détente, super power 7, 14, 41, 45, 88, 94, 98, 105, 126, 130, 141–2, 150, 152, 186, 219, 224, 227, 228, 230, 354, 355, 358, 362
Discriminate Deterrence Report 306
Double Zero Agreements *see* INF Treaty

East Germany 99, 212, 292
Eastern Europe 25, 45, 55, 58, 72, 91, 92, 105–6, 117, 124, 126, 140, 147, 163–5, 200, 206, 217, 225, 232, 256, 268–71, 303, 305, 329, 332
East–West relations
  military 5, 43, 45, 49, 58, 60–1, 72–3, 82–5, 87–95, 107, 117, 120, 127, 144, 165–7, 206–7, 216, 225–36, 244–6, 248, 268, 280, 339, 342

political 19, 41, 129, 151–3, 211–13, 219, 242–3, 270, 354–9
EEC 138
Electoral system, British 10
END (European Nuclear Disarmament) 31, 46, 51
EPC (European Political Cooperation) 317
ESECS (European Security Study) 123
ET (Emerging Technology) 285, 331–2, 361
Ethnocentrism 83, 166–7
Europe
and Britain 47, 70, 76, 126, 140, 184, 276, 284
defence 49, 101, 106, 137, 143, 162–3, 182, 196–7, 203, 239, 251, 264, 292, 286, 308, 316, 317–18, 320, 331, 361
European Defence Community 292, 361
security 26, 39, 42, 47, 54, 58, 60, 72, 78–9, 87, 90, 117, 134, 136, 138, 139, 142, 145, 146, 157, 179, 182, 188, 189, 203, 211, 217, 220, 222–3, 228–9, 230, 232, 241–2, 245–6, 248, 291, 300, 319, 325, 347, 354, 359
SAS (European Study Group on Alternative Security Policy, Germany) 50
Social democratic parties 52
unity 94, 129, 134, 135, 150
Extended Deterrence 10, 40, 42, 48, 67, 212, 234, 261
Extended Firebreak 113, 324–5, 327–8, 331, 335–7, 340, 347–8, 354, 361

F-111s 36, 147, 187
Falkland Islands 10, 23, 69, 170, 191, 273, 277, 278, 300, 316
Farrar-Hockley, Sir Anthony 319
'Finlandisation' 105, 125, 196, 232, 270–1
'First strike capability' 75, 224, 243, 244, 264, 343

Flexible Response
British political parties 12–13, 17
criticisms 58, 67, 77, 103, 112–25, 190, 192, 194, 212, 239, 255–6, 259, 263, 309, 324, 327–8, 336–7, 347, 353–4
Flexible Escalation 114, 281, 320, 321, 322, 337, 346
and the INF Treaty 36, 40, 222, 346–47
reform of 320–2, 336
supporters of 30, 259–61, 279–80, 297
FOFA (Follow On Forces Attack) 107, 171, 306, 332–3, 335
Foot, Michael 8, 31
Forsberg, Randall 46
Forward defence 87, 126, 284, 285, 287, 292, 334, 335
France 141, 149, 183, 184, 187, 189, 276, 288–9, 313–14, 318, 334, 361
Freedman, Professor Lawrence 244
Fundamentalism, US 8, 45, 53, 76, 83–4, 91–2, 94, 118, 142, 152, 167, 197, 198, 204, 223, 225, 226

Garnett, John 114
Gaulle, President Charles de 11, 21, 42, 204
Gaylor, Noel 46
Gorbachev, General Secretary Mikhail 16, 19, 27, 34–5, 38, 39, 41, 43, 54, 82–4, 91, 93, 95, 98–9, 108, 117–19, 128, 134, 146, 151, 152, 157, 158, 161–2, 164, 213, 217–28, 233, 244, 245, 246, 269, 270, 271
Gray, Colin S. 338–9, 343
Greece 47, 141
Grenada, invasion of 268, 275
Gulf, the 135, 140, 230

Hackett, General Sir John 80
Harmel Report, the 358, 362
Hart, Basil H. Liddell 117
Hattersley, Roy 22

Haig, Alexander 32, 80
Healey, Denis 7, 11, 23, 31, 115
Helsinki Final Act, the 94, 359
Heseltine, Michael 48, 274
Hitler, Adolf 90, 128, 132, 163
Hoffmann, Stanley 101, 197
Holy Loch 151
Howard, Sir Michael 306, 359
Howe, Sir Geoffrey 135, 275, 344–5
Human rights 105, 106, 161, 232
Hungary 244, 271, 296, 308
Hunt, Brigadier Kenneth 59
Huntington, Samuel 305, 306, 308

IDDS (Institute for Defense and Disarmament Studies) 47, 50
IEPG (Independent European Programme Group) 317–18
Inevitable War, Leninist Doctrine of 84, 94, 206, 226, 227
INF Treaty 11–13, 25–42, 43, 45, 47, 48, 59, 75, 76, 78, 87, 88, 94, 106, 109, 115, 118, 121, 146, 148, 161, 162, 179, 211, 216, 217, 219, 222, 225, 228, 234, 240, 346, 347, 359–62
  asymmetrical cuts 27, 35, 37, 38, 40, 56, 9, 357
  compensations and modernisations 36–7, 40, 41, 43, 146–8, 170, 219, 347, 360
  deployment 29, 30, 141
  negotiations 13, 14, 19, 26–7, 29, 32–45, 69, 87, 217, 276
  ratification 37, 228
Iran 34, 198, 199
Iraq 265
Israel 129, 265, 276
Italy 141, 318

Japan 34, 91, 129, 142, 190, 200, 202, 275, 329
Jervis, Robert 355
Just defence 49, 69, 81, 249, 286

Kaiser, Karl 306, 323, 326
Kaldor, Mary 46
Kennan, George F. 3, 83, 206, 319

Kennet, Lord 23
Kenny, Anthony 156
Khrushchev, Nikita 84, 94, 163, 164, 206, 219
Kinnock, Neil 8, 9, 18, 20, 130, 179, 180, 253, 290
Kissinger, Henry A. 227
Kohl, Chancellor Helmut 45, 186

Labour Party, Britain 6–25, 52, 66, 103, 120, 126, 131, 140, 145, 150, 151, 170, 174–6, 179–80, 213, 240, 253, 286, 288, 290, 292, 302
  defence policy 9, 15–18, 22, 131, 150–51, 175, 179, 186, 213, 277, 287, 291, 297, 302
Labour Party, New Zealand 52, 176
Lange Government, New Zealand 23, 176
'Last-resort' scenarios 66, 261, 272, 312
'Legitimate International Order' 87–97, 101, 104, 121, 127–8, 142, 144, 152, 160, 188, 215–16, 221–36, 245–6, 358, 362
Lenin, Vladimir Ilich 84, 94, 206, 226, 270
Liberal Party, Britain 6, 11, 12–13, 16, 21, 103, 213
Libya, bombing of (1986) 59, 140, 198
'Limited' nuclear war 67, 80, 212, 243, 245, 249, 255, 259, 264, 361
Lisbon Goals (1952) 113, 326
Livingstone, Ken 20
Löser, Major General Jochen 285–7, 301

McGwire, Michael 142
McLean, Scilla 46
McNamara, Robert 46, 114, 142, 239, 319, 320, 322–25
Madariaga, Salvador de 354
Maitland, Lady Olga 48
Mason, Sir Ronald 319
Mearsheimer, John 308, 330
Mertes, Alois 323

Military-industrial complex,
　US 28, 54, 217
Minimum nuclear deterrent 5, 12,
　39, 161, 201, 216, 272, 312–14,
　318–19, 323, 328, 335–45
Ministry of Defence, Britain 59,
　111, 195, 313
Missiles
　ALCMs 28, 36, 346
　anti-air 284, 300
　Blue Streak 266
　Cruise 7, 9, 10, 12, 27, 28, 35,
　　36, 42, 45, 51, 78, 97, 140, 289,
　　314–6, 346, 347
　GLCMs 26, 29, 46, 120, 346,
　　362
　ICBMs 29, 117, 342
　Lance 36
　MIRVs 216
　MX 45, 315, 343
　Pershing IAs 26, 29
　Pershing II 11, 28, 29, 30, 35, 42,
　　141, 289, 346, 347
　Polaris 7, 8, 9, 12, 28, 67, 68,
　　79, 80, 148, 151, 172, 188, 204,
　　249, 253, 256, 261, 266, 273,
　　288, 290, 318
　Poseidon 151
　short-range 26, 40, 123, 287,
　　320, 346, 360
　Skybolt 266
　SLCMs 151, 204, 342
　SS-4s 26, 27, 38
　SS-12/22s 26, 38
　SS-20s 26, 27, 28, 30, 31, 35,
　　38
　SS-23s 26, 38
　Thor 266
　Trident 8–27, 36, 42, 44, 46, 59,
　　67–8, 71, 79, 109, 136, 138,
　　148–9, 151, 161, 171–3, 186,
　　188, 207, 225, 229, 234, 236,
　　249, 253, 265–6, 272–4, 279–80,
　　287, 290, 313–19, 343, 353
Morality and nuclear weapons 60,
　69, 76, 79, 81, 127, 156, 157,
　159, 248–52, 257, 265, 279,
　280, 341–42
Müller, Albrecht von 287

Multilateralism 11, 13, 20, 24, 25,
　27, 35, 41, 87, 93, 101, 117,
　118, 161, 162, 224, 346
Mutual Assured Destruction
　(MAD) 216, 221, 243, 314,
　315, 341, 342
'Mutual Defensive Superiority' 51,
　59

NATO
　Defence Planning
　　Committee 57, 276, 302, 332
　and the INF Treaty 25–42
　Labour Party 8–11, 18,
　　286–87
　Liberal Party 21
　morality 76–9
　non-nuclear 103–53, 162–94,
　　196, 218–19, 239, 260, 287
　northern flank 141
　nuclear stockpile 37, 211, 323
　planners 36, 115, 120, 195, 347,
　　353
　reforms 5, 168, 239, 240, 281,
　　289, 312–16, 319, 320–2, 330,
　　335, 347, 353, 359, 360, 362
　southern flank 141, 149
　strategy 5–6, 11–13, 20, 27, 40–
　　2, 48, 67, 75, 78, 89, 103, 106,
　　108, 112, 114–15, 120–7, 167,
　　180, 188, 190, 234, 240, 248,
　　253–6, 259, 263–4, 279, 287,
　　303–6, 308, 312, 315–16, 319–
　　28, 330, 333, 335, 337, 339–41,
　　348, 354, 358–60
　technological and economic
　　superiority 116, 329, 343
　troop levels 110, 329
　twin-track policy 30
　Warsaw pact and 47, 56, 217,
　　225
Nazi Germany 78, 159, 295
Near-nuclear countries 68
Neild, Robert 268
Netherlands, the 30, 141
Neutralism 11, 126, 182, 183, 257–
　8, 293
Nicaragua 29, 198
Nixon, Richard 227

Index

No-early-first-use policy 12, 216, 255, 324–5, 337, 361
No-first-use policy (NFU) 41, 46, 106, 119–20, 130, 141, 148, 186, 188, 191, 216, 243, 254–5, 322–7, 361
Non-nuclear defence policy
  against 240–1, 246–51, 260–4, 269–72, 284–87, 300–9, 353, 362
  for 3–25, 52, 71, 79, 87, 101, 103, 109–10, 121, 135, 145, 150, 156–207
Non-Proliferation Treaty 19, 146, 265, 279
Non-provocative defence policy
  against 245, 270, 284–90, 301–10
  for 3–61, 76, 101, 103–53, 158, 162, 168, 179, 191, 194, 206, 213, 218, 234, 236
Non-violent resistance 5, 121
North–South relations 150, 152
Nott, John 170
Nuclear blackmail 126, 163, 193–203, 205, 266, 270, 293–7, 300, 309, 336, 353
Nuclear decoupling 41, 136, 138, 188, 254
Nuclear deterrence
  against 239–81, 309, 323, 326, 336, 338, 340–8, 362
  for 5, 21, 46–9, 58–61, 66–7, 72–85, 87, 95, 111–3, 149–50, 156, 184–5, 192, 195–6, 222, 226
Nuclear disarmament 5, 8, 11, 14, 20, 23–4, 27, 31, 34, 36–7, 59, 87, 96, 111–12, 119, 131–2, 145, 159–62, 181, 184–5, 202, 230–1, 235, 293–4, 346, 356
Nuclear free zones 37, 56, 120, 130, 141, 148, 188, 229, 257
Nuclear Freeze Movement (US) 31, 47, 97
Nuclear overkill 59, 68, 90, 117, 136, 212, 216, 222
Nuclear pacifists 157, 158

Nuclear proliferation and the Third World 82, 229–31
Nuclear test moratoriums 13, 35, 93, 98, 206
Nuclear war 77–80, 96, 161, 190, 192, 202, 242, 243, 323
Nuclear weapons, symbolism of 100, 128, 160, 168, 215
'Nuclear Winter' 66, 202, 249, 255, 263
Nunn, Senator Sam 115, 291, 333
Nye, Joseph S. 81, 96, 197

OMG (Operational Manoeuvre Group) 329–30, 333
Offensive forces 115, 116, 287, 301, 305–7, 333, 339, 342, 343
Opinion polls 14, 15, 16
Owen, David 11, 16, 319
Oxford Research Group 46, 50, 111, 177, 178, 186–7

Palme Commission Report (1982) 99, 356, 357
Peace Movement, the 8, 14, 45, 54, 77, 78, 84, 92, 97, 111, 115, 140, 157, 164, 166, 203, 240, 242, 245, 246, 248, 251–7
Pentagon, the 135, 151, 266
Perle, Richard 131, 175, 290
Plaid Cymru 11
Poland 55, 164, 271, 296
Politburo, the 104, 83, 225, 271
'Process Utopians' 95–7, 101, 147, 225
Pro-nuclear posture 95, 165, 170, 173, 184, 187, 190, 203, 205
Public opinion
  British 6–10, 17, 20, 22, 43, 44, 87, 111, 128, 162, 171, 173, 175, 181, 213
  US 32, 52, 97, 128, 134, 135, 179, 180, 181
  Western European 7, 22, 145, 53, 89, 121, 140, 143, 174, 186, 354
Pugwash Conference on Science and World Affairs 50

RAND Corporation 320
Rapacki Plan (1957) 55
Reagan Administration 7, 8, 18,
  19, 26, 30, 32–5, 39–59, 69, 84,
  91, 93–4, 98–9, 109, 118–19,
  127, 129, 130–2, 145, 160, 162,
  174–6, 179–83, 197–8, 206, 213,
  218, 222–5, 230–1, 267–8, 290,
  314, 339, 341, 345
Reciprocal actions 24, 25, 136,
  204–7, 214, 215, 220, 221, 224–
  6, 234, 246, 250, 272
Reciprocal security 355,
  357–60
Research and development,
  cooperation 317–8
Reserve forces 334
Reykjavik mini-summit (1986) 14,
  41, 69, 87, 132, 141, 161, 222,
  234, 345
Rogers, General Bernard 32, 115,
  131, 309, 320, 321, 322, 335,
  336
Ruddock, Joan 17, 47
Rugby, VLF Communication
  station 256

SACEUR 115, 130, 131, 346
Satellites, reconnaissance and
  communication 67
Schelling, Thomas 196, 197,
  259
Schmidt, Chancellor Helmut 26,
  30, 319, 334
School of Peace Studies, Bradford
  University 49
SDI (Strategic Defence
  Initiative) 13, 34, 37, 45, 46,
  53, 76, 82, 119, 132, 164, 219,
  222, 243, 244, 268, 314, 315,
  331, 335, 340–6, 353, 355
SDP (Social Democratic
  Party) 11, 12–13, 16, 21, 213
SDP–Liberal Alliance 11, 12–13,
  16, 17, 19, 21, 213, 240
'Security dilemma' 355
'Security regime' 88
Shulman, Marshall 152
Smith, Dan 256

Soviet Union
  arms negotiations 30–5, 37–42,
    88, 118, 161–2, 206, 230, 276,
    318
  and Britain 18, 79, 158, 204,
    218, 256
  defence policy 54, 224, 295,
    300, 303, 314, 338,
  Eastern Europe 54–6, 58, 82,
    92, 105–6, 133, 140, 200, 270–
    1, 305, 307–8
  foreign policy 5, 54, 72, 76, 80,
    89, 202, 224, 233, 269
  glasnost 59, 97, 100, 217, 228,
    234, 244, 269
  hegemony 106
  insecurity 107, 146, 168, 198–9,
    232–3, 269, 355
  NATO 260–3, 294, 304
  objectives 38, 75, 78, 91, 99,
    168
  perestroika 22, 269
  planners 67, 118, 124, 133, 148,
    256, 330, 339
  and Reagan Administration 7,
    31–3, 69, 99, 130, 182, 188, 268
  'Strategic Culture' 84, 226, 303,
    339
  'Soviet threat' the 16, 27, 37,
    41, 44, 46, 69, 83, 90–5, 97,
    101, 104, 124, 128, 136, 137,
    152, 163, 180, 192, 194–6, 220,
    225, 232, 248, 268, 269, 271,
    300, 330
  unilateralism 25, 35, 41, 82,
    149, 98, 218, 119, 206, 226
SPD, West Germany 50, 52, 120,
  140, 141, 174, 185
'Special relationship' (US–Britain)
  6, 13, 44, 67–9, 111, 118, 128–
  31, 136, 142, 160–1, 179–82,
  201, 234, 267, 268, 275, 288,
  312, 318
Stable peace 5, 6, 42, 72, 82, 83,
  84, 87, 95, 98, 101, 107, 134,
  142, 144, 211, 222, 225, 228,
  235, 241, 245
Stalin, Joseph 3, 93, 125, 163,
  164, 201, 207, 212, 219, 307–8

Index

Steel, David 21
Steele, Jonathon 54
Strategic interdependence 356–8
'Strategic reductionism' 167
Stromseth, Jane 321
Suez Crisis (1956) 6, 69, 128, 129, 201, 275
'Sufficiency' 41, 93
Super-power relations 19, 27, 33, 37, 39, 42, 44, 51–2, 58–9, 60, 70, 71, 72, 82, 84, 88, 93–5, 97, 99–100, 119, 121, 133, 139, 148, 152, 159, 164–6, 181, 188, 198, 214, 216, 222–3, 228, 230, 269, 318
Surprise attack 51, 55–8, 107
Sweden 47, 108, 158, 196, 201, 252, 257
Switzerland 108, 158, 252, 257

Tanks, main battle 106, 115, 116, 123, 135, 143, 170, 173, 217, 274, 284, 285, 287, 288, 300, 329, 360
Tank-free zones, Central Europe 47, 360
'Technocommandos' 285
Territorial defence, principles of 110, 284, 285, 286, 300, 304–5, 361
Terrorism, international 220, 295
Thatcher, Margaret 9, 11, 14, 16, 17, 19, 44, 45, 69, 80, 81, 94, 109, 129, 145, 161, 172, 176, 213, 218, 224, 230, 234, 263, 318, 344, 362
Thatcher government, the 10, 59, 66, 68, 71, 79, 87, 91, 109, 119, 136, 171, 176, 179, 229, 274, 318
Third World, the 68, 75, 91, 129, 138, 150, 152, 168, 180, 181, 185, 198, 225, 227–31, 243, 265, 266
'Third Zero' 40, 148, 359
'Threat Inflation' 92, 104, 108, 119, 142, 143, 147, 187
Thomson, Dr James 320, 322
Tito, Marshal 163, 207, 307

United Nations 220, 230
  Charter of 89, 96
  Conference on Disarmament (1987) 53
  International Court 220
  Security Council 220
United States
  AirLand Battle 75
  arms agreements 53–5, 272, 276, 318
  bases 7, 9, 12–13, 59, 67, 124, 126, 131–4, 139, 151, 175–8, 180, 187–8, 196, 253, 254, 256, 257, 288, 290, 291, 305, 333
  British 'independence' and 184, 248, 266–8, 280
  British politics and 9, 131, 290
  budget deficit 34, 234, 290
  communications and intelligence facilities 13, 267, 288
  Democratic Party 130, 180, 181, 289, 290, 291
  domestic policies 52, 98, 99, 110, 180, 181, 224, 290
  foreign policy 69, 76, 89, 98, 118, 127, 129, 183, 314, 228
  'Maritime Strategy' 75
  New Zealand and 22–3
  nuclear blackmail and 193, 200
  nuclear guarantees 29, 41, 114, 212, 222, 255, 307, 326–7
  nuclear strategy 46, 98, 131, 137, 159, 198–9, 244, 253–5, 343, 355
  Senate 37, 47, 180, 217, 290, 345
  unilateralism 131, 174, 178
  Western Europe and 29, 30, 41, 44, 46, 87, 120, 125–7, 131, 132, 134–8, 140, 149, 175, 196, 252, 261, 267, 290, 291, 294, 307, 332, 343, 346
Unilateralism 6, 8, 9, 12, 13, 20, 23–5, 35, 41, 93, 98, 117, 150, 151, 186, 218, 224, 240, 242, 248, 251–3, 258, 278–9, 280, 289, 293, 346, 353, 355, 358, 362
Unterseher, Lutz 287

Verification 24, 33, 40, 56, 57, 59, 93, 112, 117, 118, 146, 217, 220
Vietnam 191, 200, 234, 295

Warsaw Pact (WTO) 13, 47, 52–9, 88, 101, 105–10, 116–24, 135, 139, 142–6, 206, 212, 217, 285, 287, 297, 301–6, 321, 323, 326, 330, 332
  Political Consultative Committee (PCC) 56
Washington 14, 25, 27, 33, 132, 134, 137, 176, 178, 222, 225, 275, 357
Weaponisation of space 40, 146, 216, 244, 315, 339, 347
Weinberger, Caspar 18, 131, 175, 189, 290
Weizsacker, Professor Carl Von 285, 304
Western Europe
  Soviet relations with 4, 34, 69, 73, 80, 91, 98, 99, 104–5, 117, 134–5, 143–4, 164, 185, 192–4, 196, 248, 270, 294, 296, 324
  strategy 239, 284
  US ground-launched missiles in 26, 38, 78, 120, 240, 254

US relations with 37, 41, 114, 120, 125–41, 149, 175, 196, 234, 267, 290, 291, 294, 307, 332, 343–5
Western European Union (WEU) 91, 317–8
Westland affair 318
West Germany (FRG) 29, 36, 40, 45, 52, 87, 89, 99, 105, 110, 113, 116, 120, 122, 126, 129, 133, 140, 169, 172, 174, 181, 184–5, 187, 202, 212, 260, 275–6, 285–6, 292, 306–7, 318–9, 326–7, 335, 346, 361
Williams, Bernard 156
Wilson, Harold 7, 266
Windass, Stan 356
Women, International Assembly of 47
'World government' 96, 101
World order 228–31

Younger, George 274
Yugoslavia 105, 108, 125, 163, 164, 196, 201, 307–8

Zero option *see* INF Treaty
Zuckerman, Lord 100